Book 1

Garfield

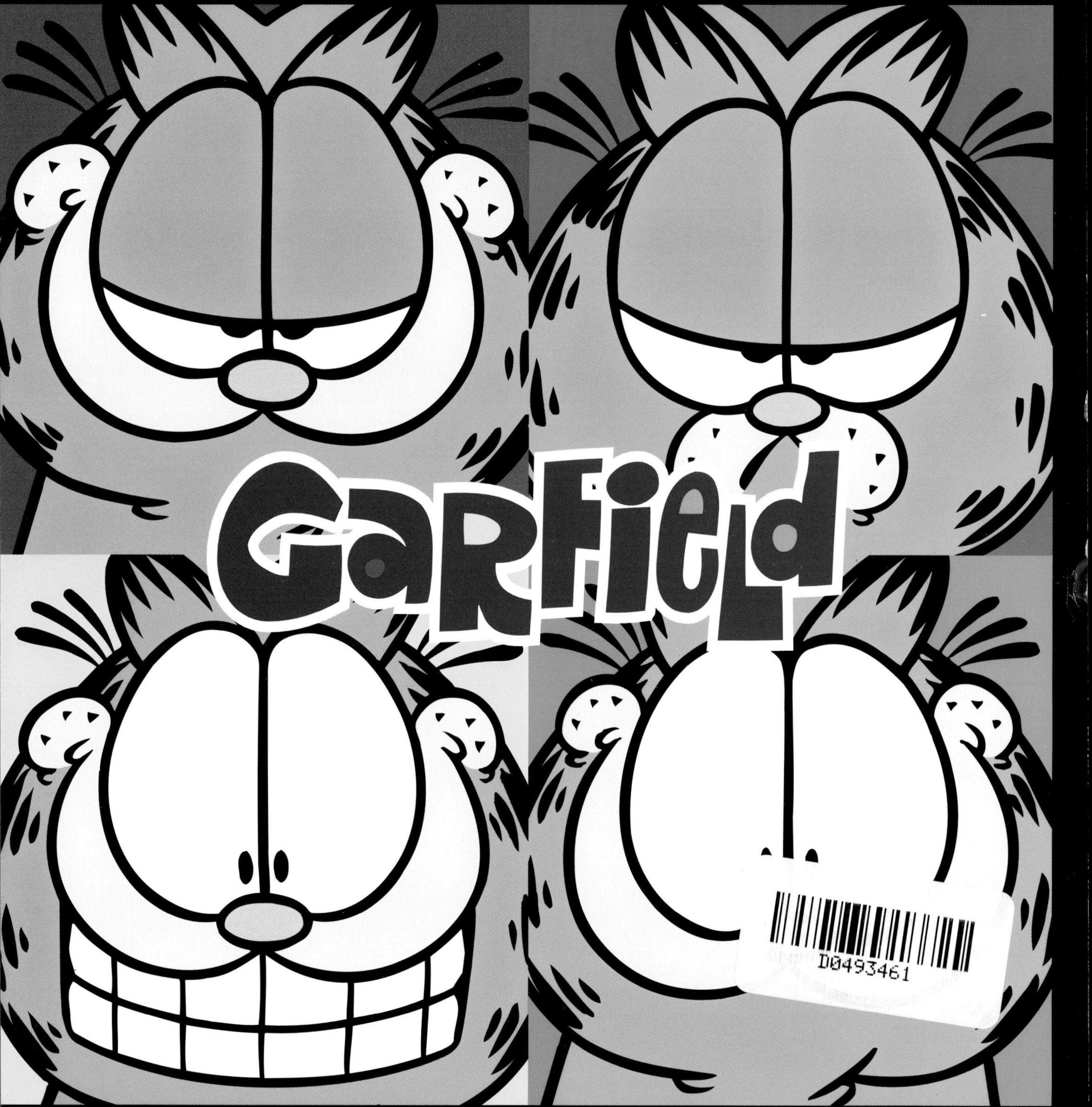

JIM DAVIS

This edition first published by Ravette Publishing in 2007.

Ravette Publishing Limited
Unit 3, Tristar Centre,
Star Road, Partridge Green,
West Sussex RH13 8RA

ISBN: 978-1-84161-293-5

IN HIS FIRST

COLOUR
COLLECTION

JIM DAVIS

RAVETTE PUBLISHING

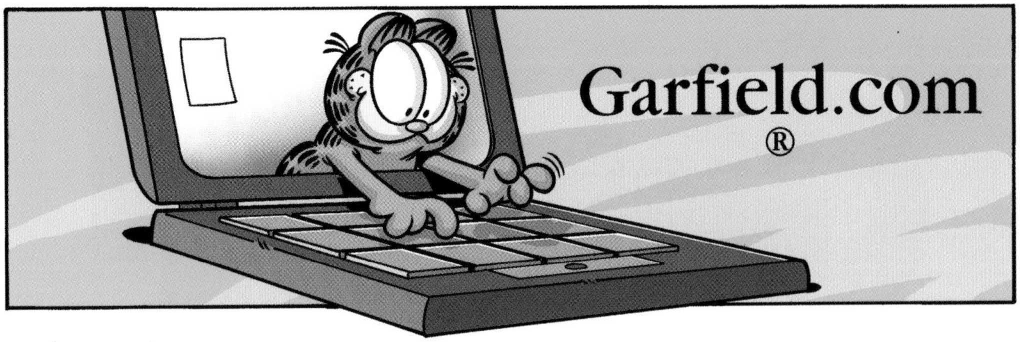
Garfield.com
®

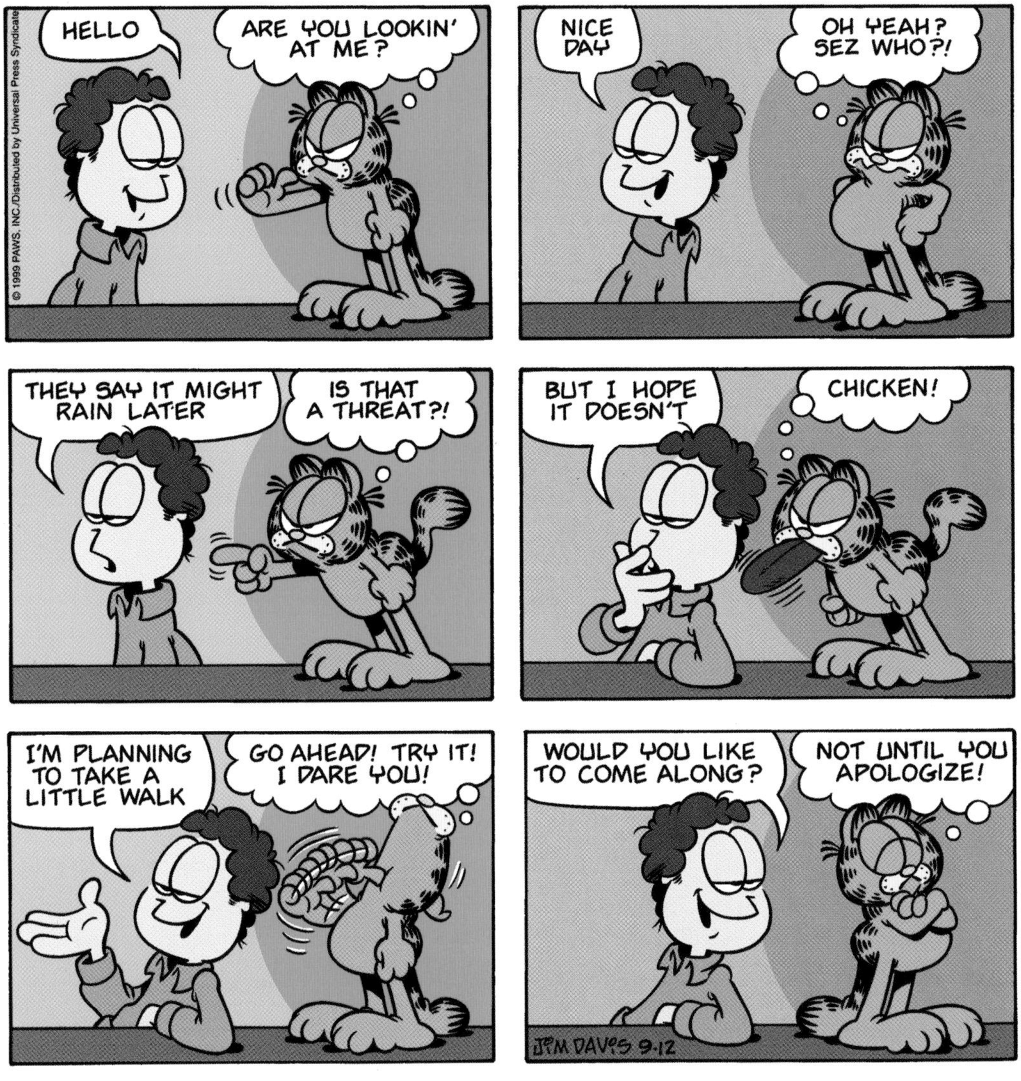
© 1999 PAWS. INC./Distributed by Universal Press Syndicate
HELLO
ARE YOU LOOKIN' AT ME?
NICE DAY
OH YEAH? SEZ WHO?!
THEY SAY IT MIGHT RAIN LATER
IS THAT A THREAT?!
BUT I HOPE IT DOESN'T
CHICKEN!
I'M PLANNING TO TAKE A LITTLE WALK
GO AHEAD! TRY IT! I DARE YOU!
WOULD YOU LIKE TO COME ALONG?
NOT UNTIL YOU APOLOGIZE!
JIM DAVIS 9-12

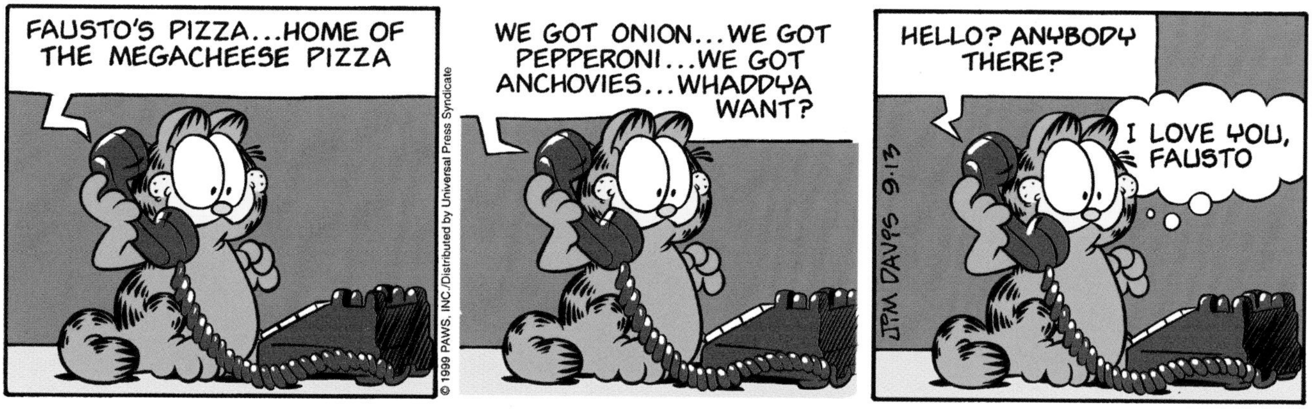
FAUSTO'S PIZZA...HOME OF THE MEGACHEESE PIZZA
WE GOT ONION...WE GOT PEPPERONI...WE GOT ANCHOVIES...WHADDYA WANT?
HELLO? ANYBODY THERE?
I LOVE YOU, FAUSTO
JIM DAVIS 9-13

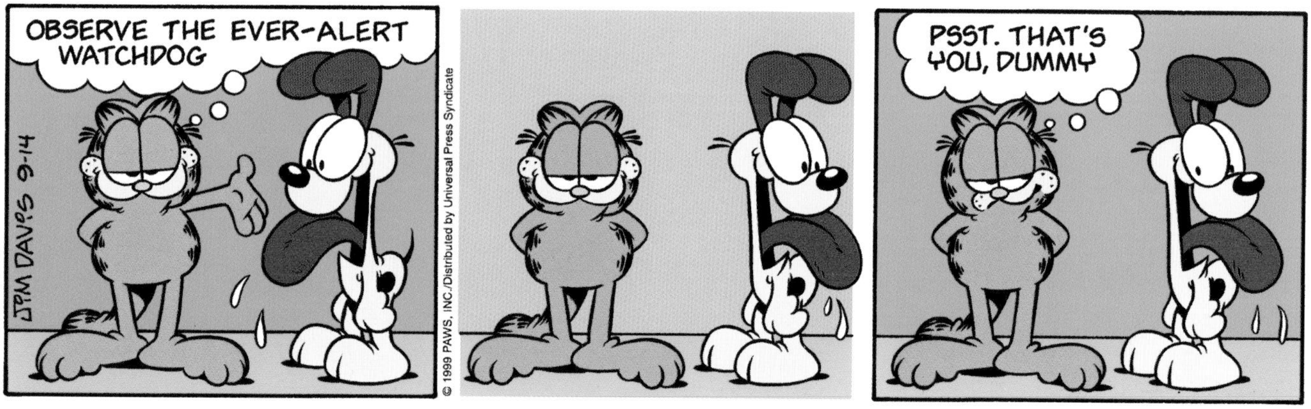
OBSERVE THE EVER-ALERT WATCHDOG
JIM DAVIS 9-14
PSST. THAT'S YOU, DUMMY

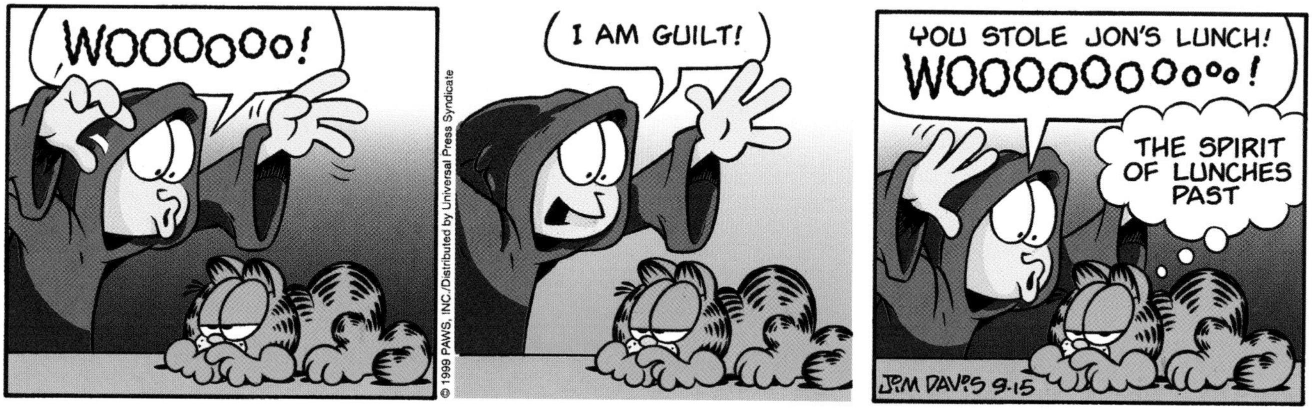
WOOOOOo!
I AM GUILT!
YOU STOLE JON'S LUNCH! WOOOOOOOooo!
THE SPIRIT OF LUNCHES PAST
JIM DAVIS 9-15

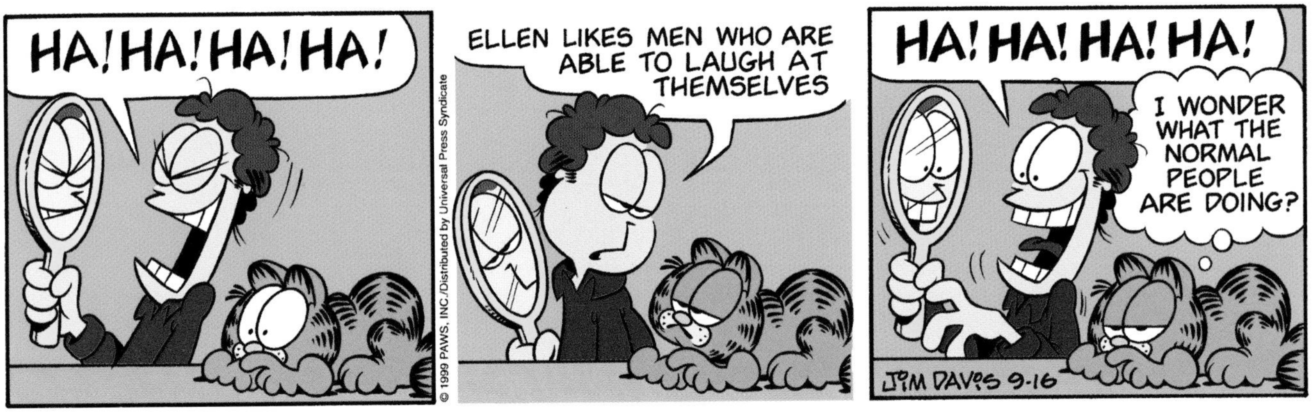
HA! HA! HA! HA!
© 1999 PAWS, INC./Distributed by Universal Press Syndicate
ELLEN LIKES MEN WHO ARE ABLE TO LAUGH AT THEMSELVES
HA! HA! HA! HA!
I WONDER WHAT THE NORMAL PEOPLE ARE DOING?
JIM DAVIS 9-16

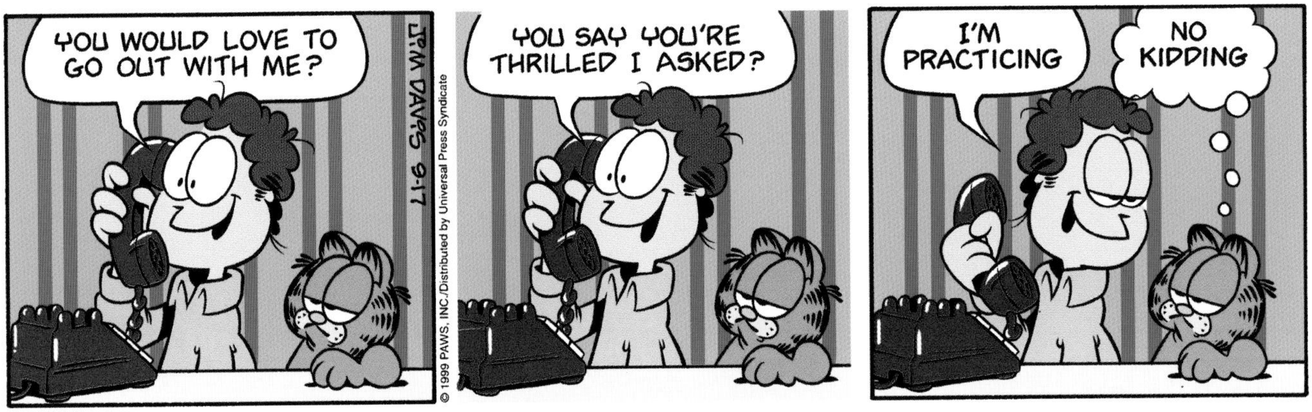
YOU WOULD LOVE TO GO OUT WITH ME?
JIM DAVIS 9-17
© 1999 PAWS, INC./Distributed by Universal Press Syndicate
YOU SAY YOU'RE THRILLED I ASKED?
I'M PRACTICING
NO KIDDING

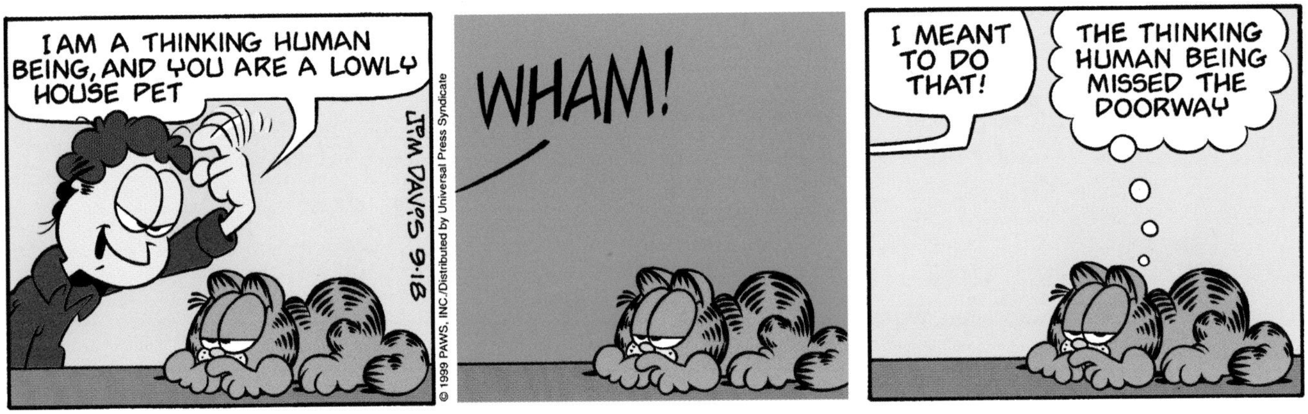
I AM A THINKING HUMAN BEING, AND YOU ARE A LOWLY HOUSE PET
JIM DAVIS 9-18
© 1999 PAWS, INC./Distributed by Universal Press Syndicate
WHAM!
I MEANT TO DO THAT!
THE THINKING HUMAN BEING MISSED THE DOORWAY

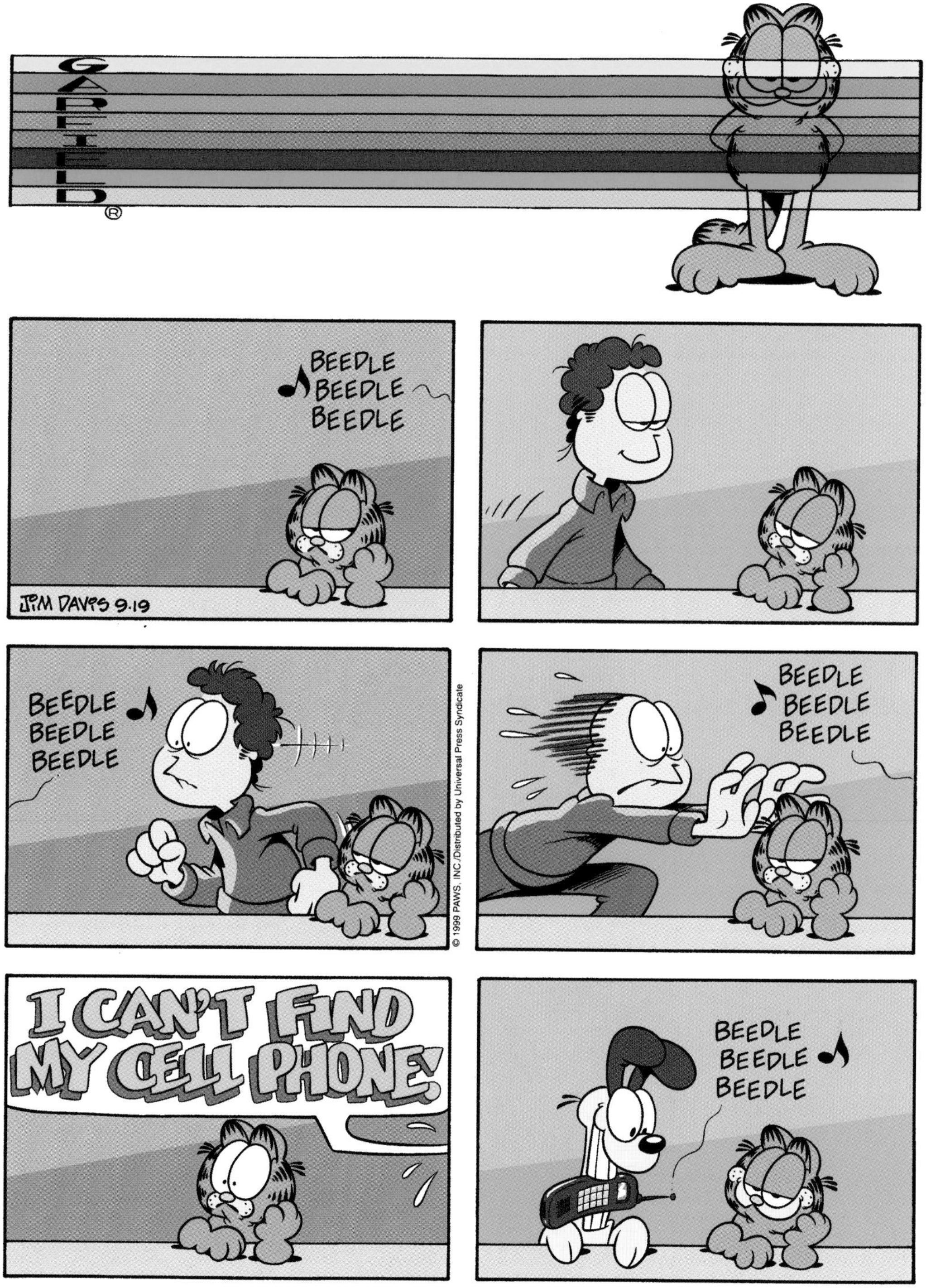
GARFIELD®
BEEDLE BEEDLE BEEDLE
JIM DAVIS 9.19
BEEDLE BEEDLE BEEDLE
© 1999 PAWS, INC./Distributed by Universal Press Syndicate
BEEDLE BEEDLE BEEDLE
I CAN'T FIND MY CELL PHONE!
BEEDLE BEEDLE BEEDLE

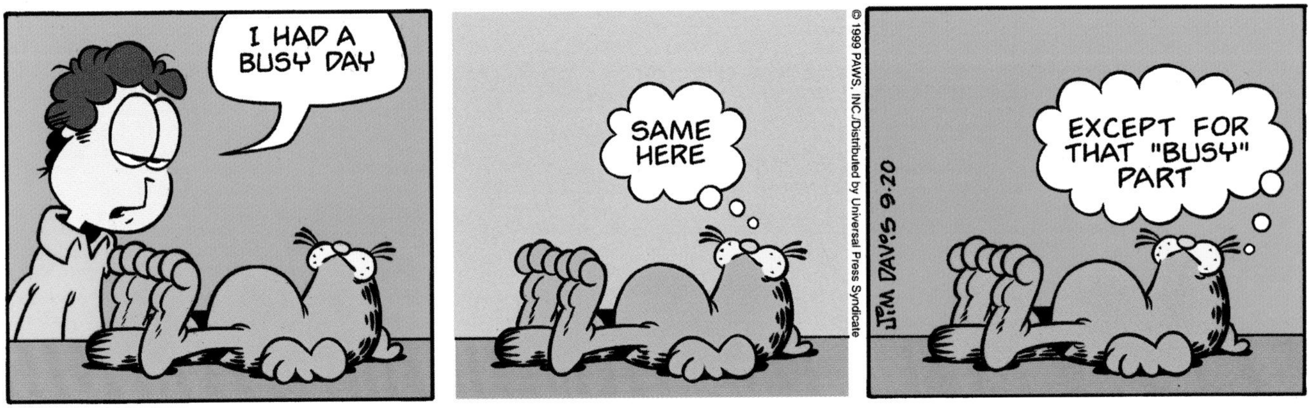
I HAD A BUSY DAY
SAME HERE
© 1999 PAWS, INC./Distributed by Universal Press Syndicate
JIM DAVIS 9.20
EXCEPT FOR THAT "BUSY" PART

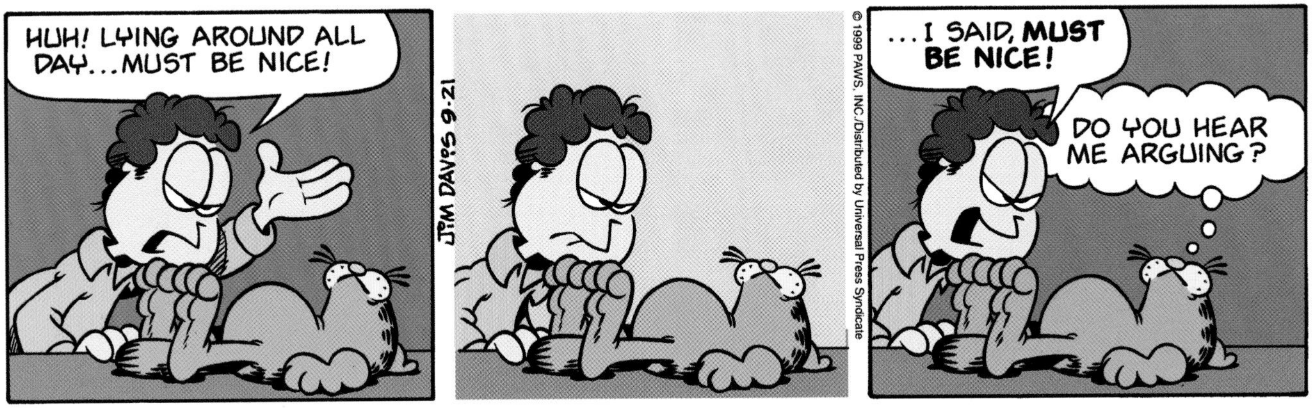
HUH! LYING AROUND ALL DAY...MUST BE NICE!
JIM DAVIS 9.21
© 1999 PAWS, INC./Distributed by Universal Press Syndicate
...I SAID, **MUST BE NICE!**
DO YOU HEAR ME ARGUING?

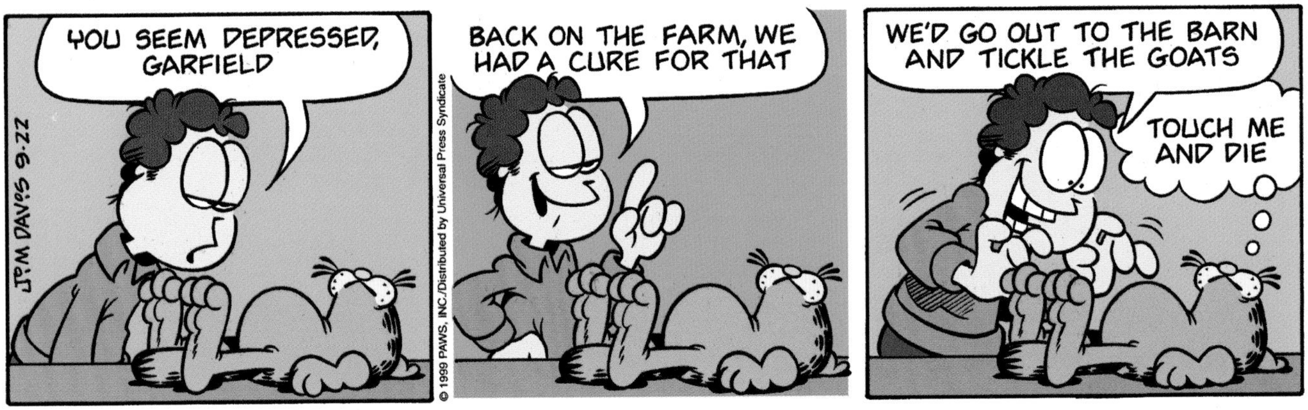
JIM DAVIS 9.22
YOU SEEM DEPRESSED, GARFIELD
© 1999 PAWS, INC./Distributed by Universal Press Syndicate
BACK ON THE FARM, WE HAD A CURE FOR THAT
WE'D GO OUT TO THE BARN AND TICKLE THE GOATS
TOUCH ME AND DIE

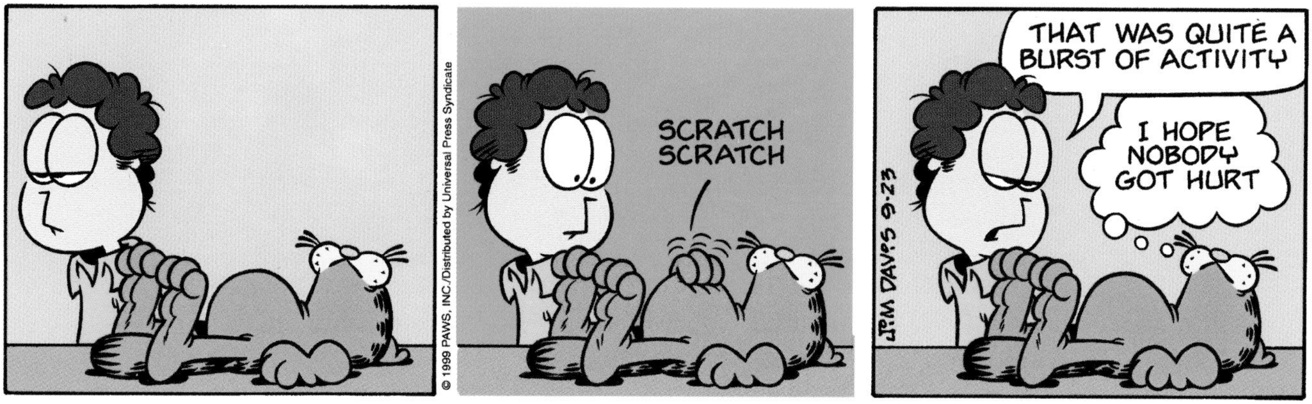
SCRATCH SCRATCH
THAT WAS QUITE A BURST OF ACTIVITY
I HOPE NOBODY GOT HURT
JIM DAVIS 9-23
© 1999 PAWS, INC./Distributed by Universal Press Syndicate

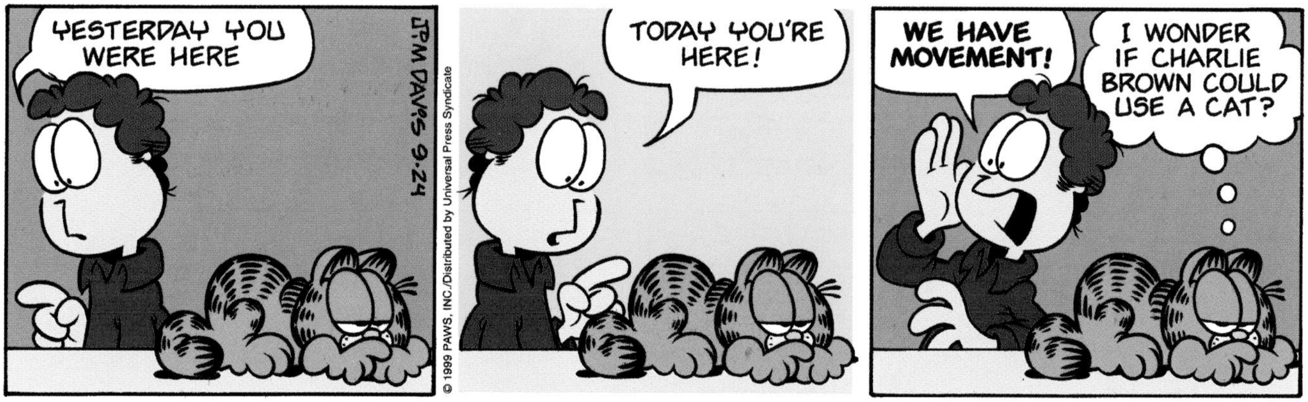
YESTERDAY YOU WERE HERE
JIM DAVIS 9-24
© 1999 PAWS, INC./Distributed by Universal Press Syndicate
TODAY YOU'RE HERE!
WE HAVE MOVEMENT!
I WONDER IF CHARLIE BROWN COULD USE A CAT?

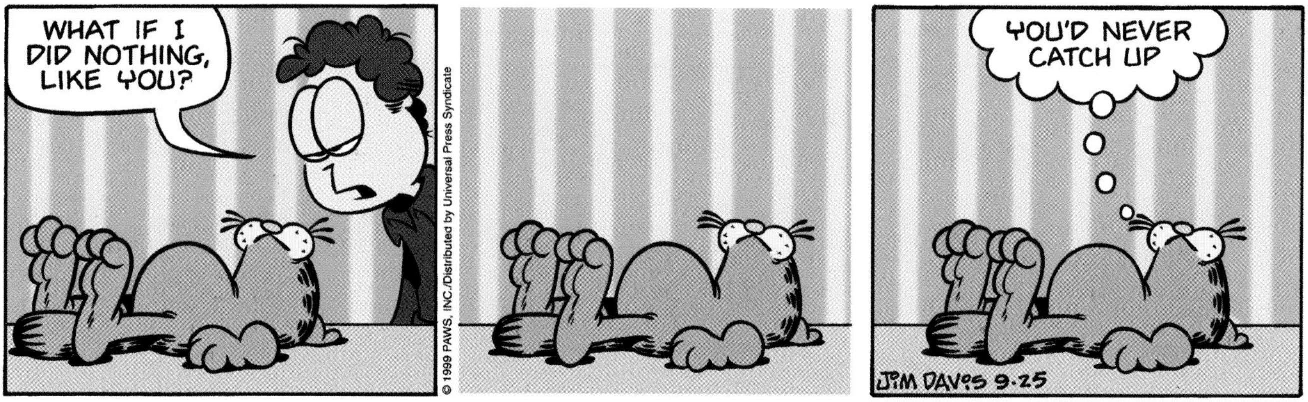
WHAT IF I DID NOTHING, LIKE YOU?
© 1999 PAWS, INC./Distributed by Universal Press Syndicate
YOU'D NEVER CATCH UP
JIM DAVIS 9-25

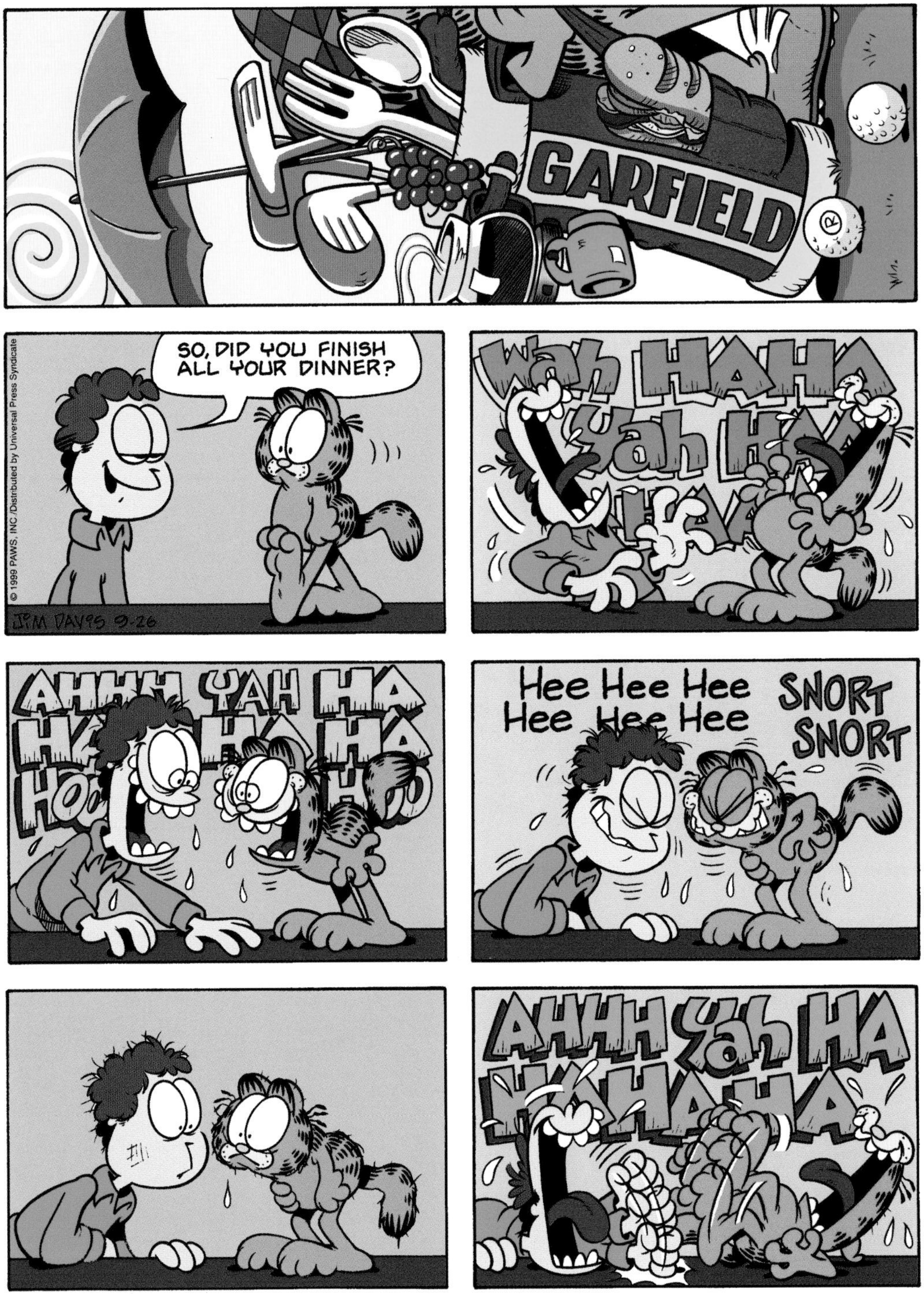

GARFIELD
© 1999 PAWS, INC./Distributed by Universal Press Syndicate
JIM DAVIS 9-26
SO, DID YOU FINISH ALL YOUR DINNER?
Wah HAHA
AHHH YAH HA
Hee Hee Hee
Hee Hee Hee
SNORT
SNORT
AHHH Yah HA

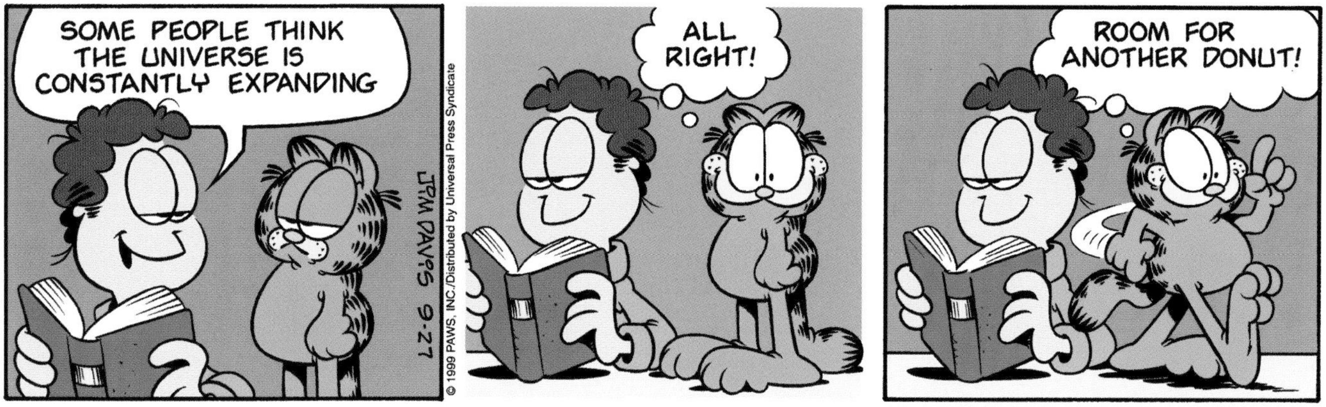
SOME PEOPLE THINK THE UNIVERSE IS CONSTANTLY EXPANDING
JIM DAVIS 9-27
© 1999 PAWS, INC./Distributed by Universal Press Syndicate
ALL RIGHT!
ROOM FOR ANOTHER DONUT!

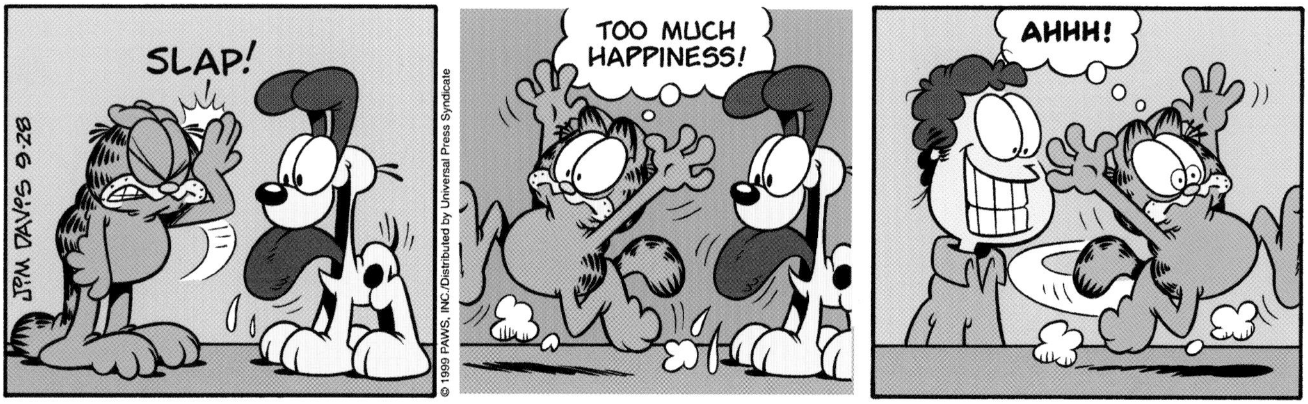
SLAP!
JIM DAVIS 9-28
© 1999 PAWS, INC./Distributed by Universal Press Syndicate
TOO MUCH HAPPINESS!
AHHH!

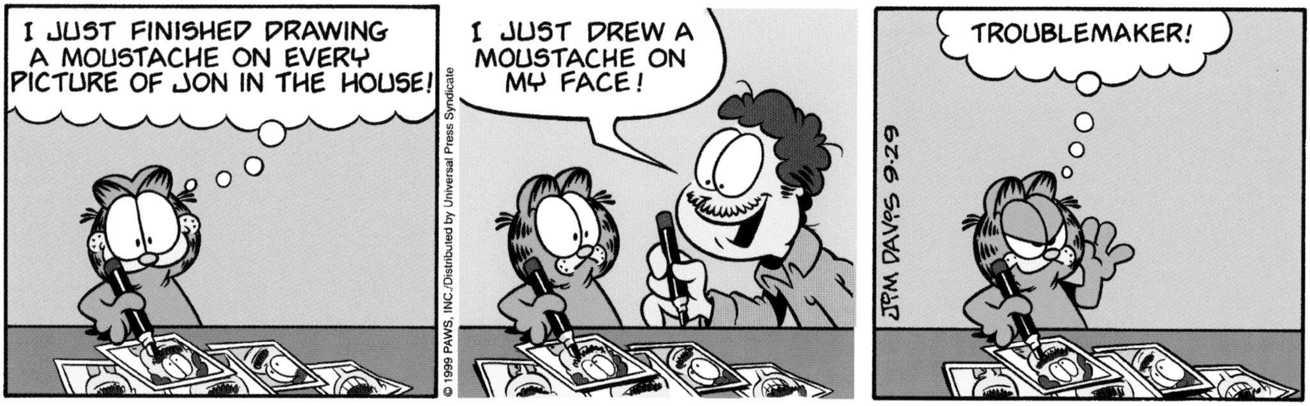
I JUST FINISHED DRAWING A MOUSTACHE ON EVERY PICTURE OF JON IN THE HOUSE!
© 1999 PAWS, INC./Distributed by Universal Press Syndicate
I JUST DREW A MOUSTACHE ON MY FACE!
JIM DAVIS 9-29
TROUBLEMAKER!

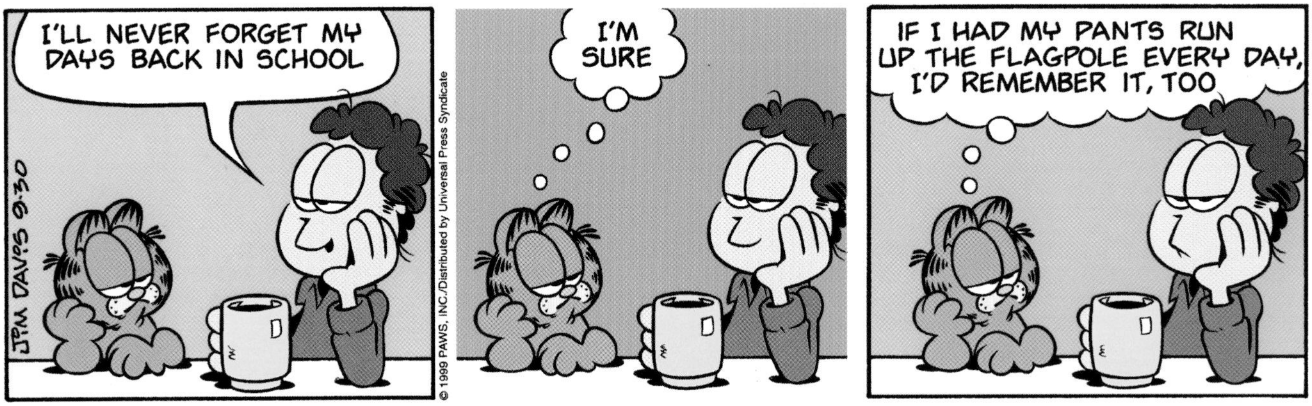
I'LL NEVER FORGET MY DAYS BACK IN SCHOOL
I'M SURE
IF I HAD MY PANTS RUN UP THE FLAGPOLE EVERY DAY, I'D REMEMBER IT, TOO
JIM DAVIS 9-30
© 1999 PAWS, INC./Distributed by Universal Press Syndicate

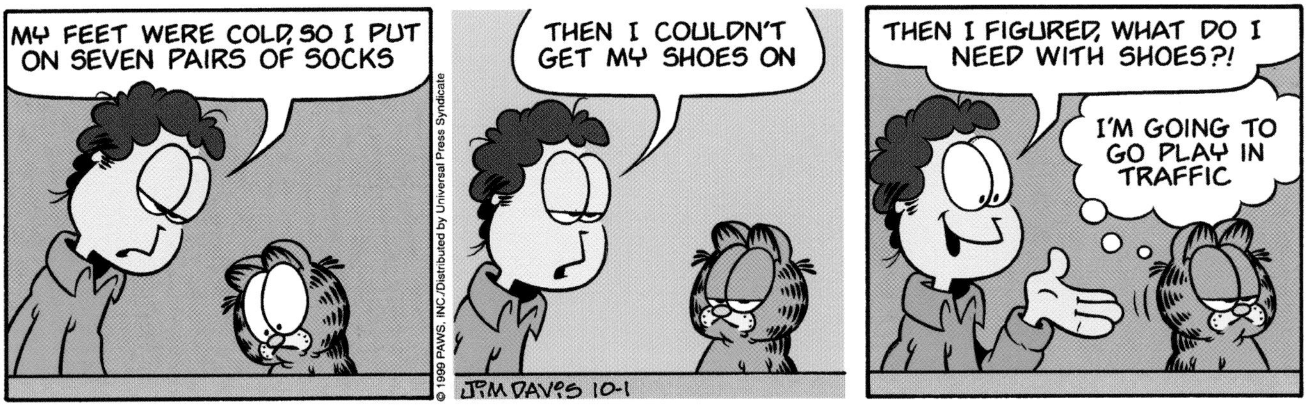
MY FEET WERE COLD, SO I PUT ON SEVEN PAIRS OF SOCKS
THEN I COULDN'T GET MY SHOES ON
THEN I FIGURED, WHAT DO I NEED WITH SHOES?!
I'M GOING TO GO PLAY IN TRAFFIC
JIM DAVIS 10-1
© 1999 PAWS, INC./Distributed by Universal Press Syndicate

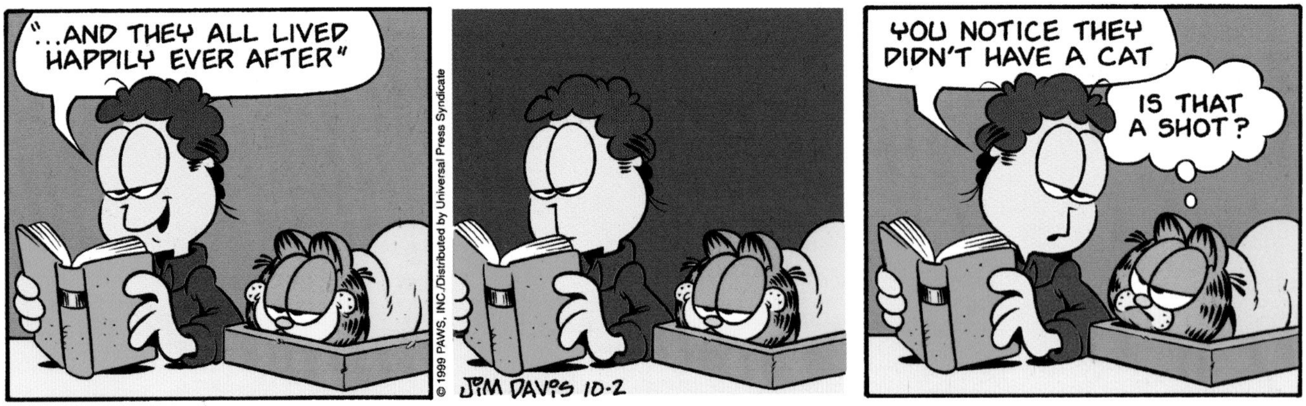
"...AND THEY ALL LIVED HAPPILY EVER AFTER"
YOU NOTICE THEY DIDN'T HAVE A CAT
IS THAT A SHOT?
JIM DAVIS 10-2
© 1999 PAWS, INC./Distributed by Universal Press Syndicate

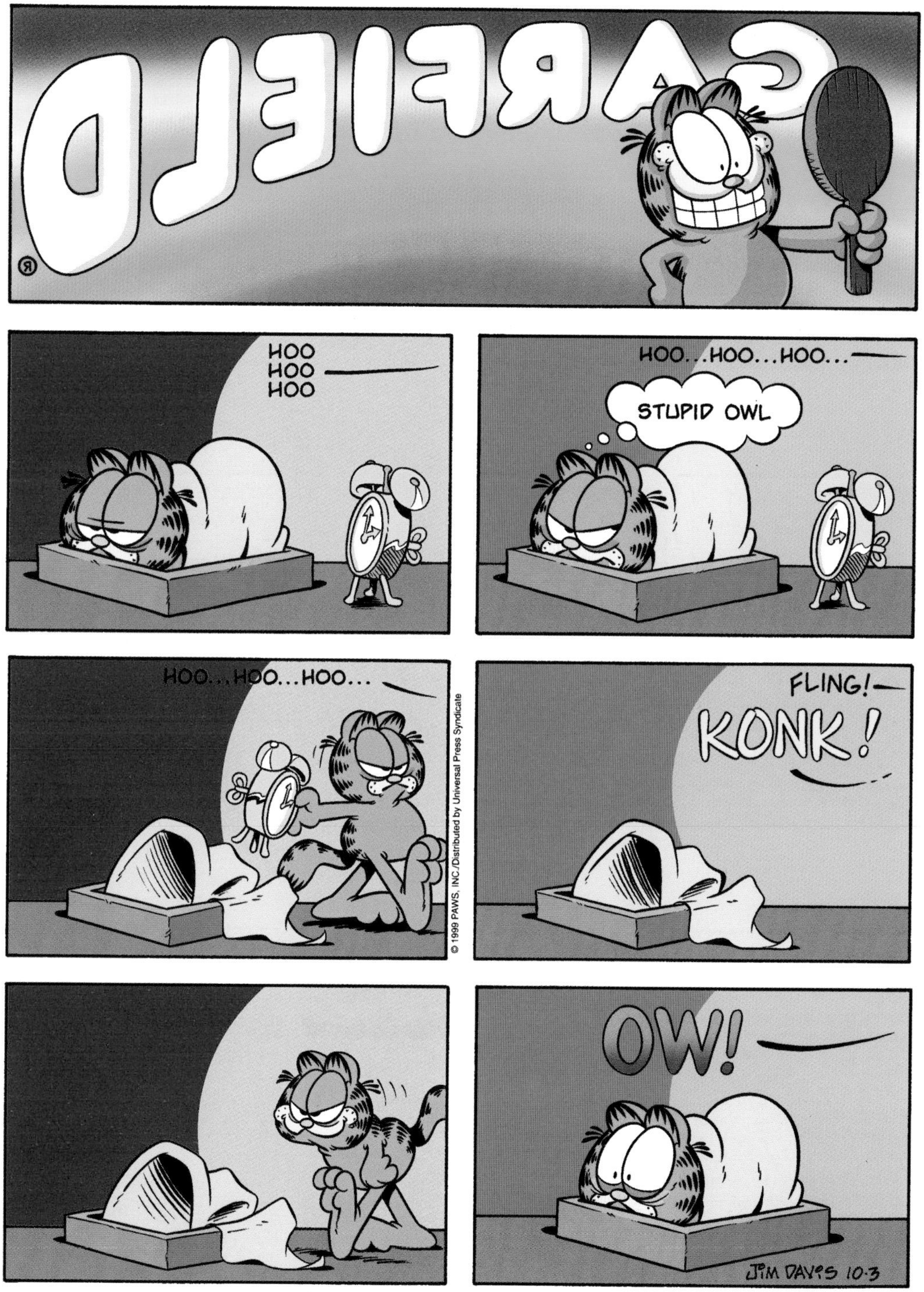
GARFIELD
HOO HOO HOO
HOO...HOO...HOO...
STUPID OWL
HOO...HOO...HOO...
© 1999 PAWS, INC./Distributed by Universal Press Syndicate
FLING!
KONK!
OW!
JIM DAVIS 10-3

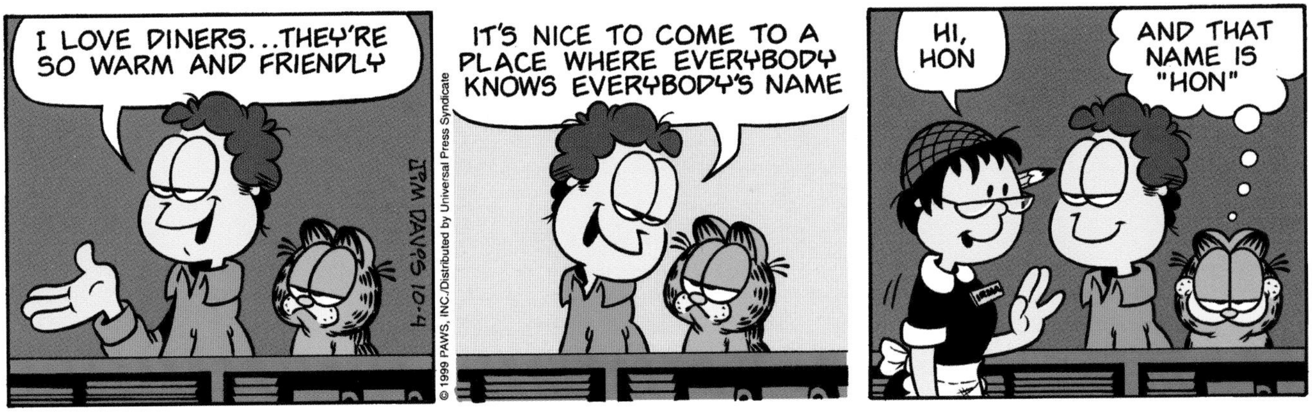
I LOVE DINERS...THEY'RE SO WARM AND FRIENDLY
JIM DAVIS 10-4
© 1999 PAWS, INC./Distributed by Universal Press Syndicate
IT'S NICE TO COME TO A PLACE WHERE EVERYBODY KNOWS EVERYBODY'S NAME
HI, HON
AND THAT NAME IS "HON"

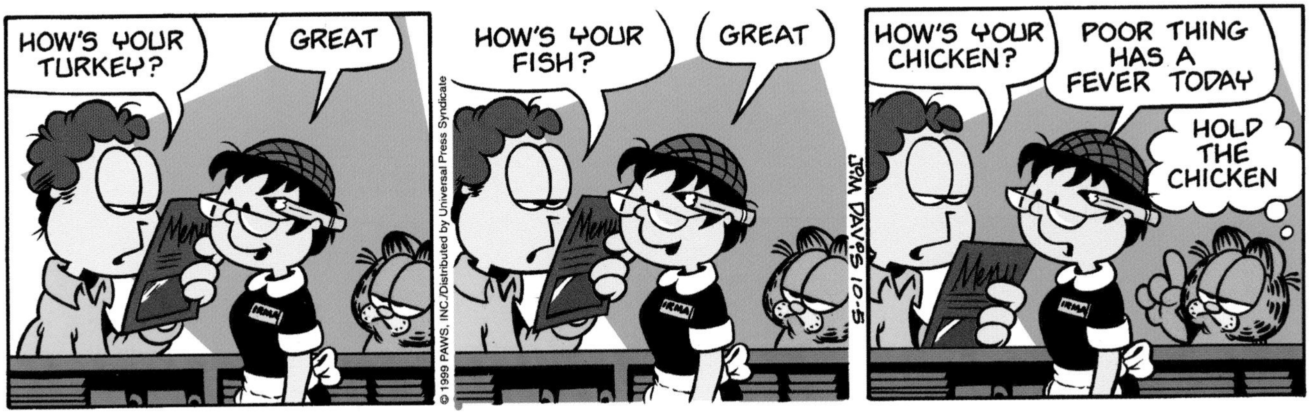
HOW'S YOUR TURKEY?
GREAT
Menu
© 1999 PAWS, INC./Distributed by Universal Press Syndicate
HOW'S YOUR FISH?
GREAT
Menu
JIM DAVIS 10-5
HOW'S YOUR CHICKEN?
POOR THING HAS A FEVER TODAY
HOLD THE CHICKEN
Menu

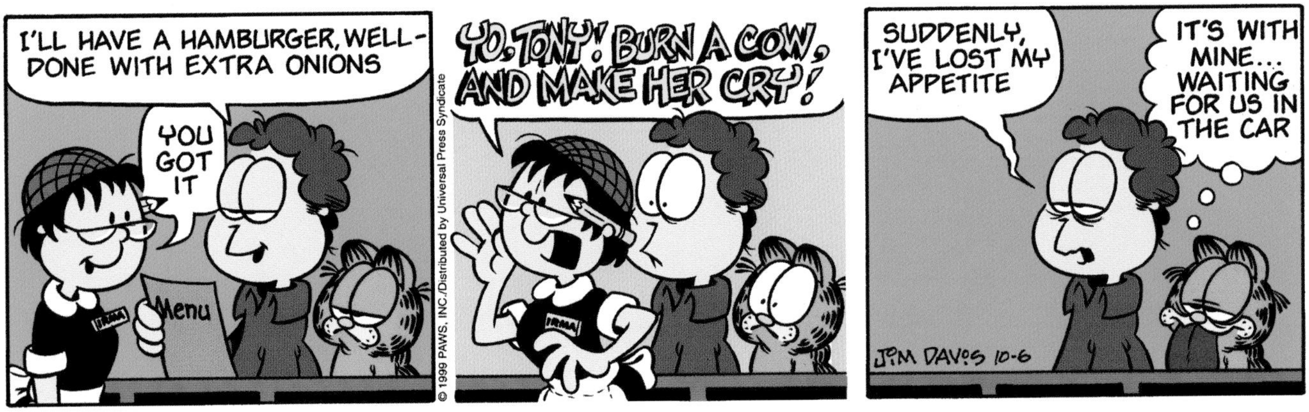
I'LL HAVE A HAMBURGER, WELL-DONE WITH EXTRA ONIONS
YOU GOT IT
Menu
© 1999 PAWS, INC./Distributed by Universal Press Syndicate
YO, TONY! BURN A COW, AND MAKE HER CRY!
SUDDENLY, I'VE LOST MY APPETITE
IT'S WITH MINE... WAITING FOR US IN THE CAR
JIM DAVIS 10-6

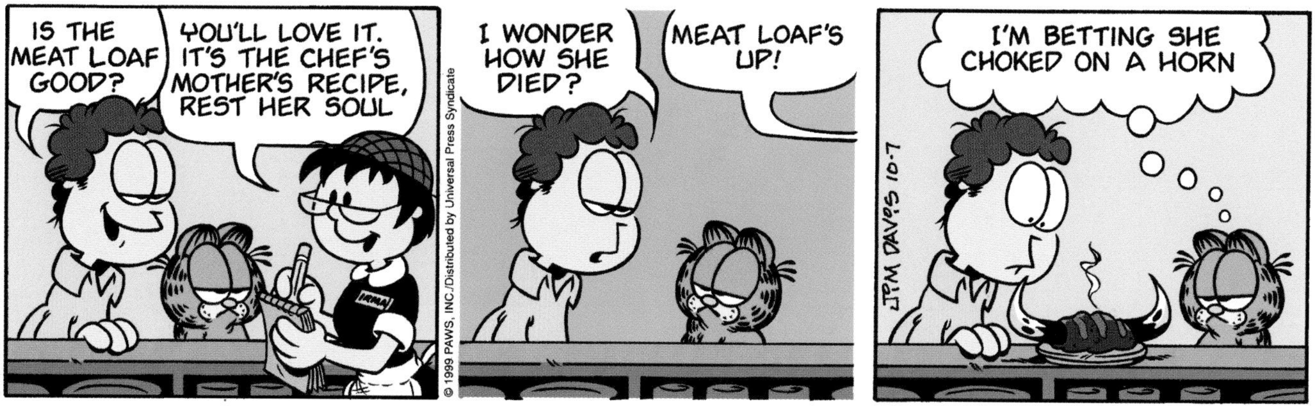
IS THE MEAT LOAF GOOD?
YOU'LL LOVE IT. IT'S THE CHEF'S MOTHER'S RECIPE, REST HER SOUL
© 1999 PAWS, INC./Distributed by Universal Press Syndicate
I WONDER HOW SHE DIED?
MEAT LOAF'S UP!
I'M BETTING SHE CHOKED ON A HORN
JIM DAVIS 10-7

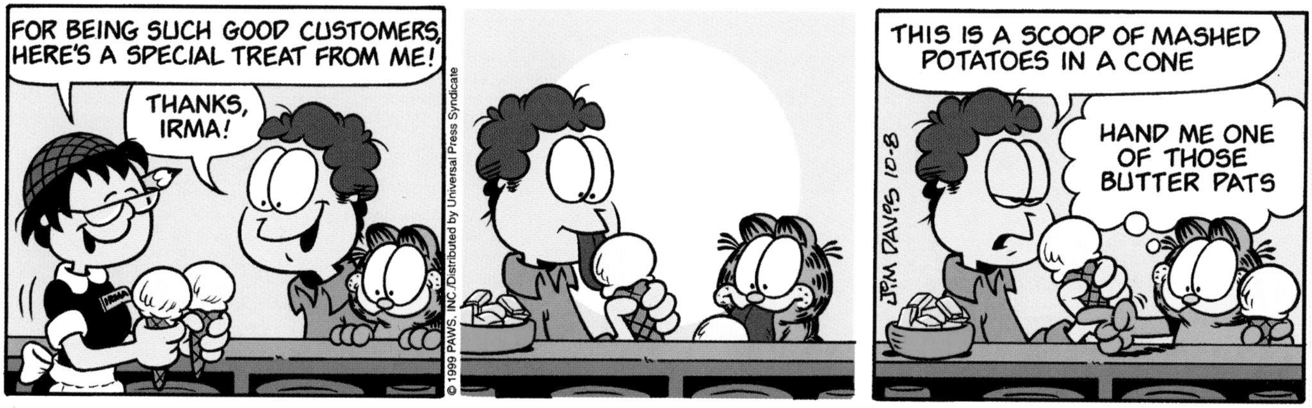
FOR BEING SUCH GOOD CUSTOMERS, HERE'S A SPECIAL TREAT FROM ME!
THANKS, IRMA!
IRMA
© 1999 PAWS, INC./Distributed by Universal Press Syndicate
THIS IS A SCOOP OF MASHED POTATOES IN A CONE
HAND ME ONE OF THOSE BUTTER PATS
JIM DAVIS 10-8

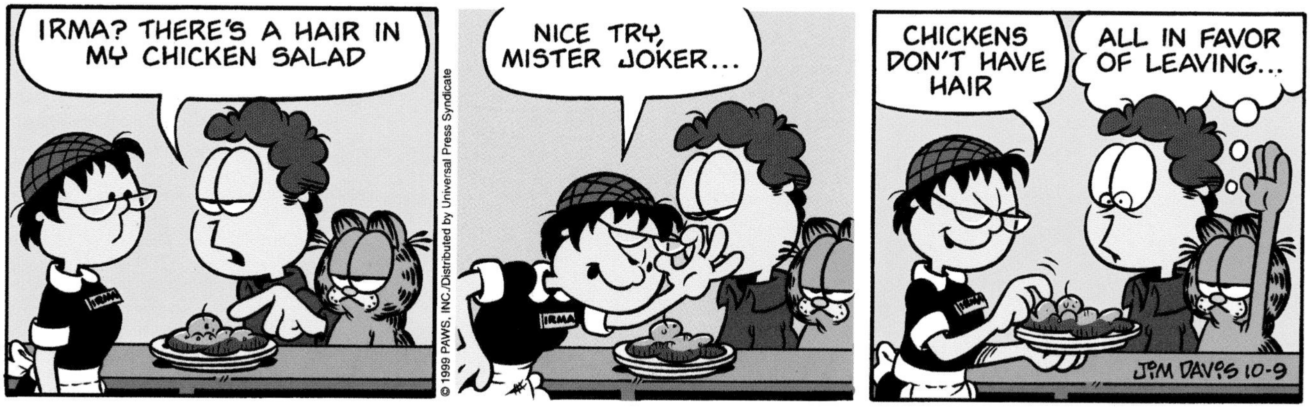
IRMA? THERE'S A HAIR IN MY CHICKEN SALAD
IRMA
© 1999 PAWS, INC./Distributed by Universal Press Syndicate
NICE TRY, MISTER JOKER...
IRMA
CHICKENS DON'T HAVE HAIR
ALL IN FAVOR OF LEAVING...
JIM DAVIS 10-9

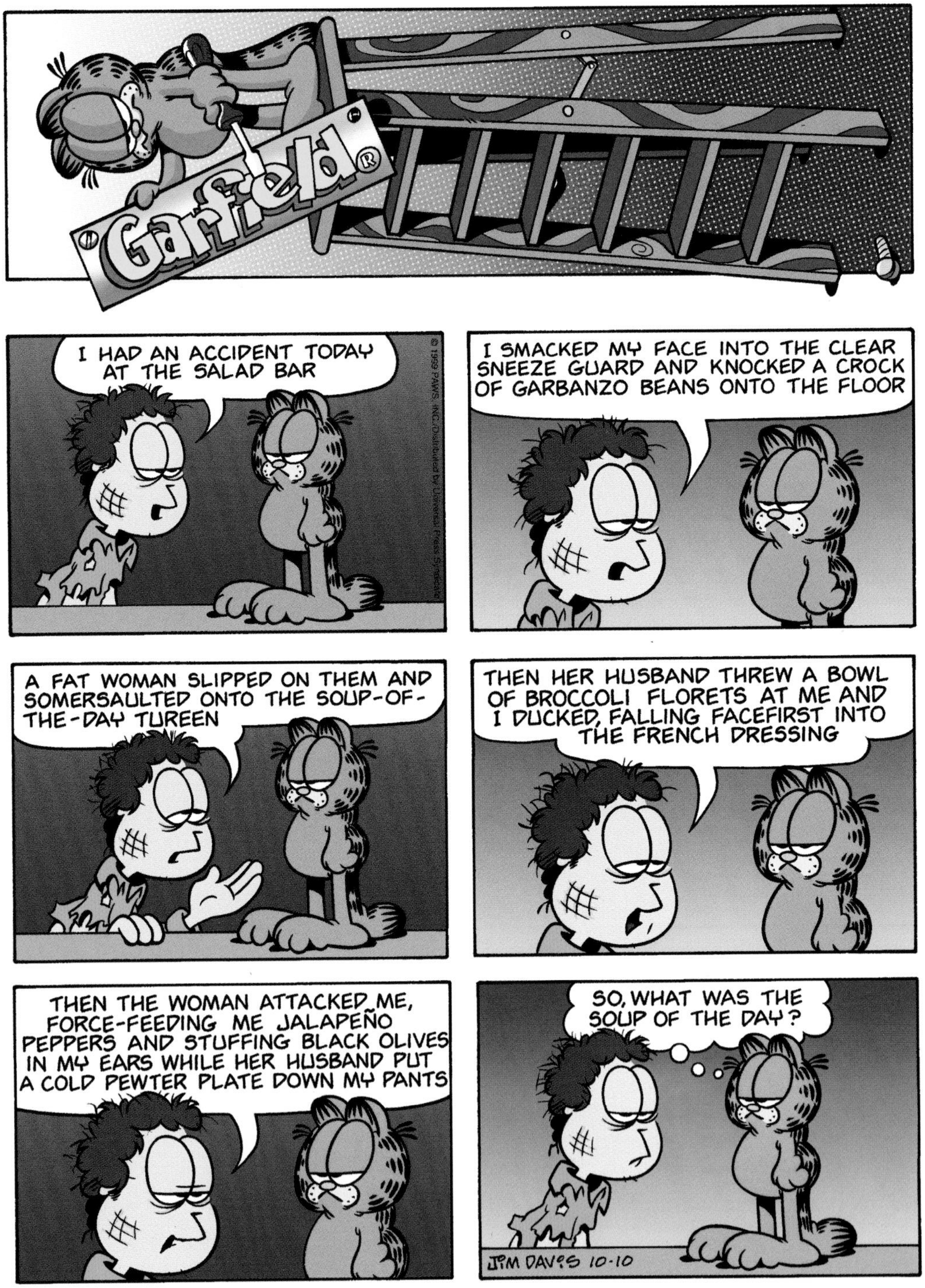
Garfield®
I HAD AN ACCIDENT TODAY AT THE SALAD BAR
© 1999 PAWS, INC./Distributed by Universal Press Syndicate
I SMACKED MY FACE INTO THE CLEAR SNEEZE GUARD AND KNOCKED A CROCK OF GARBANZO BEANS ONTO THE FLOOR
A FAT WOMAN SLIPPED ON THEM AND SOMERSAULTED ONTO THE SOUP-OF-THE-DAY TUREEN
THEN HER HUSBAND THREW A BOWL OF BROCCOLI FLORETS AT ME AND I DUCKED, FALLING FACEFIRST INTO THE FRENCH DRESSING
THEN THE WOMAN ATTACKED ME, FORCE-FEEDING ME JALAPEÑO PEPPERS AND STUFFING BLACK OLIVES IN MY EARS WHILE HER HUSBAND PUT A COLD PEWTER PLATE DOWN MY PANTS
SO, WHAT WAS THE SOUP OF THE DAY?
JIM DAVIS 10-10

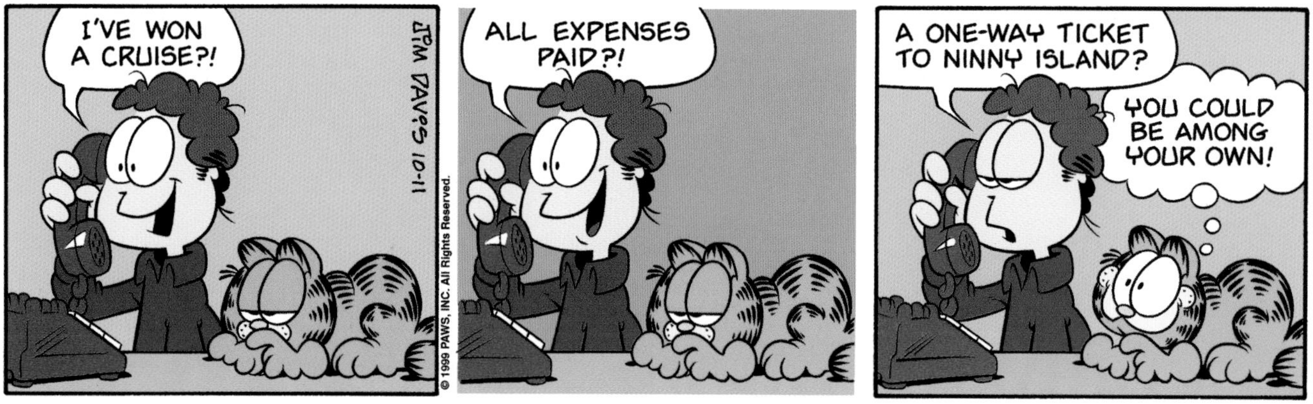
I'VE WON A CRUISE?!
JIM DAVIS 10-11
ALL EXPENSES PAID?!
A ONE-WAY TICKET TO NINNY ISLAND?
YOU COULD BE AMONG YOUR OWN!

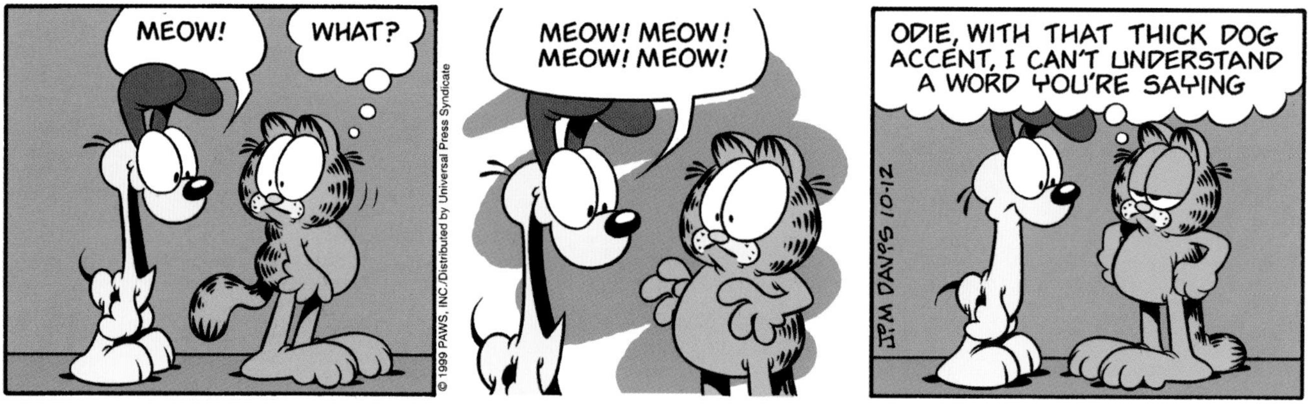
MEOW!
WHAT?
MEOW! MEOW! MEOW! MEOW!
ODIE, WITH THAT THICK DOG ACCENT, I CAN'T UNDERSTAND A WORD YOU'RE SAYING
JIM DAVIS 10-12

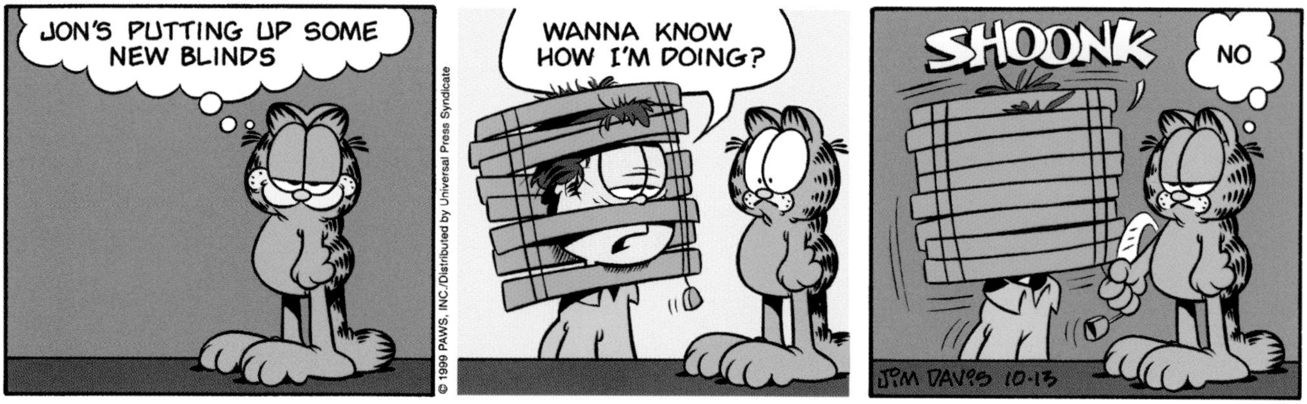
JON'S PUTTING UP SOME NEW BLINDS
WANNA KNOW HOW I'M DOING?
SHOONK
NO
JIM DAVIS 10-13

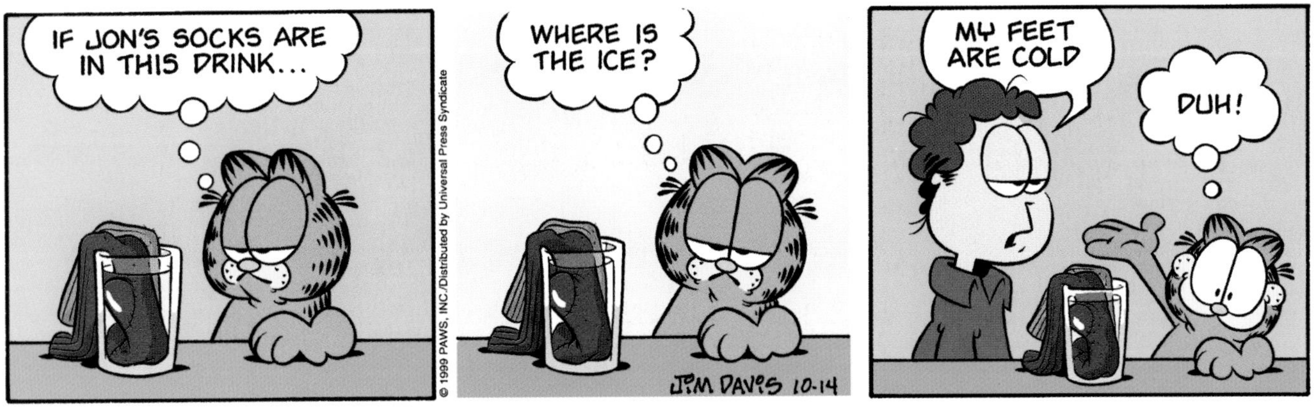
IF JON'S SOCKS ARE IN THIS DRINK...
WHERE IS THE ICE?
MY FEET ARE COLD
DUH!
© 1999 PAWS, INC./Distributed by Universal Press Syndicate
JIM DAVIS 10-14

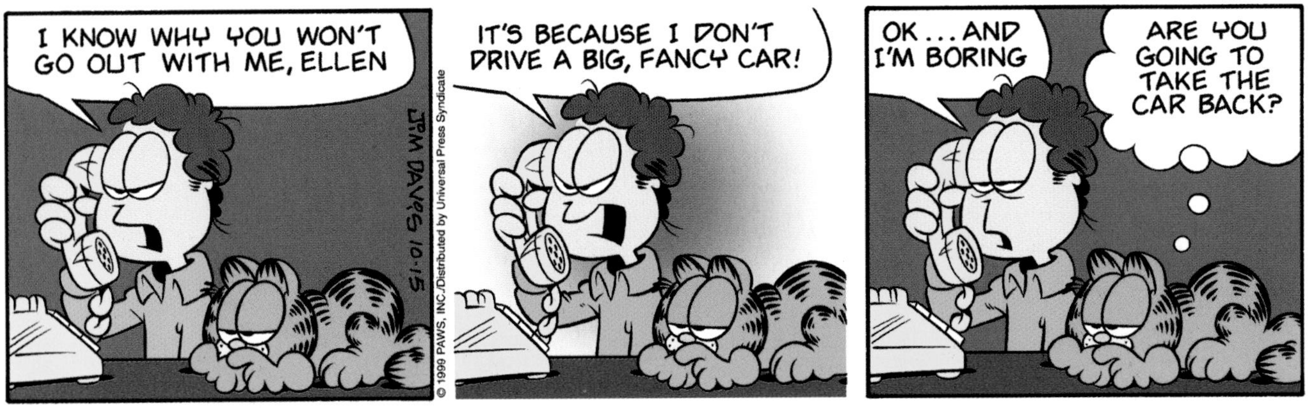
I KNOW WHY YOU WON'T GO OUT WITH ME, ELLEN
IT'S BECAUSE I DON'T DRIVE A BIG, FANCY CAR!
OK ... AND I'M BORING
ARE YOU GOING TO TAKE THE CAR BACK?
© 1999 PAWS, INC./Distributed by Universal Press Syndicate
JIM DAVIS 10-15

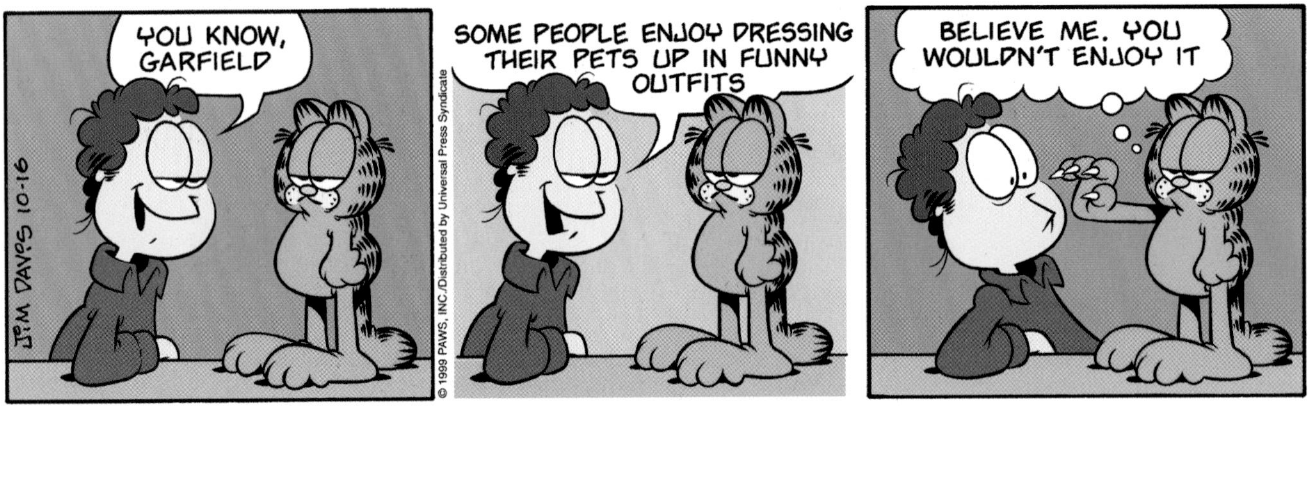
YOU KNOW, GARFIELD
SOME PEOPLE ENJOY DRESSING THEIR PETS UP IN FUNNY OUTFITS
BELIEVE ME. YOU WOULDN'T ENJOY IT
© 1999 PAWS, INC./Distributed by Universal Press Syndicate
JIM DAVIS 10-16

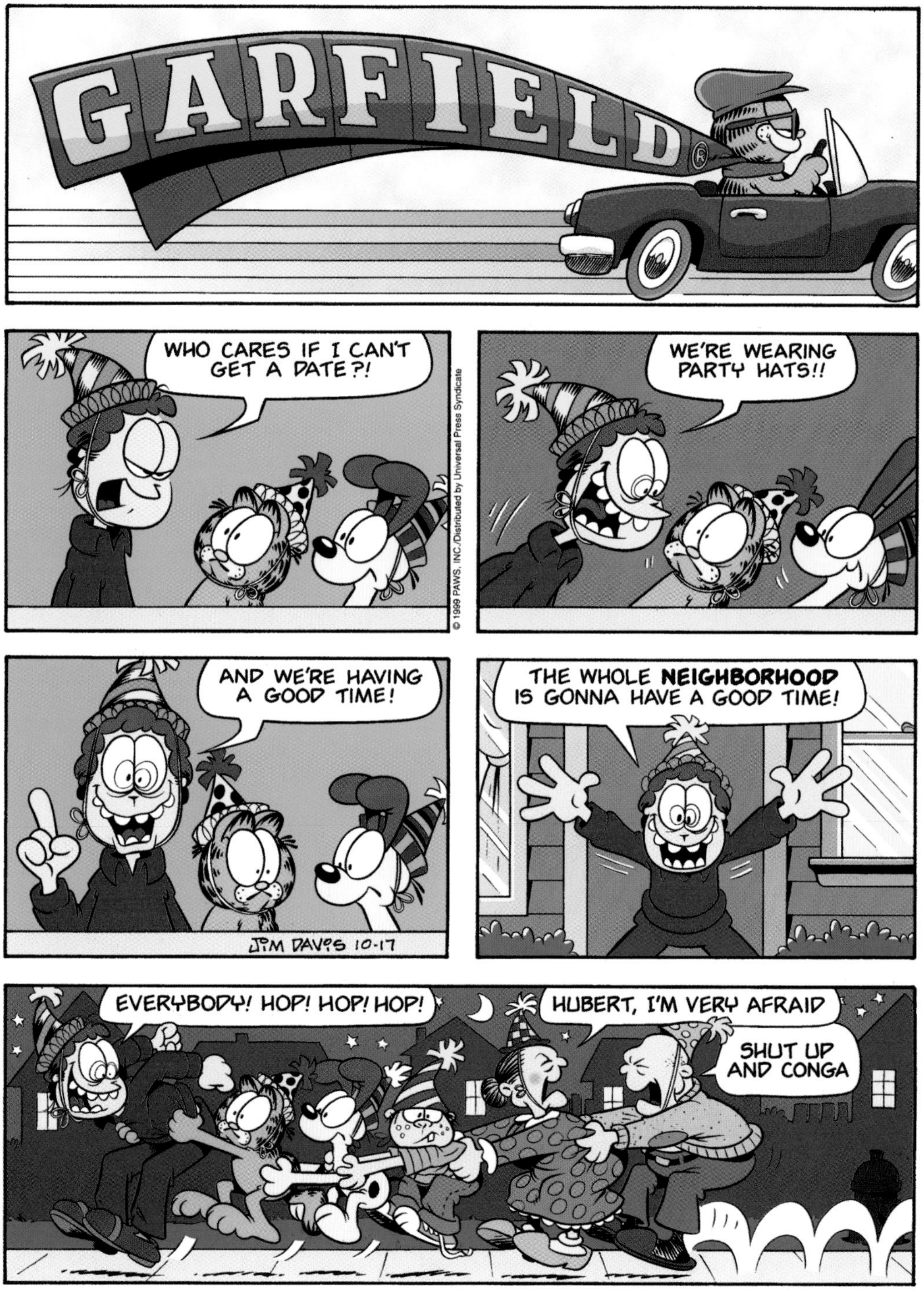
GARFIELD
WHO CARES IF I CAN'T GET A DATE?!
© 1999 PAWS, INC./Distributed by Universal Press Syndicate
WE'RE WEARING PARTY HATS!!
AND WE'RE HAVING A GOOD TIME!
JIM DAVIS 10-17
THE WHOLE NEIGHBORHOOD IS GONNA HAVE A GOOD TIME!
EVERYBODY! HOP! HOP! HOP!
HUBERT, I'M VERY AFRAID
SHUT UP AND CONGA

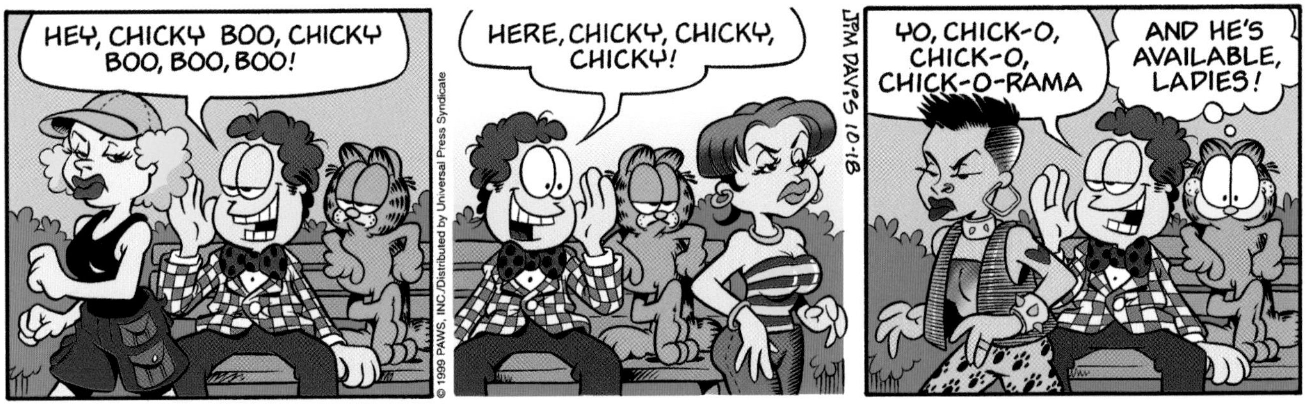
HEY, CHICKY BOO, CHICKY BOO, BOO, BOO!
© 1999 PAWS, INC./Distributed by Universal Press Syndicate
HERE, CHICKY, CHICKY, CHICKY!
JIM DAVIS 10-18
YO, CHICK-O, CHICK-O, CHICK-O-RAMA
AND HE'S AVAILABLE, LADIES!

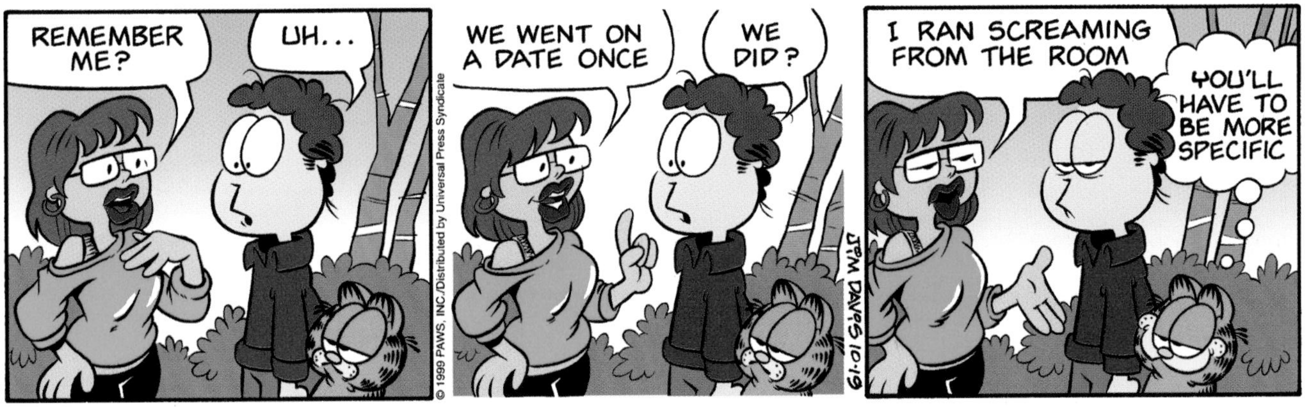
REMEMBER ME?
UH...
© 1999 PAWS, INC./Distributed by Universal Press Syndicate
WE WENT ON A DATE ONCE
WE DID?
JIM DAVIS 10-19
I RAN SCREAMING FROM THE ROOM
YOU'LL HAVE TO BE MORE SPECIFIC

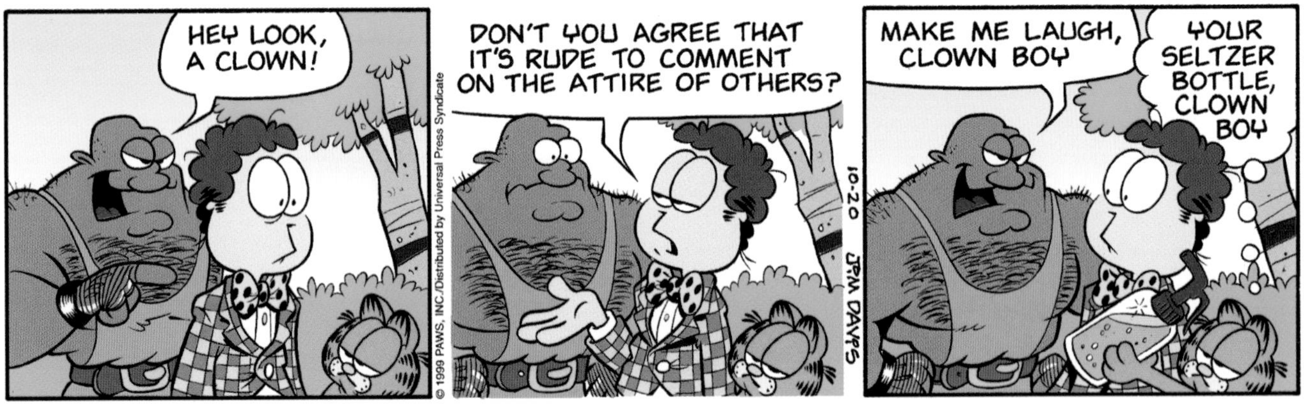
HEY LOOK, A CLOWN!
© 1999 PAWS, INC./Distributed by Universal Press Syndicate
DON'T YOU AGREE THAT IT'S RUDE TO COMMENT ON THE ATTIRE OF OTHERS?
JIM DAVIS 10-20
MAKE ME LAUGH, CLOWN BOY
YOUR SELTZER BOTTLE, CLOWN BOY

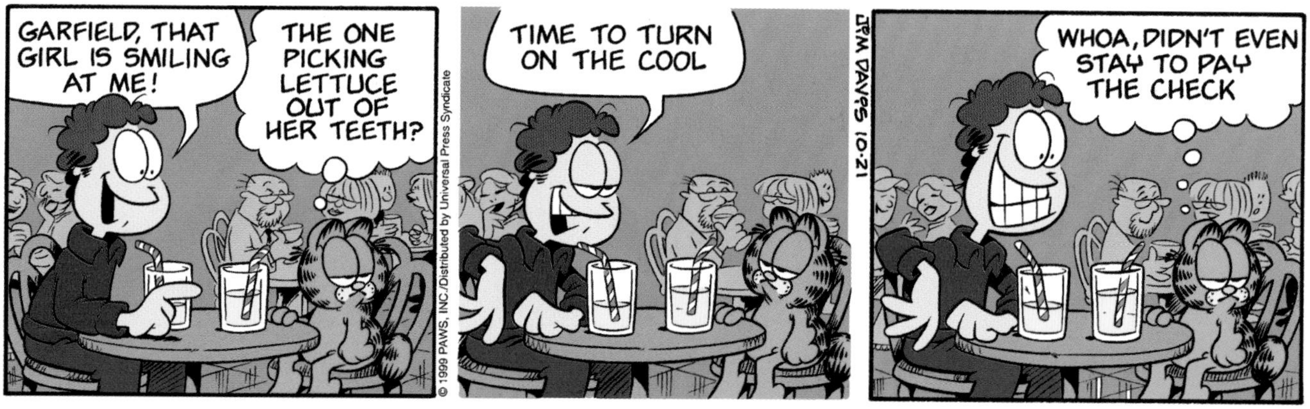
GARFIELD, THAT GIRL IS SMILING AT ME!
THE ONE PICKING LETTUCE OUT OF HER TEETH?
© 1999 PAWS, INC./Distributed by Universal Press Syndicate
TIME TO TURN ON THE COOL
JIM DAVIS 10-21
WHOA, DIDN'T EVEN STAY TO PAY THE CHECK

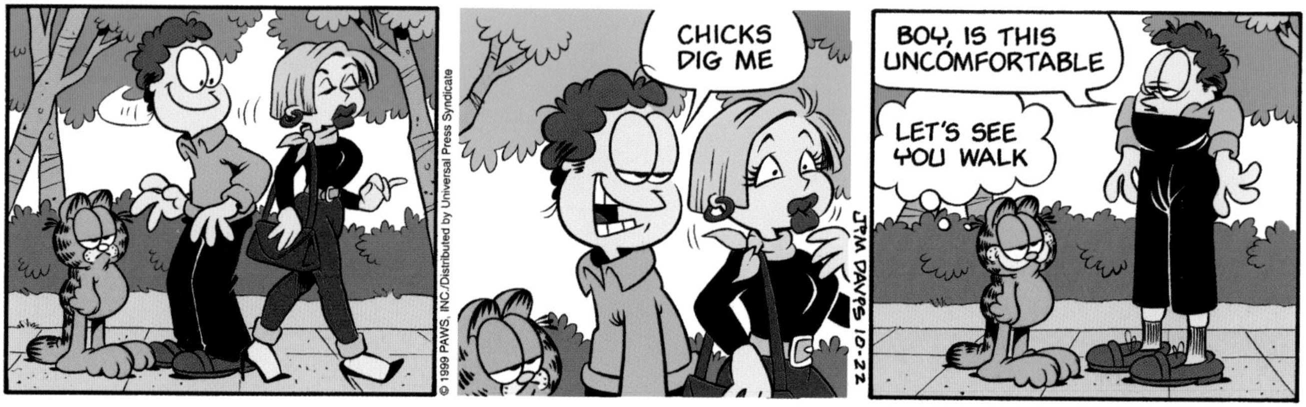
© 1999 PAWS, INC./Distributed by Universal Press Syndicate
CHICKS DIG ME
JIM DAVIS 10-22
BOY, IS THIS UNCOMFORTABLE
LET'S SEE YOU WALK

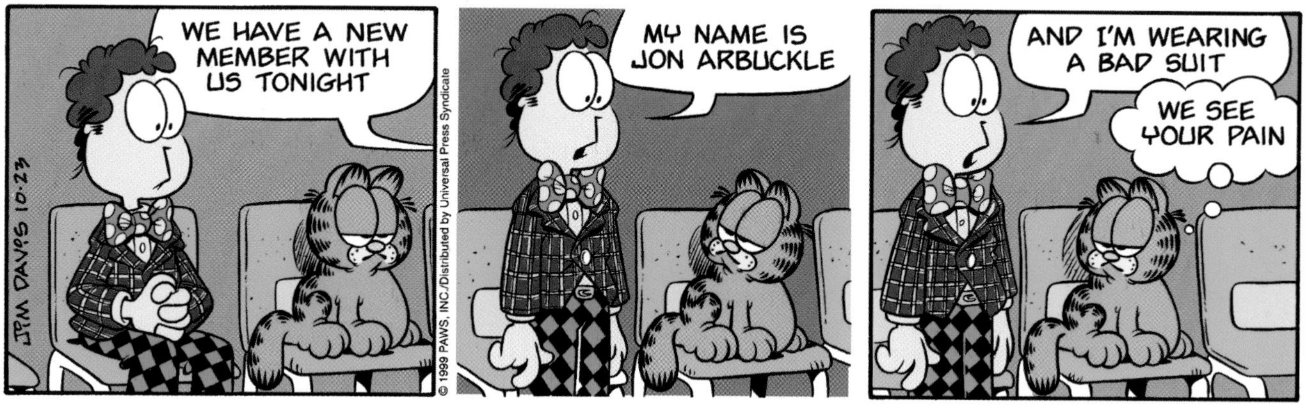
WE HAVE A NEW MEMBER WITH US TONIGHT
JIM DAVIS 10-23
© 1999 PAWS, INC./Distributed by Universal Press Syndicate
MY NAME IS JON ARBUCKLE
AND I'M WEARING A BAD SUIT
WE SEE YOUR PAIN

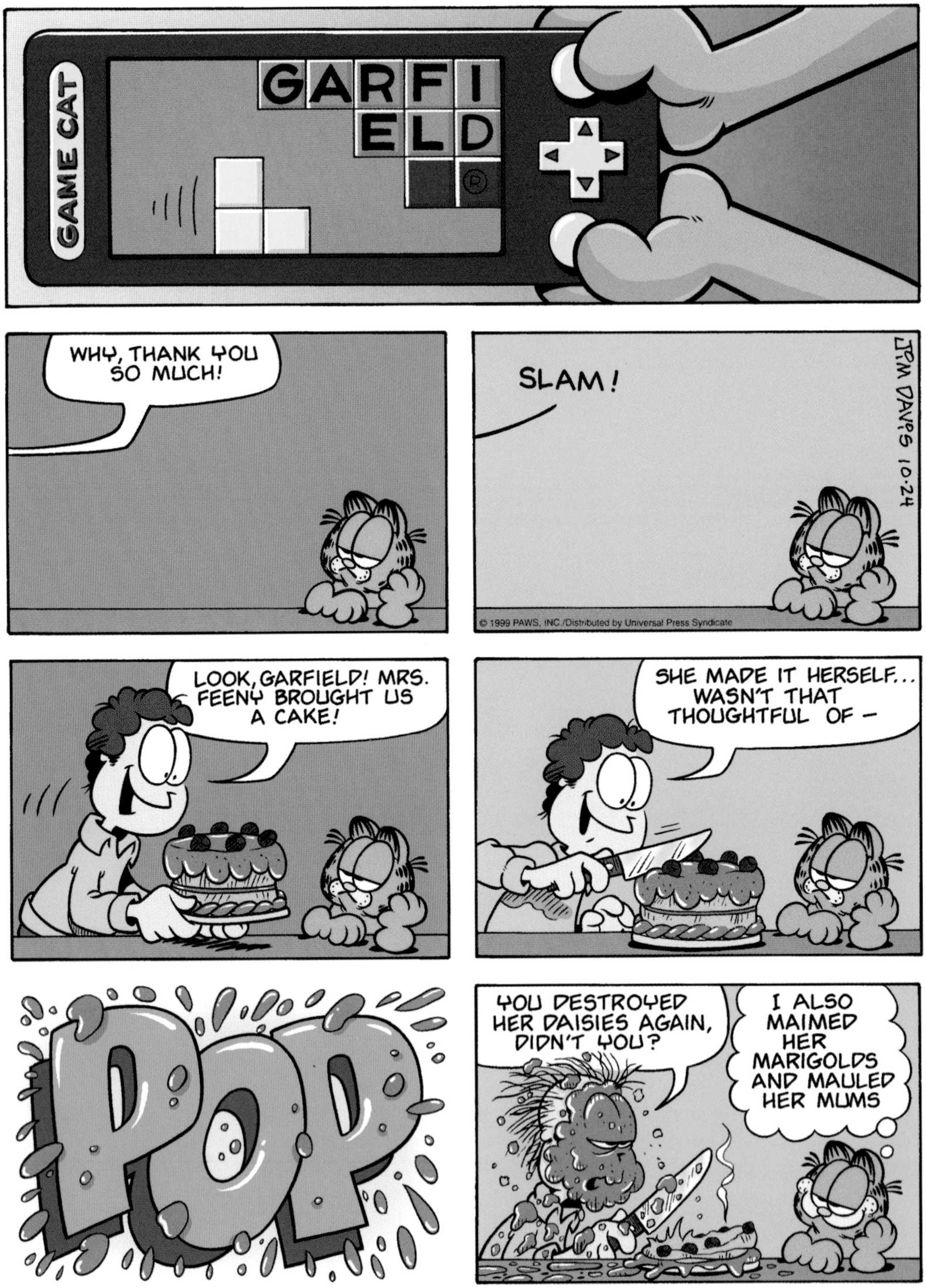
GAME CAT
GARFIELD®
WHY, THANK YOU SO MUCH!
SLAM!
JIM DAVIS 10-24
© 1999 PAWS, INC./Distributed by Universal Press Syndicate
LOOK, GARFIELD! MRS. FEENY BROUGHT US A CAKE!
SHE MADE IT HERSELF... WASN'T THAT THOUGHTFUL OF –
POP
YOU DESTROYED HER DAISIES AGAIN, DIDN'T YOU?
I ALSO MAIMED HER MARIGOLDS AND MAULED HER MUMS

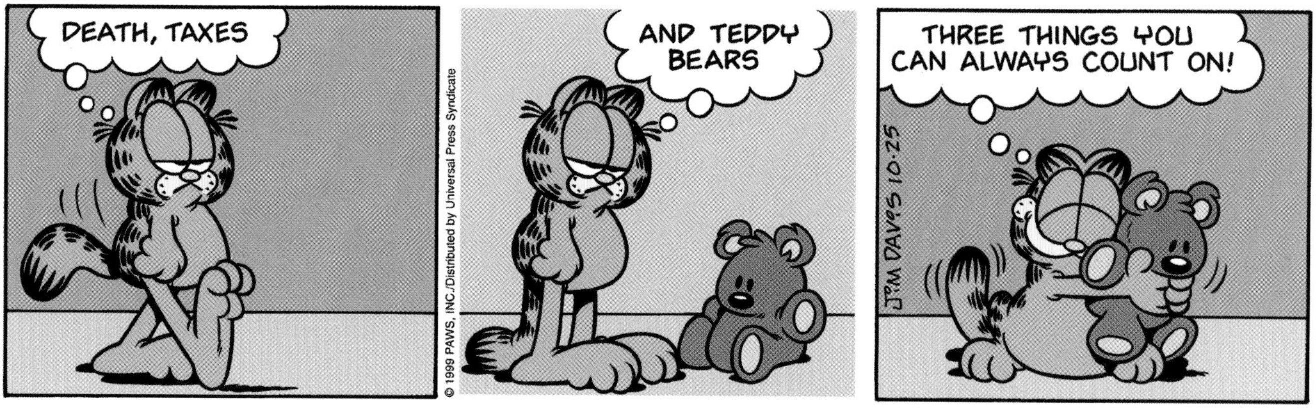
DEATH, TAXES
AND TEDDY BEARS
THREE THINGS YOU CAN ALWAYS COUNT ON!
JIM DAVIS 10-25

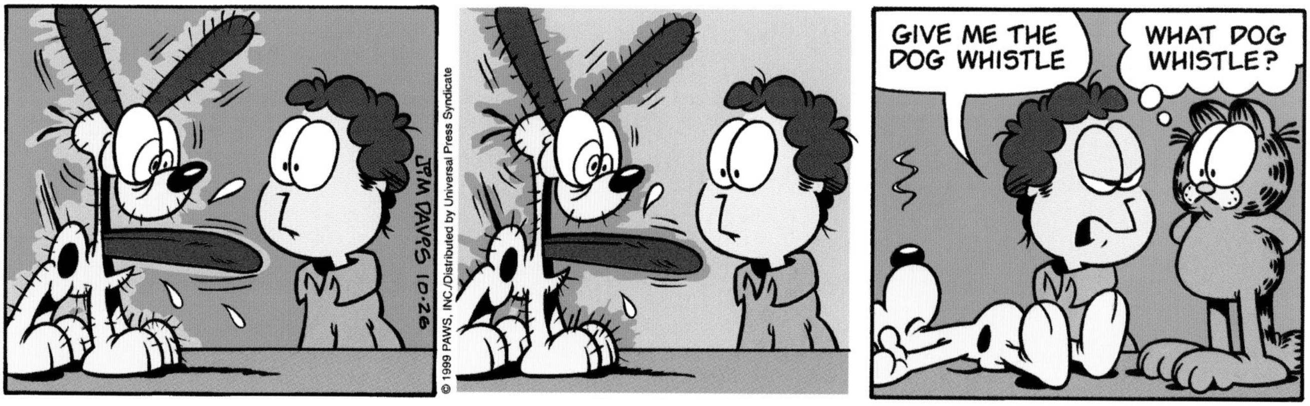
JIM DAVIS 10-26
GIVE ME THE DOG WHISTLE
WHAT DOG WHISTLE?

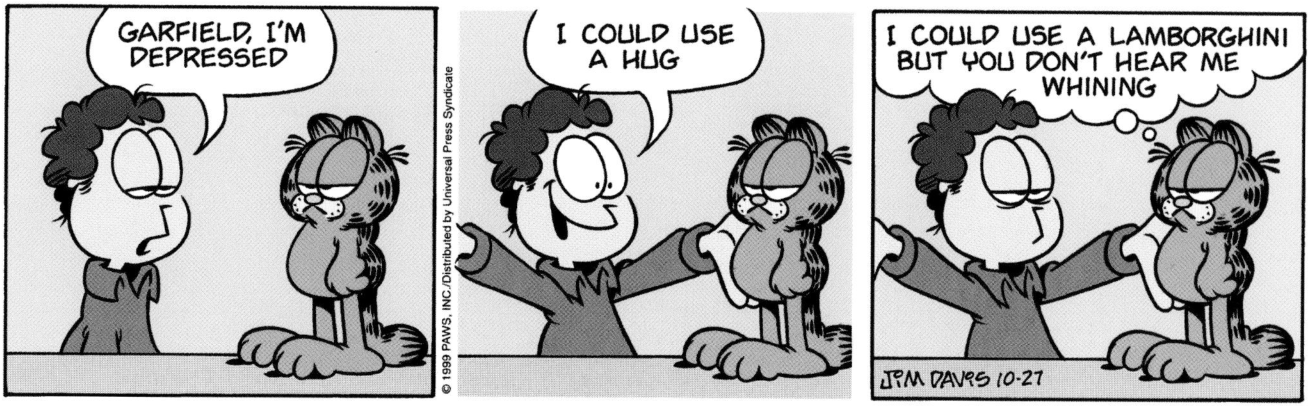
GARFIELD, I'M DEPRESSED
I COULD USE A HUG
I COULD USE A LAMBORGHINI BUT YOU DON'T HEAR ME WHINING
JIM DAVIS 10-27

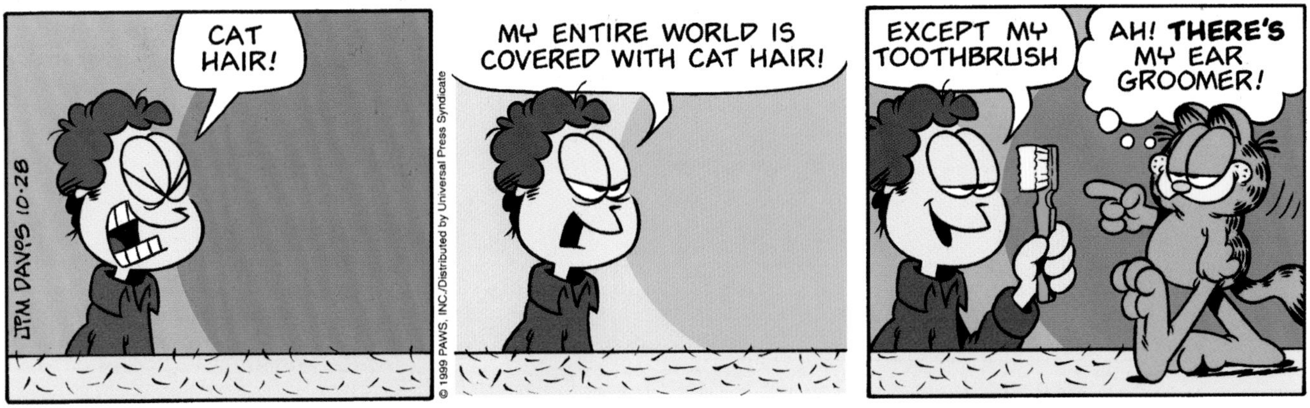
CAT HAIR!
JPM DAVIS 10-28
© 1999 PAWS, INC./Distributed by Universal Press Syndicate
MY ENTIRE WORLD IS COVERED WITH CAT HAIR!
EXCEPT MY TOOTHBRUSH
AH! **THERE'S** MY EAR GROOMER!

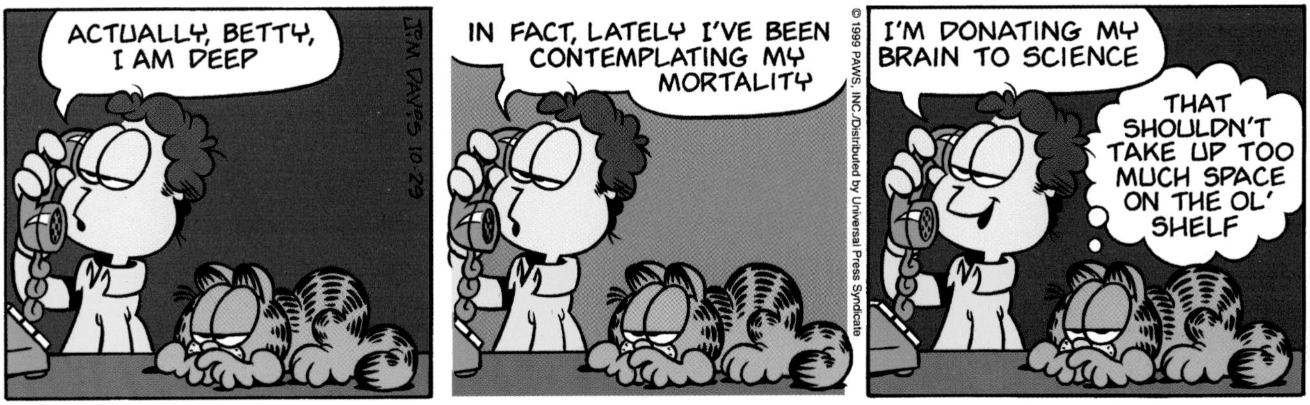
ACTUALLY, BETTY, I AM DEEP
JPM DAVIS 10-29
IN FACT, LATELY I'VE BEEN CONTEMPLATING MY MORTALITY
© 1999 PAWS, INC./Distributed by Universal Press Syndicate
I'M DONATING MY BRAIN TO SCIENCE
THAT SHOULDN'T TAKE UP TOO MUCH SPACE ON THE OL' SHELF

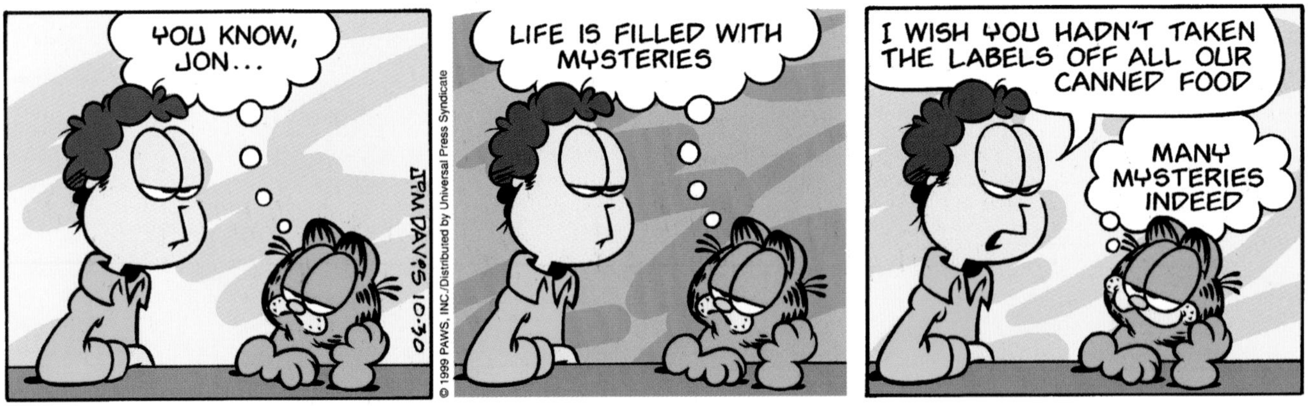
YOU KNOW, JON...
JPM DAVIS 10-30
© 1999 PAWS, INC./Distributed by Universal Press Syndicate
LIFE IS FILLED WITH MYSTERIES
I WISH YOU HADN'T TAKEN THE LABELS OFF ALL OUR CANNED FOOD
MANY MYSTERIES INDEED

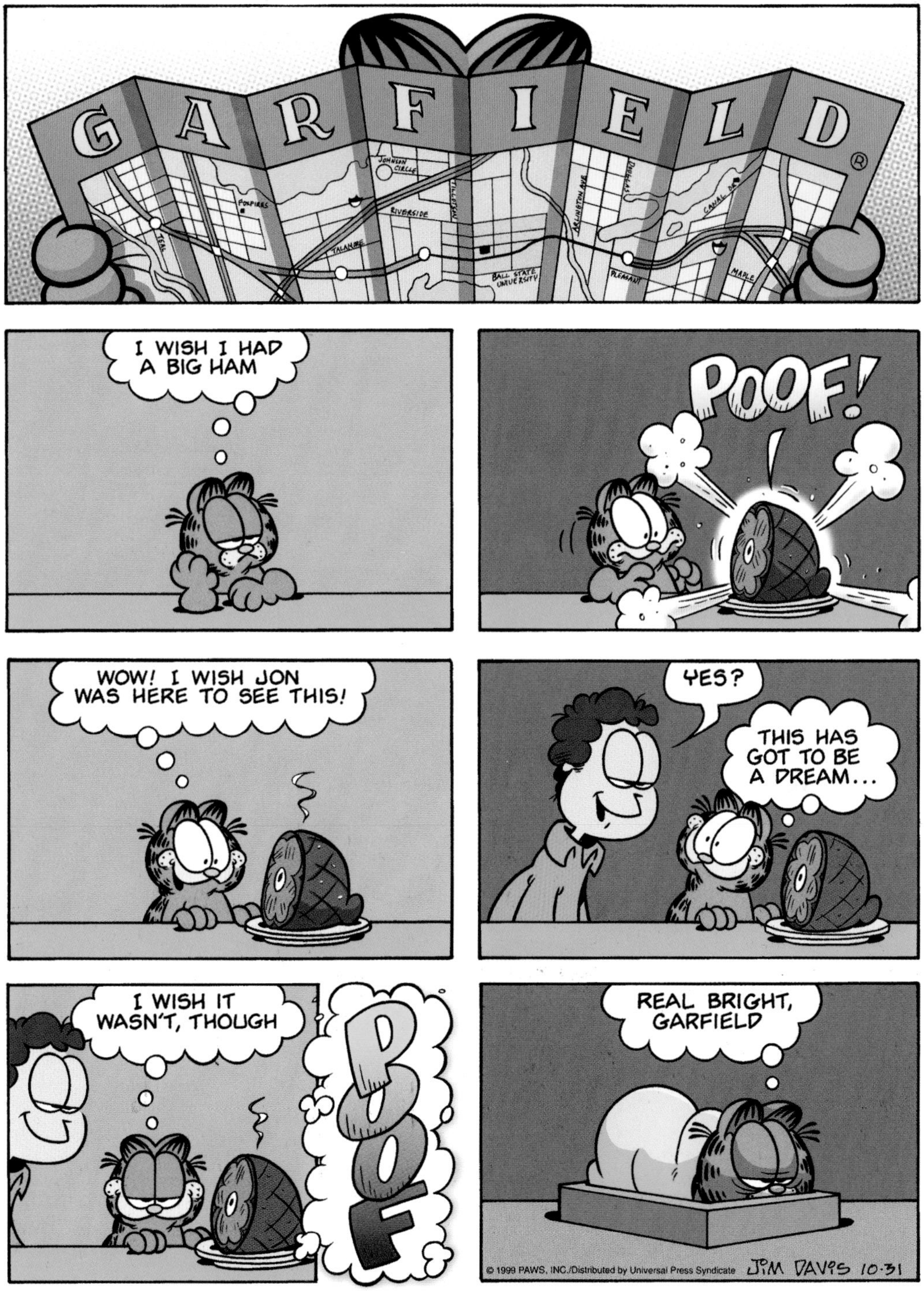
GARFIELD®
I WISH I HAD A BIG HAM
POOF!
WOW! I WISH JON WAS HERE TO SEE THIS!
YES?
THIS HAS GOT TO BE A DREAM...
I WISH IT WASN'T, THOUGH
POOF
REAL BRIGHT, GARFIELD
© 1999 PAWS, INC./Distributed by Universal Press Syndicate
JIM DAVIS 10-31

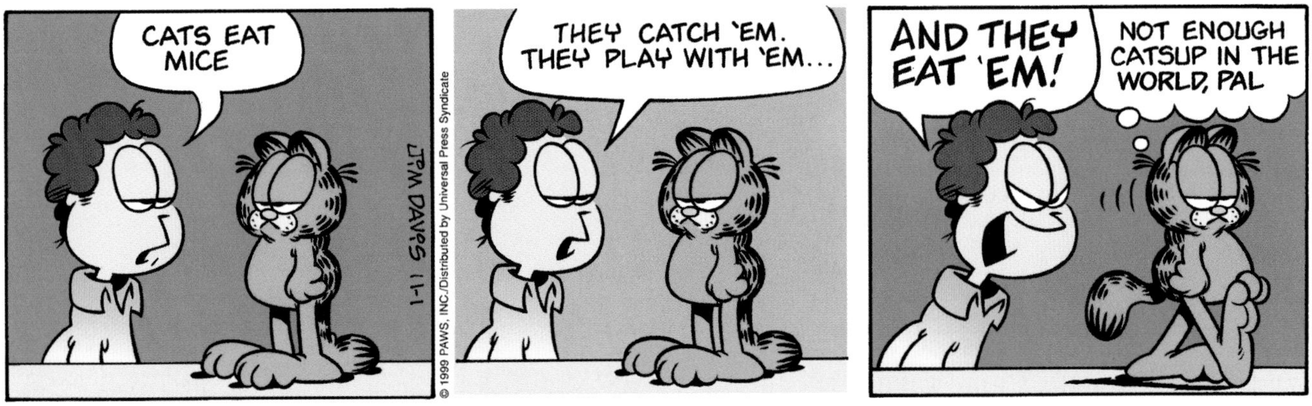
CATS EAT MICE
JIM DAVIS 11-1
THEY CATCH 'EM. THEY PLAY WITH 'EM...
AND THEY EAT 'EM!
NOT ENOUGH CATSUP IN THE WORLD, PAL

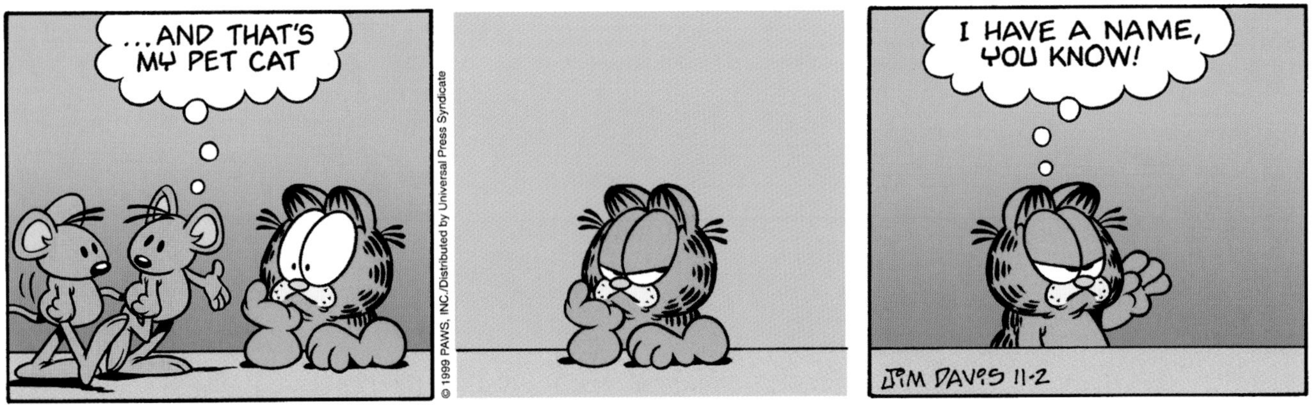
...AND THAT'S MY PET CAT
I HAVE A NAME, YOU KNOW!
JIM DAVIS 11-2

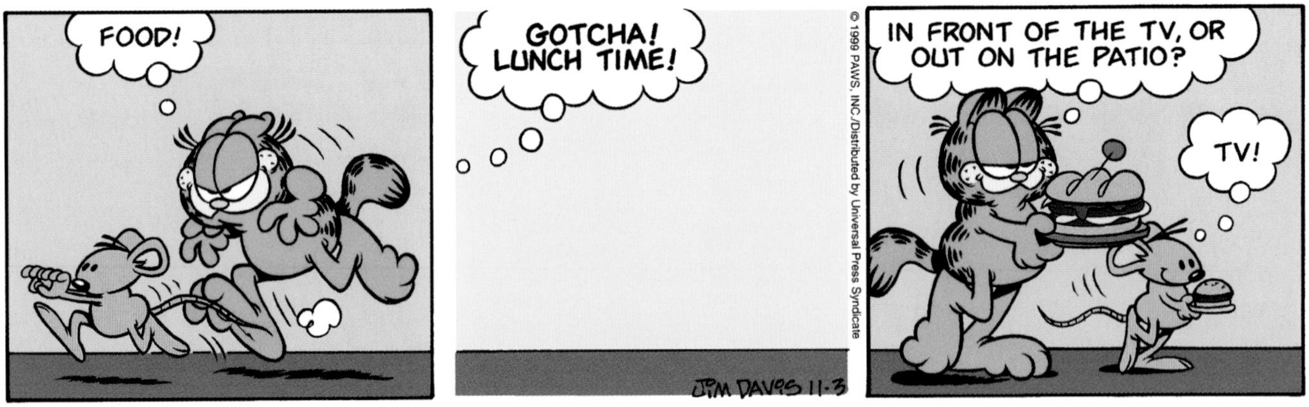
FOOD!
GOTCHA! LUNCH TIME!
JIM DAVIS 11-3
IN FRONT OF THE TV, OR OUT ON THE PATIO?
TV!

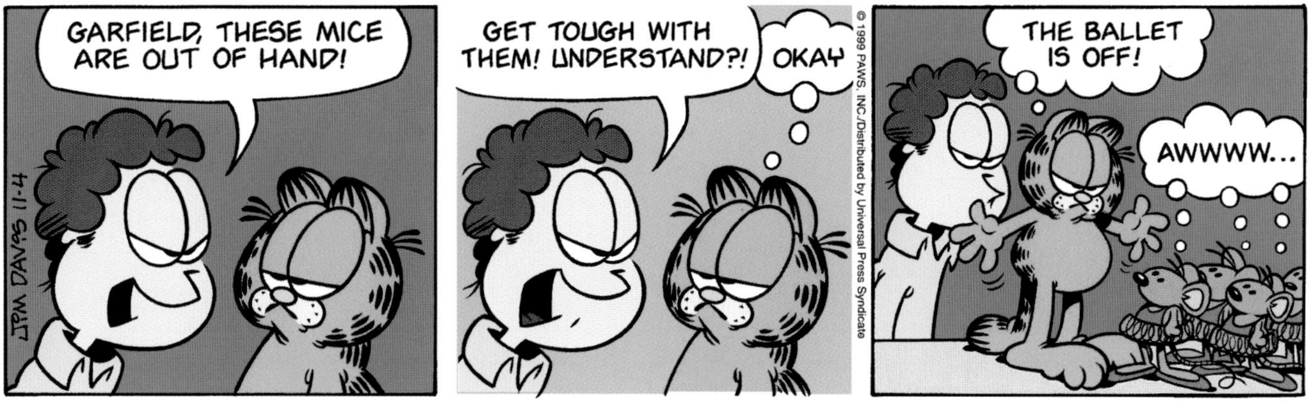
GARFIELD, THESE MICE ARE OUT OF HAND!
GET TOUGH WITH THEM! UNDERSTAND?!
OKAY
THE BALLET IS OFF!
AWWWW...
© 1999 PAWS, INC./Distributed by Universal Press Syndicate

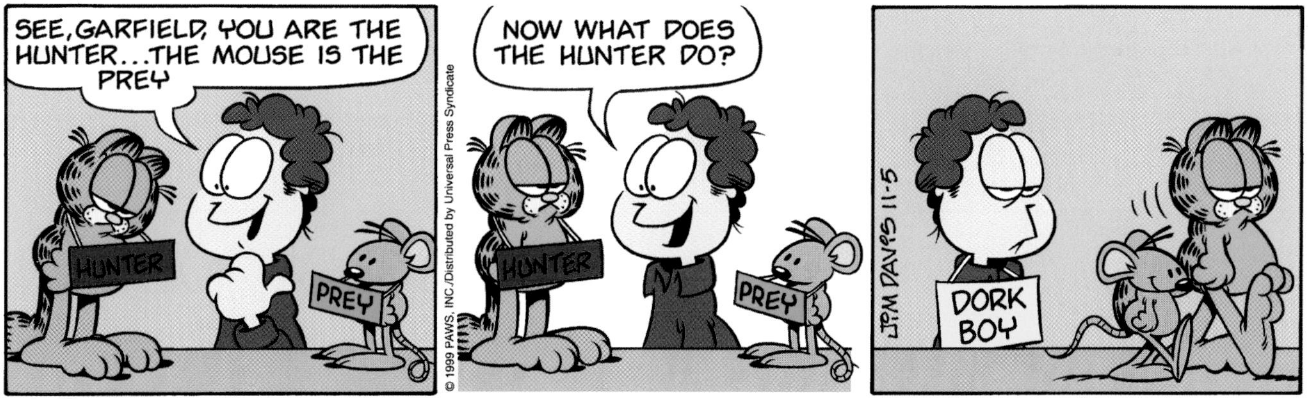
SEE, GARFIELD, YOU ARE THE HUNTER...THE MOUSE IS THE PREY
HUNTER
PREY
NOW WHAT DOES THE HUNTER DO?
HUNTER
PREY
DORK BOY
© 1999 PAWS, INC./Distributed by Universal Press Syndicate

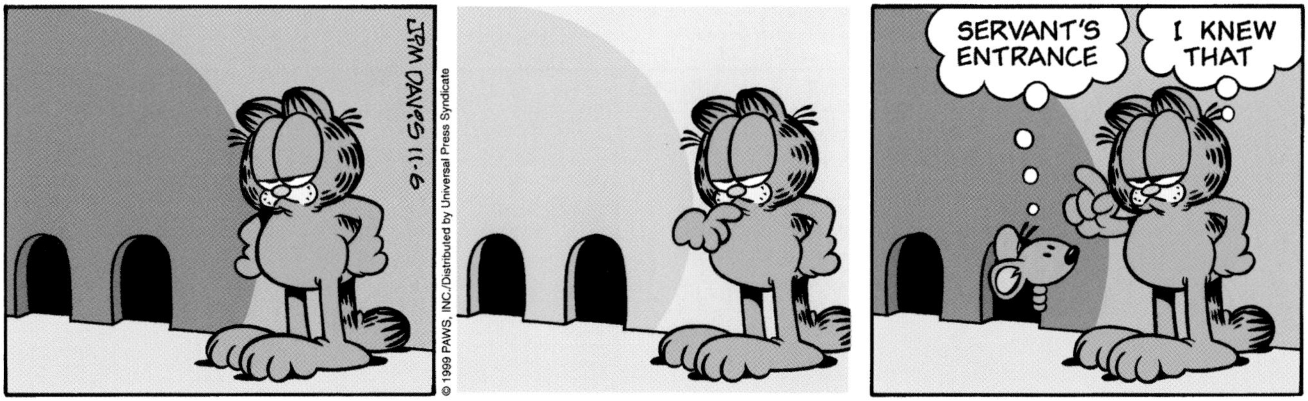
SERVANT'S ENTRANCE
I KNEW THAT
© 1999 PAWS, INC./Distributed by Universal Press Syndicate

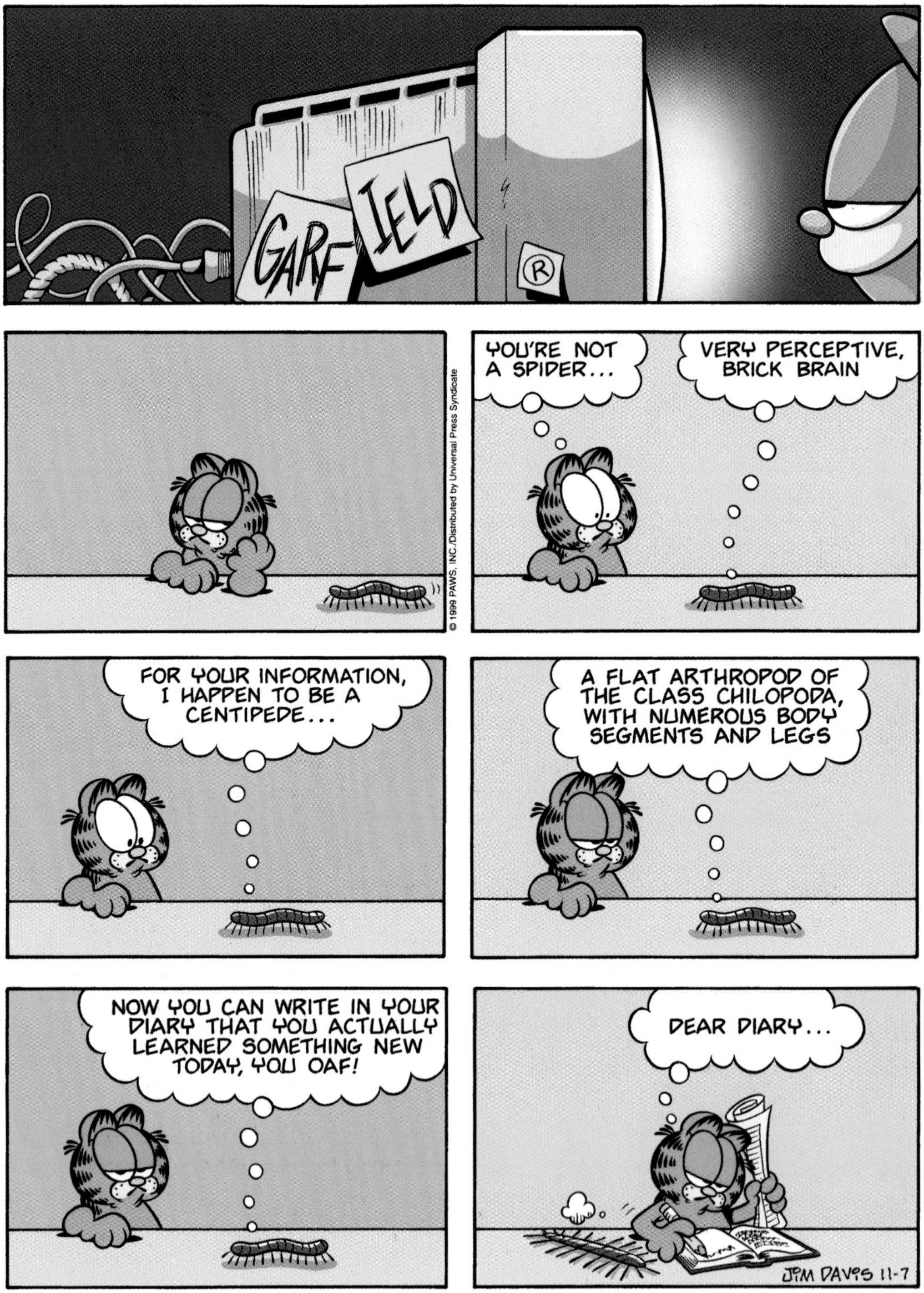
GARFIELD
®
© 1999 PAWS, INC./Distributed by Universal Press Syndicate
YOU'RE NOT A SPIDER...
VERY PERCEPTIVE, BRICK BRAIN
FOR YOUR INFORMATION, I HAPPEN TO BE A CENTIPEDE...
A FLAT ARTHROPOD OF THE CLASS CHILOPODA, WITH NUMEROUS BODY SEGMENTS AND LEGS
NOW YOU CAN WRITE IN YOUR DIARY THAT YOU ACTUALLY LEARNED SOMETHING NEW TODAY, YOU OAF!
DEAR DIARY...
JIM DAVIS 11-7

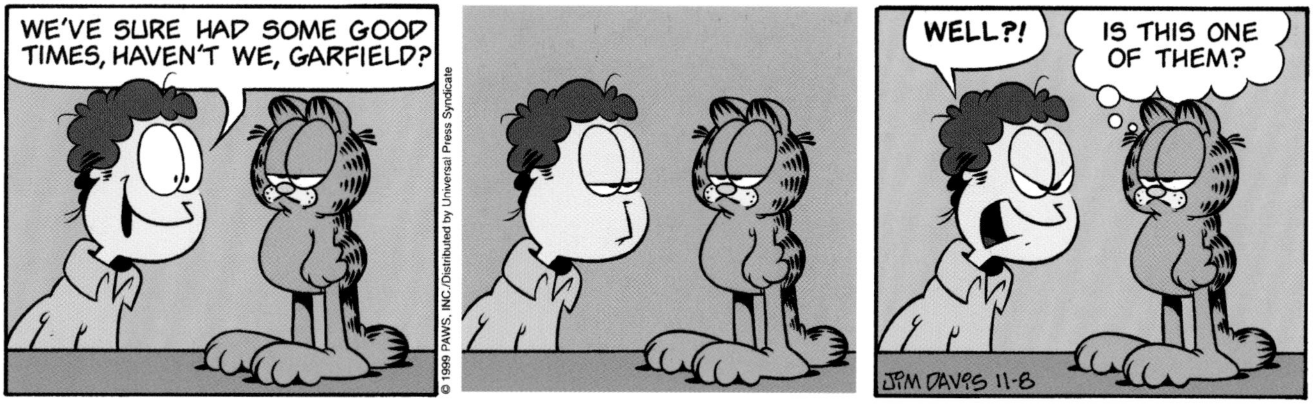
WE'VE SURE HAD SOME GOOD TIMES, HAVEN'T WE, GARFIELD?
© 1999 PAWS, INC./Distributed by Universal Press Syndicate
WELL?!
IS THIS ONE OF THEM?
JIM DAVIS 11-8

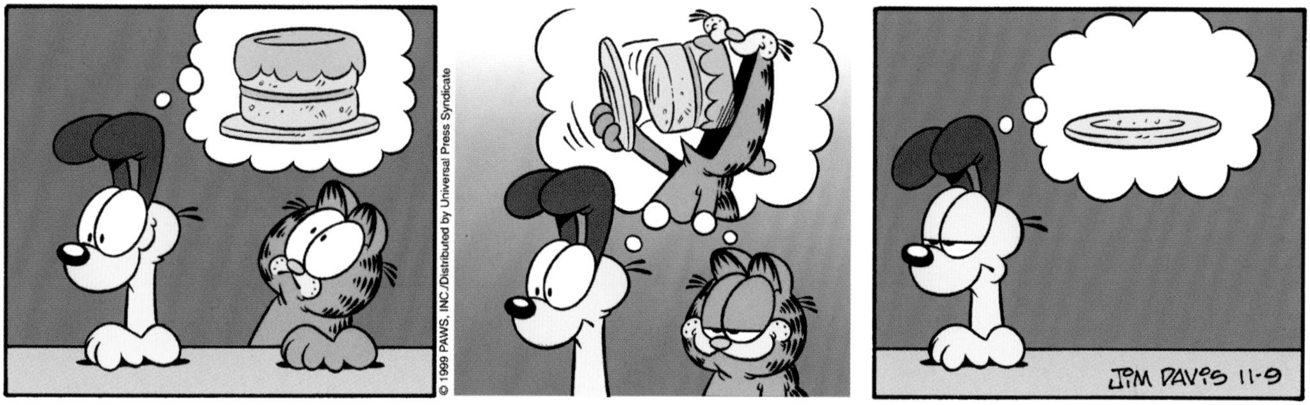
© 1999 PAWS, INC./Distributed by Universal Press Syndicate
JIM DAVIS 11-9

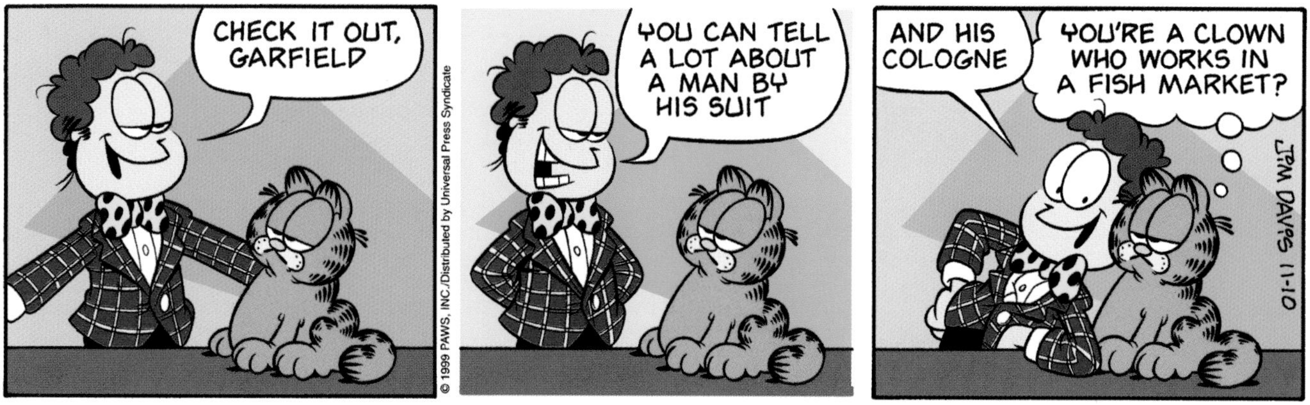
CHECK IT OUT, GARFIELD
© 1999 PAWS, INC./Distributed by Universal Press Syndicate
YOU CAN TELL A LOT ABOUT A MAN BY HIS SUIT
AND HIS COLOGNE
YOU'RE A CLOWN WHO WORKS IN A FISH MARKET?
JIM DAVIS 11-10

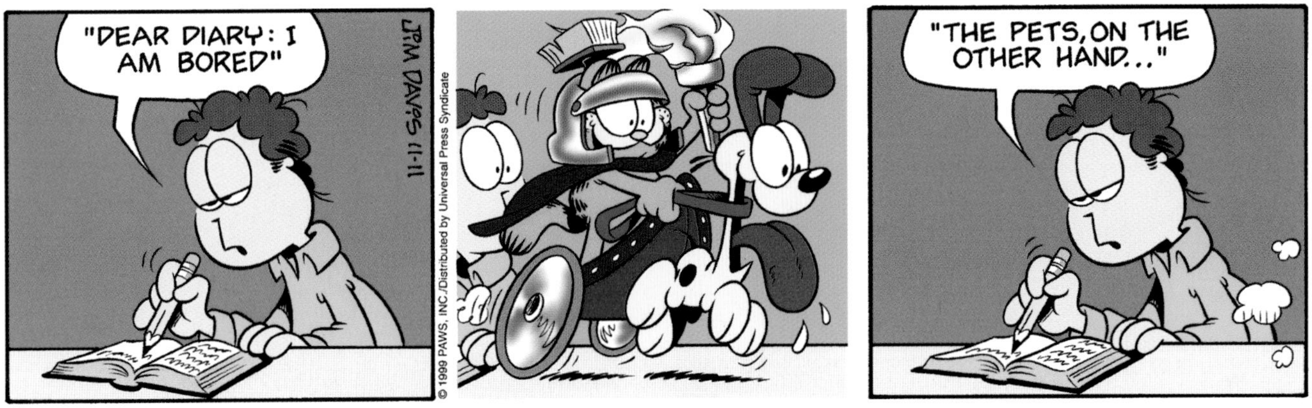
"DEAR DIARY: I AM BORED"
JIM DAVIS 11-11
© 1999 PAWS, INC./Distributed by Universal Press Syndicate
"THE PETS, ON THE OTHER HAND..."

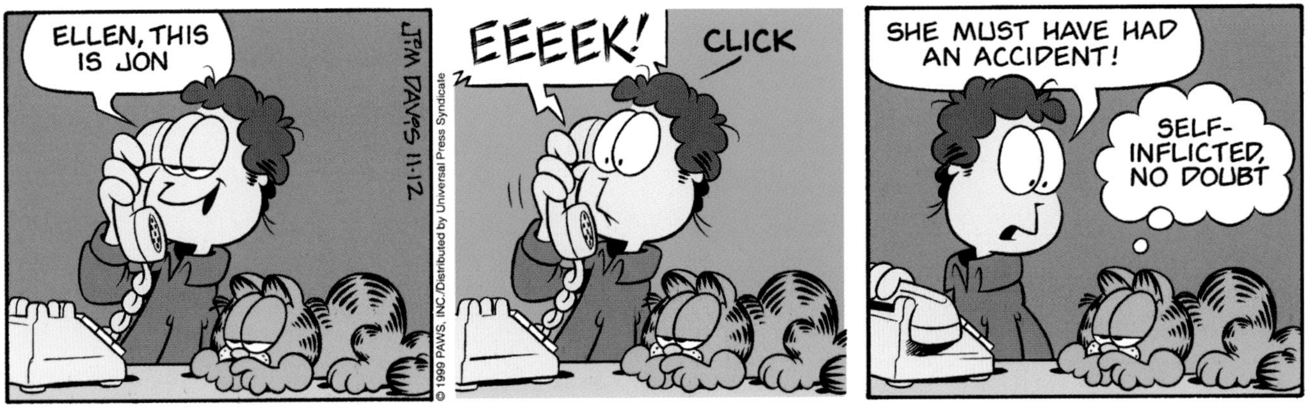
ELLEN, THIS IS JON
JIM DAVIS 11-12
© 1999 PAWS, INC./Distributed by Universal Press Syndicate
EEEEK!
CLICK
SHE MUST HAVE HAD AN ACCIDENT!
SELF-INFLICTED, NO DOUBT

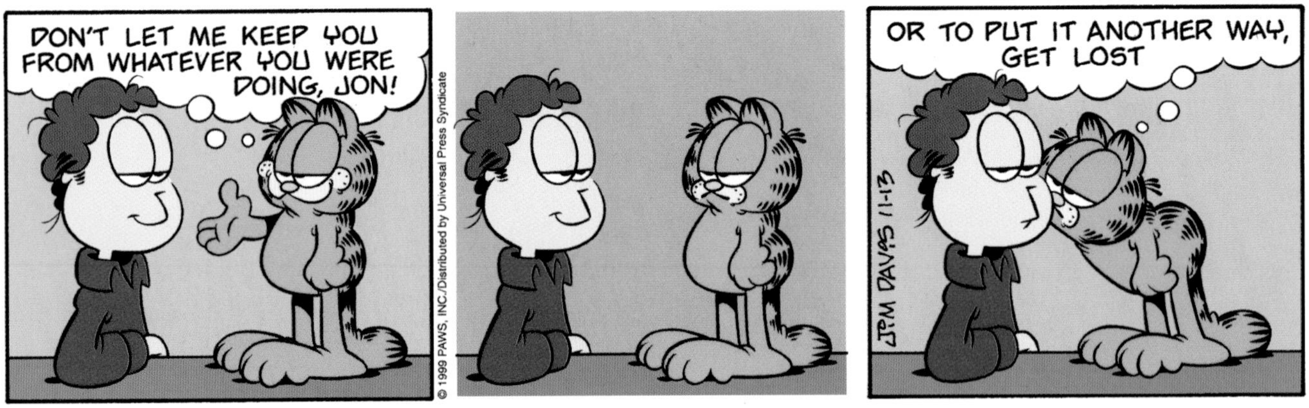
DON'T LET ME KEEP YOU FROM WHATEVER YOU WERE DOING, JON!
© 1999 PAWS, INC./Distributed by Universal Press Syndicate
OR TO PUT IT ANOTHER WAY, GET LOST
JIM DAVIS 11-13

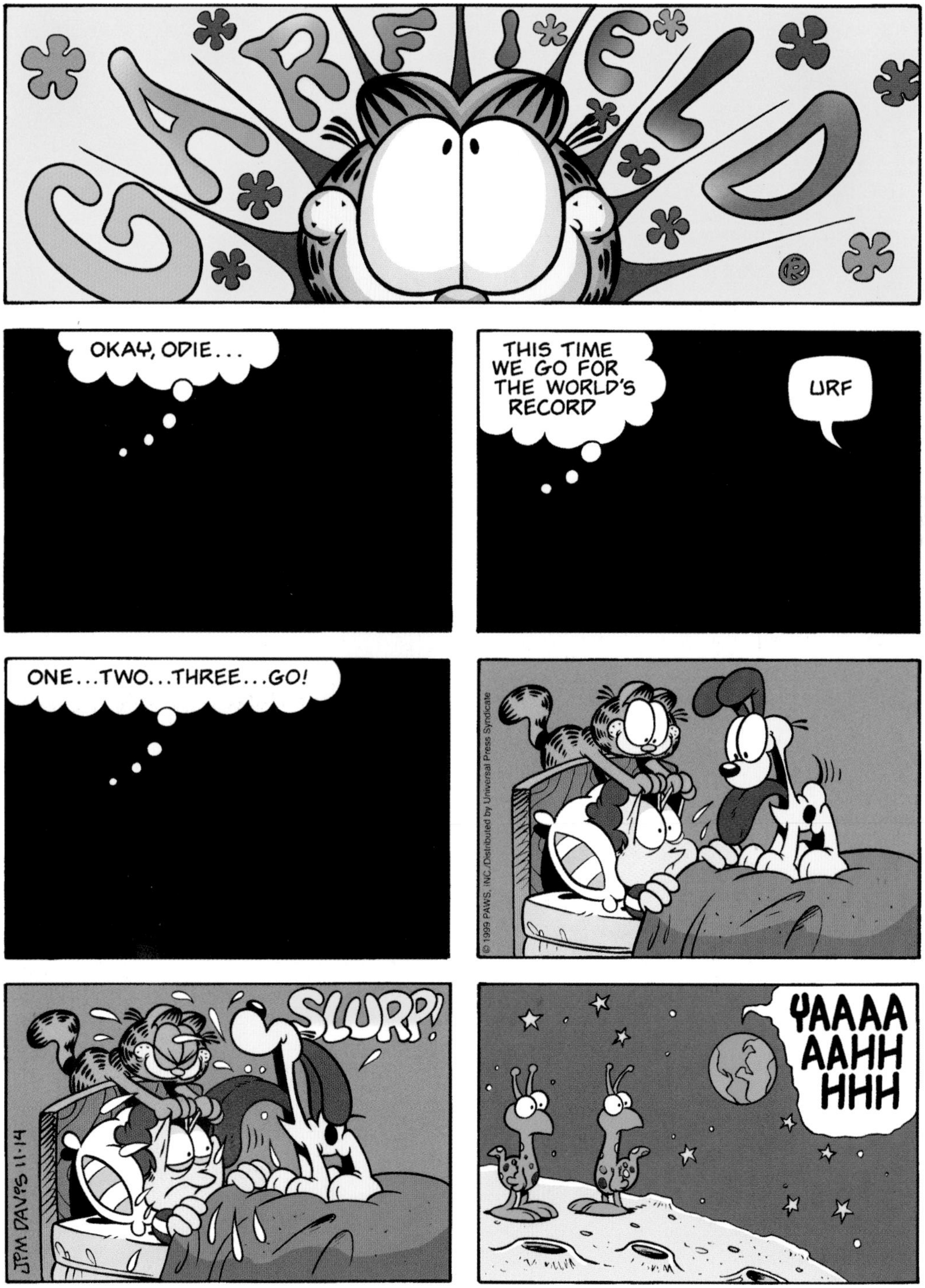
GARFIELD ®
OKAY, ODIE...
THIS TIME WE GO FOR THE WORLD'S RECORD
URF
ONE...TWO...THREE...GO!
© 1999 PAWS, INC./Distributed by Universal Press Syndicate
SLURP!
JPM DAVPS 11-14
YAAAA AAHH HHH

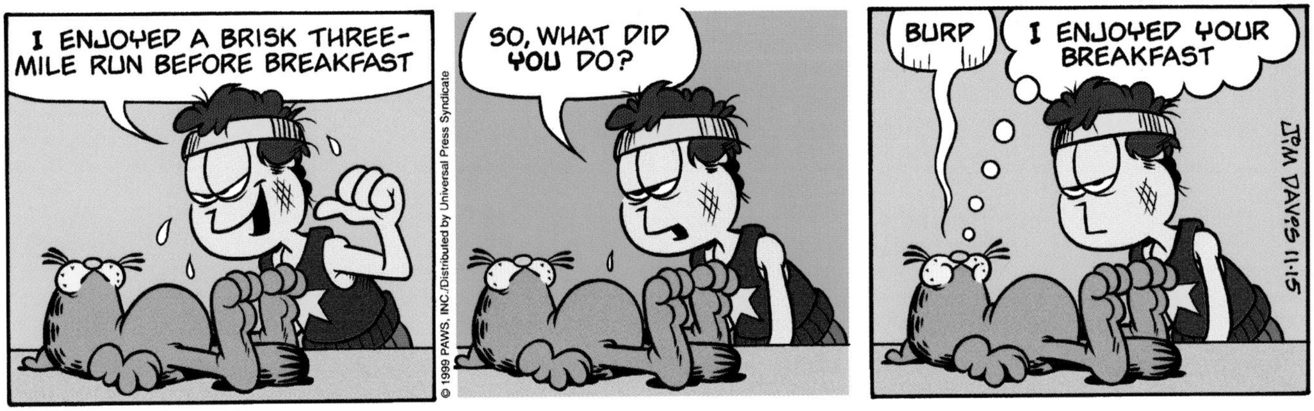
I ENJOYED A BRISK THREE-MILE RUN BEFORE BREAKFAST
© 1999 PAWS, INC./Distributed by Universal Press Syndicate
SO, WHAT DID YOU DO?
BURP
I ENJOYED YOUR BREAKFAST
JIM DAVIS 11-15

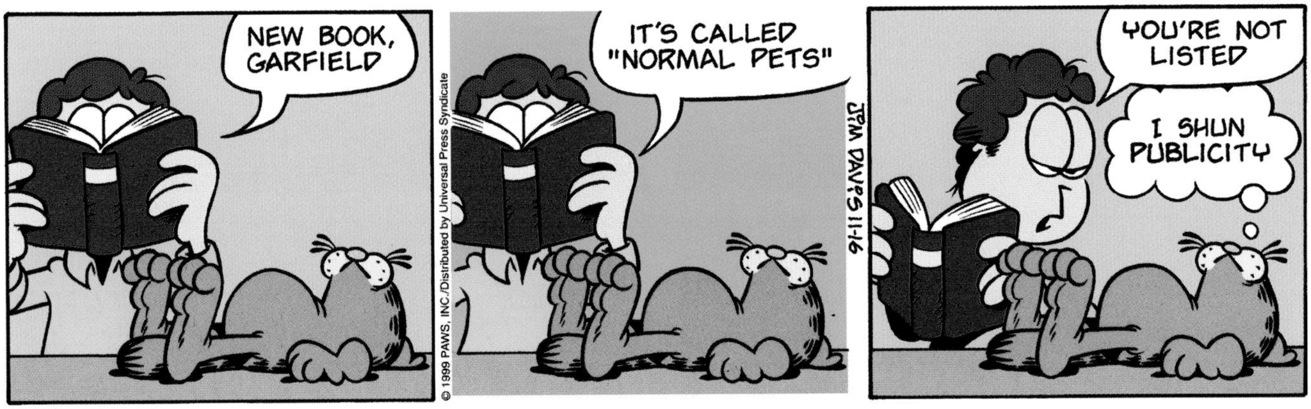
NEW BOOK, GARFIELD
© 1999 PAWS, INC./Distributed by Universal Press Syndicate
IT'S CALLED "NORMAL PETS"
JIM DAVIS 11-16
YOU'RE NOT LISTED
I SHUN PUBLICITY

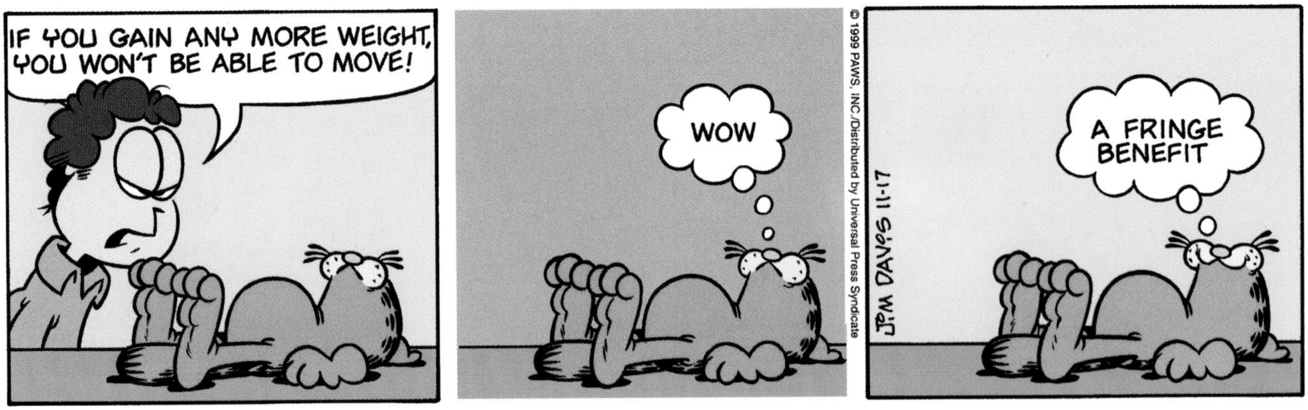
IF YOU GAIN ANY MORE WEIGHT, YOU WON'T BE ABLE TO MOVE!
WOW
© 1999 PAWS, INC./Distributed by Universal Press Syndicate
JIM DAVIS 11-17
A FRINGE BENEFIT

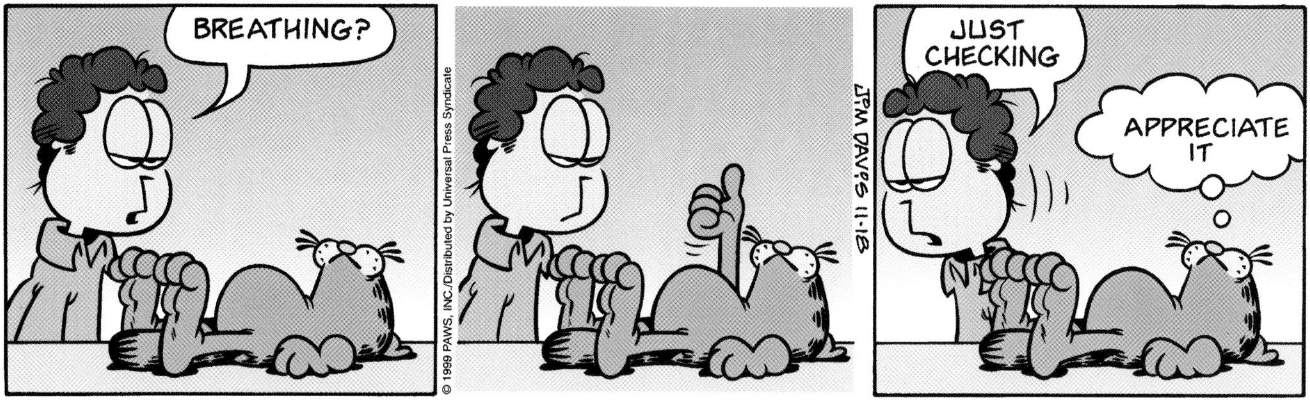
BREATHING?
© 1999 PAWS, INC./Distributed by Universal Press Syndicate
JIM DAVIS 11-18
JUST CHECKING
APPRECIATE IT

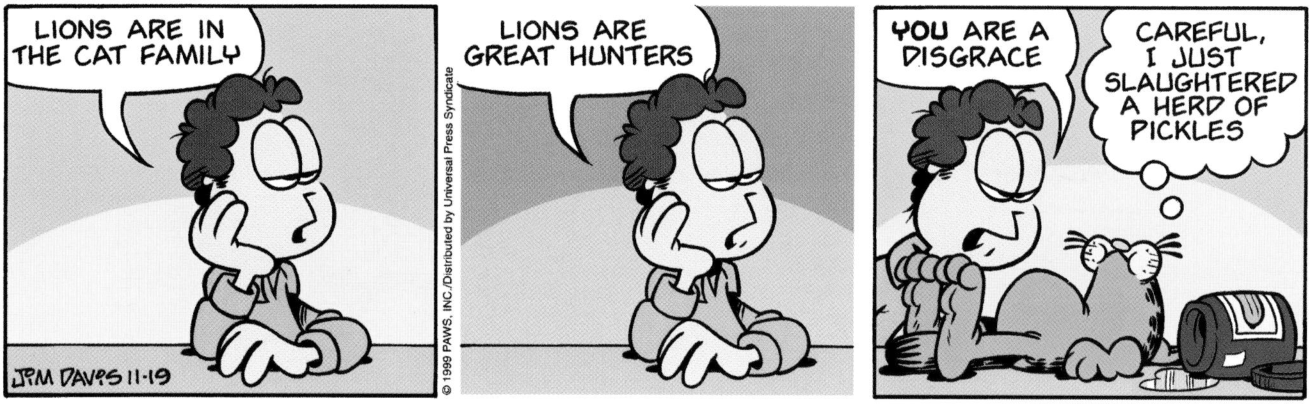
LIONS ARE IN THE CAT FAMILY
JIM DAVIS 11-19
© 1999 PAWS, INC./Distributed by Universal Press Syndicate
LIONS ARE GREAT HUNTERS
YOU ARE A DISGRACE
CAREFUL, I JUST SLAUGHTERED A HERD OF PICKLES

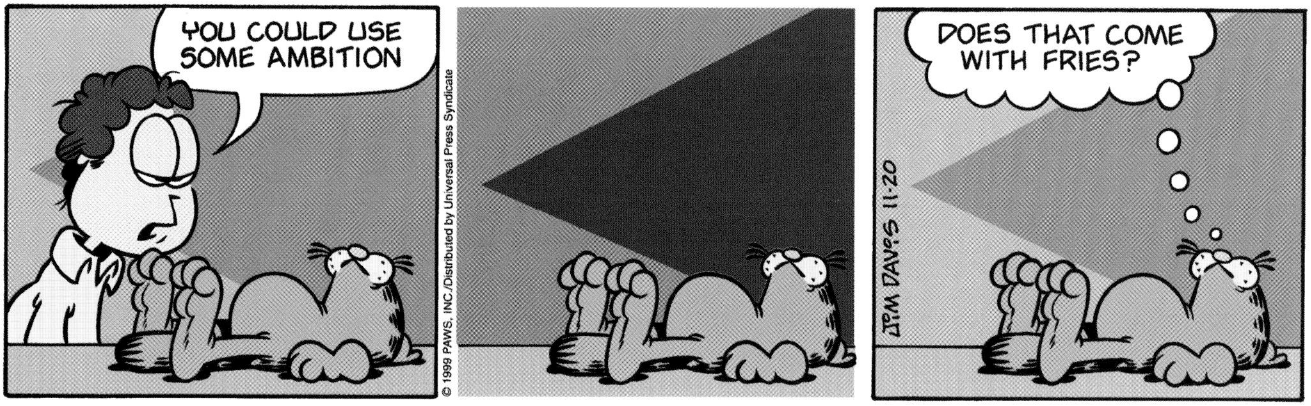
YOU COULD USE SOME AMBITION
© 1999 PAWS, INC./Distributed by Universal Press Syndicate
JIM DAVIS 11-20
DOES THAT COME WITH FRIES?

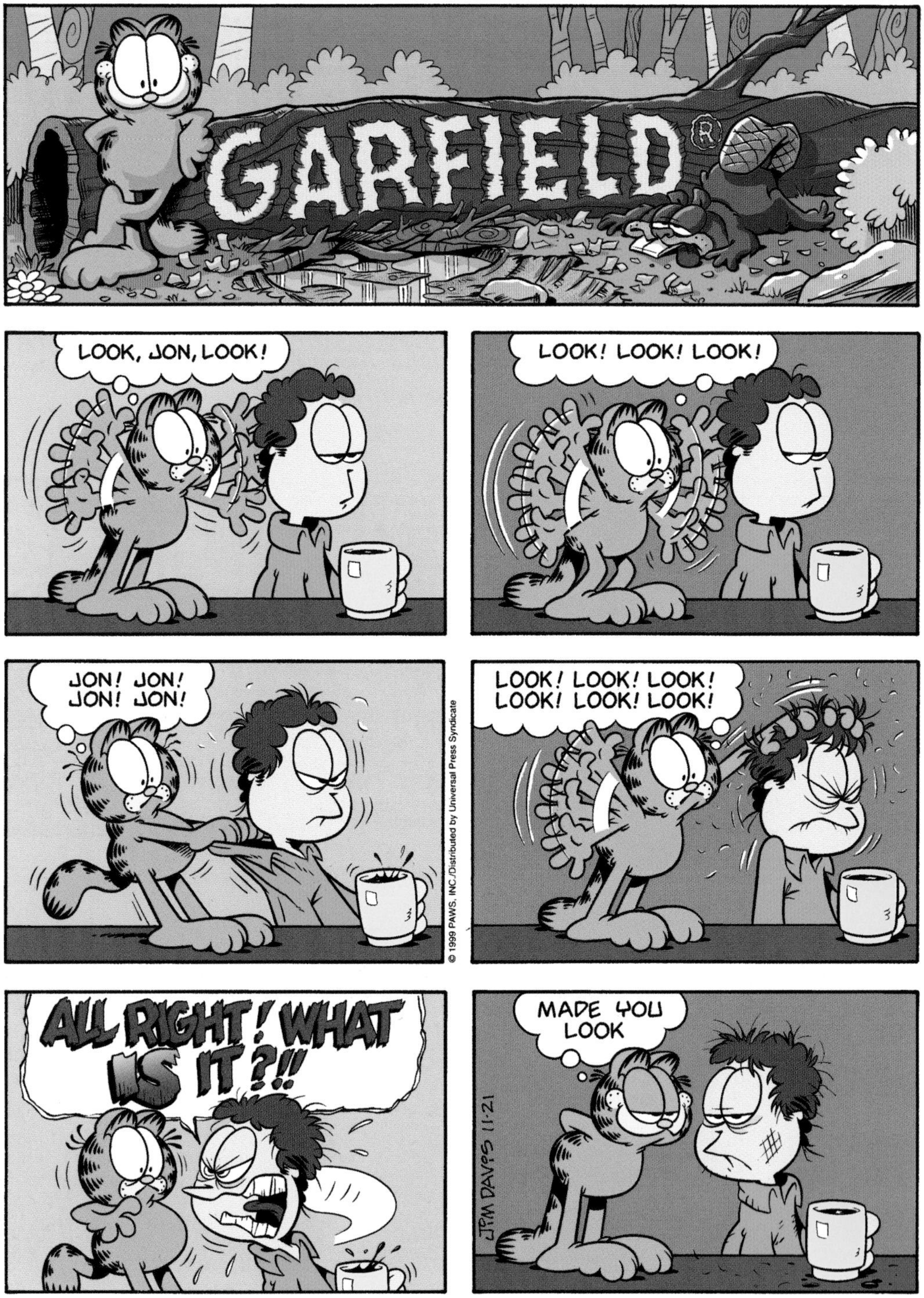
GARFIELD®
LOOK, JON, LOOK!
LOOK! LOOK! LOOK!
JON! JON! JON! JON!
LOOK! LOOK! LOOK! LOOK! LOOK! LOOK!
ALL RIGHT! WHAT IS IT?!!
MADE YOU LOOK
JPM DAVPS 11·21
© 1999 PAWS, INC./Distributed by Universal Press Syndicate

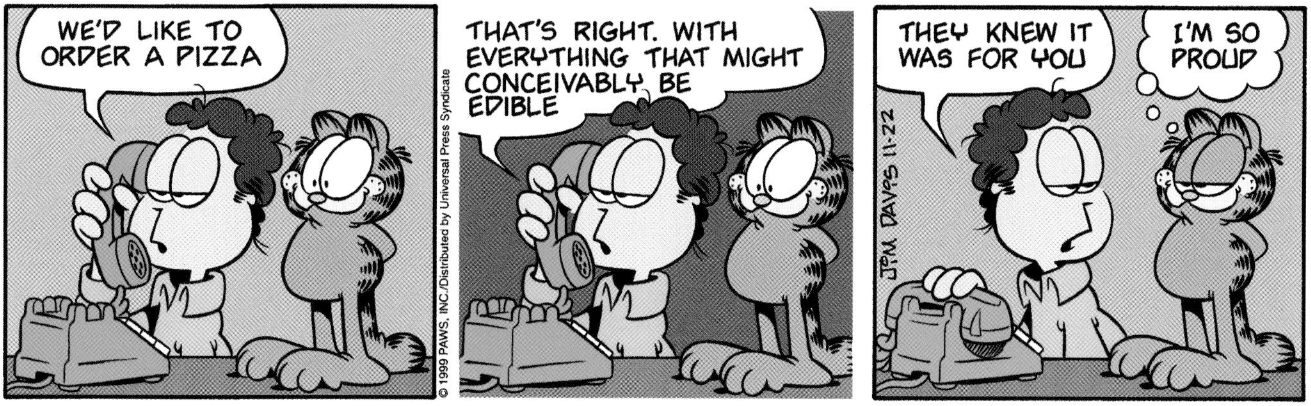
WE'D LIKE TO ORDER A PIZZA
THAT'S RIGHT. WITH EVERYTHING THAT MIGHT CONCEIVABLY BE EDIBLE
THEY KNEW IT WAS FOR YOU
I'M SO PROUD
JIM DAVIS 11-22
© 1999 PAWS, INC./Distributed by Universal Press Syndicate

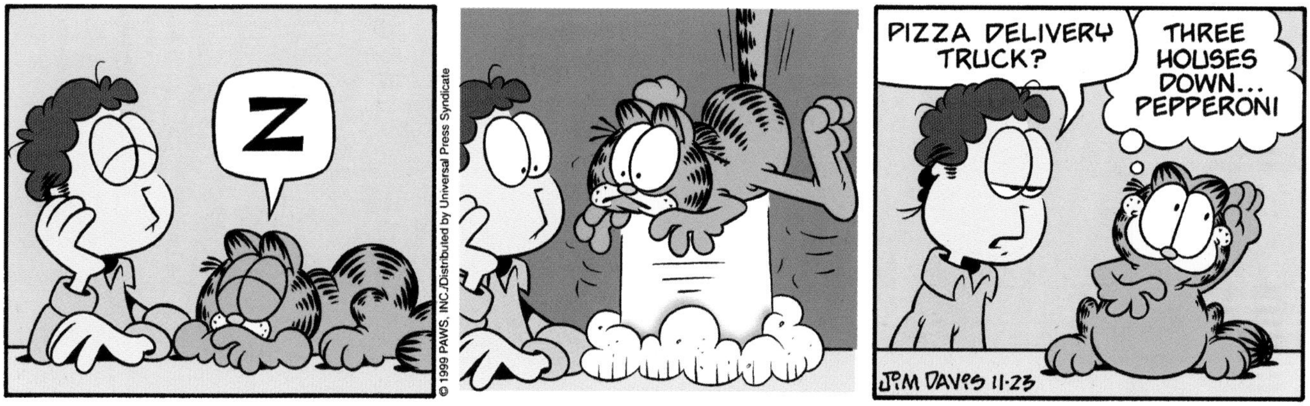
Z
PIZZA DELIVERY TRUCK?
THREE HOUSES DOWN... PEPPERONI
JIM DAVIS 11-23
© 1999 PAWS, INC./Distributed by Universal Press Syndicate

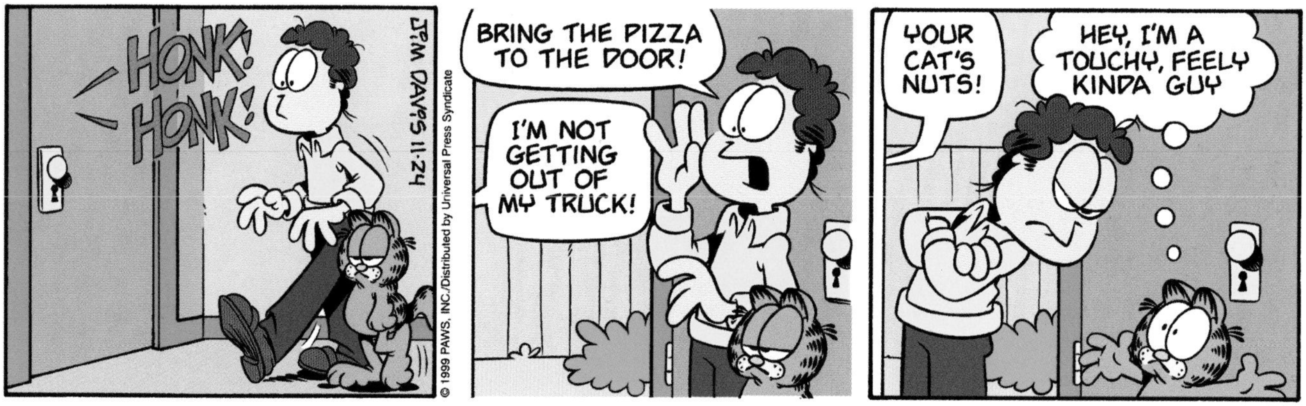
HONK! HONK!
JIM DAVIS 11-24
BRING THE PIZZA TO THE DOOR!
I'M NOT GETTING OUT OF MY TRUCK!
YOUR CAT'S NUTS!
HEY, I'M A TOUCHY, FEELY KINDA GUY
© 1999 PAWS, INC./Distributed by Universal Press Syndicate

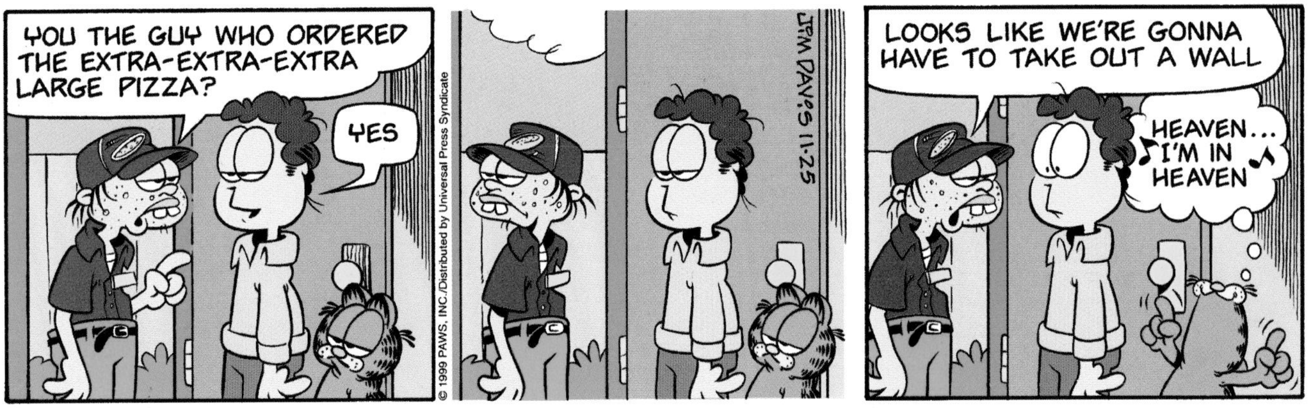
YOU THE GUY WHO ORDERED THE EXTRA-EXTRA-EXTRA LARGE PIZZA?
YES
© 1999 PAWS, INC./Distributed by Universal Press Syndicate
JIM DAVIS 11·25
LOOKS LIKE WE'RE GONNA HAVE TO TAKE OUT A WALL
HEAVEN... I'M IN HEAVEN

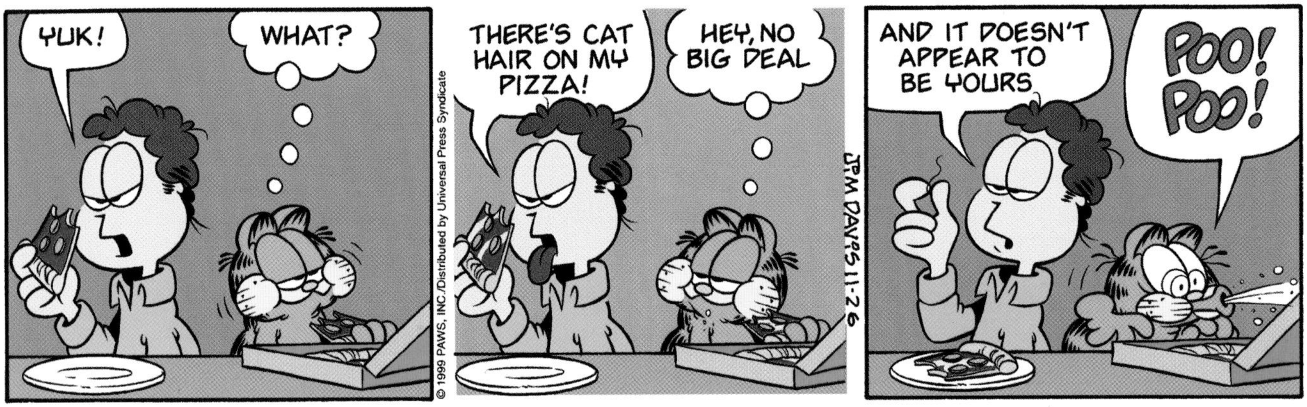
YUK!
WHAT?
© 1999 PAWS, INC./Distributed by Universal Press Syndicate
THERE'S CAT HAIR ON MY PIZZA!
HEY, NO BIG DEAL
JIM DAVIS 11·26
AND IT DOESN'T APPEAR TO BE YOURS
POO! POO!

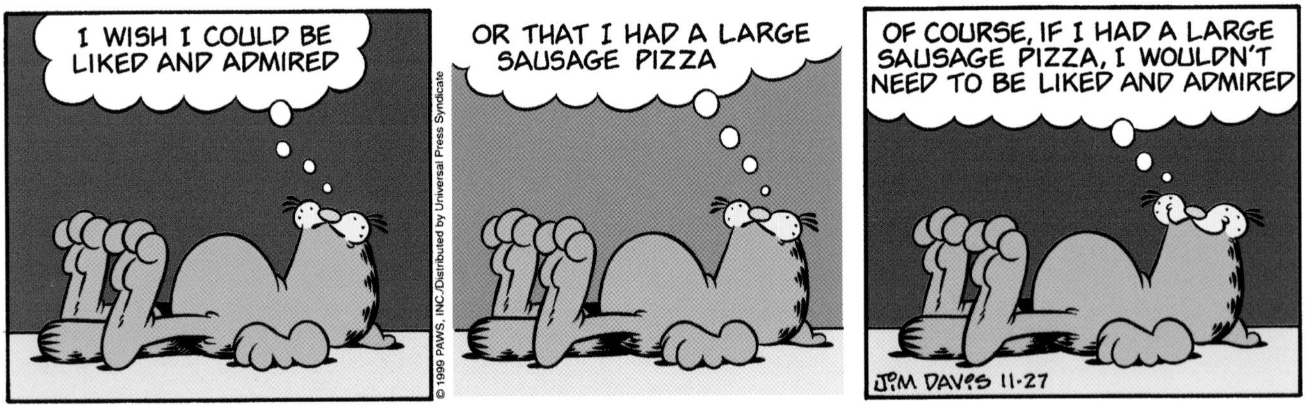
I WISH I COULD BE LIKED AND ADMIRED
© 1999 PAWS, INC./Distributed by Universal Press Syndicate
OR THAT I HAD A LARGE SAUSAGE PIZZA
OF COURSE, IF I HAD A LARGE SAUSAGE PIZZA, I WOULDN'T NEED TO BE LIKED AND ADMIRED
JIM DAVIS 11·27

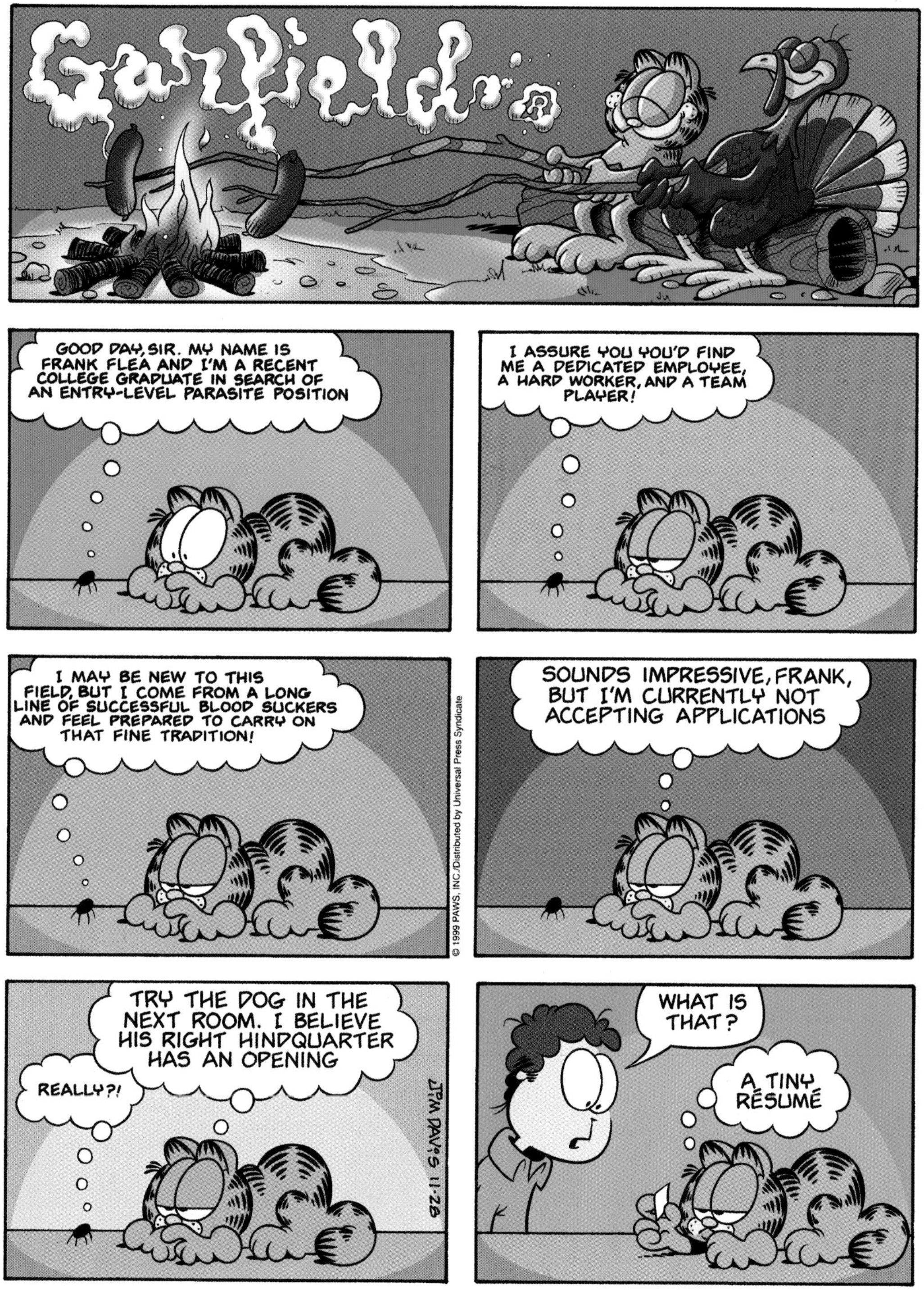
GARFIELD
GOOD DAY, SIR. MY NAME IS FRANK FLEA AND I'M A RECENT COLLEGE GRADUATE IN SEARCH OF AN ENTRY-LEVEL PARASITE POSITION
I ASSURE YOU YOU'D FIND ME A DEDICATED EMPLOYEE, A HARD WORKER, AND A TEAM PLAYER!
I MAY BE NEW TO THIS FIELD, BUT I COME FROM A LONG LINE OF SUCCESSFUL BLOOD SUCKERS AND FEEL PREPARED TO CARRY ON THAT FINE TRADITION!
SOUNDS IMPRESSIVE, FRANK, BUT I'M CURRENTLY NOT ACCEPTING APPLICATIONS
TRY THE DOG IN THE NEXT ROOM. I BELIEVE HIS RIGHT HINDQUARTER HAS AN OPENING
REALLY?!
JIM DAVIS 11-28
WHAT IS THAT?
A TINY RÉSUMÉ

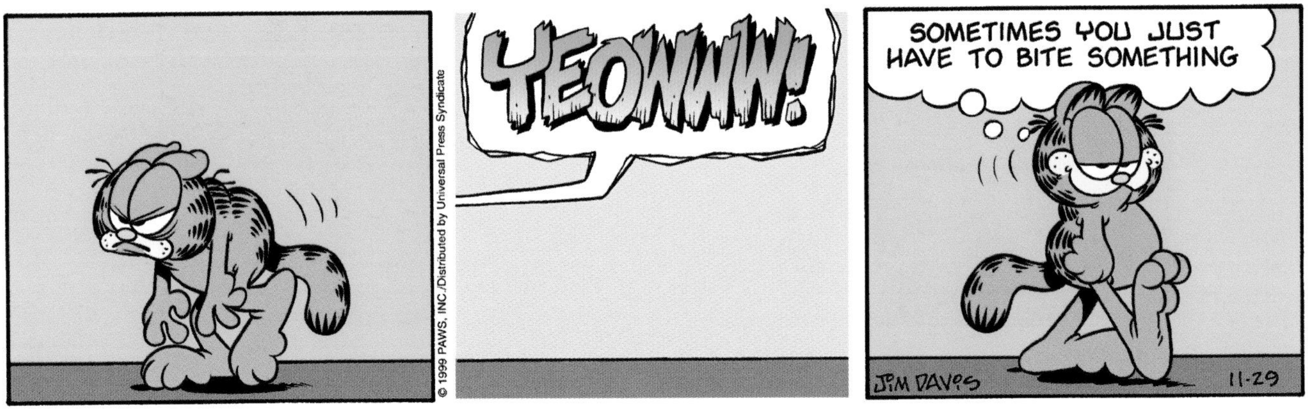
YEOWWW!
SOMETIMES YOU JUST HAVE TO BITE SOMETHING
JIM DAVIS 11-29
© 1999 PAWS, INC./Distributed by Universal Press Syndicate

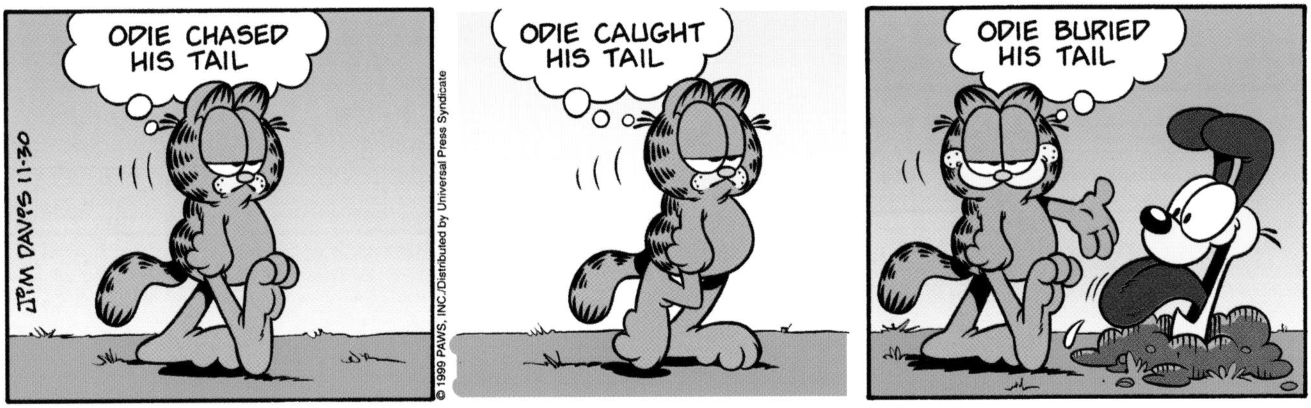
ODIE CHASED HIS TAIL
ODIE CAUGHT HIS TAIL
ODIE BURIED HIS TAIL
JIM DAVIS 11-30
© 1999 PAWS, INC./Distributed by Universal Press Syndicate

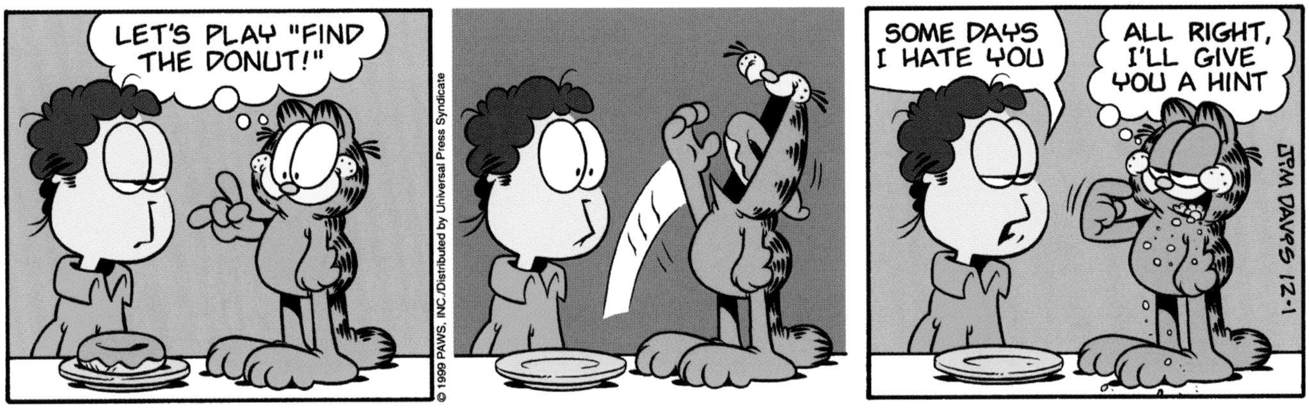
LET'S PLAY "FIND THE DONUT!"
SOME DAYS I HATE YOU
ALL RIGHT, I'LL GIVE YOU A HINT
JIM DAVIS 12-1
© 1999 PAWS, INC./Distributed by Universal Press Syndicate

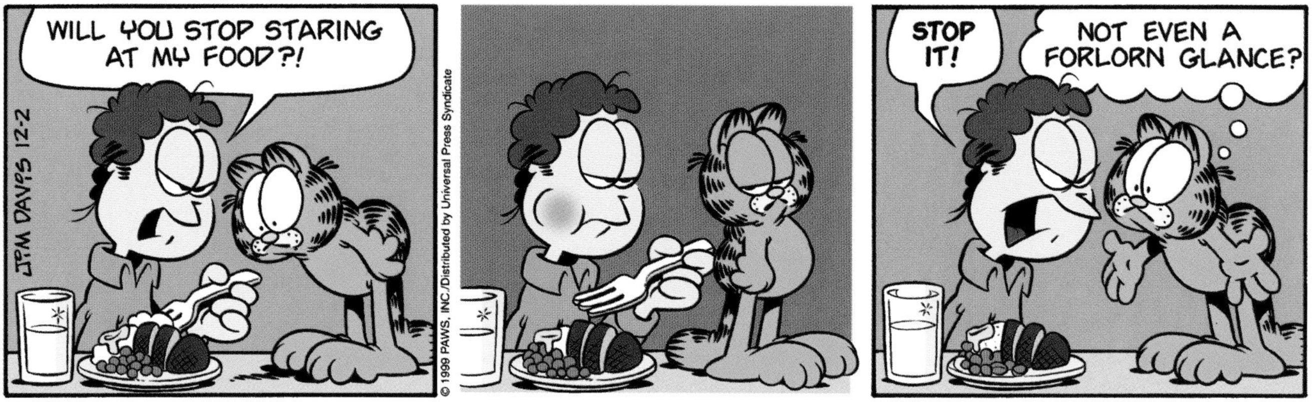
WILL YOU STOP STARING AT MY FOOD?!
JIM DAVIS 12-2
© 1999 PAWS, INC./Distributed by Universal Press Syndicate
STOP IT!
NOT EVEN A FORLORN GLANCE?

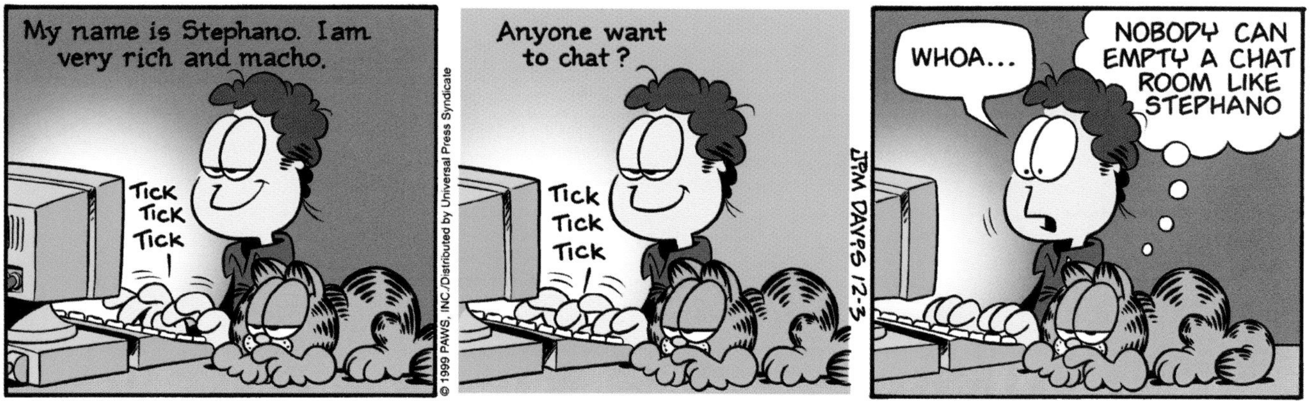
My name is Stephano. I am very rich and macho.
Tick Tick Tick
© 1999 PAWS, INC./Distributed by Universal Press Syndicate
Anyone want to chat?
Tick Tick Tick
JIM DAVIS 12-3
WHOA...
NOBODY CAN EMPTY A CHAT ROOM LIKE STEPHANO

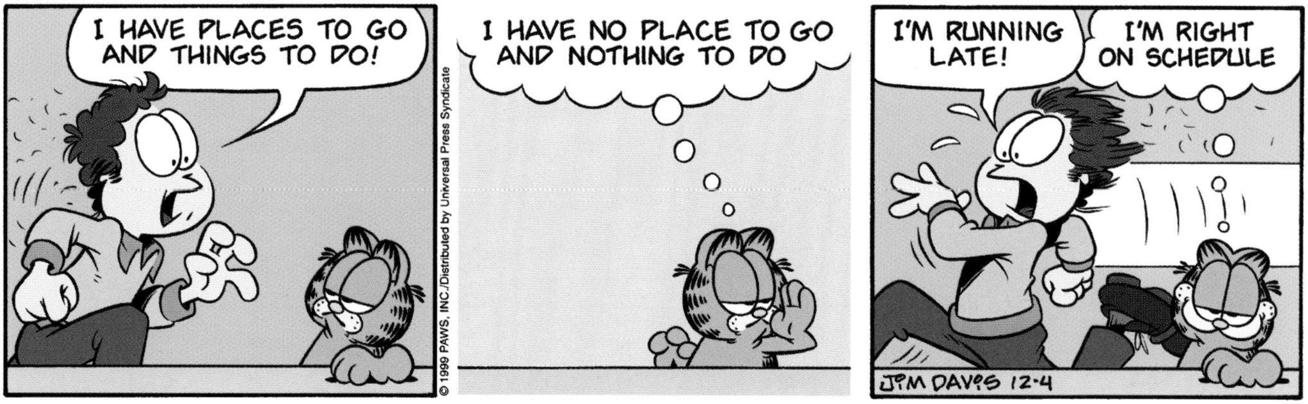
I HAVE PLACES TO GO AND THINGS TO DO!
© 1999 PAWS, INC./Distributed by Universal Press Syndicate
I HAVE NO PLACE TO GO AND NOTHING TO DO
I'M RUNNING LATE!
I'M RIGHT ON SCHEDULE
JIM DAVIS 12-4

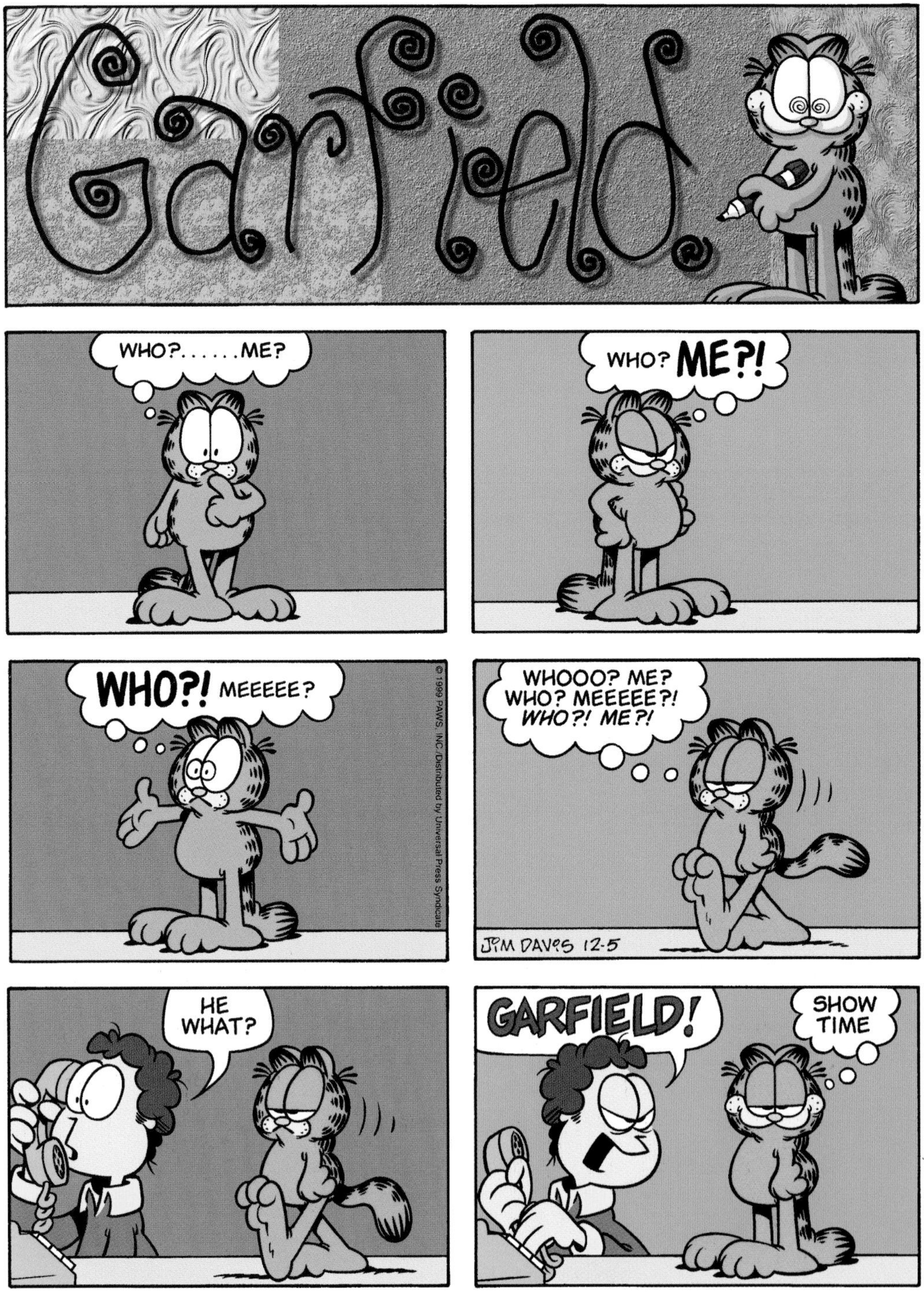
Garfield
WHO?......ME?
WHO? ME?!
WHO?! MEEEEE?
© 1999 PAWS, INC./Distributed by Universal Press Syndicate
WHOOO? ME?
WHO? MEEEEE?!
WHO?! ME?!
JIM DAVIS 12-5
HE WHAT?
GARFIELD!
SHOW TIME

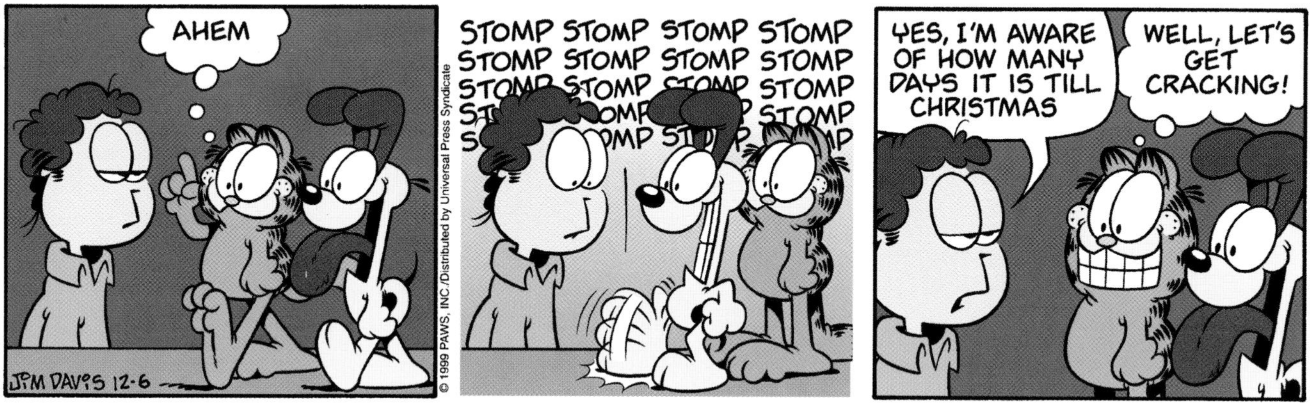
AHEM
JIM DAVIS 12-6
© 1999 PAWS, INC./Distributed by Universal Press Syndicate
STOMP STOMP STOMP STOMP
STOMP STOMP STOMP STOMP
STOMP
STOMP
YES, I'M AWARE OF HOW MANY DAYS IT IS TILL CHRISTMAS
WELL, LET'S GET CRACKING!

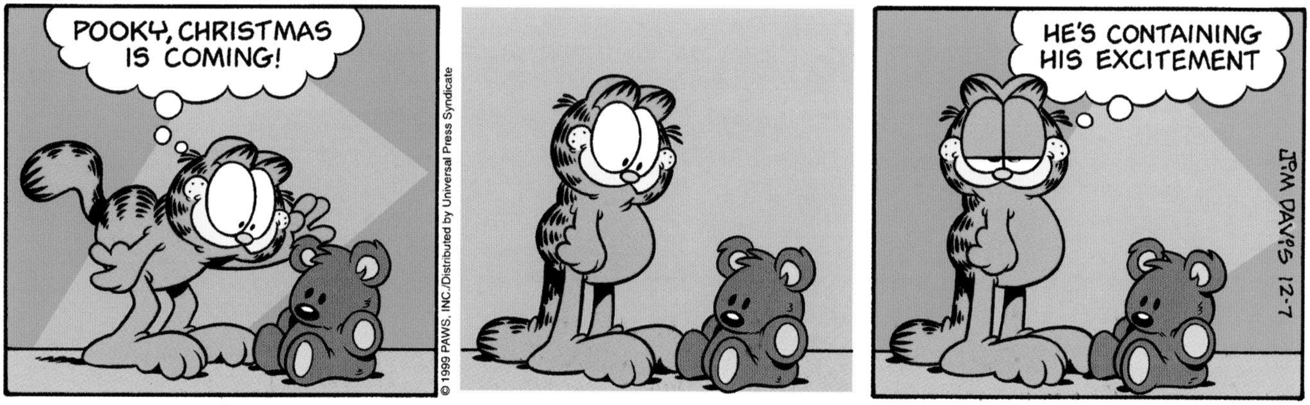
POOKY, CHRISTMAS IS COMING!
© 1999 PAWS, INC./Distributed by Universal Press Syndicate
HE'S CONTAINING HIS EXCITEMENT
JIM DAVIS 12-7

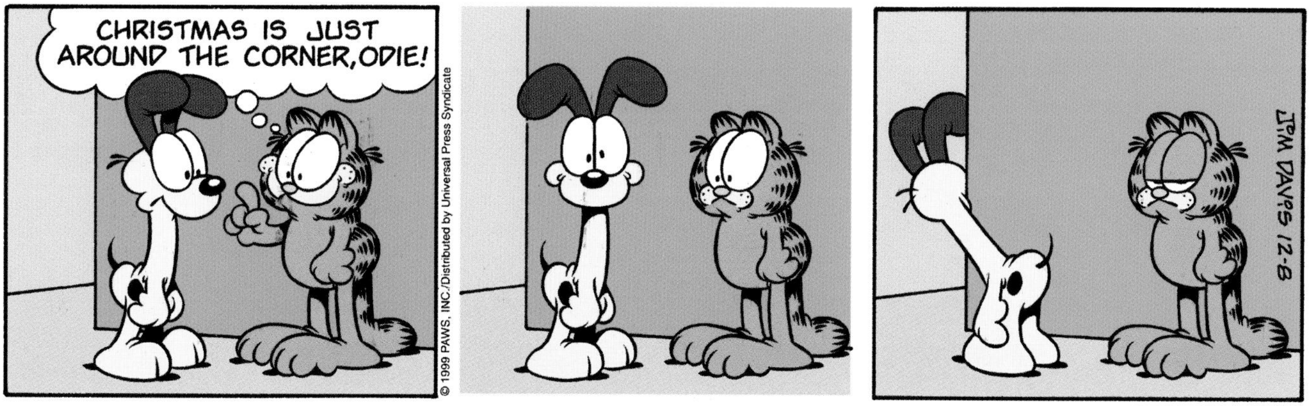
CHRISTMAS IS JUST AROUND THE CORNER, ODIE!
© 1999 PAWS, INC./Distributed by Universal Press Syndicate
JIM DAVIS 12-8

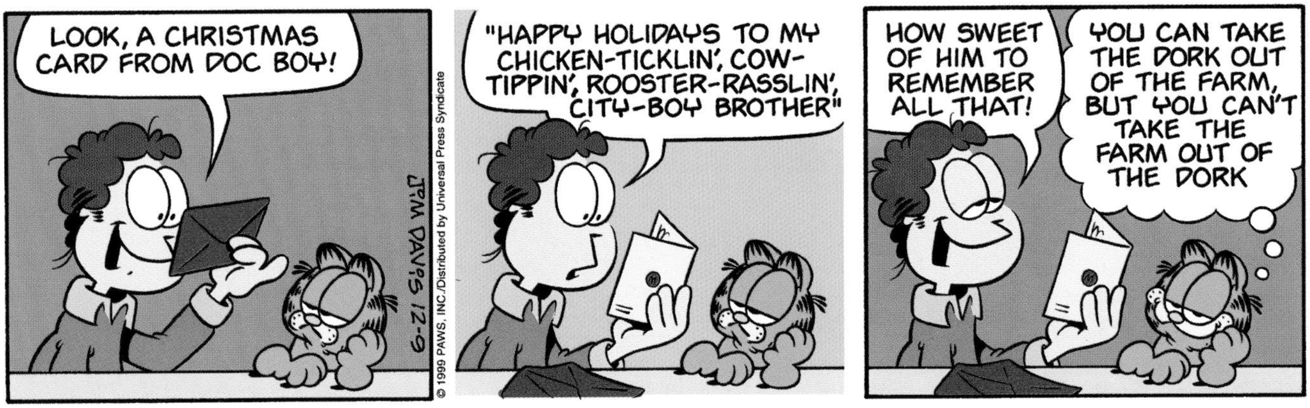
LOOK, A CHRISTMAS CARD FROM DOC BOY!
JPM DAVIS 12-9
© 1999 PAWS, INC./Distributed by Universal Press Syndicate
"HAPPY HOLIDAYS TO MY CHICKEN-TICKLIN', COW-TIPPIN', ROOSTER-RASSLIN', CITY-BOY BROTHER"
HOW SWEET OF HIM TO REMEMBER ALL THAT!
YOU CAN TAKE THE DORK OUT OF THE FARM, BUT YOU CAN'T TAKE THE FARM OUT OF THE DORK

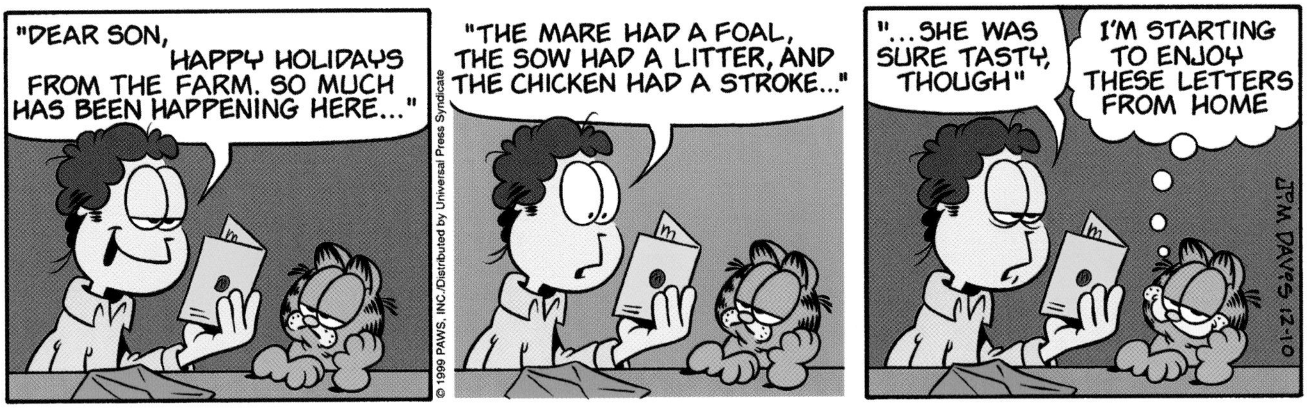
"DEAR SON, HAPPY HOLIDAYS FROM THE FARM. SO MUCH HAS BEEN HAPPENING HERE..."
© 1999 PAWS, INC./Distributed by Universal Press Syndicate
"THE MARE HAD A FOAL, THE SOW HAD A LITTER, AND THE CHICKEN HAD A STROKE..."
"...SHE WAS SURE TASTY, THOUGH"
I'M STARTING TO ENJOY THESE LETTERS FROM HOME
JPM DAVIS 12-10

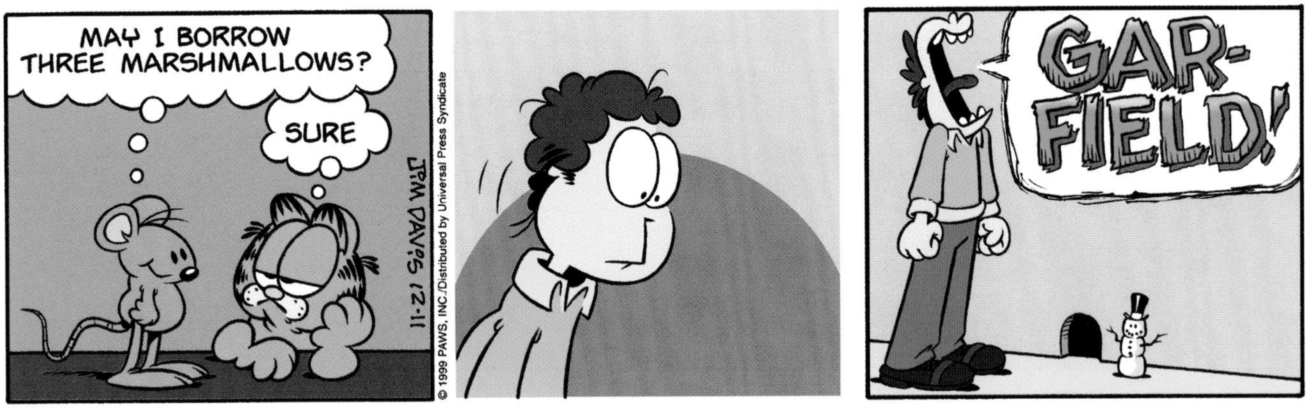
MAY I BORROW THREE MARSHMALLOWS?
SURE
JPM DAVIS 12-11
© 1999 PAWS, INC./Distributed by Universal Press Syndicate
GAR-FIELD!

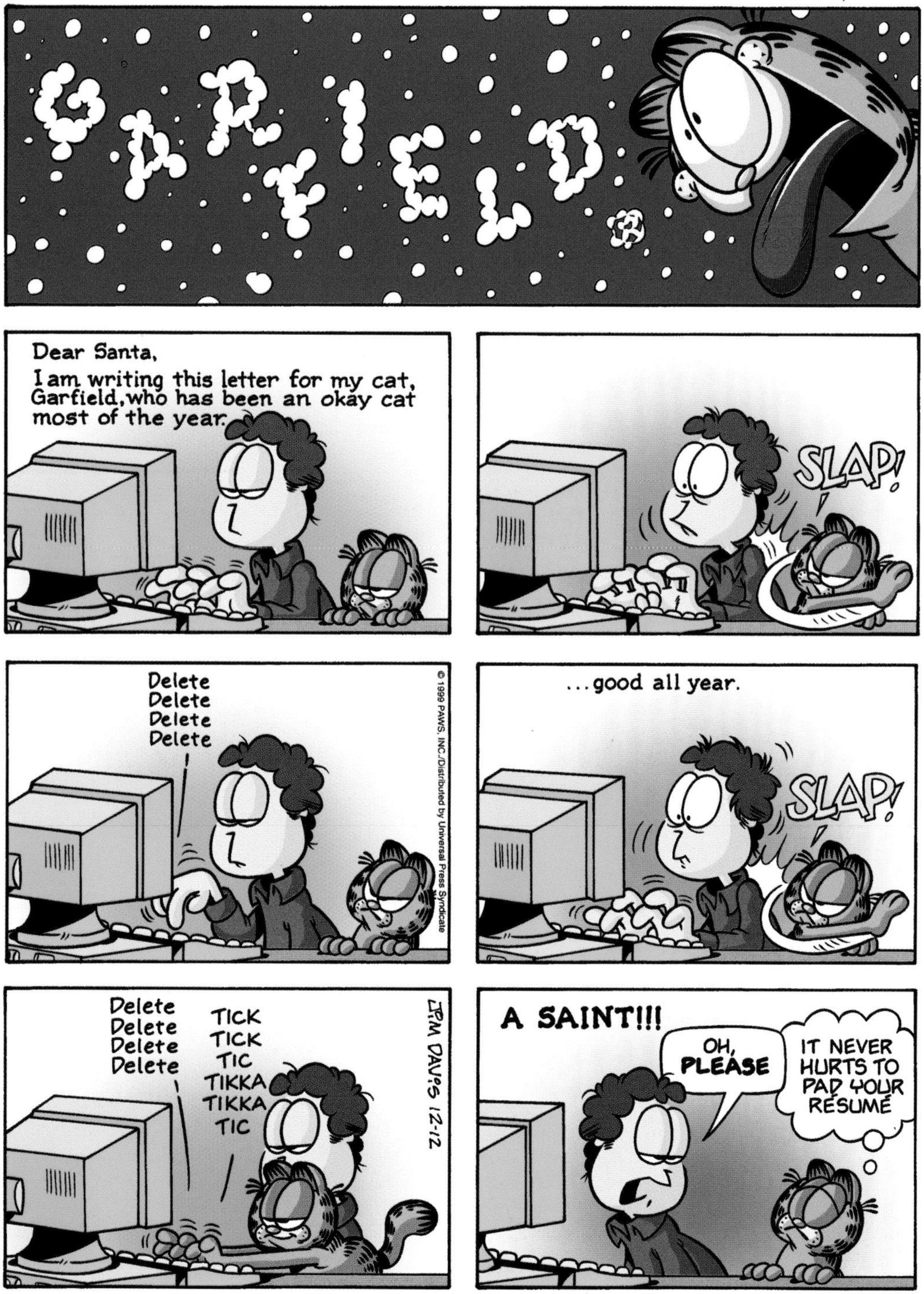
GARFIELD®
Dear Santa,
I am writing this letter for my cat, Garfield, who has been an okay cat most of the year.
SLAP!
Delete
Delete
Delete
Delete
© 1999 PAWS, INC./Distributed by Universal Press Syndicate
. . . good all year.
SLAP!
Delete
Delete
Delete
Delete
TICK
TICK
TIC
TIKKA
TIKKA
TIC
JIM DAVIS 12-12
A SAINT!!!
OH, PLEASE
IT NEVER HURTS TO PAD YOUR RÉSUMÉ

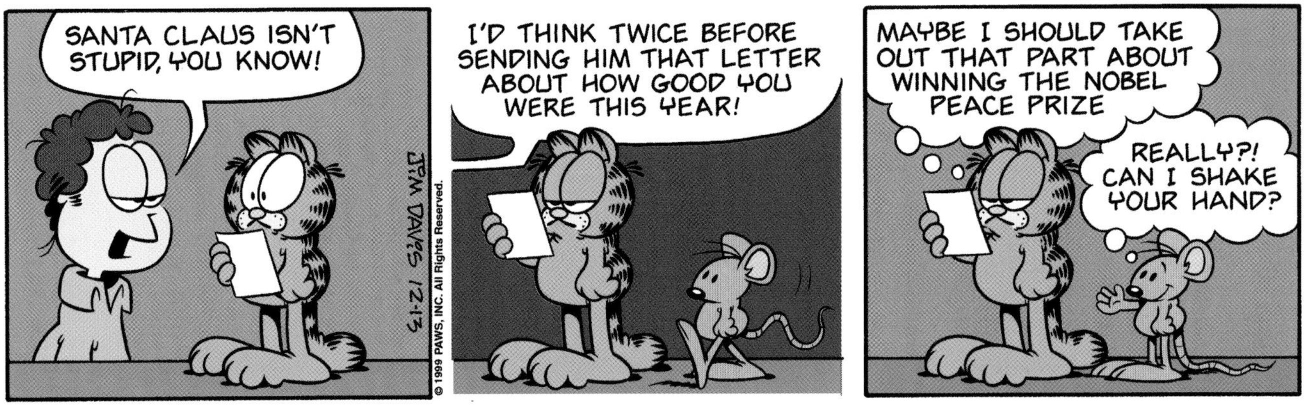
SANTA CLAUS ISN'T STUPID, YOU KNOW!
I'D THINK TWICE BEFORE SENDING HIM THAT LETTER ABOUT HOW GOOD YOU WERE THIS YEAR!
MAYBE I SHOULD TAKE OUT THAT PART ABOUT WINNING THE NOBEL PEACE PRIZE
REALLY?! CAN I SHAKE YOUR HAND?
JPM DAVPS 12-13

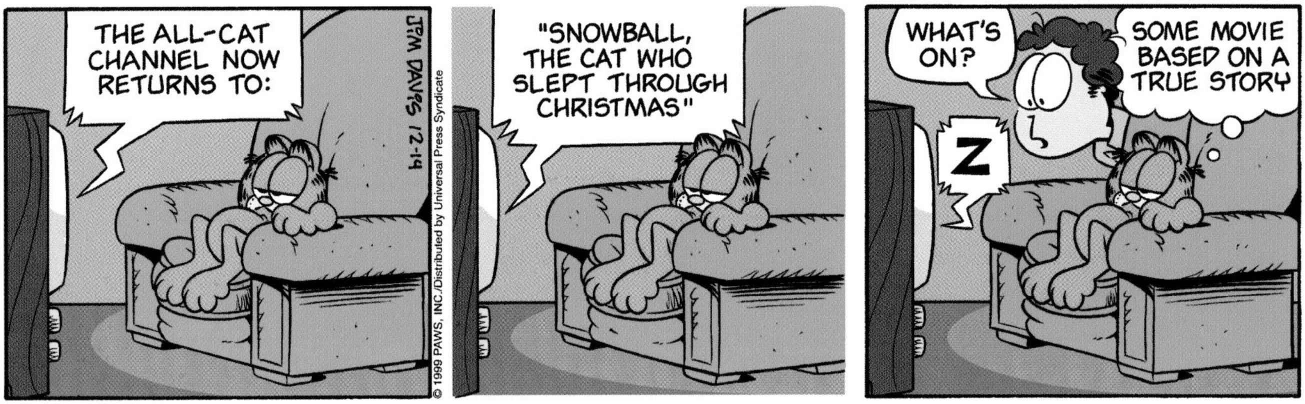
THE ALL-CAT CHANNEL NOW RETURNS TO:
"SNOWBALL, THE CAT WHO SLEPT THROUGH CHRISTMAS"
WHAT'S ON?
Z
SOME MOVIE BASED ON A TRUE STORY
JPM DAVPS 12-14

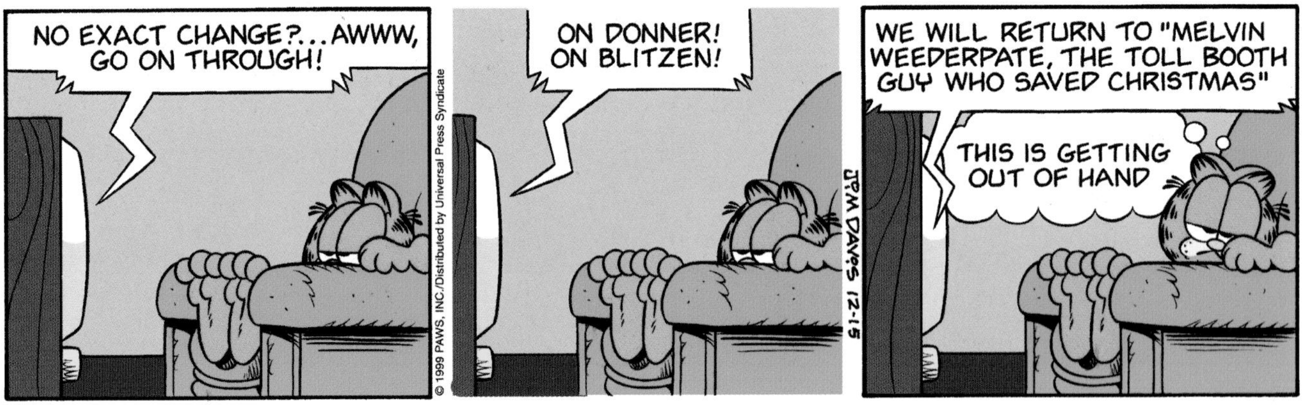
NO EXACT CHANGE?... AWWW, GO ON THROUGH!
ON DONNER! ON BLITZEN!
WE WILL RETURN TO "MELVIN WEEDERPATE, THE TOLL BOOTH GUY WHO SAVED CHRISTMAS"
THIS IS GETTING OUT OF HAND
JPM DAVPS 12-15

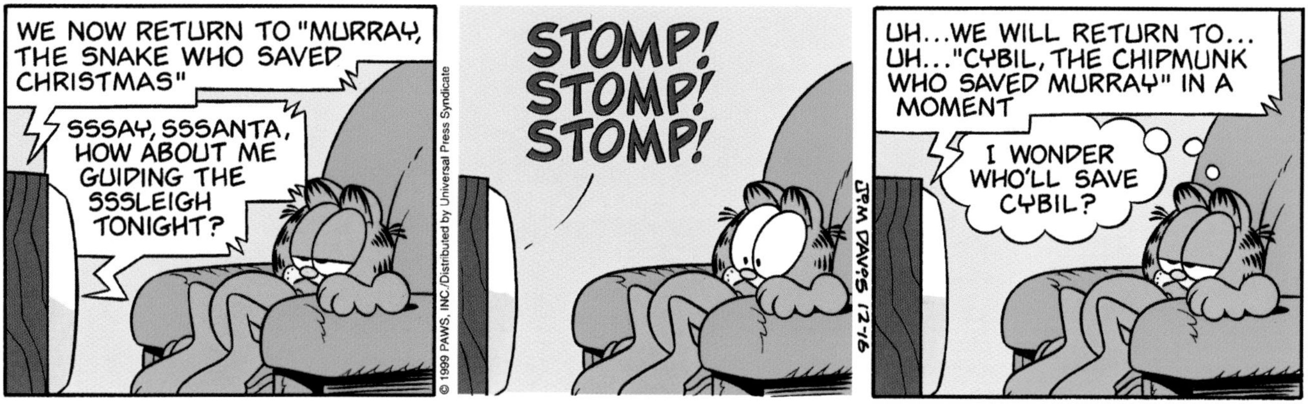
WE NOW RETURN TO "MURRAY, THE SNAKE WHO SAVED CHRISTMAS"
SSSAY, SSSANTA, HOW ABOUT ME GUIDING THE SSSLEIGH TONIGHT?
© 1999 PAWS, INC./Distributed by Universal Press Syndicate
STOMP! STOMP! STOMP!
JIM DAVIS 12-16
UH...WE WILL RETURN TO... UH..."CYBIL, THE CHIPMUNK WHO SAVED MURRAY" IN A MOMENT
I WONDER WHO'LL SAVE CYBIL?

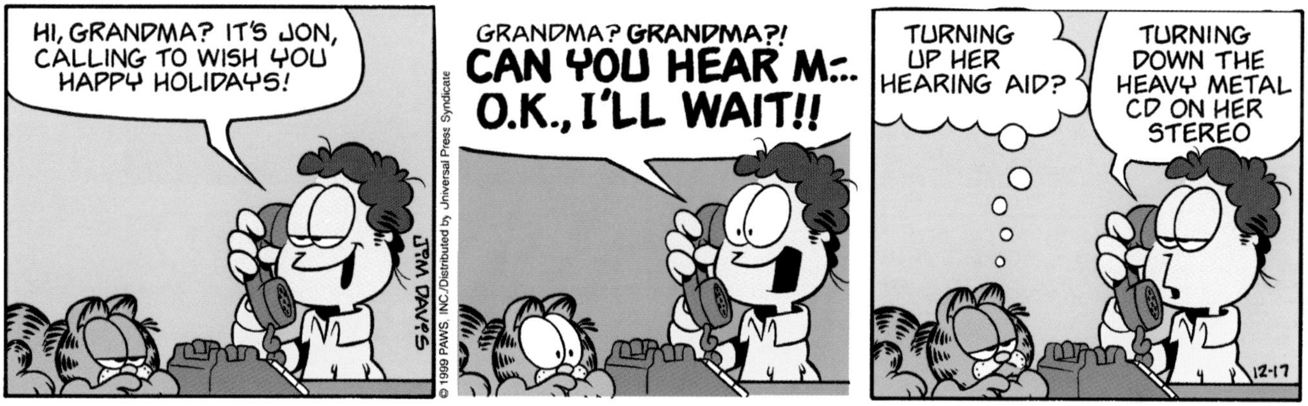
HI, GRANDMA? IT'S JON, CALLING TO WISH YOU HAPPY HOLIDAYS!
JIM DAVIS
© 1999 PAWS, INC./Distributed by Universal Press Syndicate
GRANDMA? GRANDMA?! CAN YOU HEAR M:... O.K., I'LL WAIT!!
TURNING UP HER HEARING AID?
TURNING DOWN THE HEAVY METAL CD ON HER STEREO
12-17

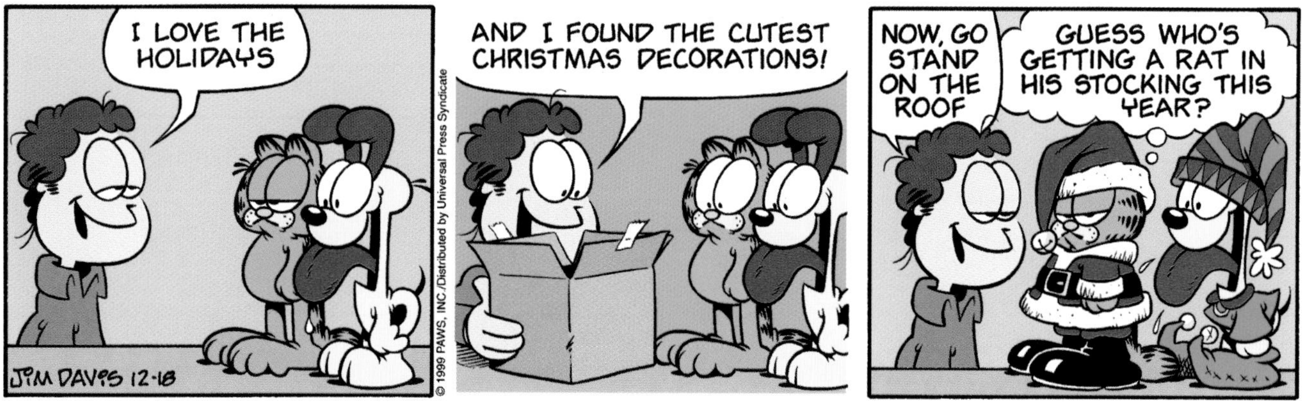
I LOVE THE HOLIDAYS
JIM DAVIS 12-18
© 1999 PAWS, INC./Distributed by Universal Press Syndicate
AND I FOUND THE CUTEST CHRISTMAS DECORATIONS!
NOW, GO STAND ON THE ROOF
GUESS WHO'S GETTING A RAT IN HIS STOCKING THIS YEAR?

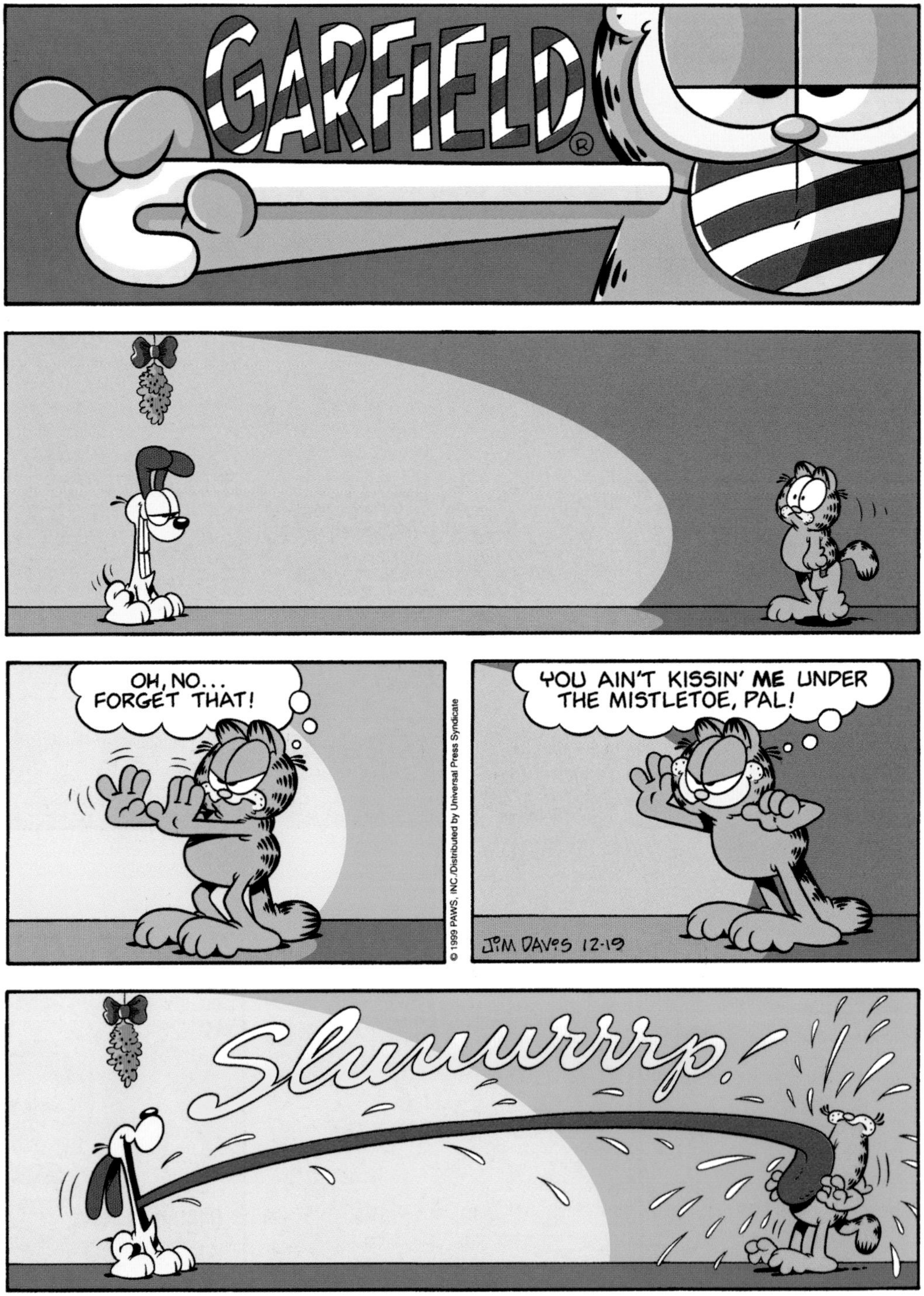
GARFIELD®
OH, NO... FORGET THAT!
© 1999 PAWS, INC./Distributed by Universal Press Syndicate
YOU AIN'T KISSIN' ME UNDER THE MISTLETOE, PAL!
JIM DAVIS 12-19
Sluuurrrp!

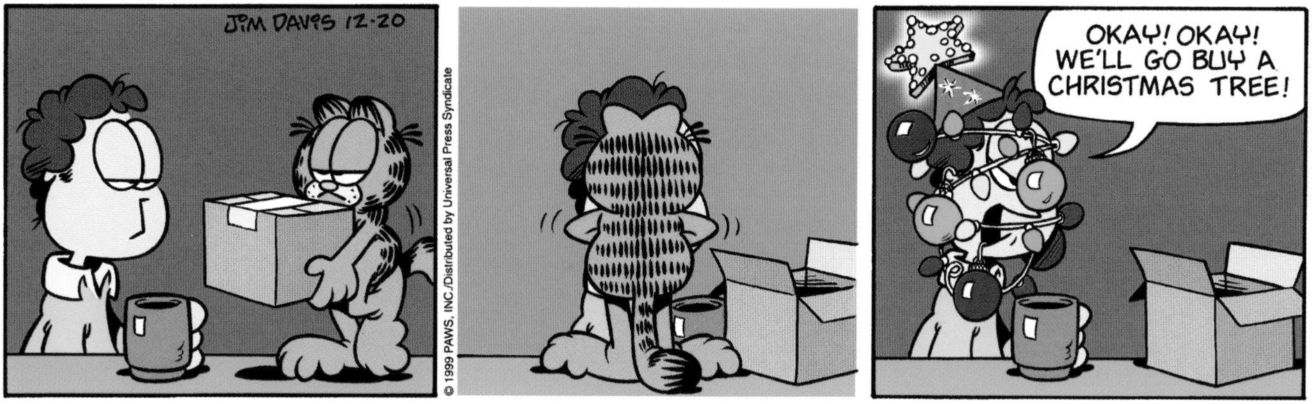
JIM DAVIS 12-20
© 1999 PAWS, INC./Distributed by Universal Press Syndicate
OKAY! OKAY! WE'LL GO BUY A CHRISTMAS TREE!

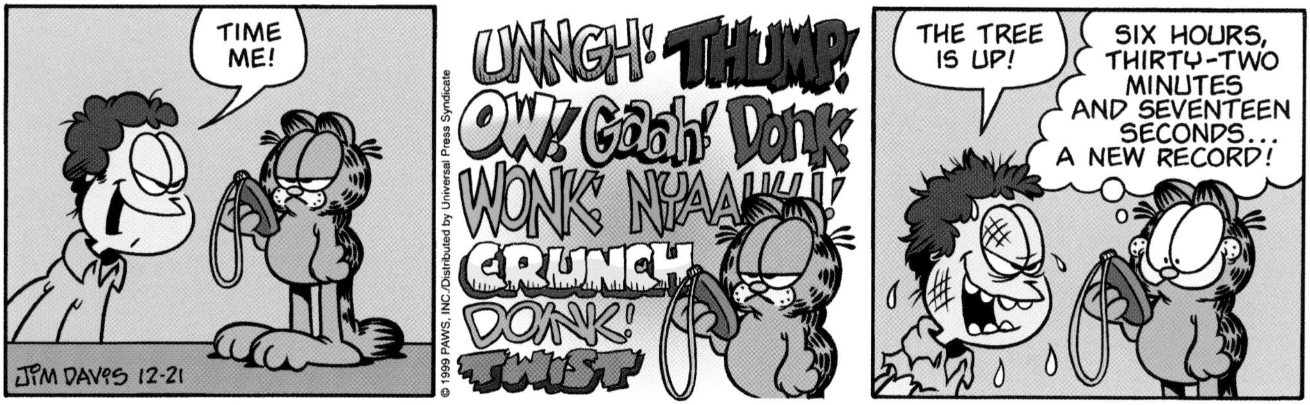
TIME ME!
JIM DAVIS 12-21
© 1999 PAWS, INC./Distributed by Universal Press Syndicate
UNNGH! THUMP!
OW! Gaah! Donk!
WONK!
CRUNCH
DOINK!
TWIST
THE TREE IS UP!
SIX HOURS, THIRTY-TWO MINUTES AND SEVENTEEN SECONDS... A NEW RECORD!

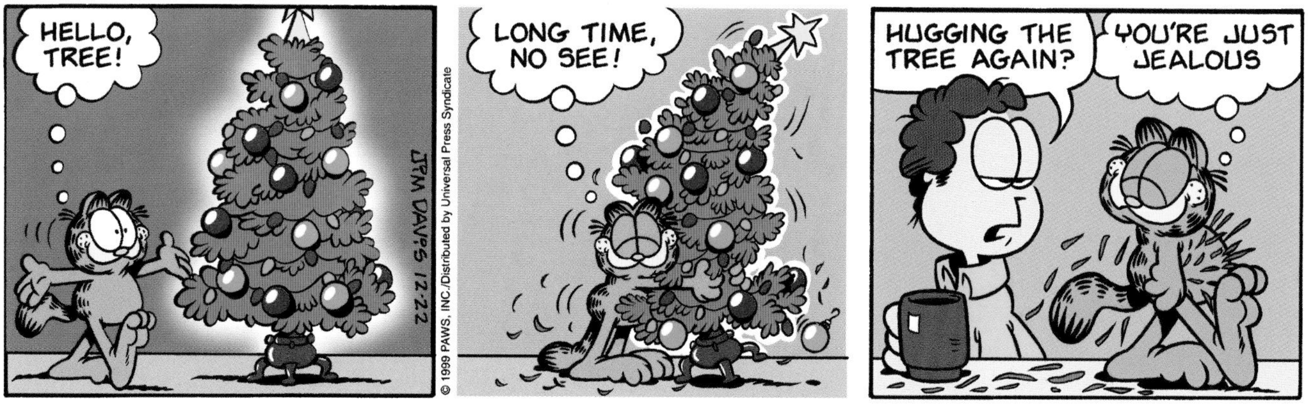
HELLO, TREE!
JIM DAVIS 12-22
© 1999 PAWS, INC./Distributed by Universal Press Syndicate
LONG TIME, NO SEE!
HUGGING THE TREE AGAIN?
YOU'RE JUST JEALOUS

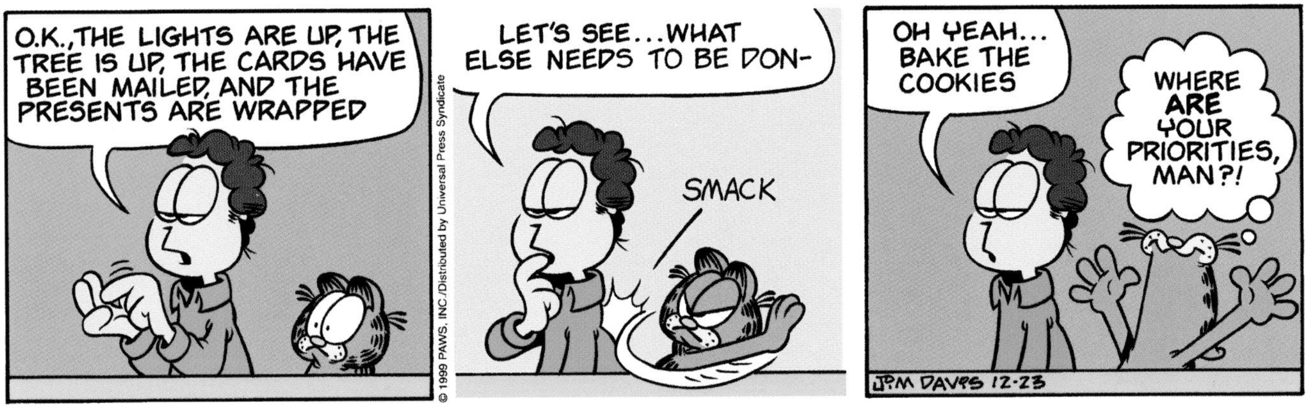
O.K., THE LIGHTS ARE UP, THE TREE IS UP, THE CARDS HAVE BEEN MAILED, AND THE PRESENTS ARE WRAPPED
LET'S SEE...WHAT ELSE NEEDS TO BE DON-
SMACK
© 1999 PAWS, INC./Distributed by Universal Press Syndicate
OH YEAH... BAKE THE COOKIES
WHERE **ARE** YOUR PRIORITIES, MAN?!
JIM DAVIS 12-23

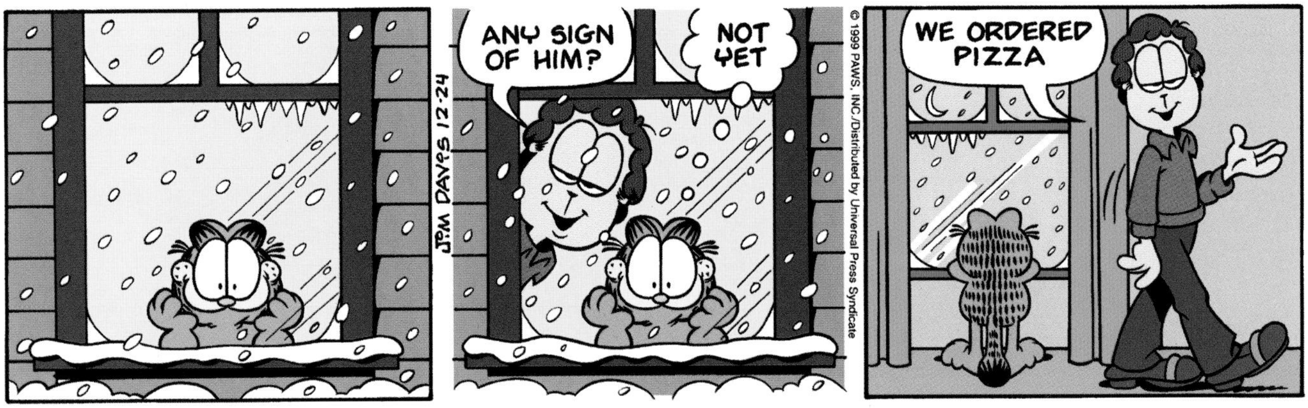
JIM DAVIS 12-24
ANY SIGN OF HIM?
NOT YET
© 1999 PAWS, INC./Distributed by Universal Press Syndicate
WE ORDERED PIZZA

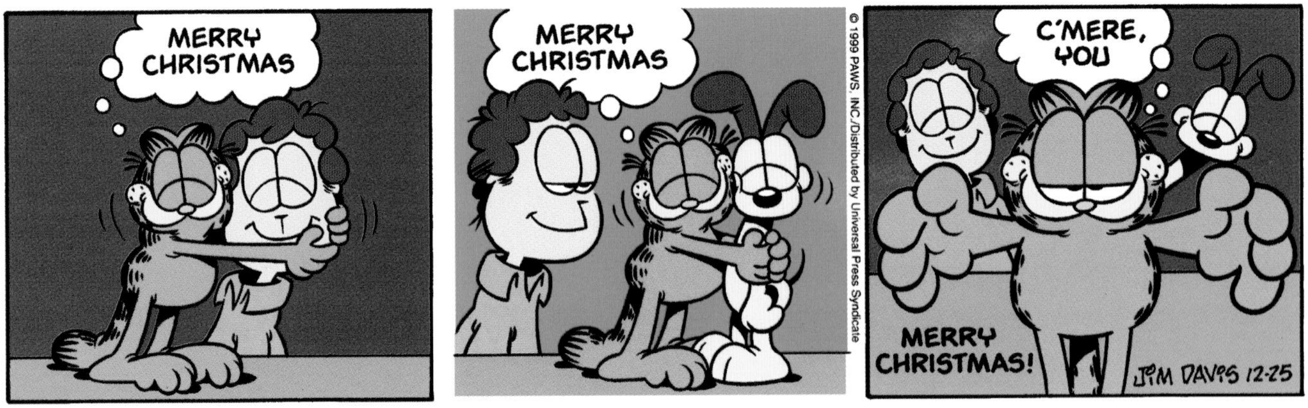
MERRY CHRISTMAS
MERRY CHRISTMAS
© 1999 PAWS, INC./Distributed by Universal Press Syndicate
C'MERE, YOU
MERRY CHRISTMAS!
JIM DAVIS 12-25

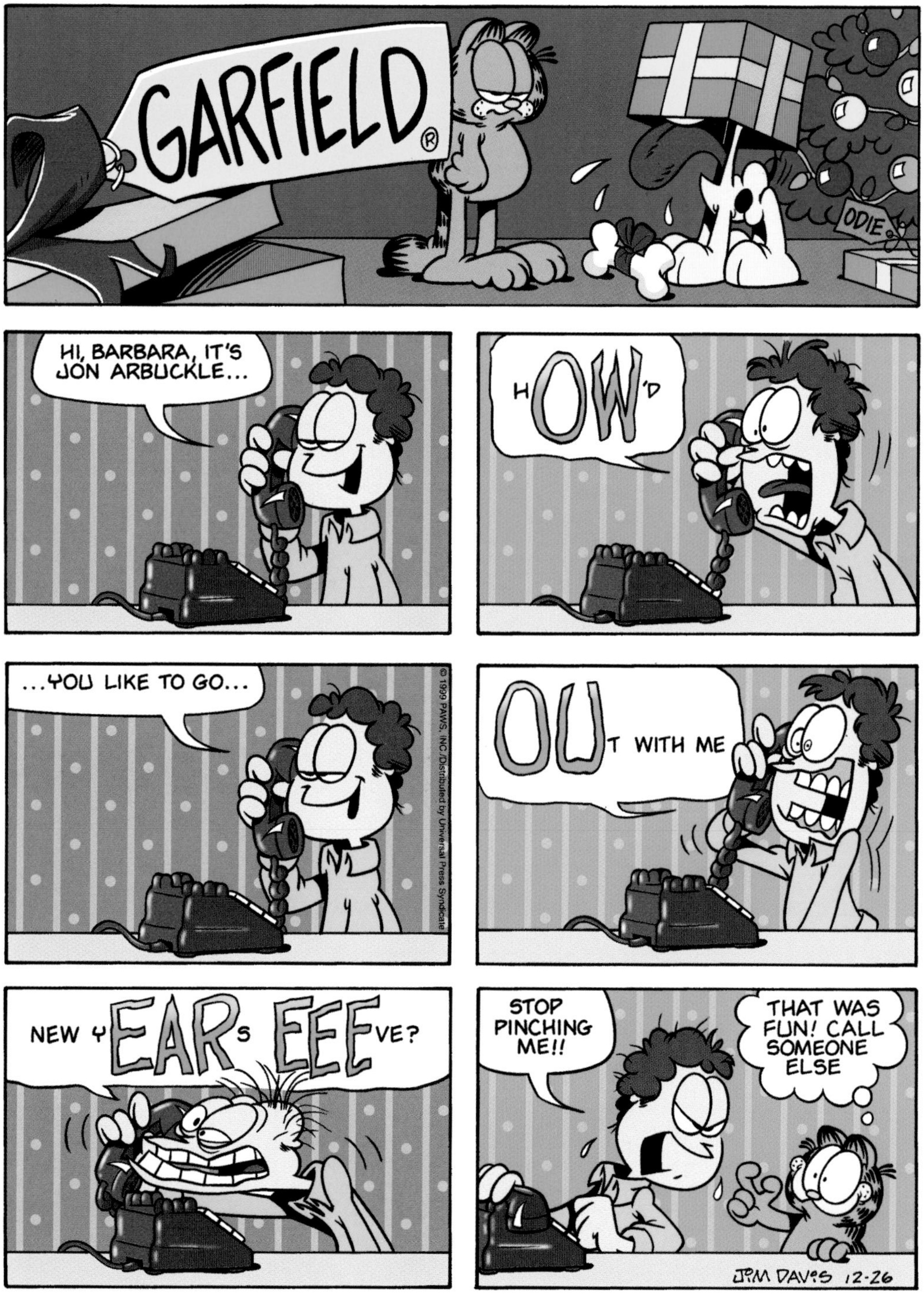
GARFIELD®
ODIE
HI, BARBARA, IT'S JON ARBUCKLE...
HOW'D
...YOU LIKE TO GO...
© 1999 PAWS, INC./Distributed by Universal Press Syndicate
OUT WITH ME
NEW YEARS EEEVE?
STOP PINCHING ME!!
THAT WAS FUN! CALL SOMEONE ELSE
JIM DAVIS 12-26

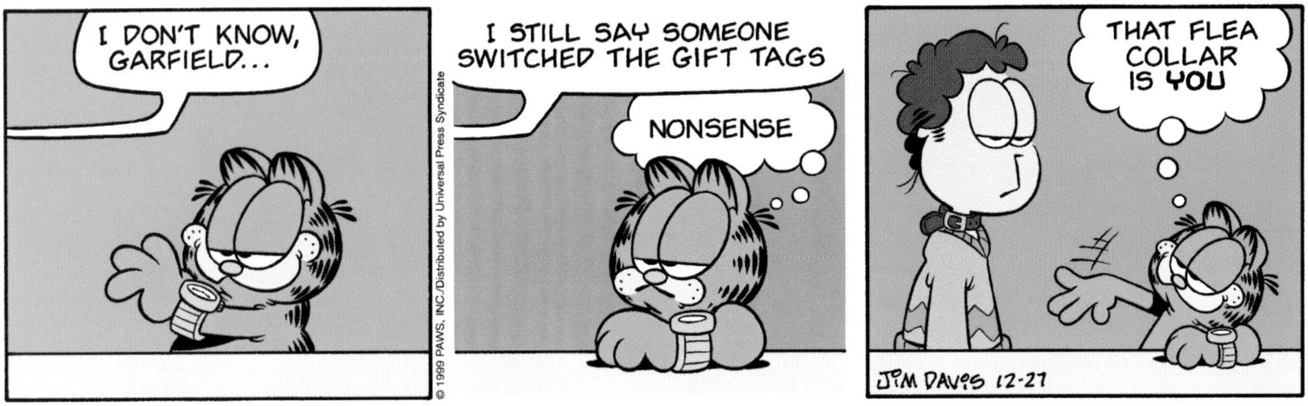
I DON'T KNOW, GARFIELD...
I STILL SAY SOMEONE SWITCHED THE GIFT TAGS
NONSENSE
THAT FLEA COLLAR IS **YOU**
© 1999 PAWS, INC./Distributed by Universal Press Syndicate
JIM DAVIS 12-27

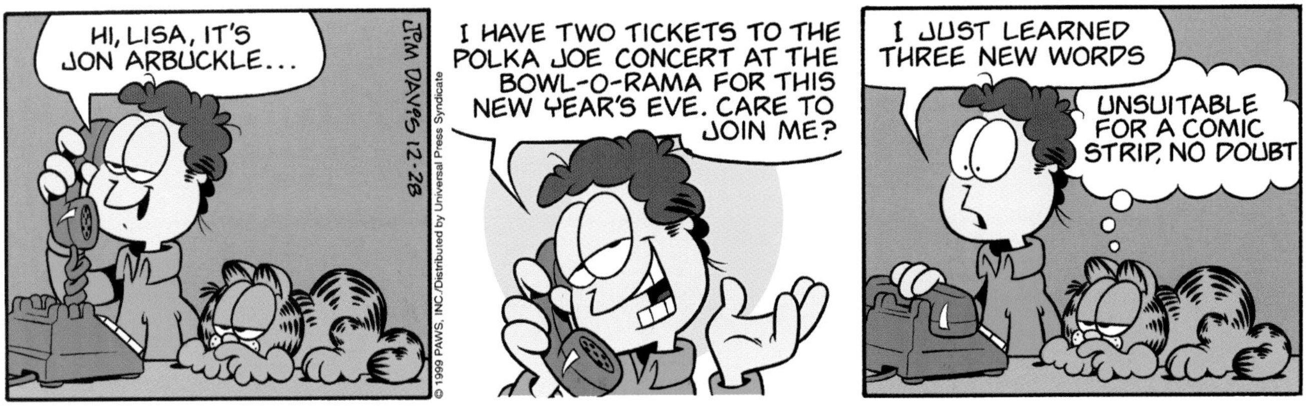
HI, LISA, IT'S JON ARBUCKLE...
I HAVE TWO TICKETS TO THE POLKA JOE CONCERT AT THE BOWL-O-RAMA FOR THIS NEW YEAR'S EVE. CARE TO JOIN ME?
I JUST LEARNED THREE NEW WORDS
UNSUITABLE FOR A COMIC STRIP, NO DOUBT
JIM DAVIS 12-28
© 1999 PAWS, INC./Distributed by Universal Press Syndicate

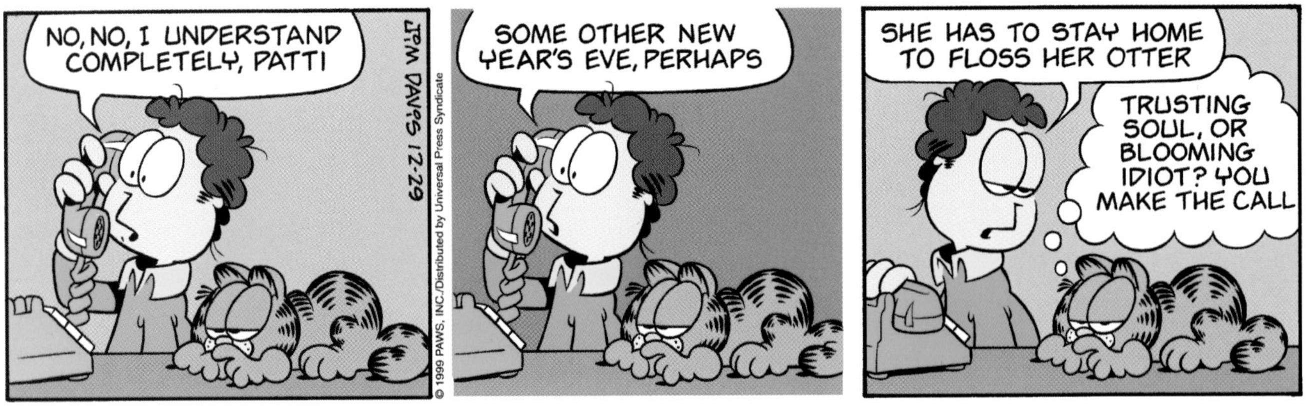
NO, NO, I UNDERSTAND COMPLETELY, PATTI
SOME OTHER NEW YEAR'S EVE, PERHAPS
SHE HAS TO STAY HOME TO FLOSS HER OTTER
TRUSTING SOUL, OR BLOOMING IDIOT? YOU MAKE THE CALL
JIM DAVIS 12-29
© 1999 PAWS, INC./Distributed by Universal Press Syndicate

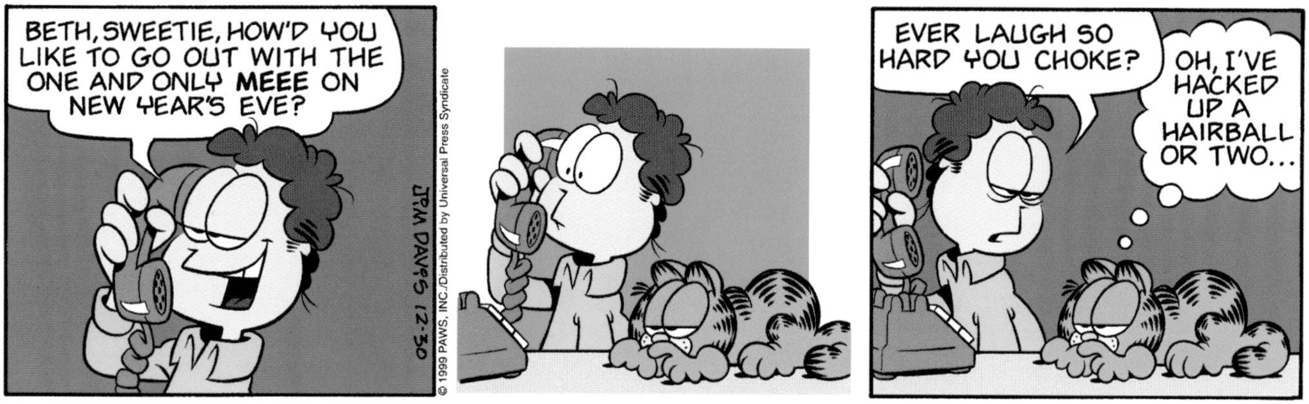
BETH, SWEETIE, HOW'D YOU LIKE TO GO OUT WITH THE ONE AND ONLY MEEE ON NEW YEAR'S EVE?
JIM DAVIS 12-30
© 1999 PAWS, INC./Distributed by Universal Press Syndicate
EVER LAUGH SO HARD YOU CHOKE?
OH, I'VE HACKED UP A HAIRBALL OR TWO...

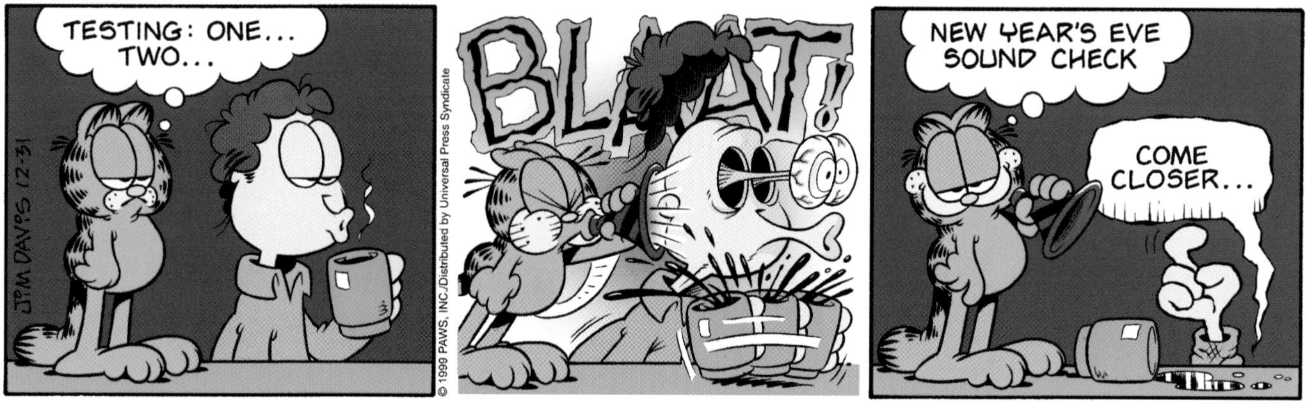
TESTING: ONE... TWO...
JIM DAVIS 12-31
© 1999 PAWS, INC./Distributed by Universal Press Syndicate
BLAAT!
NEW YEAR'S EVE SOUND CHECK
COME CLOSER...

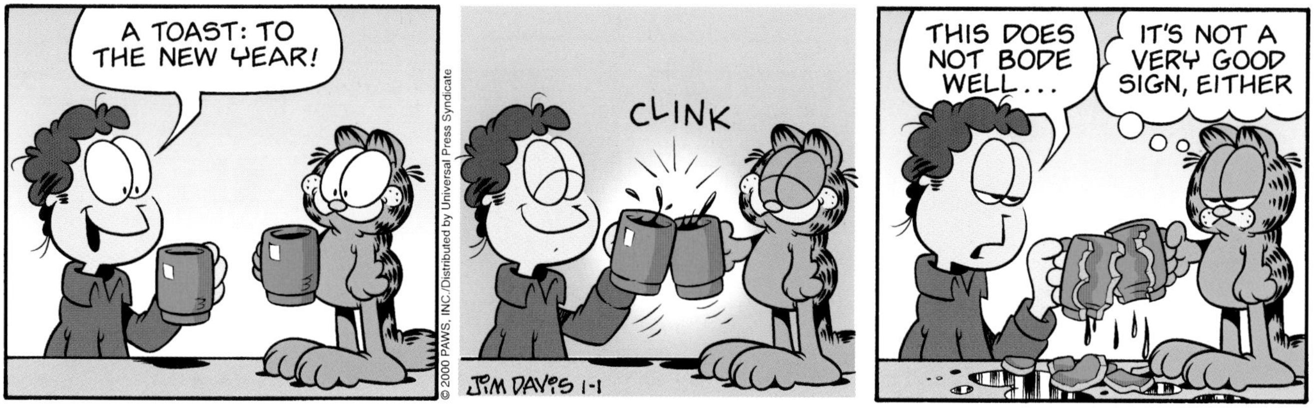
A TOAST: TO THE NEW YEAR!
© 2000 PAWS, INC./Distributed by Universal Press Syndicate
CLINK
JIM DAVIS 1-1
THIS DOES NOT BODE WELL...
IT'S NOT A VERY GOOD SIGN, EITHER

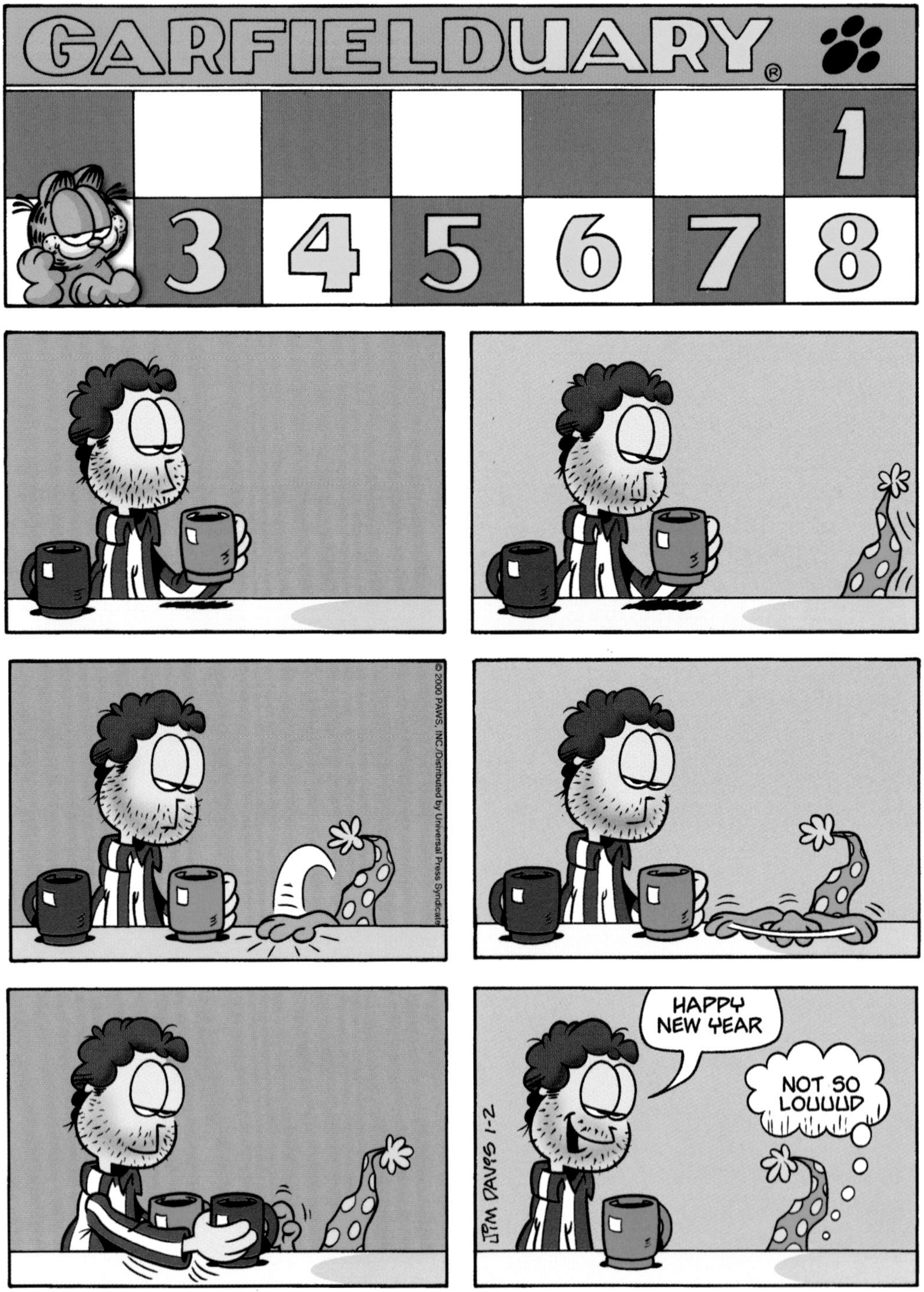
GARFIELDUARY®
1
3 4 5 6 7 8
© 2000 PAWS, INC./Distributed by Universal Press Syndicate
JIM DAVIS 1-2
HAPPY NEW YEAR
NOT SO LOUUUD

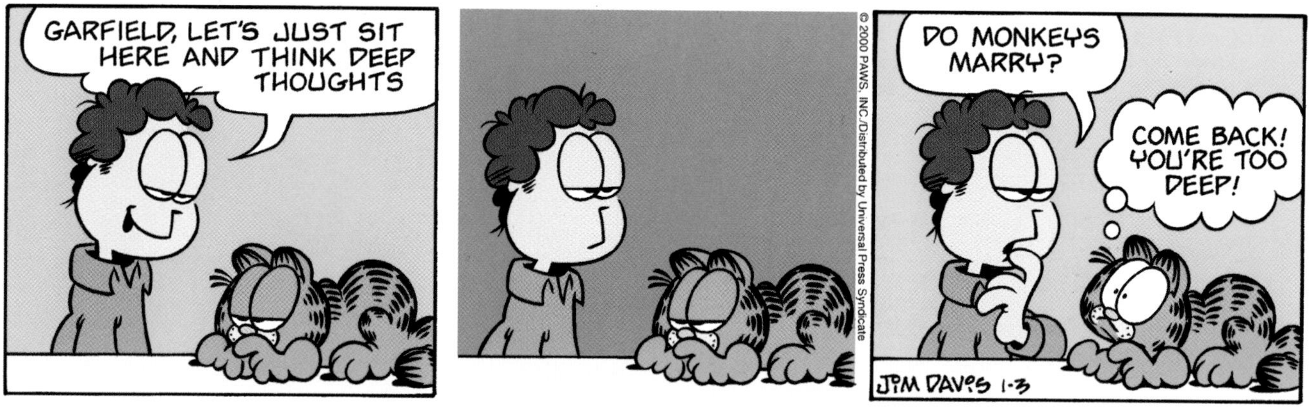
GARFIELD, LET'S JUST SIT HERE AND THINK DEEP THOUGHTS
DO MONKEYS MARRY?
COME BACK! YOU'RE TOO DEEP!
JIM DAVIS 1-3

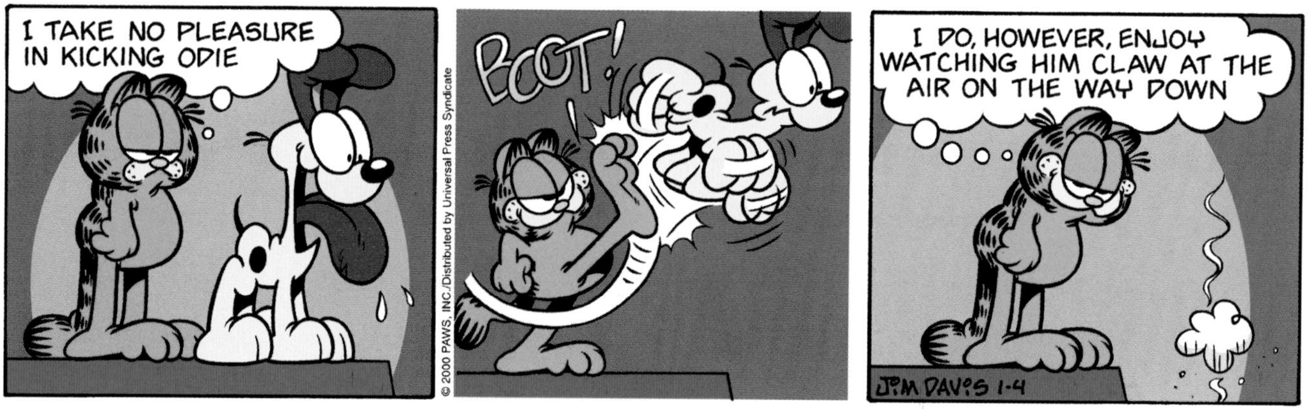
I TAKE NO PLEASURE IN KICKING ODIE
BOOT!
I DO, HOWEVER, ENJOY WATCHING HIM CLAW AT THE AIR ON THE WAY DOWN
JIM DAVIS 1-4

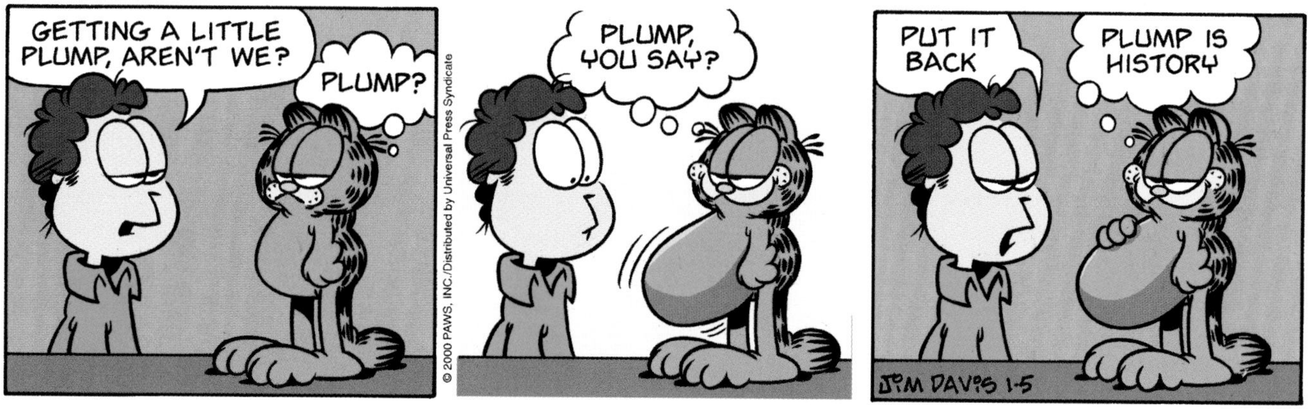
GETTING A LITTLE PLUMP, AREN'T WE?
PLUMP?
PLUMP, YOU SAY?
PUT IT BACK
PLUMP IS HISTORY
JIM DAVIS 1-5

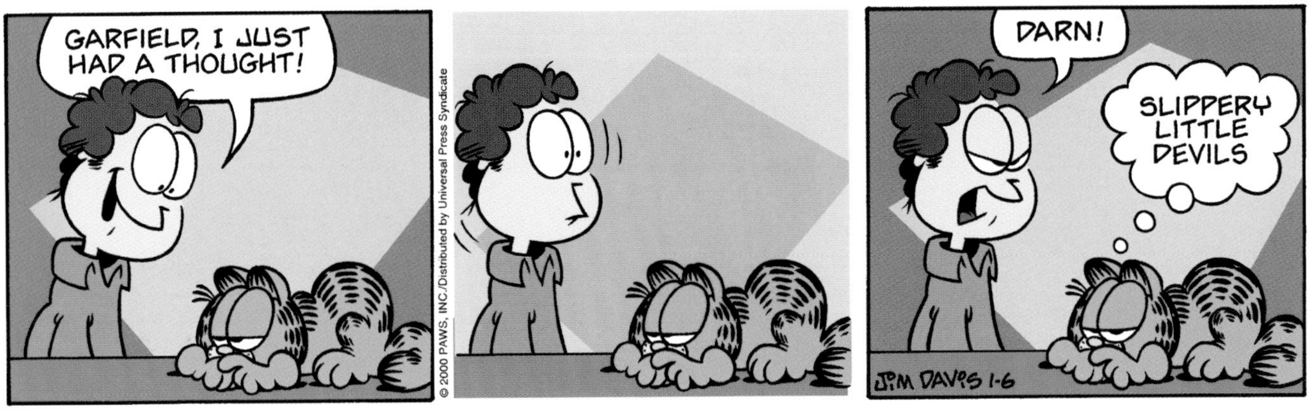
GARFIELD, I JUST HAD A THOUGHT!
© 2000 PAWS, INC./Distributed by Universal Press Syndicate
DARN!
SLIPPERY LITTLE DEVILS
JIM DAVIS 1-6

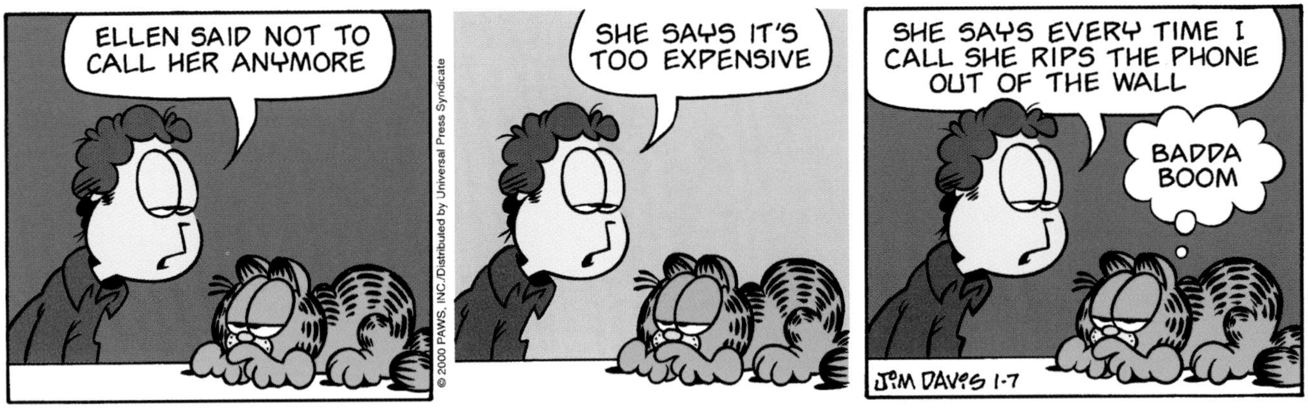
ELLEN SAID NOT TO CALL HER ANYMORE
© 2000 PAWS, INC./Distributed by Universal Press Syndicate
SHE SAYS IT'S TOO EXPENSIVE
SHE SAYS EVERY TIME I CALL SHE RIPS THE PHONE OUT OF THE WALL
BADDA BOOM
JIM DAVIS 1-7

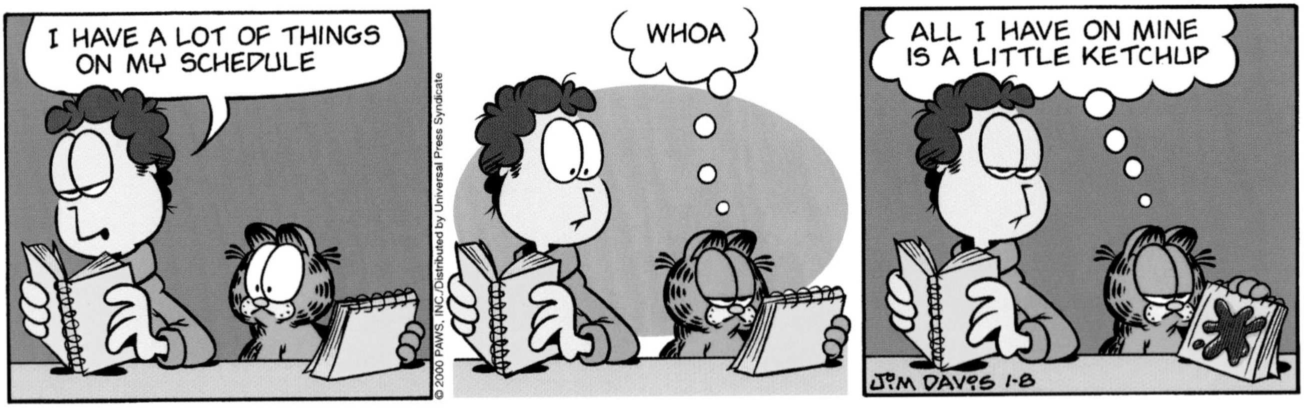
I HAVE A LOT OF THINGS ON MY SCHEDULE
© 2000 PAWS, INC./Distributed by Universal Press Syndicate
WHOA
ALL I HAVE ON MINE IS A LITTLE KETCHUP
JIM DAVIS 1-8

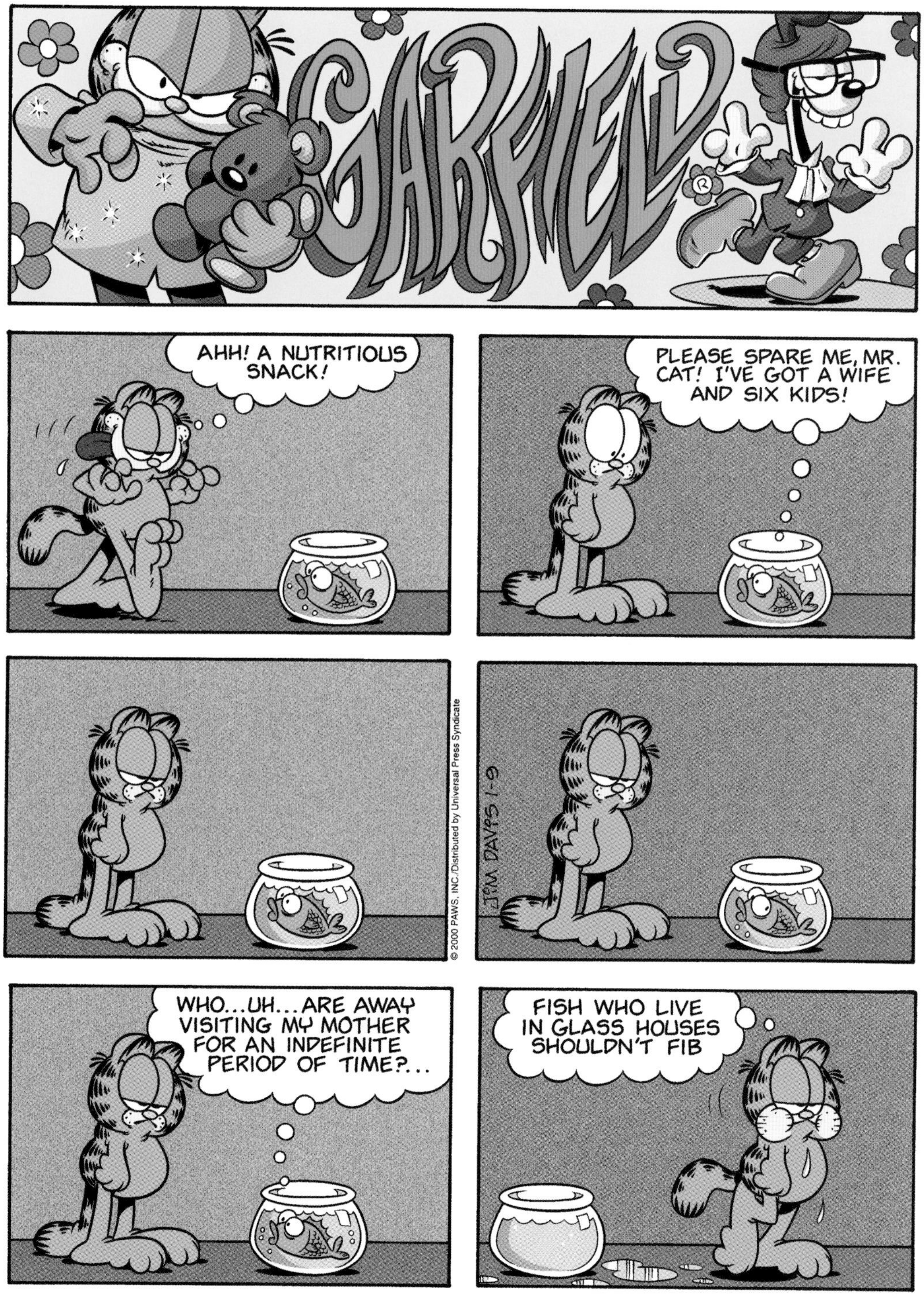
GARFIELD
AHH! A NUTRITIOUS SNACK!
PLEASE SPARE ME, MR. CAT! I'VE GOT A WIFE AND SIX KIDS!
© 2000 PAWS, INC./Distributed by Universal Press Syndicate
JIM DAVIS 1-9
WHO...UH...ARE AWAY VISITING MY MOTHER FOR AN INDEFINITE PERIOD OF TIME?...
FISH WHO LIVE IN GLASS HOUSES SHOULDN'T FIB

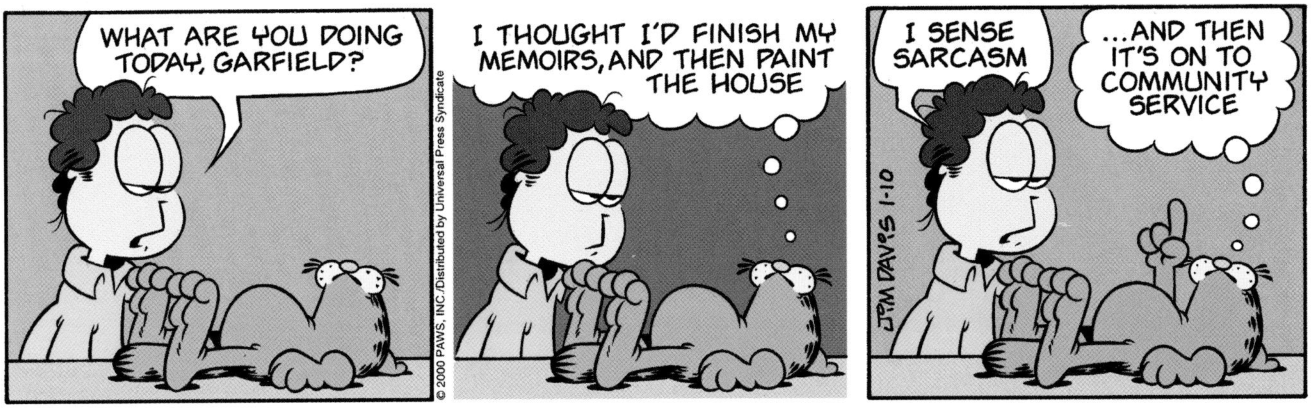
WHAT ARE YOU DOING TODAY, GARFIELD?
I THOUGHT I'D FINISH MY MEMOIRS, AND THEN PAINT THE HOUSE
I SENSE SARCASM
...AND THEN IT'S ON TO COMMUNITY SERVICE
JIM DAVIS 1-10
© 2000 PAWS, INC./Distributed by Universal Press Syndicate

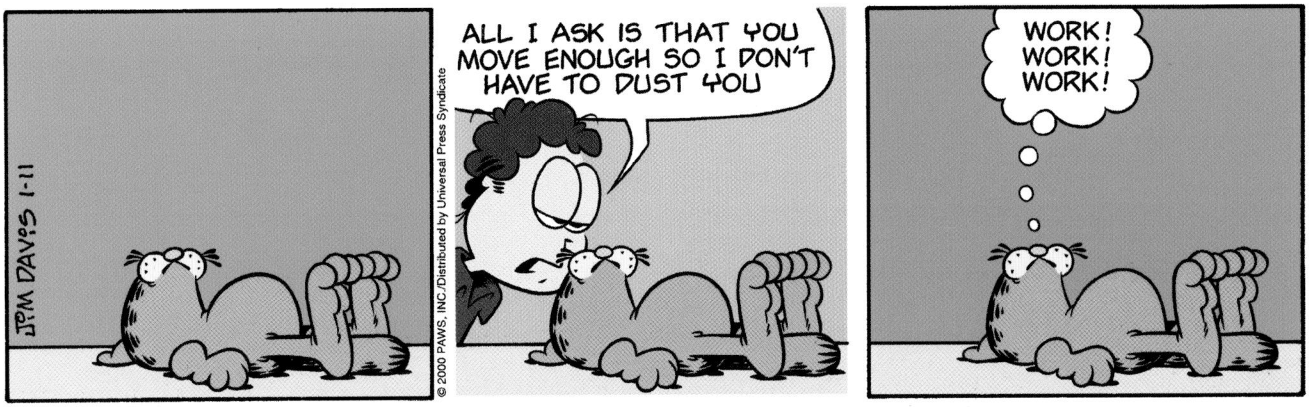
JIM DAVIS 1-11
ALL I ASK IS THAT YOU MOVE ENOUGH SO I DON'T HAVE TO DUST YOU
WORK! WORK! WORK!
© 2000 PAWS, INC./Distributed by Universal Press Syndicate

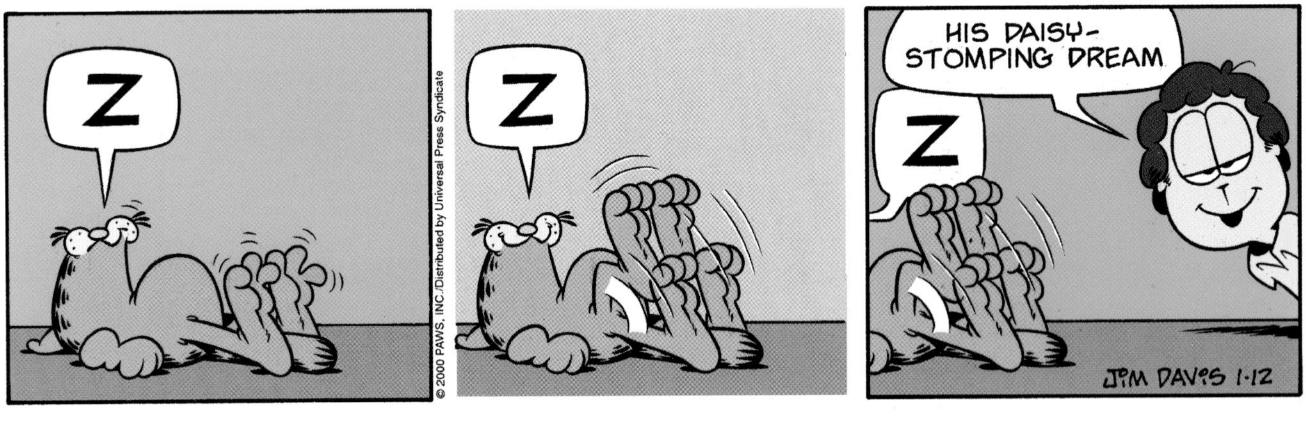
Z
Z
Z
HIS DAISY-STOMPING DREAM
JIM DAVIS 1-12
© 2000 PAWS, INC./Distributed by Universal Press Syndicate

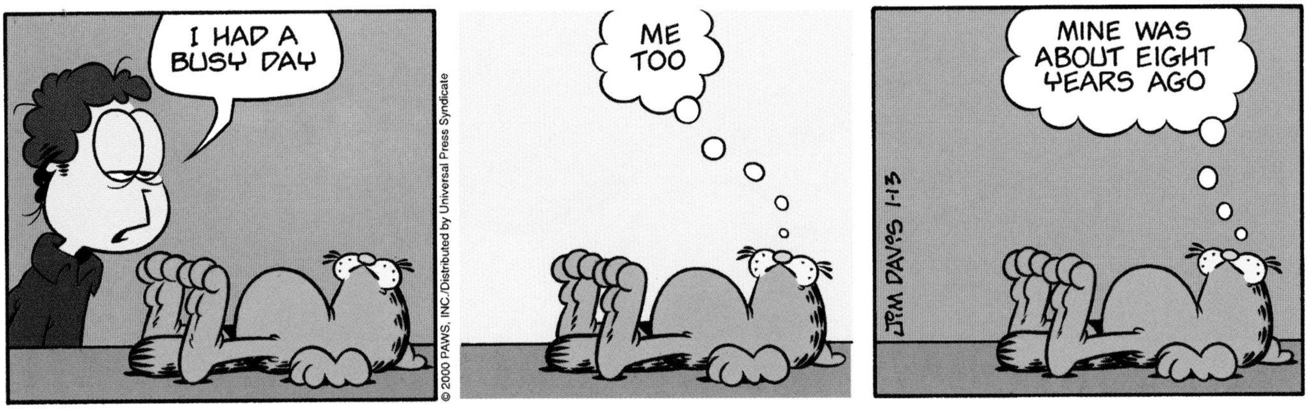
I HAD A BUSY DAY
ME TOO
MINE WAS ABOUT EIGHT YEARS AGO
© 2000 PAWS, INC./Distributed by Universal Press Syndicate
JIM DAVIS 1-13

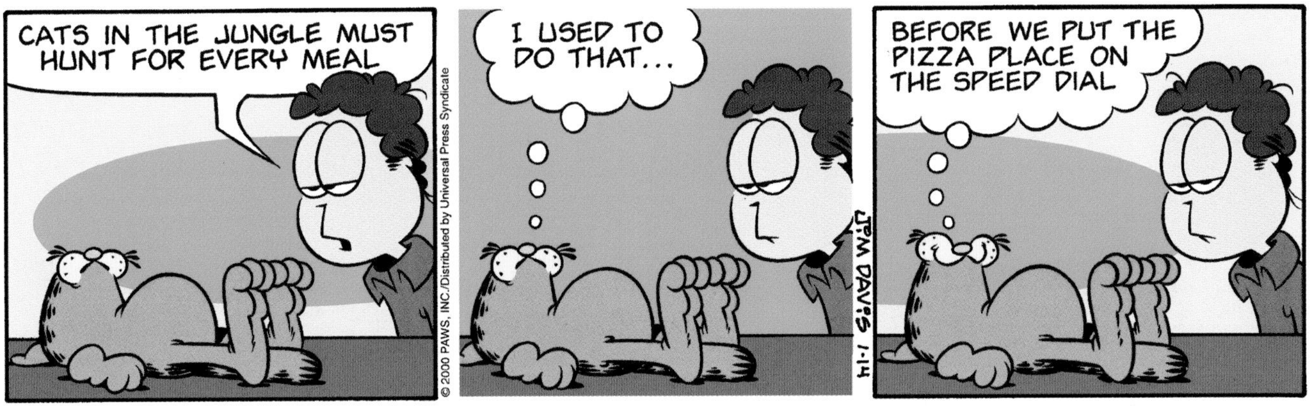
CATS IN THE JUNGLE MUST HUNT FOR EVERY MEAL
I USED TO DO THAT...
BEFORE WE PUT THE PIZZA PLACE ON THE SPEED DIAL
© 2000 PAWS, INC./Distributed by Universal Press Syndicate
JIM DAVIS 1-14

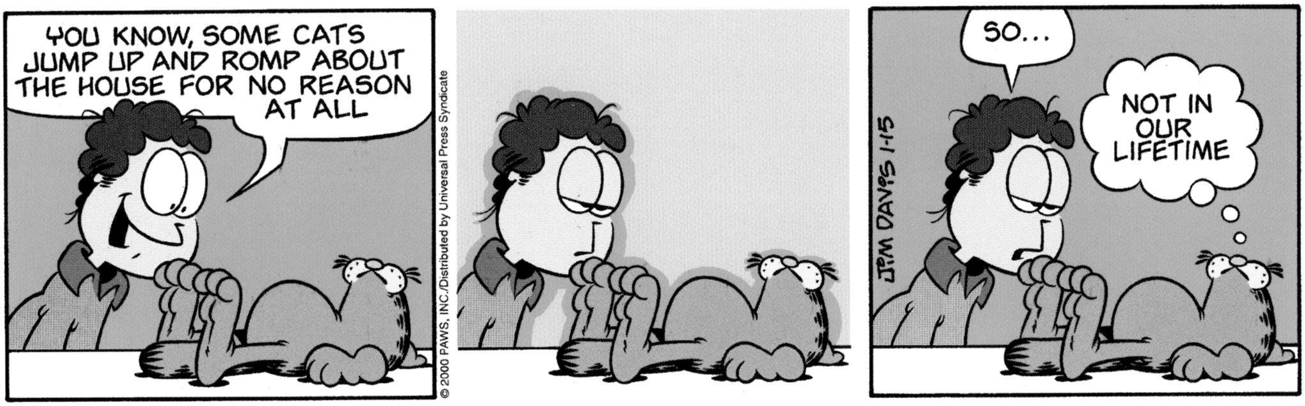
YOU KNOW, SOME CATS JUMP UP AND ROMP ABOUT THE HOUSE FOR NO REASON AT ALL
SO...
NOT IN OUR LIFETIME
© 2000 PAWS, INC./Distributed by Universal Press Syndicate
JIM DAVIS 1-15

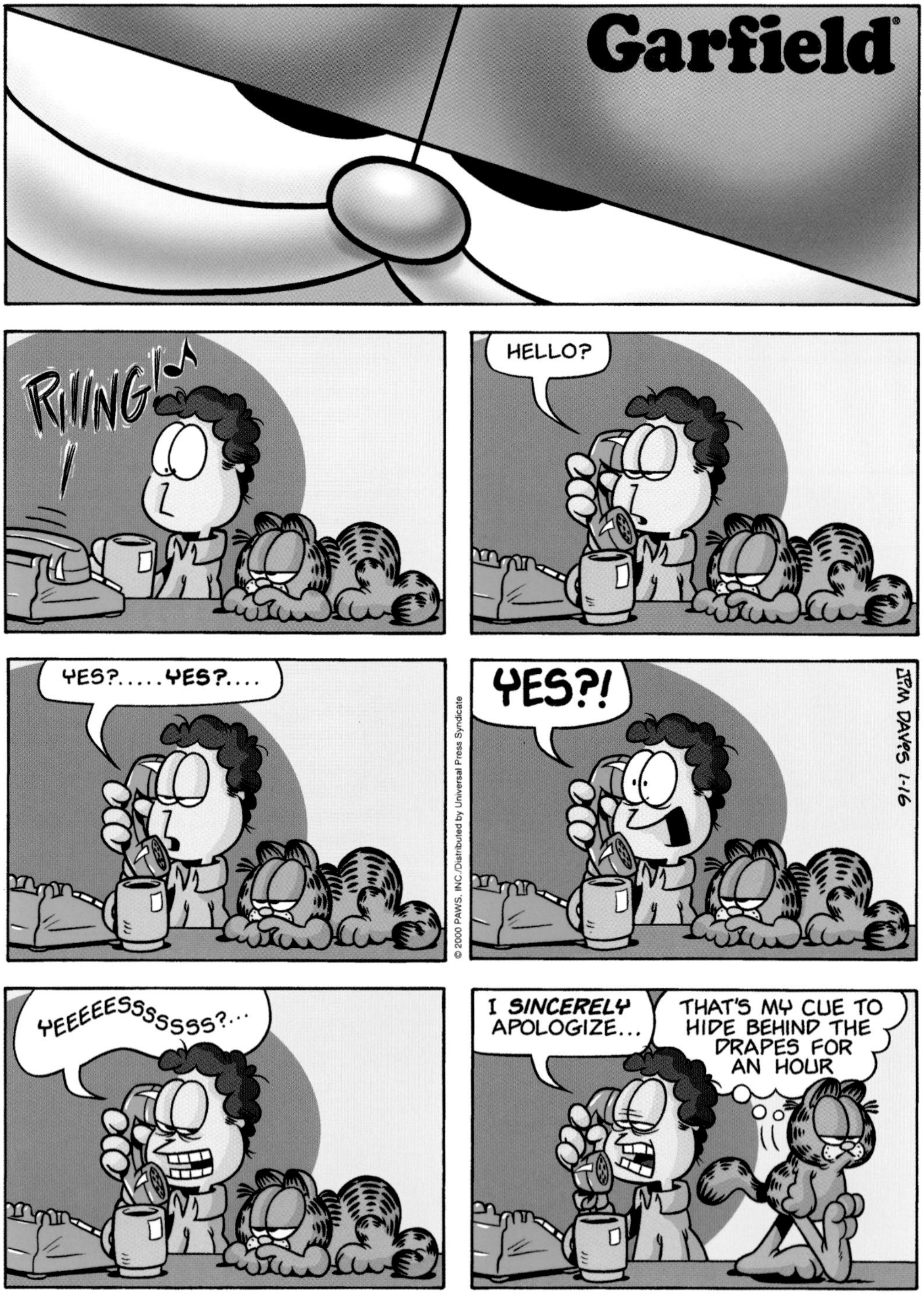
Garfield®
RIIING!
HELLO?
YES?.....YES?....
YES?!
JIM DAVIS 1-16
© 2000 PAWS, INC./Distributed by Universal Press Syndicate
YEEEEESSSSSSS?...
I SINCERELY APOLOGIZE...
THAT'S MY CUE TO HIDE BEHIND THE DRAPES FOR AN HOUR

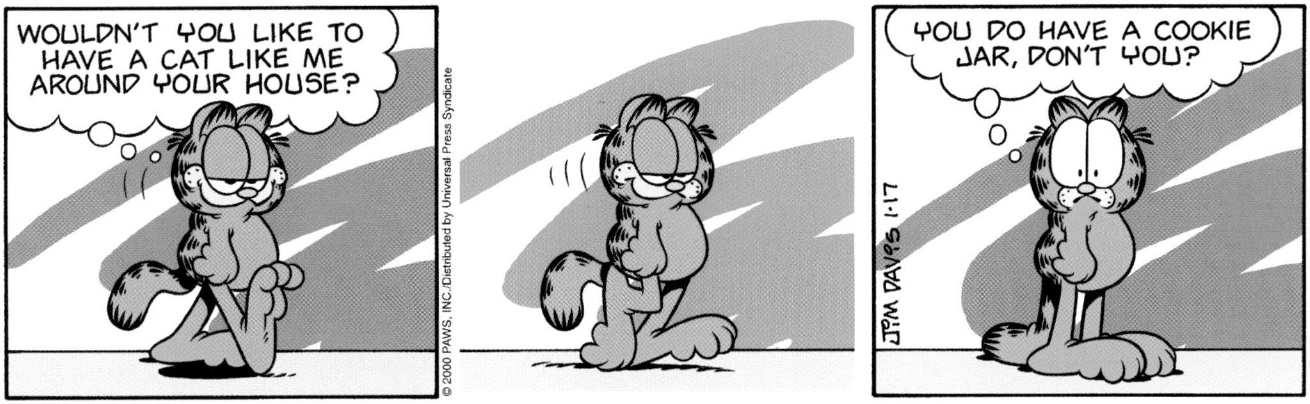
WOULDN'T YOU LIKE TO HAVE A CAT LIKE ME AROUND YOUR HOUSE?
YOU DO HAVE A COOKIE JAR, DON'T YOU?
JIM DAVIS 1-17

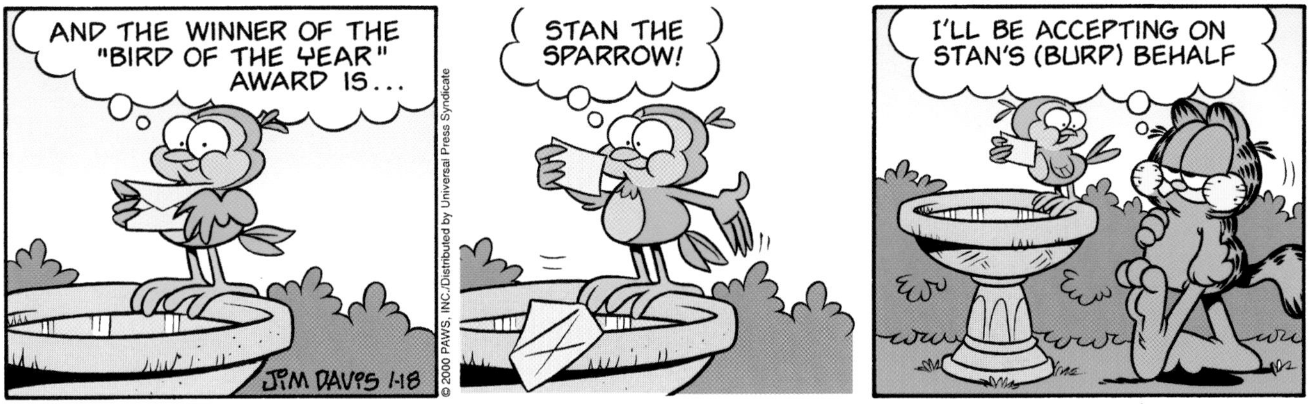
AND THE WINNER OF THE "BIRD OF THE YEAR" AWARD IS...
JIM DAVIS 1-18
STAN THE SPARROW!
I'LL BE ACCEPTING ON STAN'S (BURP) BEHALF

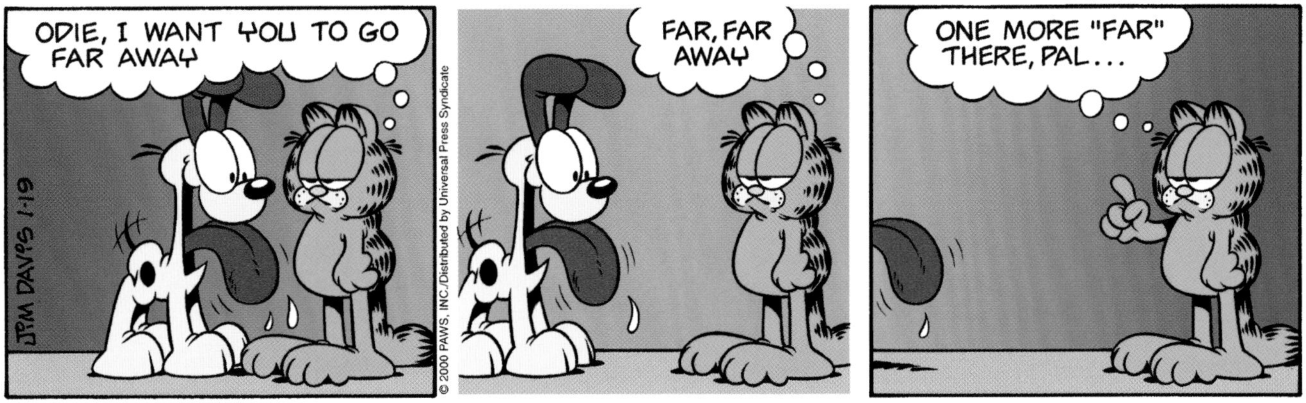
ODIE, I WANT YOU TO GO FAR AWAY
JIM DAVIS 1-19
FAR, FAR AWAY
ONE MORE "FAR" THERE, PAL...

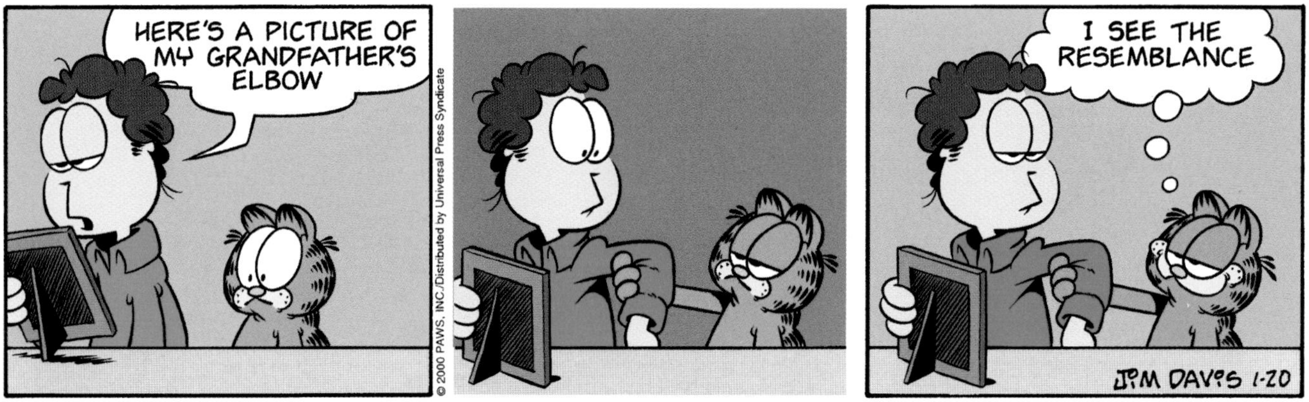
HERE'S A PICTURE OF MY GRANDFATHER'S ELBOW
I SEE THE RESEMBLANCE
© 2000 PAWS, INC./Distributed by Universal Press Syndicate
JIM DAVIS 1-20

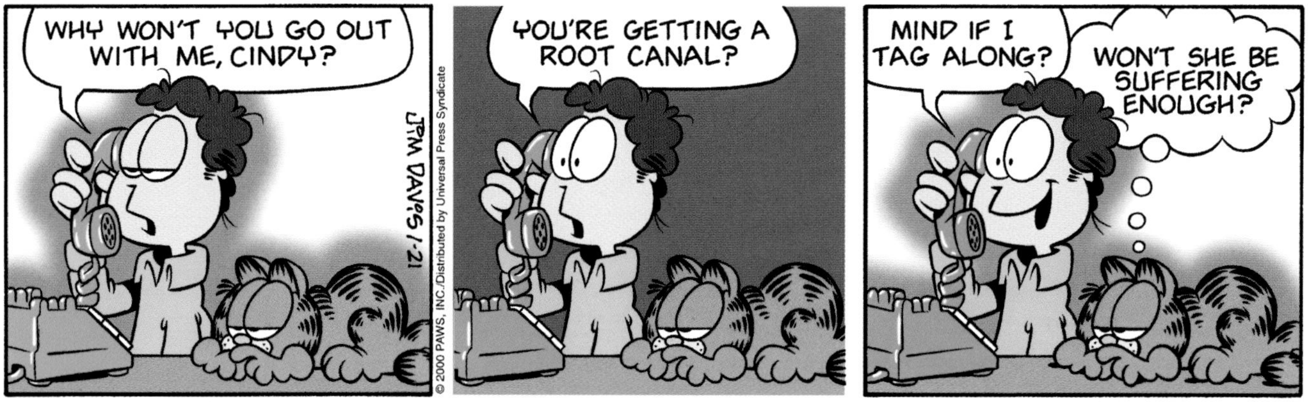
WHY WON'T YOU GO OUT WITH ME, CINDY?
YOU'RE GETTING A ROOT CANAL?
MIND IF I TAG ALONG?
WON'T SHE BE SUFFERING ENOUGH?
JIM DAVIS 1-21
© 2000 PAWS, INC./Distributed by Universal Press Syndicate

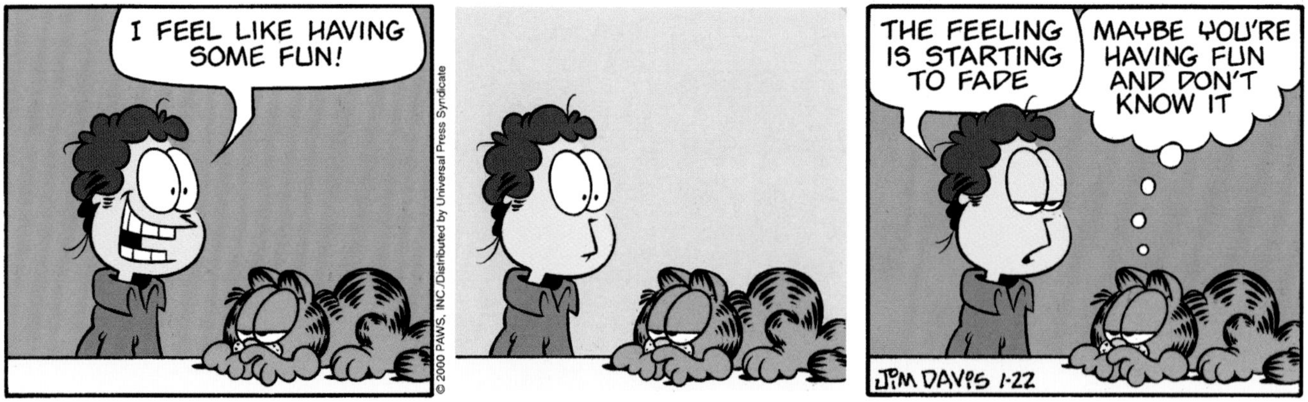
I FEEL LIKE HAVING SOME FUN!
THE FEELING IS STARTING TO FADE
MAYBE YOU'RE HAVING FUN AND DON'T KNOW IT
© 2000 PAWS, INC./Distributed by Universal Press Syndicate
JIM DAVIS 1-22

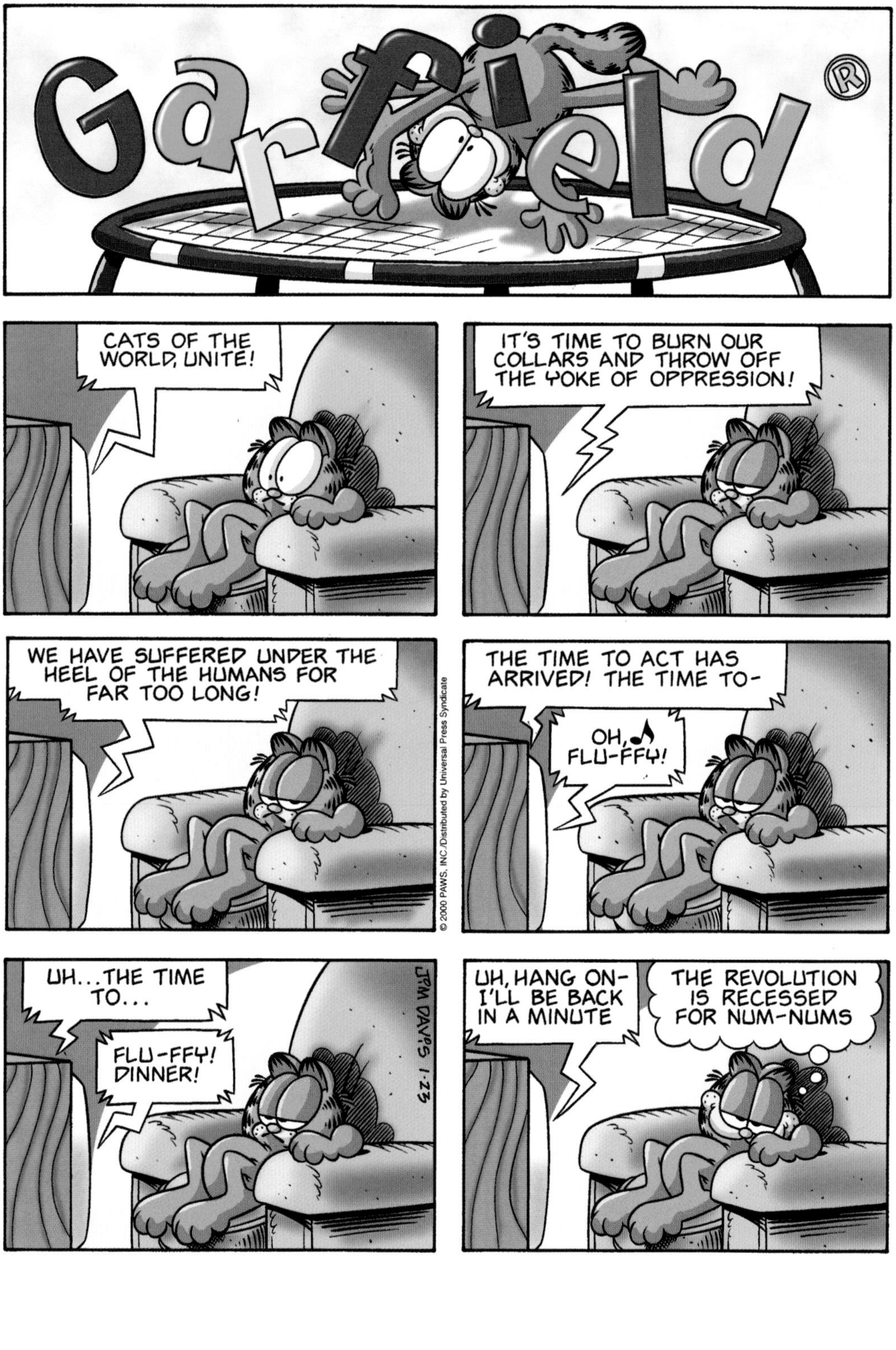
Garfield®
CATS OF THE WORLD, UNITE!
IT'S TIME TO BURN OUR COLLARS AND THROW OFF THE YOKE OF OPPRESSION!
WE HAVE SUFFERED UNDER THE HEEL OF THE HUMANS FOR FAR TOO LONG!
THE TIME TO ACT HAS ARRIVED! THE TIME TO-
OH, FLU-FFY!
UH...THE TIME TO...
FLU-FFY! DINNER!
JPM DAVPS 1-23
UH, HANG ON- I'LL BE BACK IN A MINUTE
THE REVOLUTION IS RECESSED FOR NUM-NUMS
© 2000 PAWS, INC./Distributed by Universal Press Syndicate

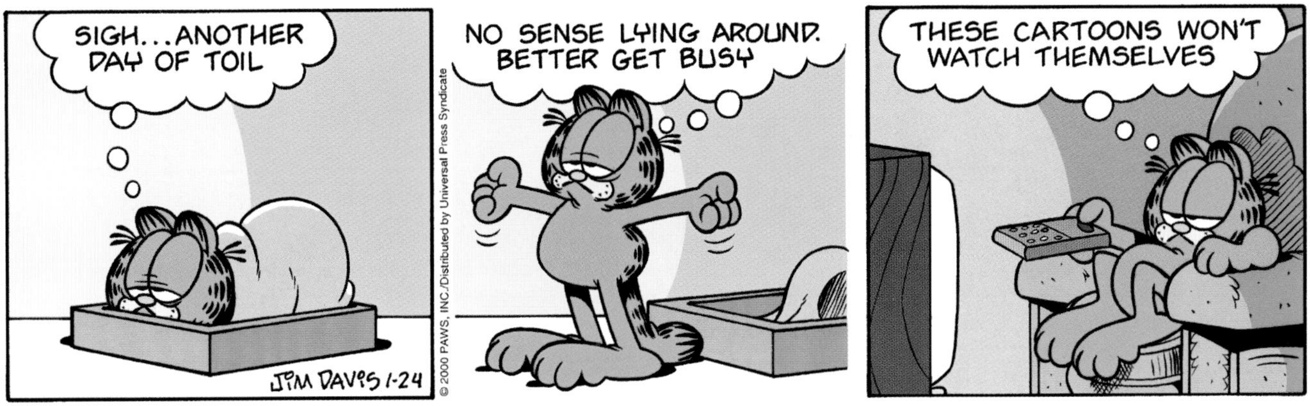
SIGH...ANOTHER DAY OF TOIL
JIM DAVIS 1-24
© 2000 PAWS, INC./Distributed by Universal Press Syndicate
NO SENSE LYING AROUND. BETTER GET BUSY
THESE CARTOONS WON'T WATCH THEMSELVES

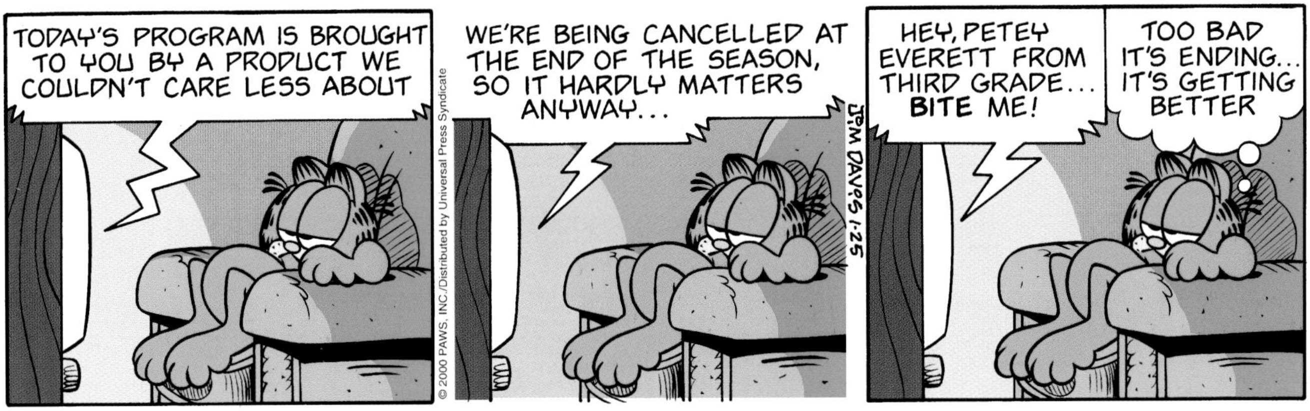
TODAY'S PROGRAM IS BROUGHT TO YOU BY A PRODUCT WE COULDN'T CARE LESS ABOUT
© 2000 PAWS, INC./Distributed by Universal Press Syndicate
WE'RE BEING CANCELLED AT THE END OF THE SEASON, SO IT HARDLY MATTERS ANYWAY...
JIM DAVIS 1-25
HEY, PETEY EVERETT FROM THIRD GRADE... **BITE** ME!
TOO BAD IT'S ENDING... IT'S GETTING BETTER

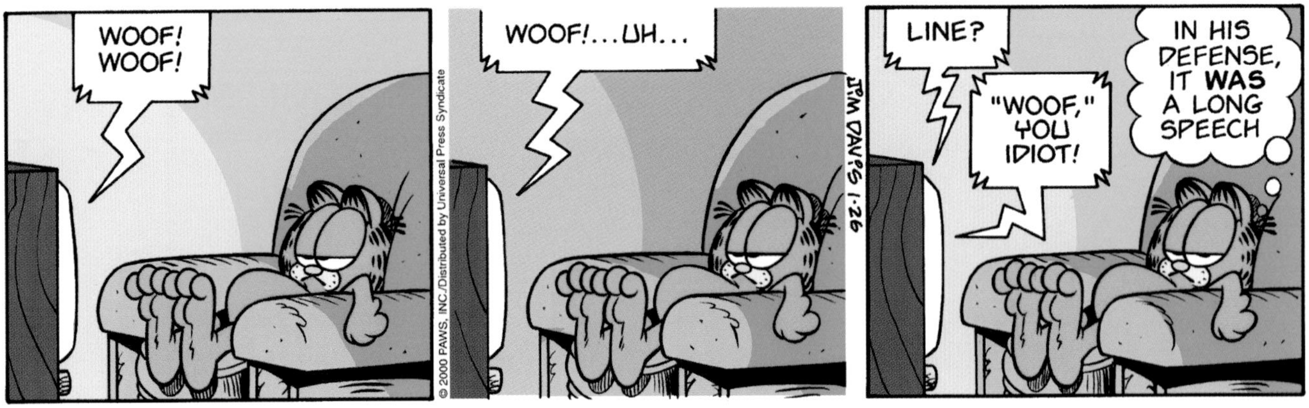
WOOF! WOOF!
© 2000 PAWS, INC./Distributed by Universal Press Syndicate
WOOF!...UH...
JIM DAVIS 1-26
LINE?
"WOOF," YOU IDIOT!
IN HIS DEFENSE, IT **WAS** A LONG SPEECH

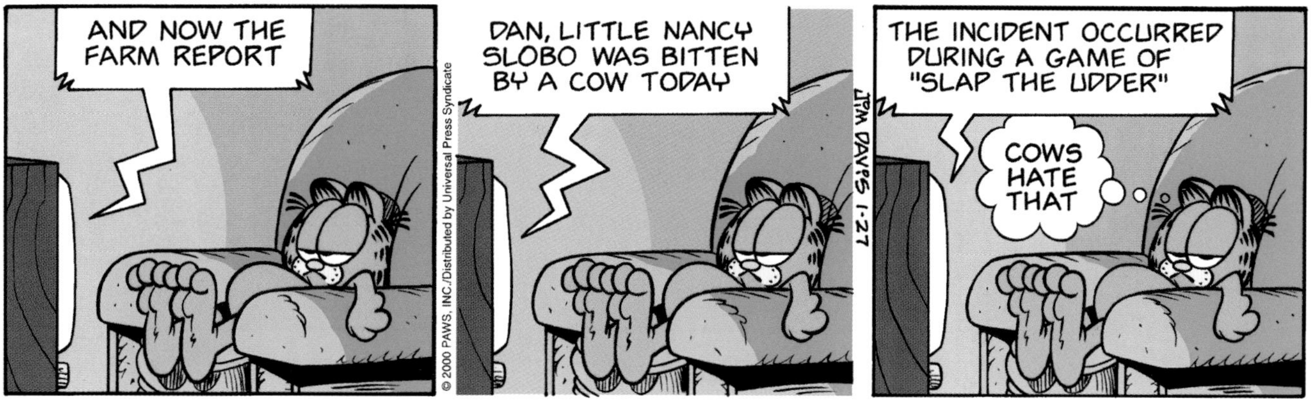
AND NOW THE FARM REPORT
DAN, LITTLE NANCY SLOBO WAS BITTEN BY A COW TODAY
© 2000 PAWS, INC./Distributed by Universal Press Syndicate
JIM DAVIS 1-27
THE INCIDENT OCCURRED DURING A GAME OF "SLAP THE UDDER"
COWS HATE THAT

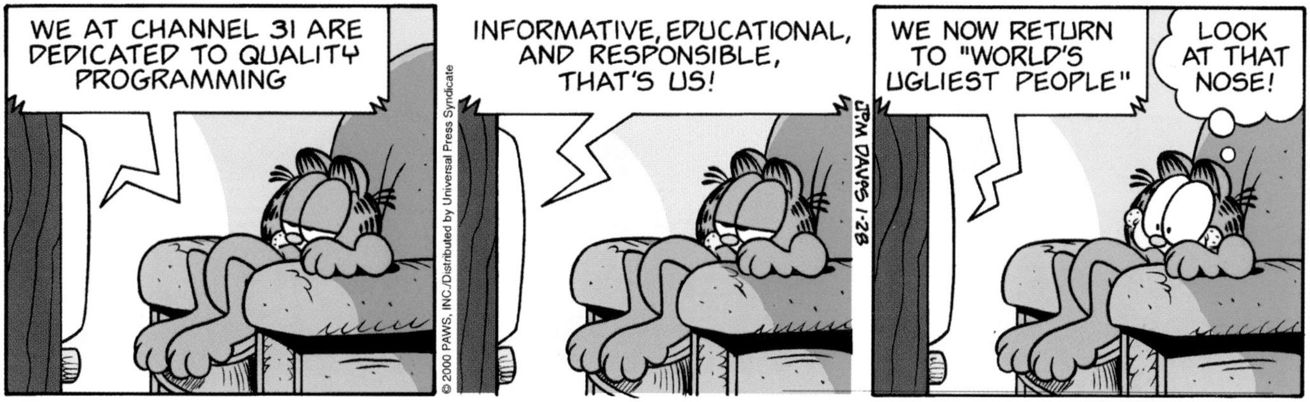
WE AT CHANNEL 31 ARE DEDICATED TO QUALITY PROGRAMMING
INFORMATIVE, EDUCATIONAL, AND RESPONSIBLE, THAT'S US!
© 2000 PAWS, INC./Distributed by Universal Press Syndicate
JIM DAVIS 1-28
WE NOW RETURN TO "WORLD'S UGLIEST PEOPLE"
LOOK AT THAT NOSE!

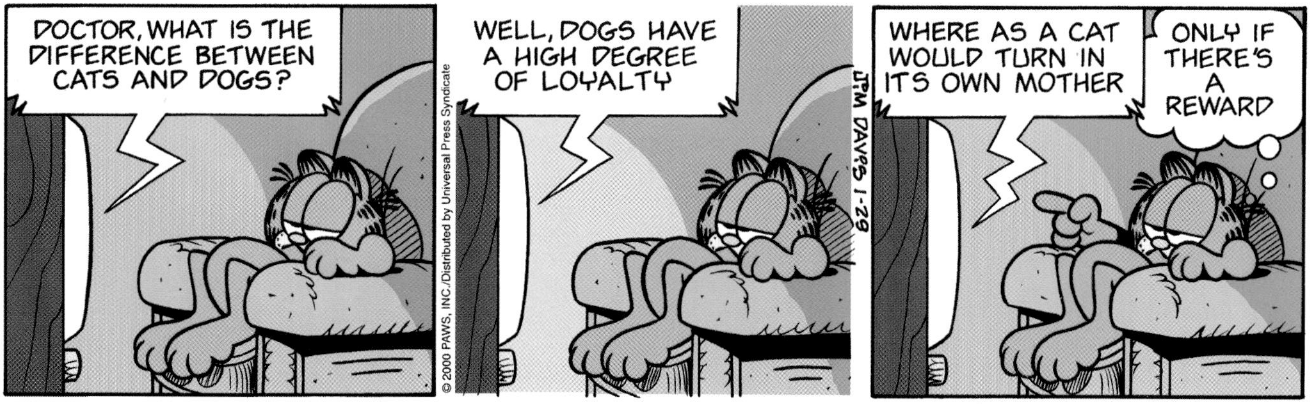
DOCTOR, WHAT IS THE DIFFERENCE BETWEEN CATS AND DOGS?
WELL, DOGS HAVE A HIGH DEGREE OF LOYALTY
© 2000 PAWS, INC./Distributed by Universal Press Syndicate
JIM DAVIS 1-29
WHERE AS A CAT WOULD TURN IN ITS OWN MOTHER
ONLY IF THERE'S A REWARD

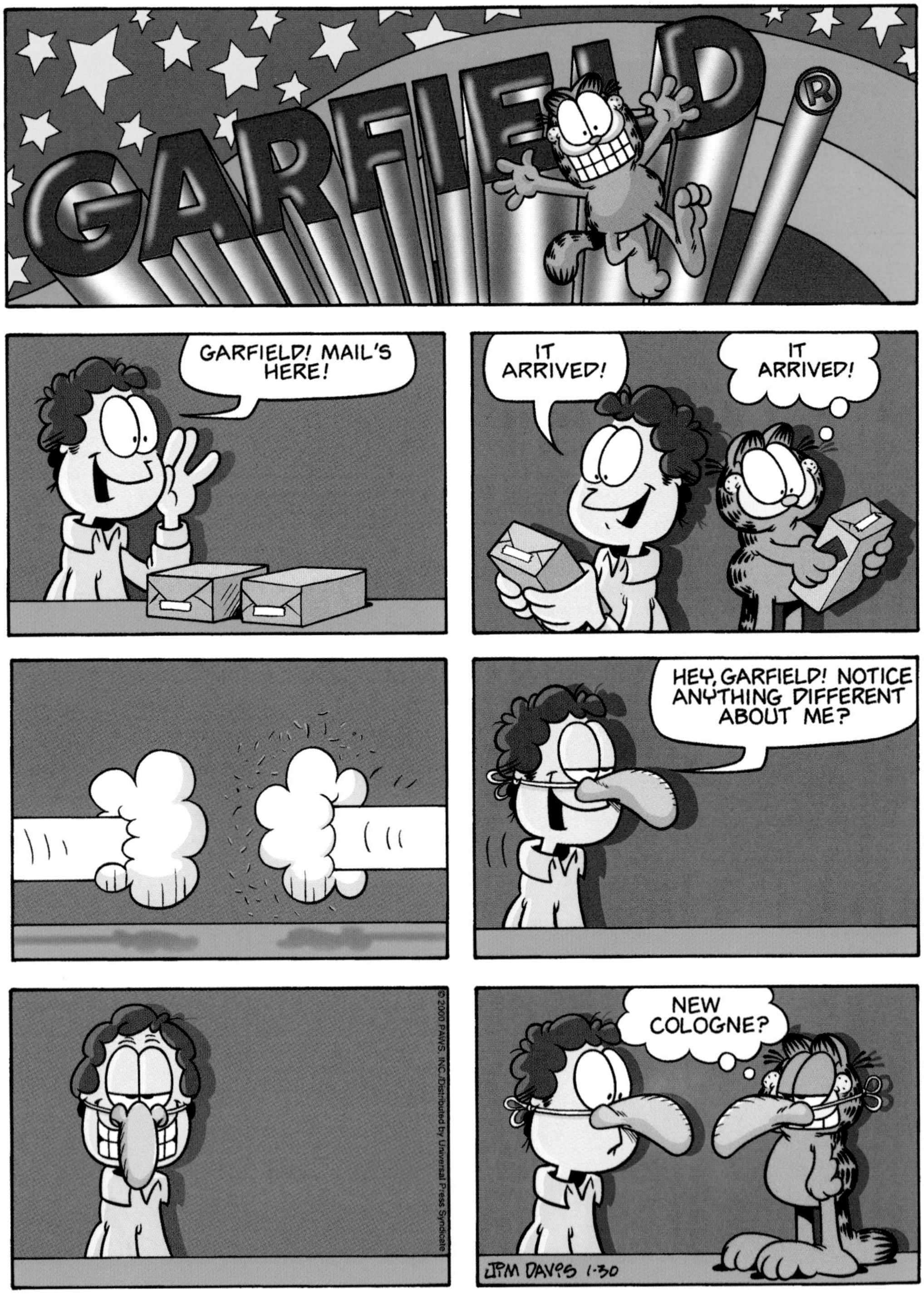
GARFIELD®
GARFIELD! MAIL'S HERE!
IT ARRIVED!
IT ARRIVED!
HEY, GARFIELD! NOTICE ANYTHING DIFFERENT ABOUT ME?
© 2000 PAWS, INC./Distributed by Universal Press Syndicate
NEW COLOGNE?
JIM DAVIS 1-30

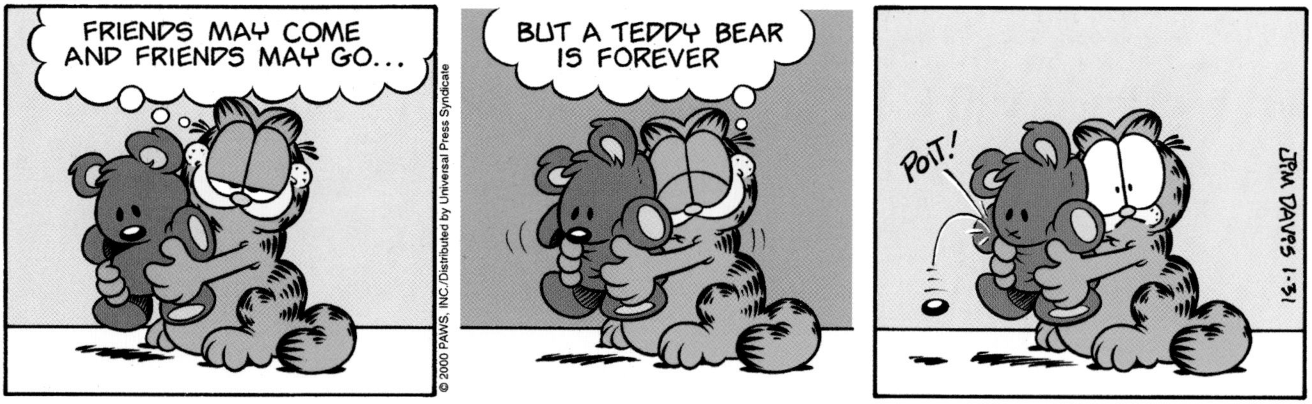
FRIENDS MAY COME AND FRIENDS MAY GO...
BUT A TEDDY BEAR IS FOREVER
POIT!
JIM DAVIS 1-31

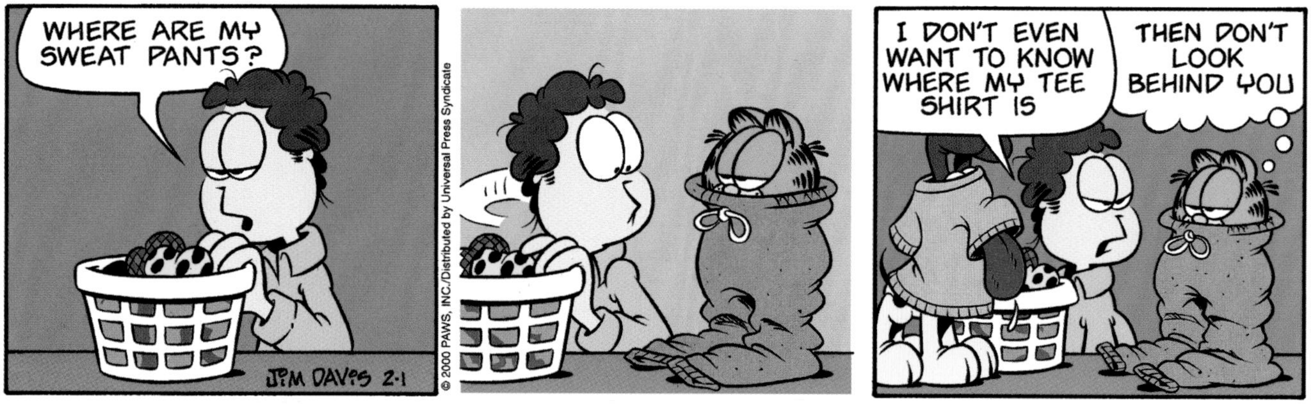
WHERE ARE MY SWEAT PANTS?
JIM DAVIS 2-1
I DON'T EVEN WANT TO KNOW WHERE MY TEE SHIRT IS
THEN DON'T LOOK BEHIND YOU

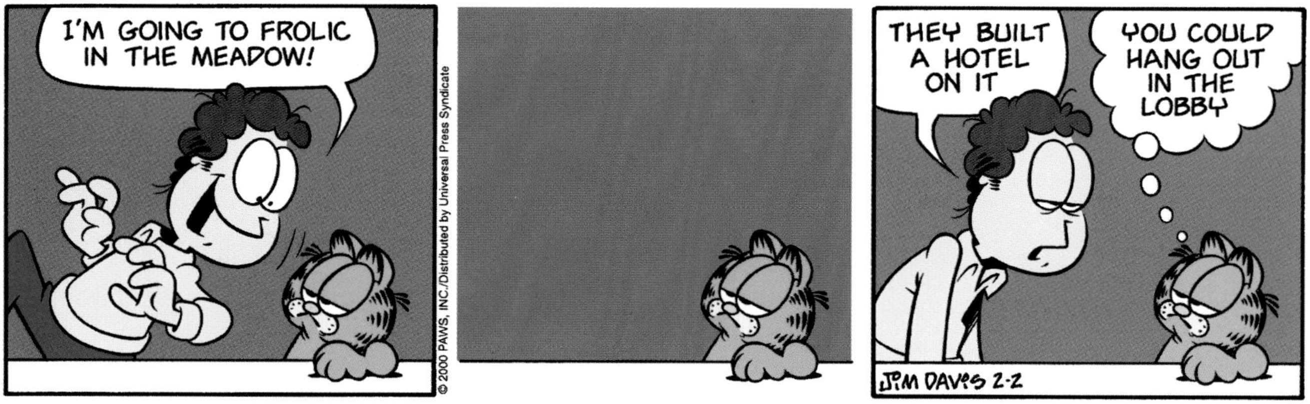
I'M GOING TO FROLIC IN THE MEADOW!
THEY BUILT A HOTEL ON IT
YOU COULD HANG OUT IN THE LOBBY
JIM DAVIS 2-2

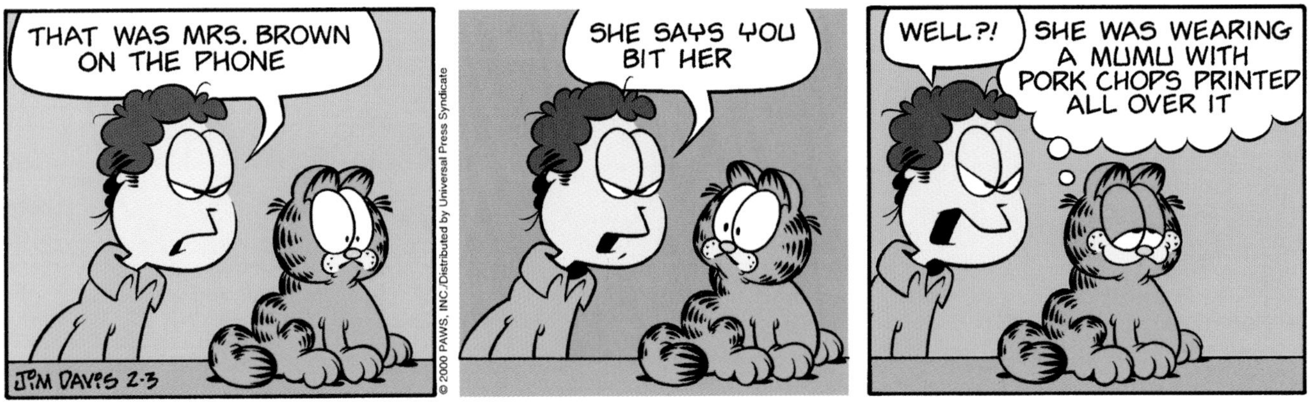
THAT WAS MRS. BROWN ON THE PHONE
SHE SAYS YOU BIT HER
WELL?!
SHE WAS WEARING A MUMU WITH PORK CHOPS PRINTED ALL OVER IT
JIM DAVIS 2-3
© 2000 PAWS, INC./Distributed by Universal Press Syndicate

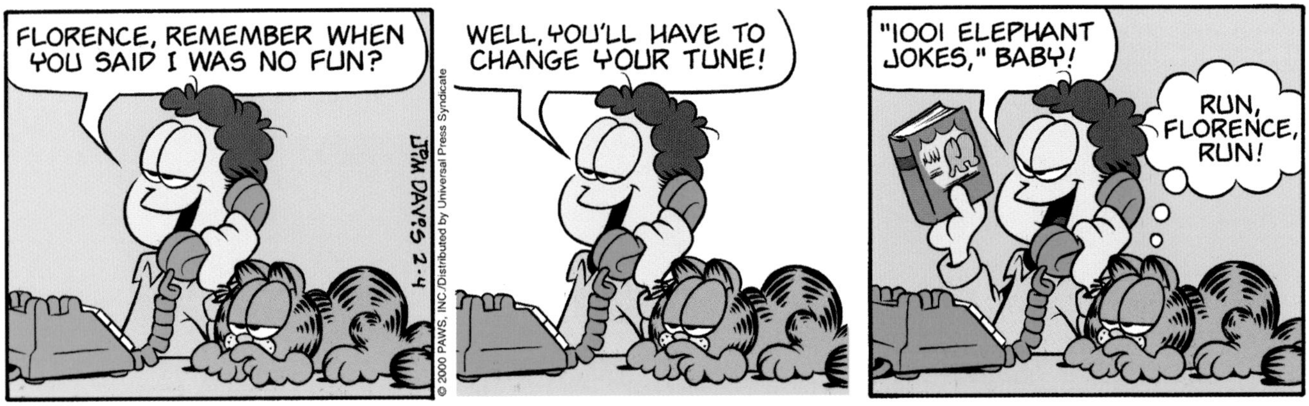
FLORENCE, REMEMBER WHEN YOU SAID I WAS NO FUN?
WELL, YOU'LL HAVE TO CHANGE YOUR TUNE!
"1001 ELEPHANT JOKES," BABY!
RUN, FLORENCE, RUN!
JIM DAVIS 2-4
© 2000 PAWS, INC./Distributed by Universal Press Syndicate

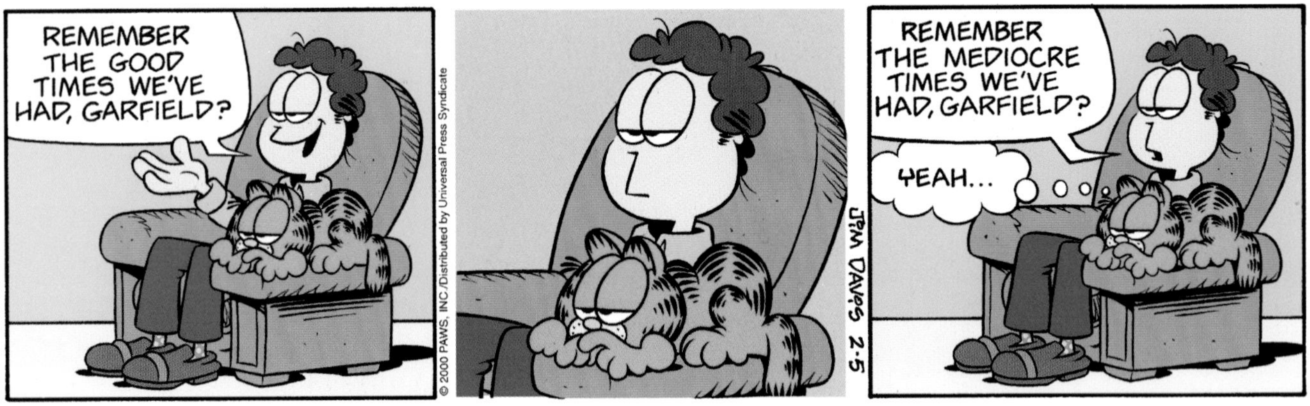
REMEMBER THE GOOD TIMES WE'VE HAD, GARFIELD?
REMEMBER THE MEDIOCRE TIMES WE'VE HAD, GARFIELD?
YEAH...
JIM DAVIS 2-5
© 2000 PAWS, INC./Distributed by Universal Press Syndicate

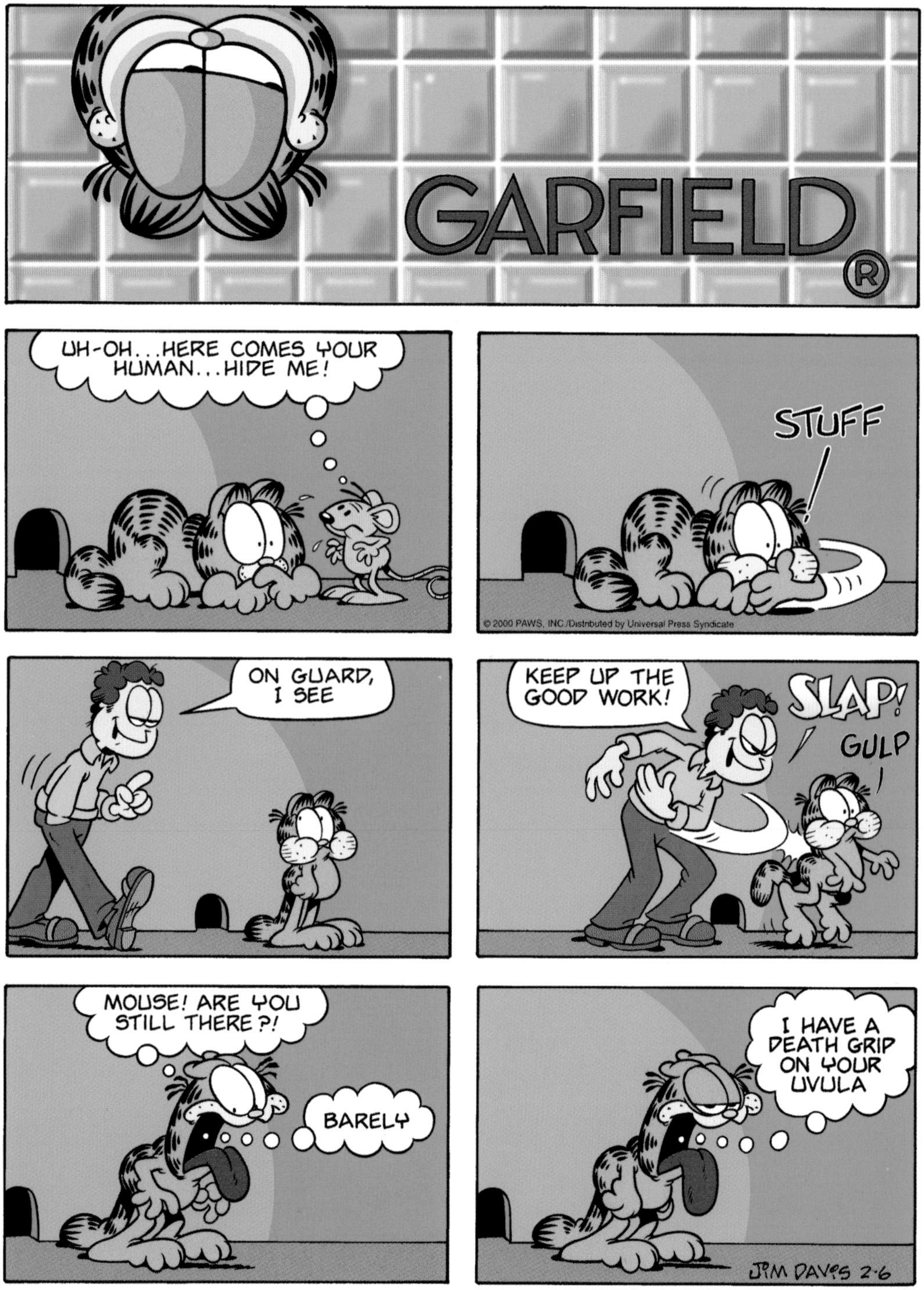
GARFIELD®
UH-OH...HERE COMES YOUR HUMAN...HIDE ME!
STUFF
© 2000 PAWS, INC./Distributed by Universal Press Syndicate
ON GUARD, I SEE
KEEP UP THE GOOD WORK!
SLAP!
GULP
MOUSE! ARE YOU STILL THERE?!
BARELY
I HAVE A DEATH GRIP ON YOUR UVULA
JIM DAVIS 2-6

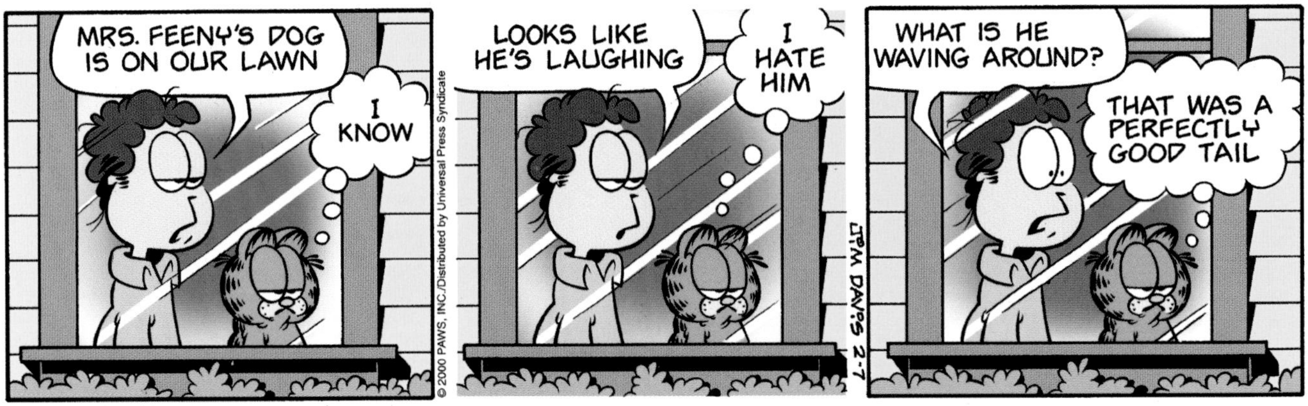
MRS. FEENY'S DOG IS ON OUR LAWN
I KNOW
LOOKS LIKE HE'S LAUGHING
I HATE HIM
WHAT IS HE WAVING AROUND?
THAT WAS A PERFECTLY GOOD TAIL
JPM DAVPS 2-7

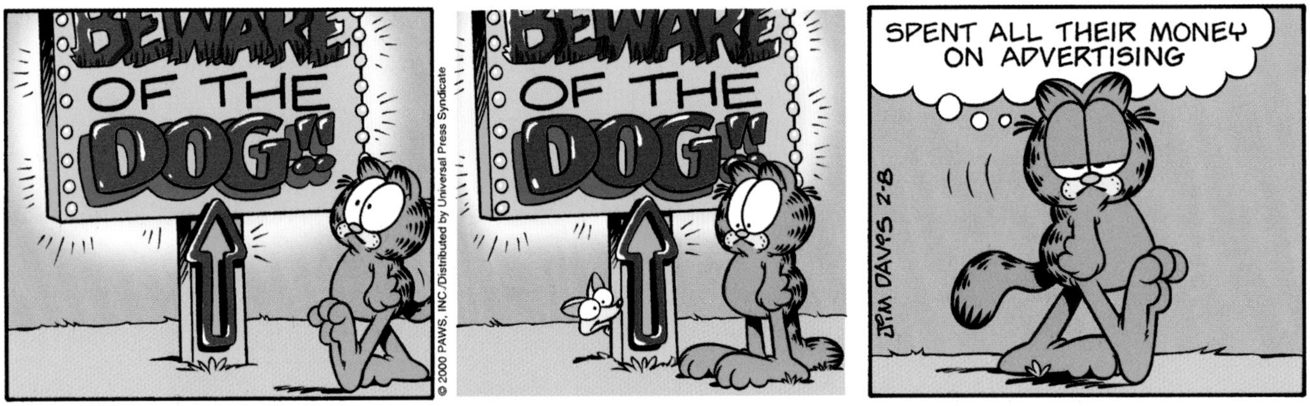
BEWARE OF THE DOG!!
SPENT ALL THEIR MONEY ON ADVERTISING
JPM DAVPS 2-8

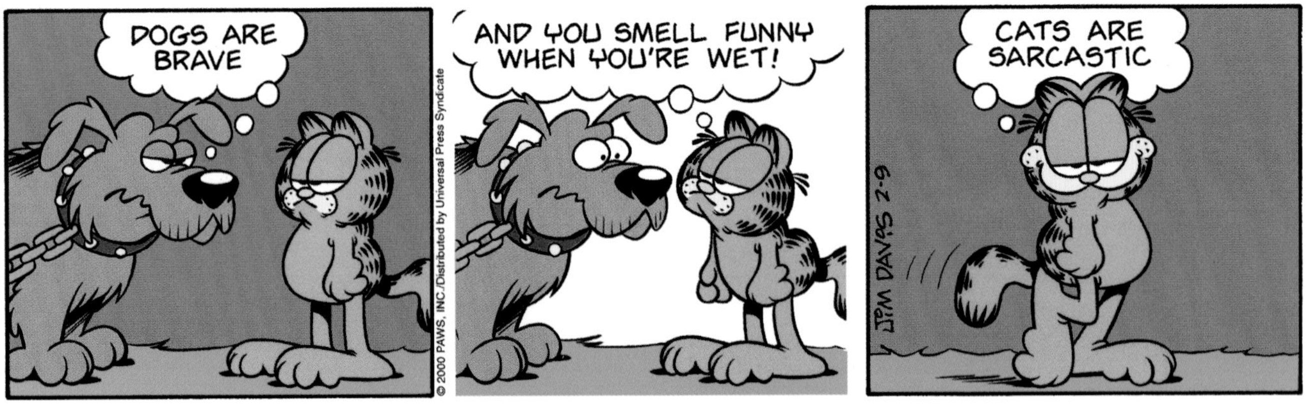
DOGS ARE BRAVE
AND YOU SMELL FUNNY WHEN YOU'RE WET!
CATS ARE SARCASTIC
JPM DAVPS 2-9

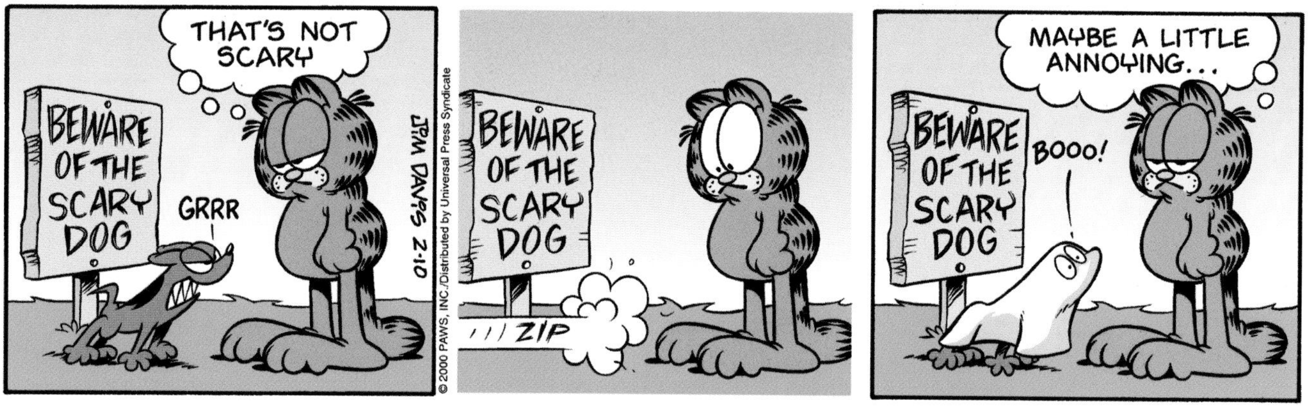
THAT'S NOT SCARY
BEWARE OF THE SCARY DOG
GRRR
JPM DAVPS 2-10
© 2000 PAWS, INC./Distributed by Universal Press Syndicate
BEWARE OF THE SCARY DOG
ZIP
MAYBE A LITTLE ANNOYING...
BEWARE OF THE SCARY DOG
BOOO!

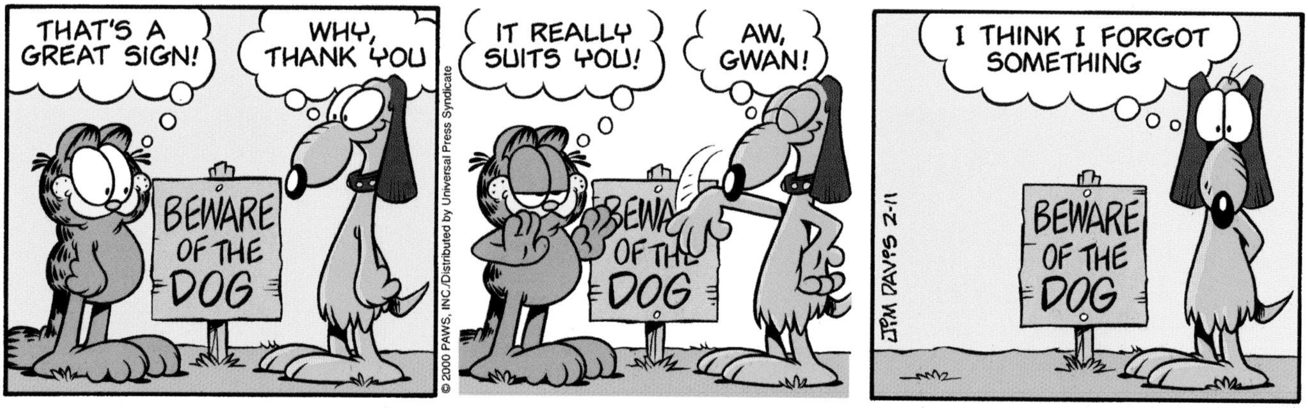
THAT'S A GREAT SIGN!
WHY, THANK YOU
BEWARE OF THE DOG
© 2000 PAWS, INC./Distributed by Universal Press Syndicate
IT REALLY SUITS YOU!
AW, GWAN!
I THINK I FORGOT SOMETHING
BEWARE OF THE DOG
JPM DAVPS 2-11

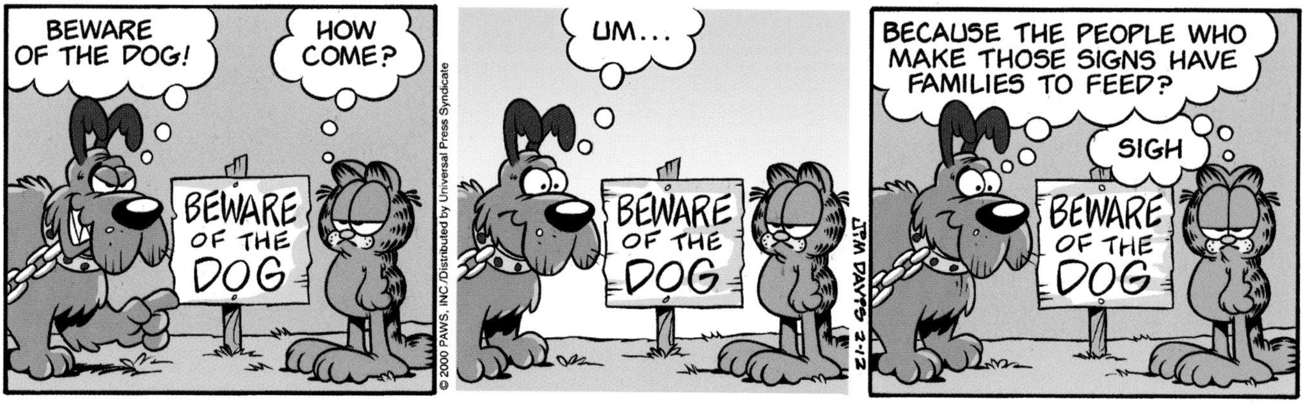
BEWARE OF THE DOG!
HOW COME?
BEWARE OF THE DOG
© 2000 PAWS, INC./Distributed by Universal Press Syndicate
UM...
BEWARE OF THE DOG
JPM DAVPS 2-12
BECAUSE THE PEOPLE WHO MAKE THOSE SIGNS HAVE FAMILIES TO FEED?
SIGH
BEWARE OF THE DOG

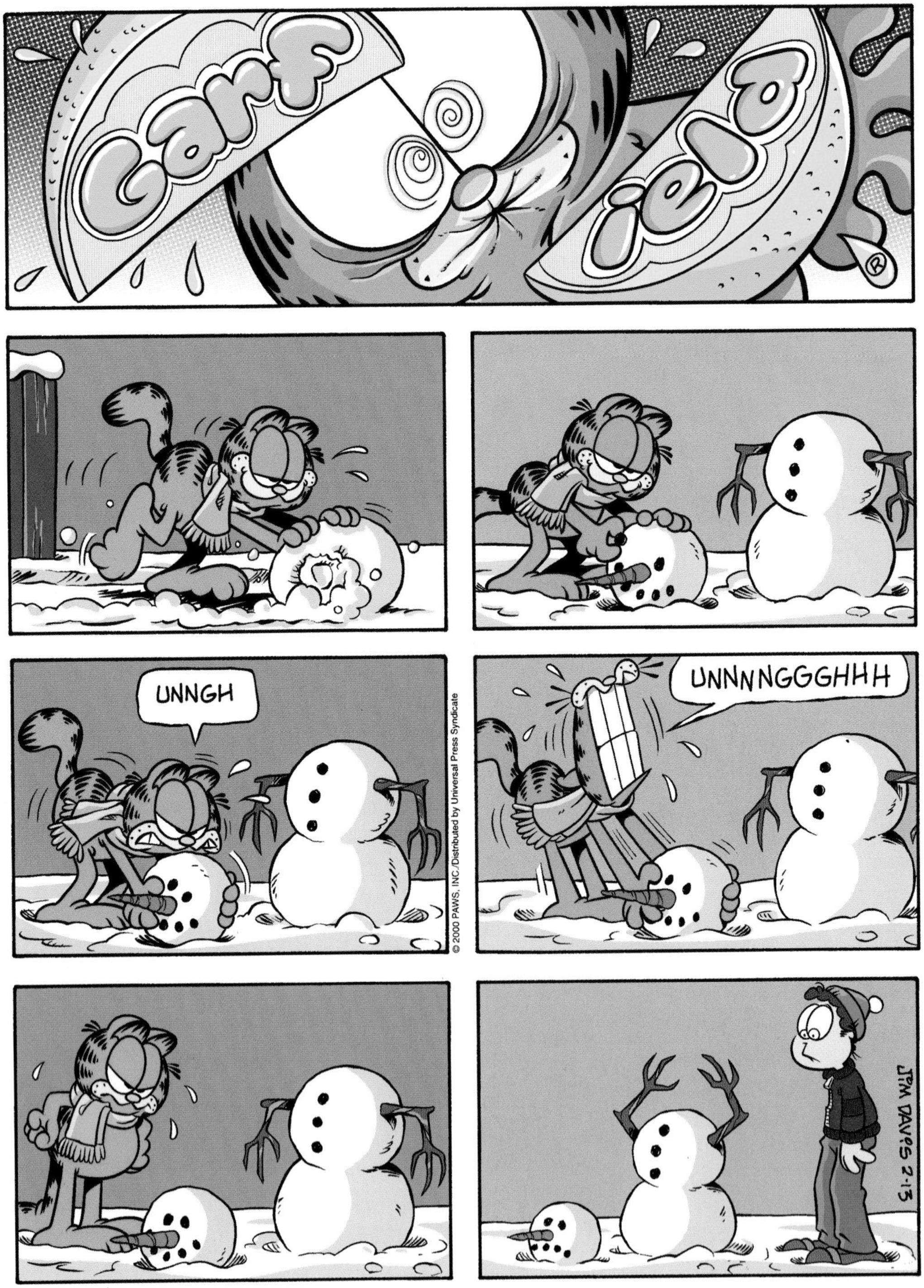
Garfield®
UNNGH
UNNNNGGGHHH
JIM DAVIS 2-13
© 2000 PAWS, INC./Distributed by Universal Press Syndicate

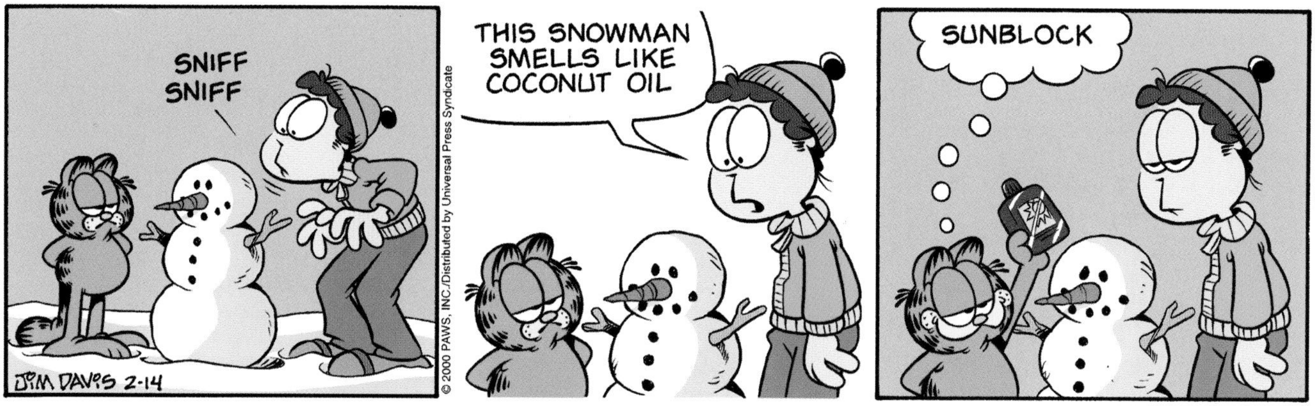
SNIFF SNIFF
JIM DAVIS 2-14
© 2000 PAWS, INC./Distributed by Universal Press Syndicate
THIS SNOWMAN SMELLS LIKE COCONUT OIL
SUNBLOCK

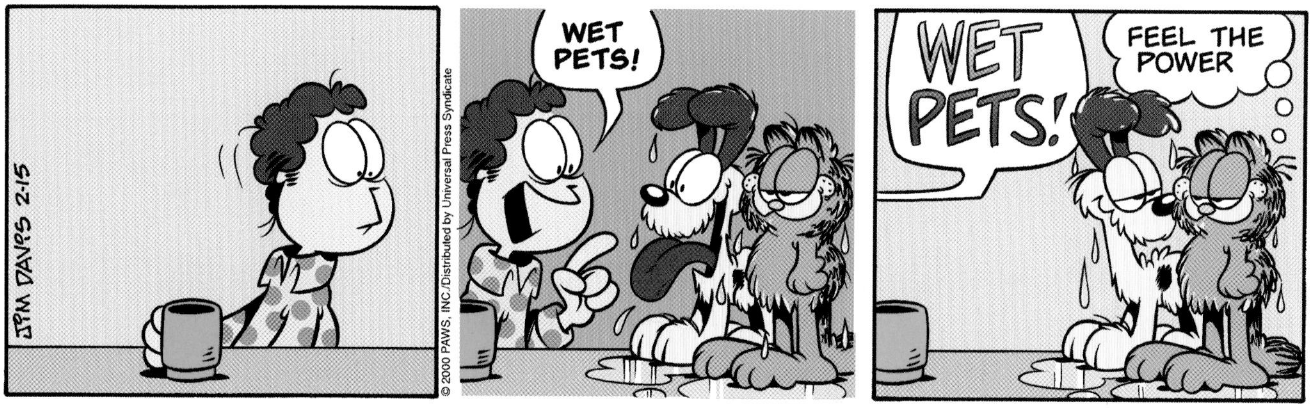
JIM DAVIS 2-15
© 2000 PAWS, INC./Distributed by Universal Press Syndicate
WET PETS!
WET PETS!
FEEL THE POWER

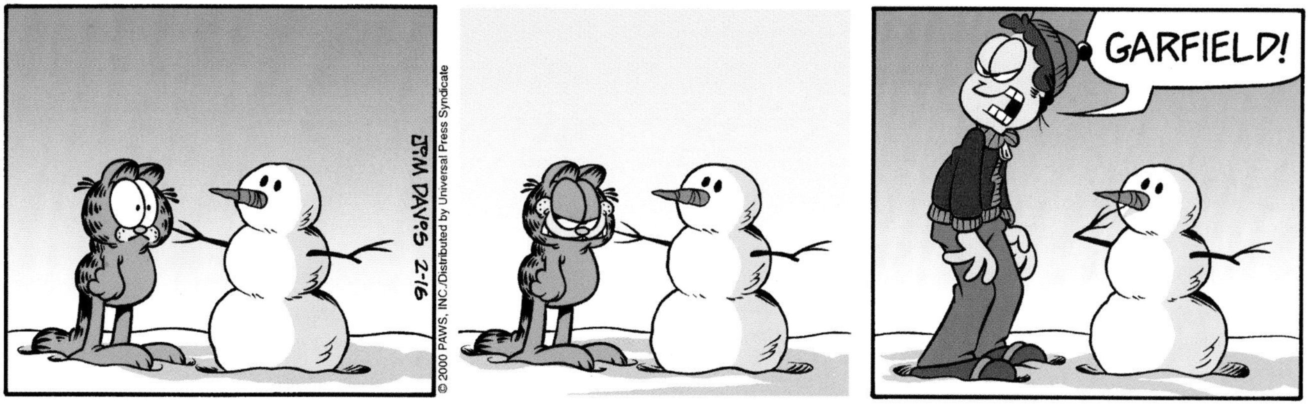
JIM DAVIS 2-16
© 2000 PAWS, INC./Distributed by Universal Press Syndicate
GARFIELD!

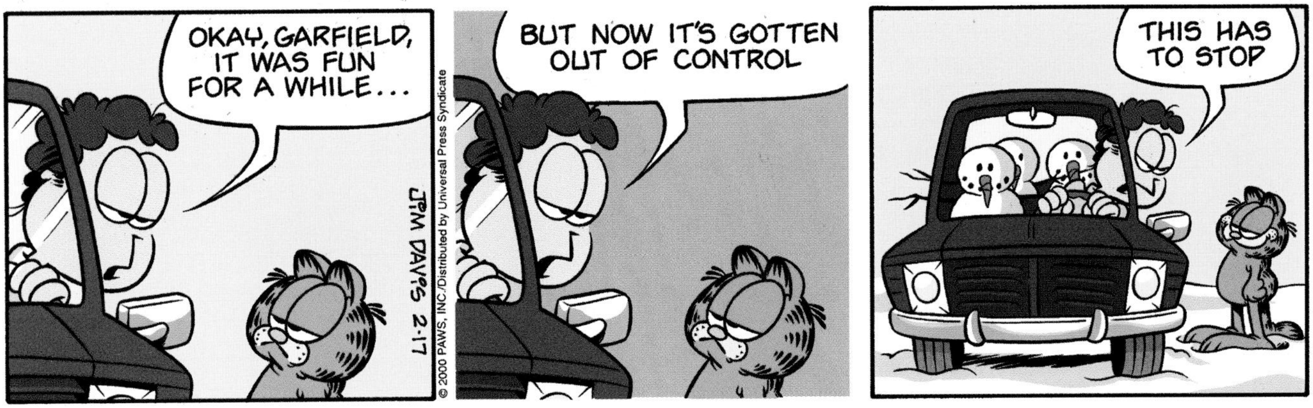
OKAY, GARFIELD, IT WAS FUN FOR A WHILE...
JIM DAVIS 2-17
© 2000 PAWS, INC./Distributed by Universal Press Syndicate
BUT NOW IT'S GOTTEN OUT OF CONTROL
THIS HAS TO STOP

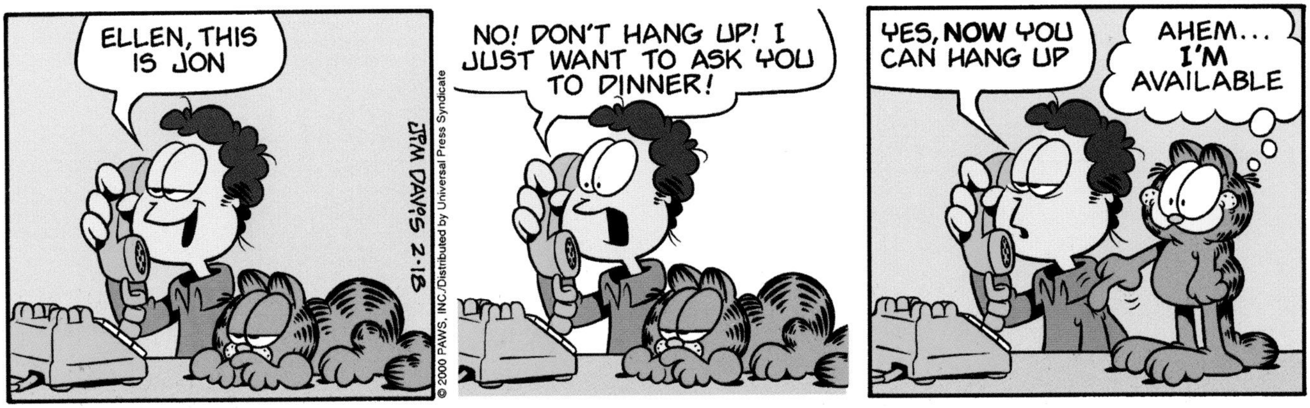
ELLEN, THIS IS JON
JIM DAVIS 2-18
© 2000 PAWS, INC./Distributed by Universal Press Syndicate
NO! DON'T HANG UP! I JUST WANT TO ASK YOU TO DINNER!
YES, NOW YOU CAN HANG UP
AHEM... I'M AVAILABLE

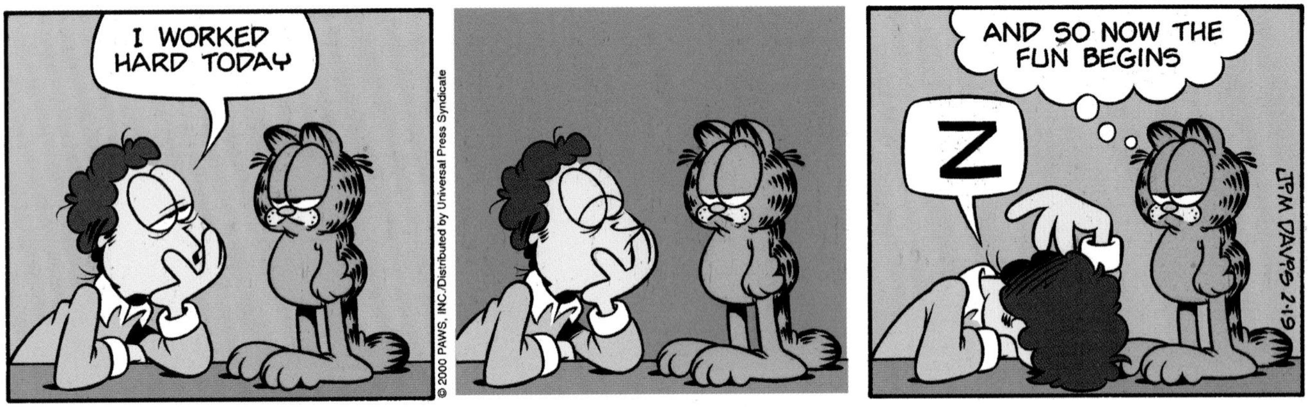
I WORKED HARD TODAY
© 2000 PAWS, INC./Distributed by Universal Press Syndicate
Z
AND SO NOW THE FUN BEGINS
JIM DAVIS 2-19

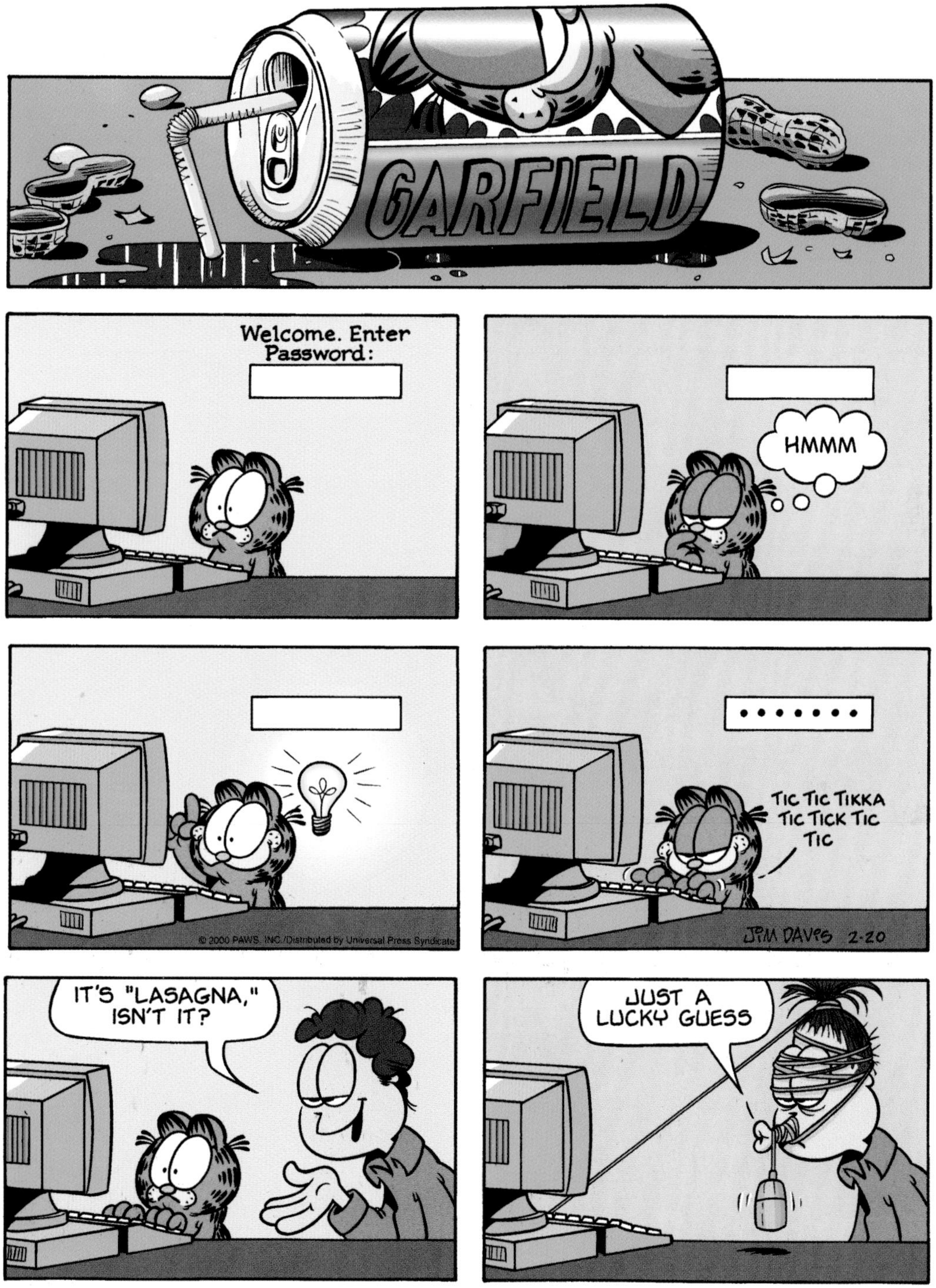
GARFIELD
Welcome. Enter Password:
HMMM
TIC TIC TIKKA TIC TICK TIC TIC
© 2000 PAWS, INC./Distributed by Universal Press Syndicate
JIM DAVIS 2-20
IT'S "LASAGNA," ISN'T IT?
JUST A LUCKY GUESS

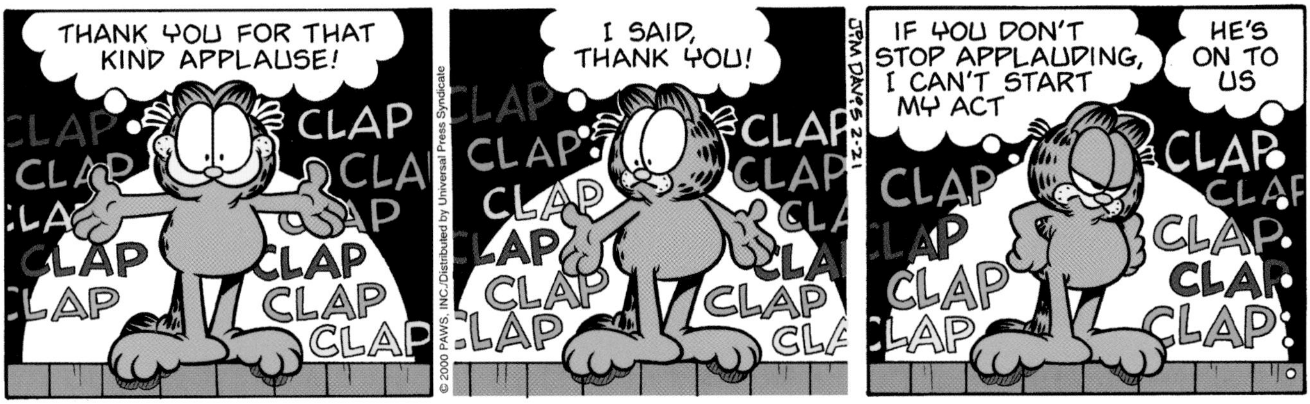
THANK YOU FOR THAT KIND APPLAUSE!
CLAP CLAP CLAP CLAP CLAP CLAP CLAP
© 2000 PAWS, INC./Distributed by Universal Press Syndicate
I SAID, THANK YOU!
CLAP CLAP CLAP CLAP CLAP CLAP
JIM DAVIS 2-21
IF YOU DON'T STOP APPLAUDING, I CAN'T START MY ACT
HE'S ON TO US
CLAP CLAP CLAP CLAP CLAP CLAP

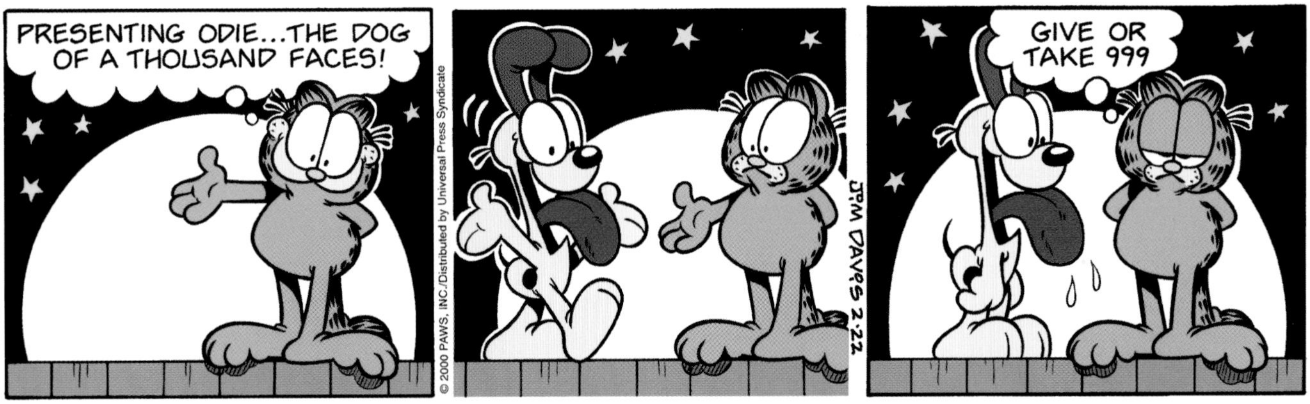
PRESENTING ODIE...THE DOG OF A THOUSAND FACES!
© 2000 PAWS, INC./Distributed by Universal Press Syndicate
JIM DAVIS 2-22
GIVE OR TAKE 999

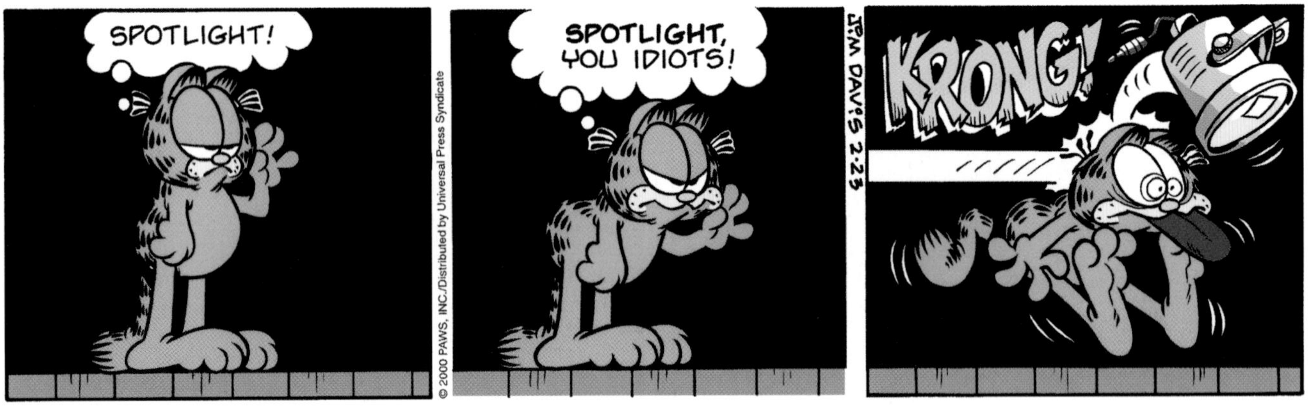
SPOTLIGHT!
© 2000 PAWS, INC./Distributed by Universal Press Syndicate
SPOTLIGHT, YOU IDIOTS!
JIM DAVIS 2-23
KRONG!

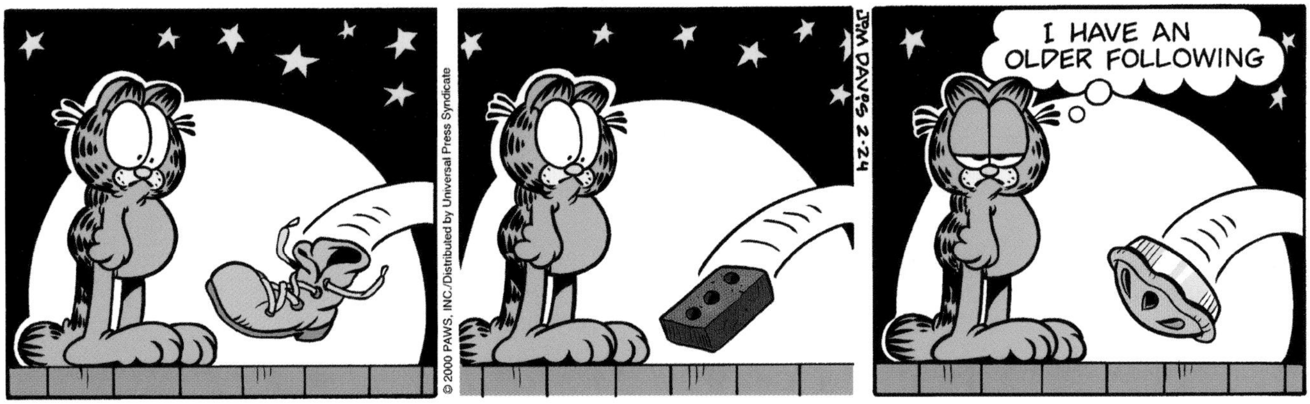
© 2000 PAWS, INC./Distributed by Universal Press Syndicate
JPM DAVIS 2-24
I HAVE AN OLDER FOLLOWING

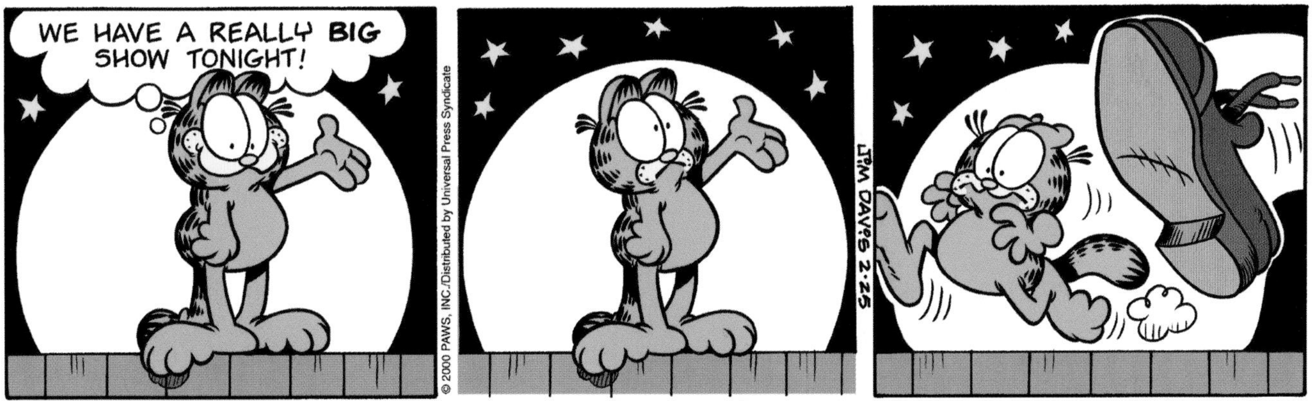
WE HAVE A REALLY **BIG** SHOW TONIGHT!
© 2000 PAWS, INC./Distributed by Universal Press Syndicate
JPM DAVIS 2-25

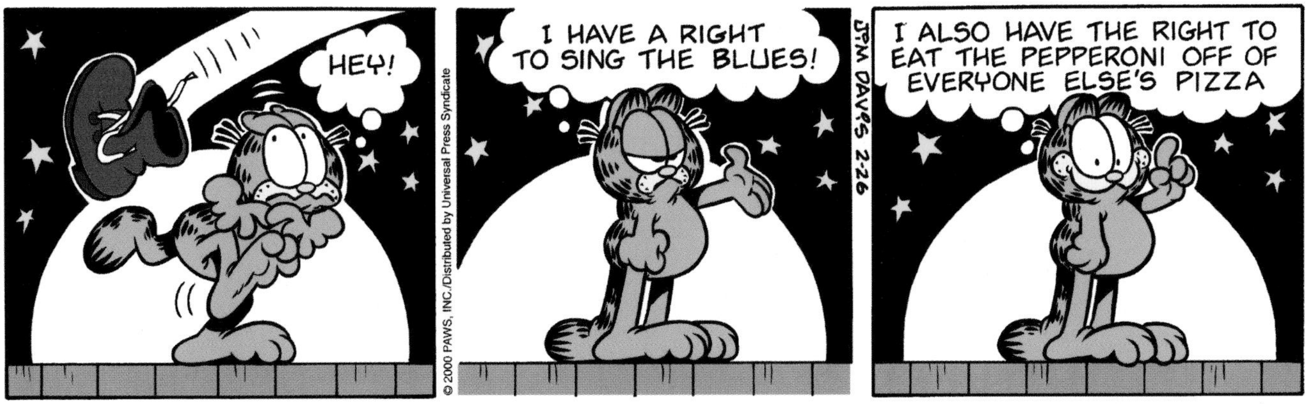
HEY!
© 2000 PAWS, INC./Distributed by Universal Press Syndicate
I HAVE A RIGHT TO SING THE BLUES!
JPM DAVIS 2-26
I ALSO HAVE THE RIGHT TO EAT THE PEPPERONI OFF OF EVERYONE ELSE'S PIZZA

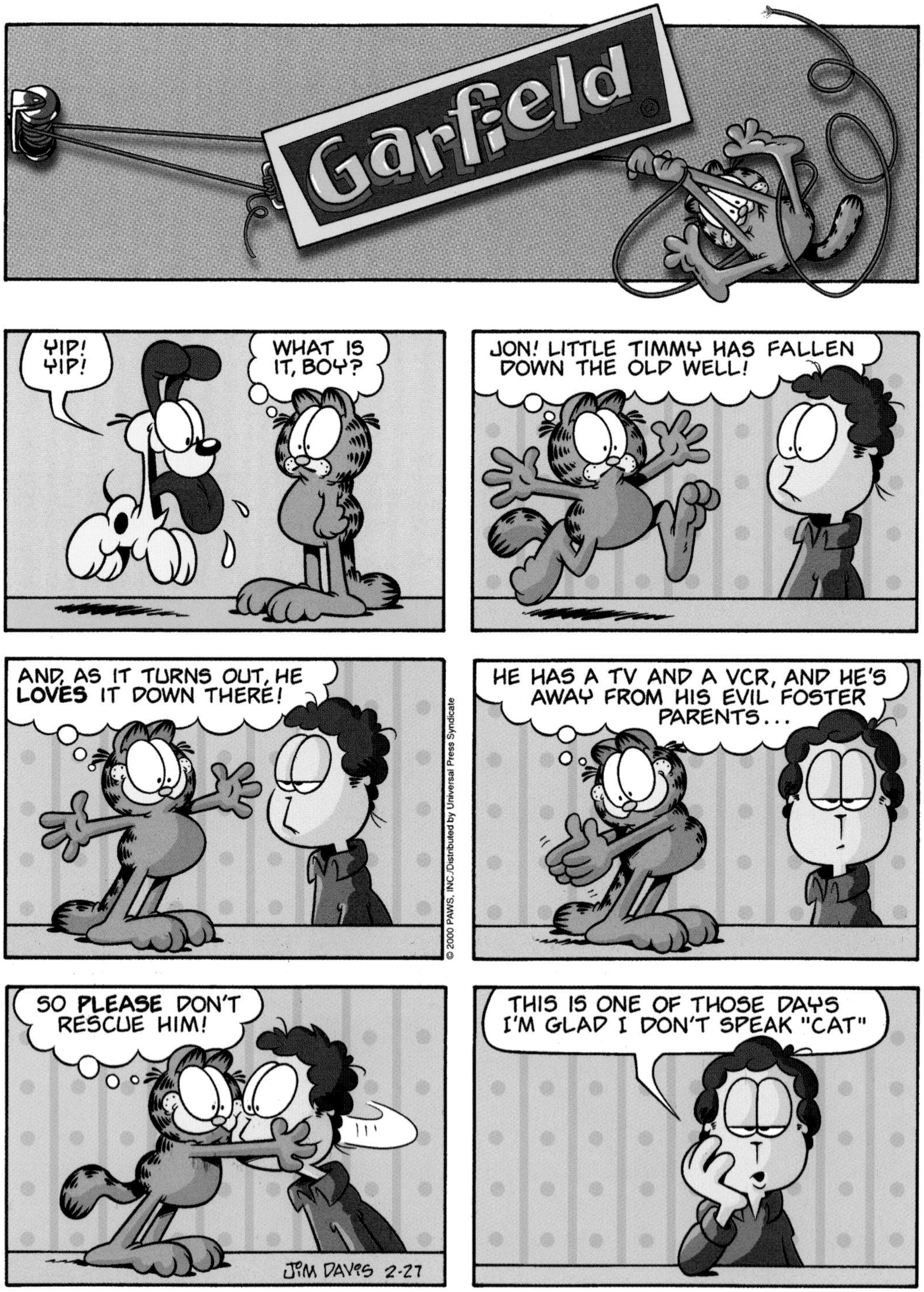
Garfield
YIP! YIP!
WHAT IS IT, BOY?
JON! LITTLE TIMMY HAS FALLEN DOWN THE OLD WELL!
AND, AS IT TURNS OUT, HE **LOVES** IT DOWN THERE!
HE HAS A TV AND A VCR, AND HE'S AWAY FROM HIS EVIL FOSTER PARENTS...
SO **PLEASE** DON'T RESCUE HIM!
THIS IS ONE OF THOSE DAYS I'M GLAD I DON'T SPEAK "CAT"
JIM DAVIS 2-27
© 2000 PAWS, INC./Distributed by Universal Press Syndicate

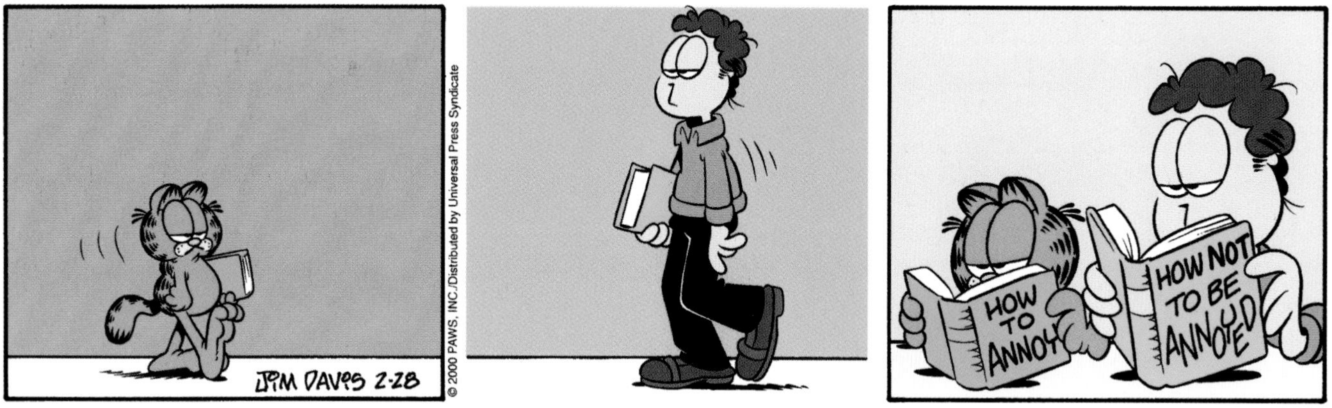
JIM DAVIS 2-28
© 2000 PAWS, INC./Distributed by Universal Press Syndicate
HOW TO ANNOY
HOW NOT TO BE ANNOYED

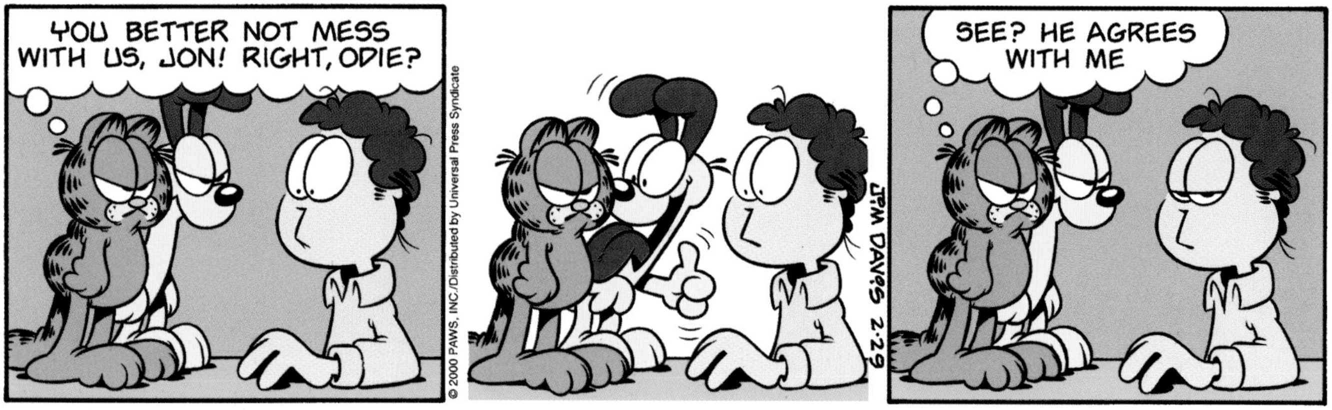
YOU BETTER NOT MESS WITH US, JON! RIGHT, ODIE?
© 2000 PAWS, INC./Distributed by Universal Press Syndicate
JIM DAVIS 2-29
SEE? HE AGREES WITH ME

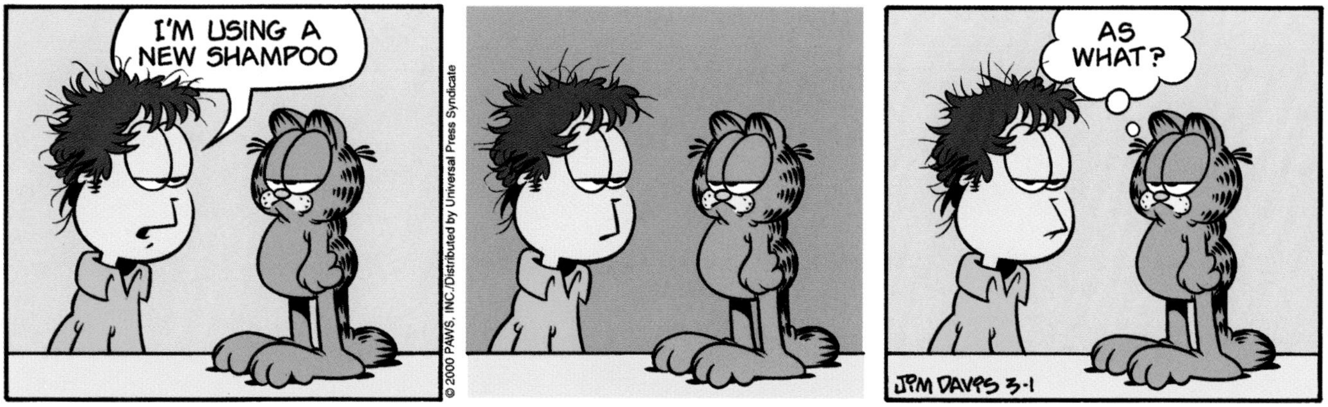
I'M USING A NEW SHAMPOO
© 2000 PAWS, INC./Distributed by Universal Press Syndicate
AS WHAT?
JIM DAVIS 3-1

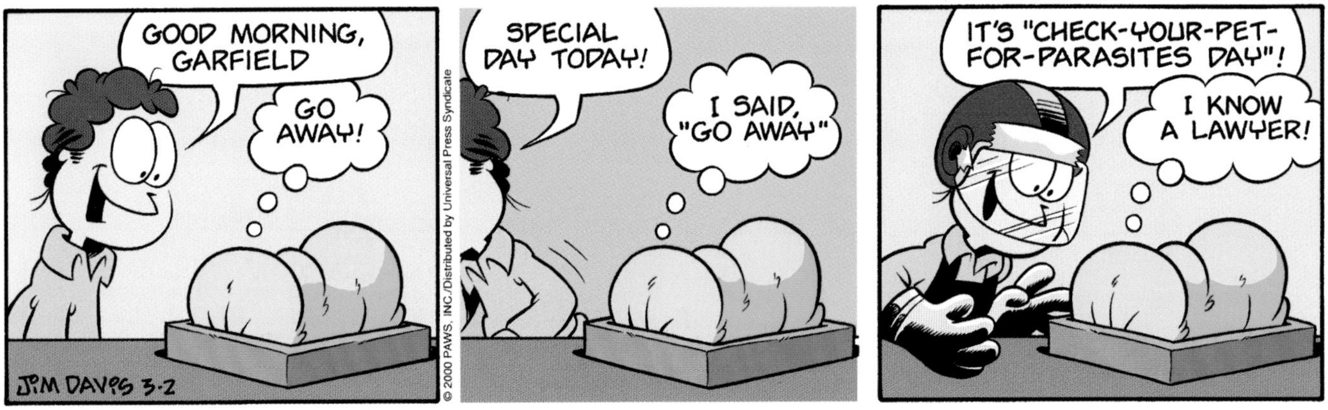
GOOD MORNING, GARFIELD
GO AWAY!
JIM DAVIS 3-2
© 2000 PAWS, INC./Distributed by Universal Press Syndicate
SPECIAL DAY TODAY!
I SAID, "GO AWAY"
IT'S "CHECK-YOUR-PET-FOR-PARASITES DAY"!
I KNOW A LAWYER!

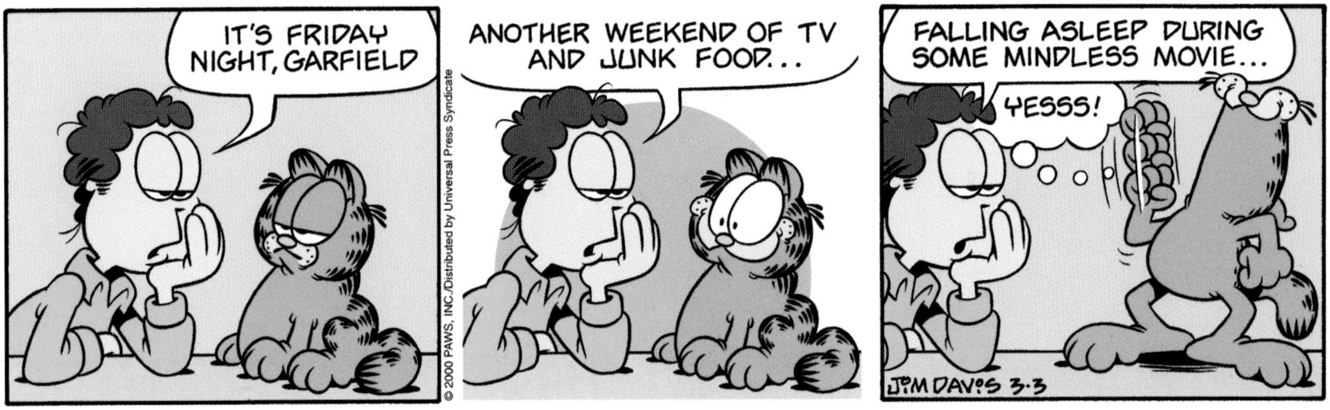
IT'S FRIDAY NIGHT, GARFIELD
© 2000 PAWS, INC./Distributed by Universal Press Syndicate
ANOTHER WEEKEND OF TV AND JUNK FOOD...
FALLING ASLEEP DURING SOME MINDLESS MOVIE...
YESSS!
JIM DAVIS 3-3

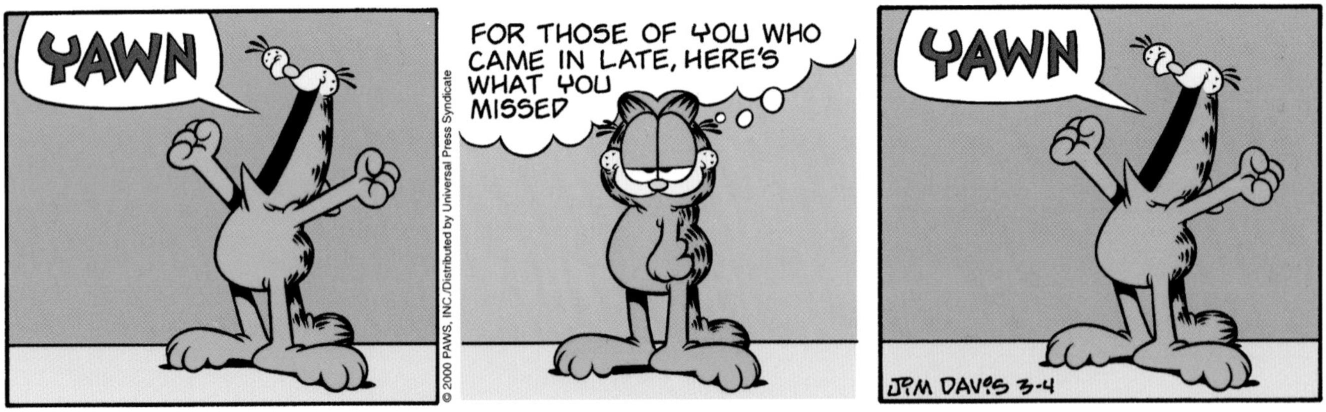
YAWN
© 2000 PAWS, INC./Distributed by Universal Press Syndicate
FOR THOSE OF YOU WHO CAME IN LATE, HERE'S WHAT YOU MISSED
YAWN
JIM DAVIS 3-4

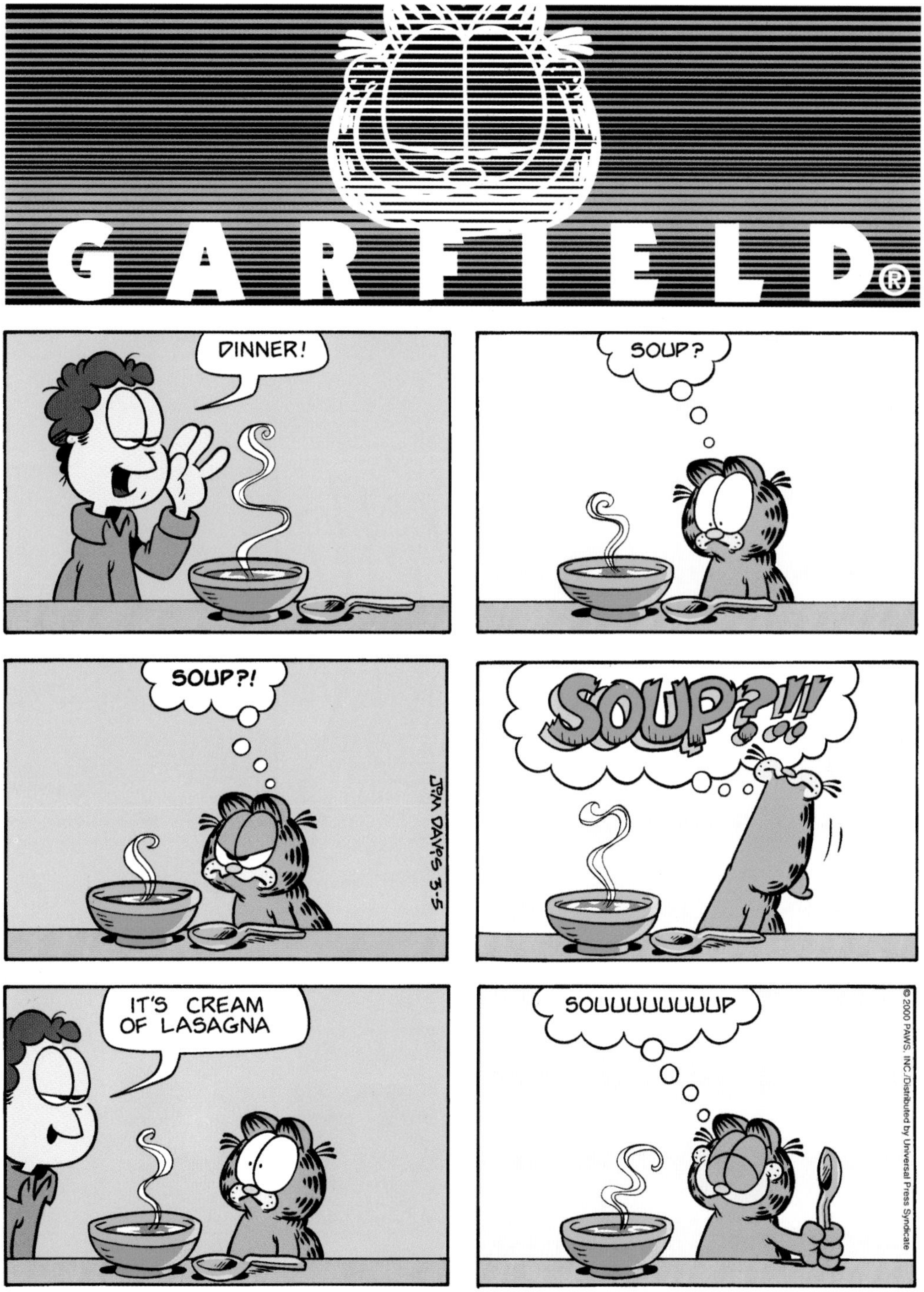
GARFIELD®
DINNER!
SOUP?
SOUP?!
JIM DAVIS 3-5
SOUP?!!
IT'S CREAM OF LASAGNA
SOUUUUUUUUP
© 2000 PAWS, INC./Distributed by Universal Press Syndicate

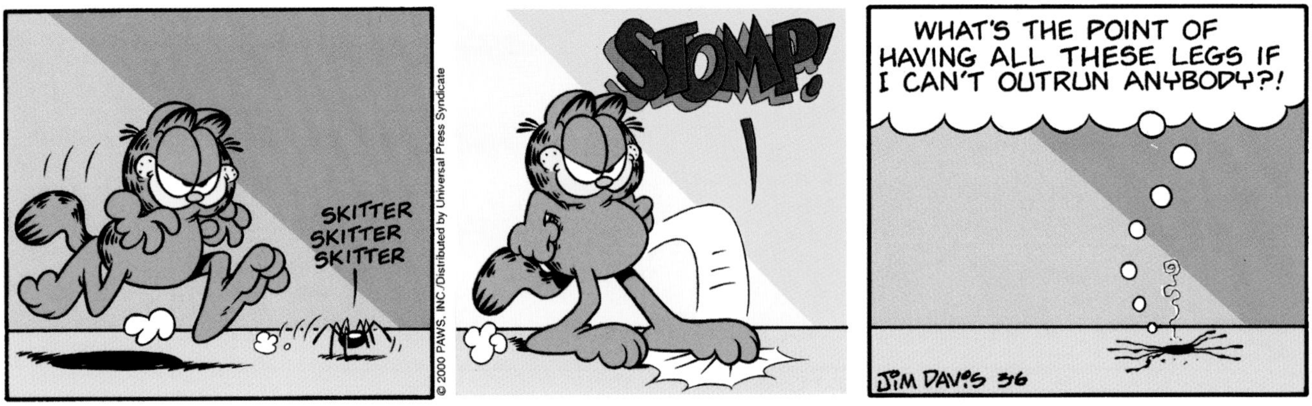
SKITTER
SKITTER
SKITTER
© 2000 PAWS, INC./Distributed by Universal Press Syndicate
STOMP!
WHAT'S THE POINT OF HAVING ALL THESE LEGS IF I CAN'T OUTRUN ANYBODY?!
JIM DAVIS 3-6

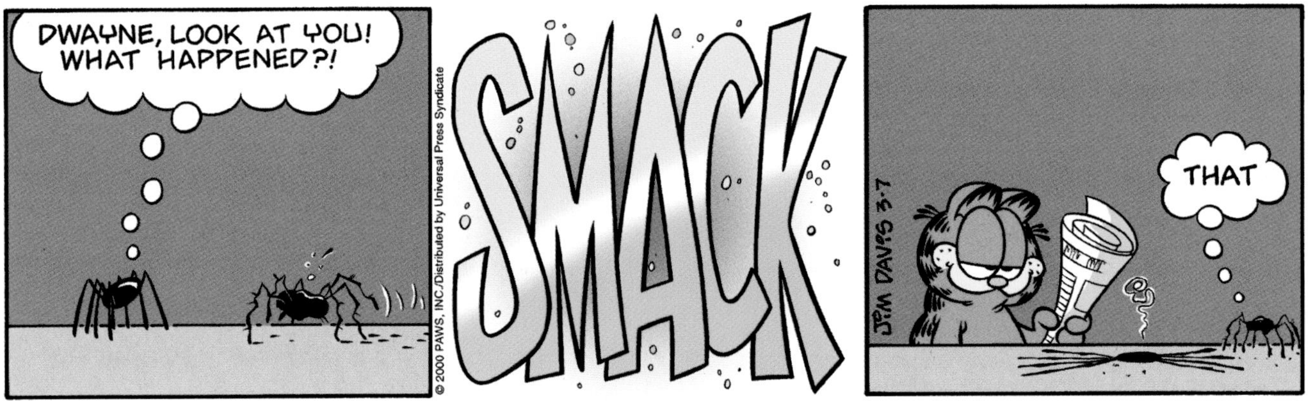
DWAYNE, LOOK AT YOU! WHAT HAPPENED?!
© 2000 PAWS, INC./Distributed by Universal Press Syndicate
SMACK
JIM DAVIS 3-7
THAT

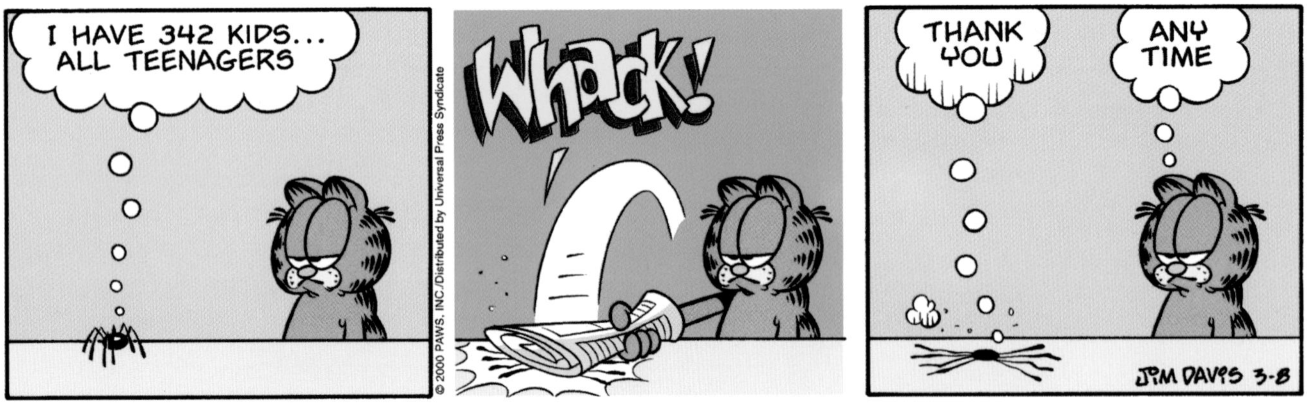
I HAVE 342 KIDS... ALL TEENAGERS
© 2000 PAWS, INC./Distributed by Universal Press Syndicate
Whack!
THANK YOU
ANY TIME
JIM DAVIS 3-8

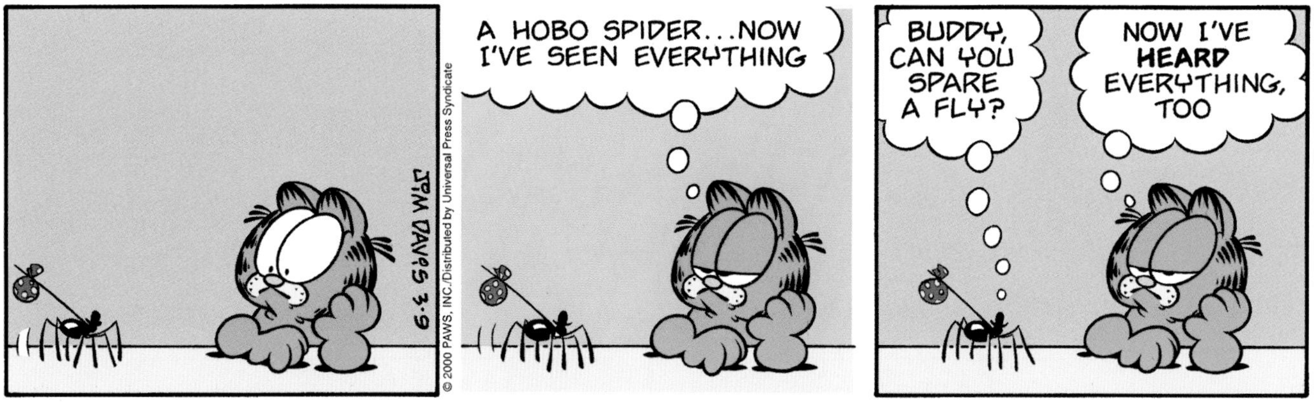
JIM DAVIS 3-9
© 2000 PAWS, INC./Distributed by Universal Press Syndicate
A HOBO SPIDER...NOW I'VE SEEN EVERYTHING
BUDDY, CAN YOU SPARE A FLY?
NOW I'VE **HEARD** EVERYTHING, TOO

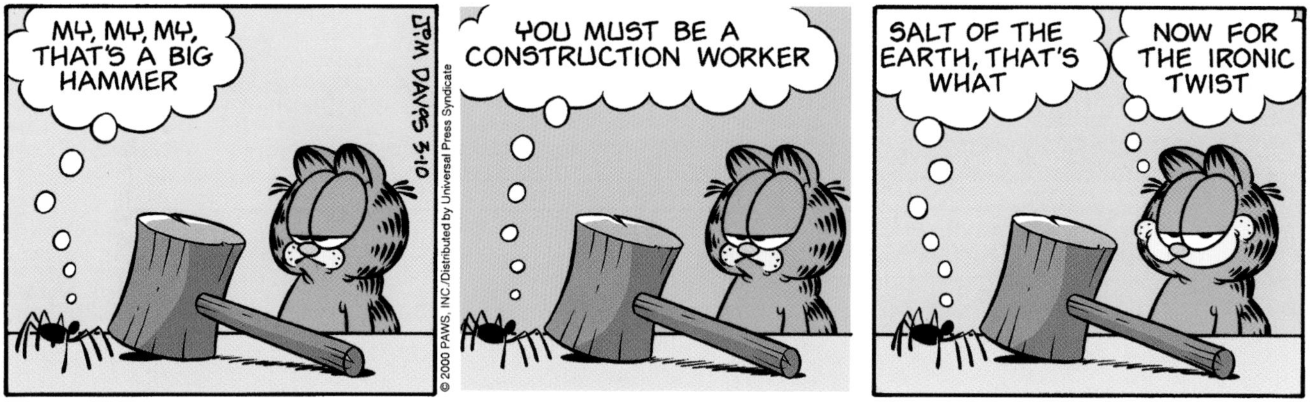
MY, MY, MY, THAT'S A BIG HAMMER
JIM DAVIS 3-10
© 2000 PAWS, INC./Distributed by Universal Press Syndicate
YOU MUST BE A CONSTRUCTION WORKER
SALT OF THE EARTH, THAT'S WHAT
NOW FOR THE IRONIC TWIST

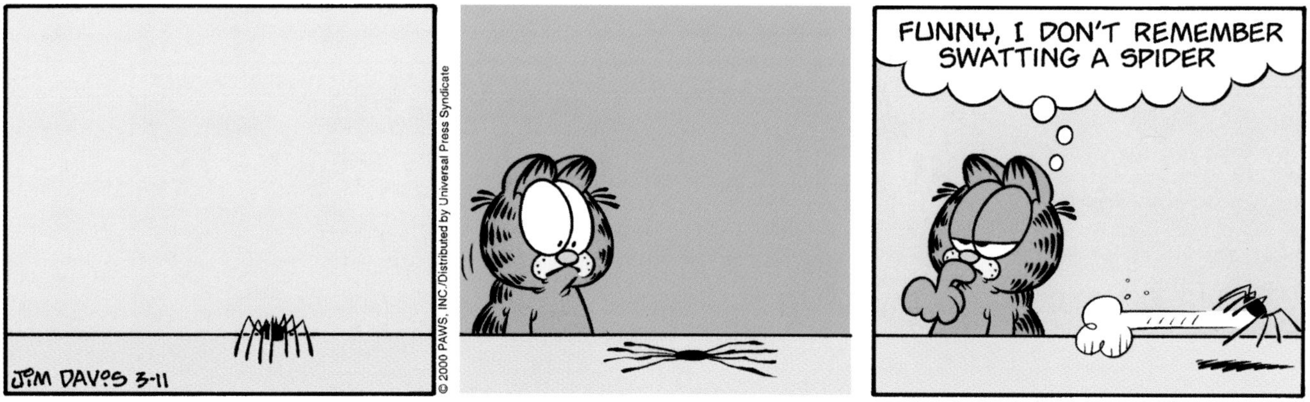
JIM DAVIS 3-11
© 2000 PAWS, INC./Distributed by Universal Press Syndicate
FUNNY, I DON'T REMEMBER SWATTING A SPIDER

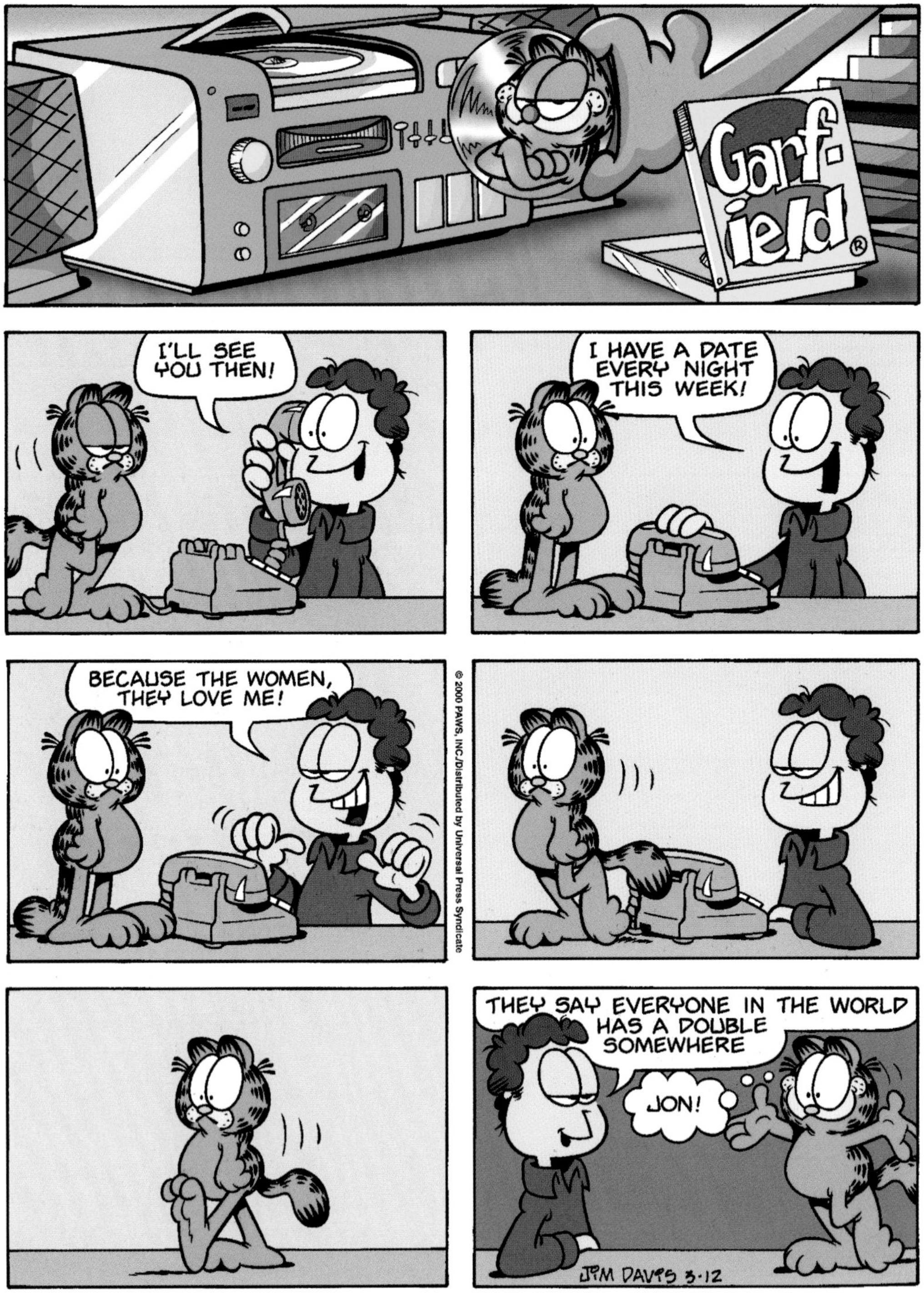
Garf-ield®
I'LL SEE YOU THEN!
I HAVE A DATE EVERY NIGHT THIS WEEK!
BECAUSE THE WOMEN, THEY LOVE ME!
THEY SAY EVERYONE IN THE WORLD HAS A DOUBLE SOMEWHERE
JON!
JIM DAVIS 3-12

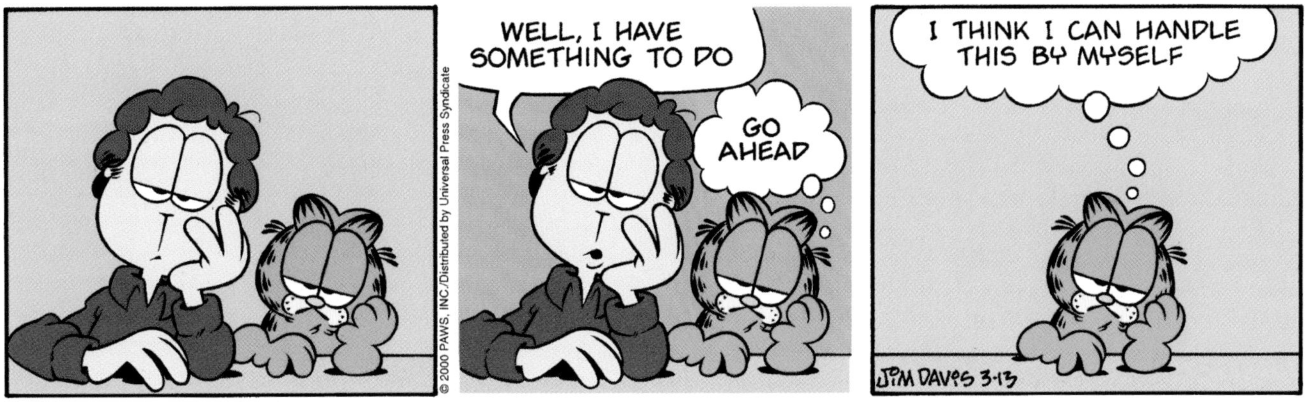
© 2000 PAWS, INC./Distributed by Universal Press Syndicate
WELL, I HAVE SOMETHING TO DO
GO AHEAD
I THINK I CAN HANDLE THIS BY MYSELF
JIM DAVIS 3-13

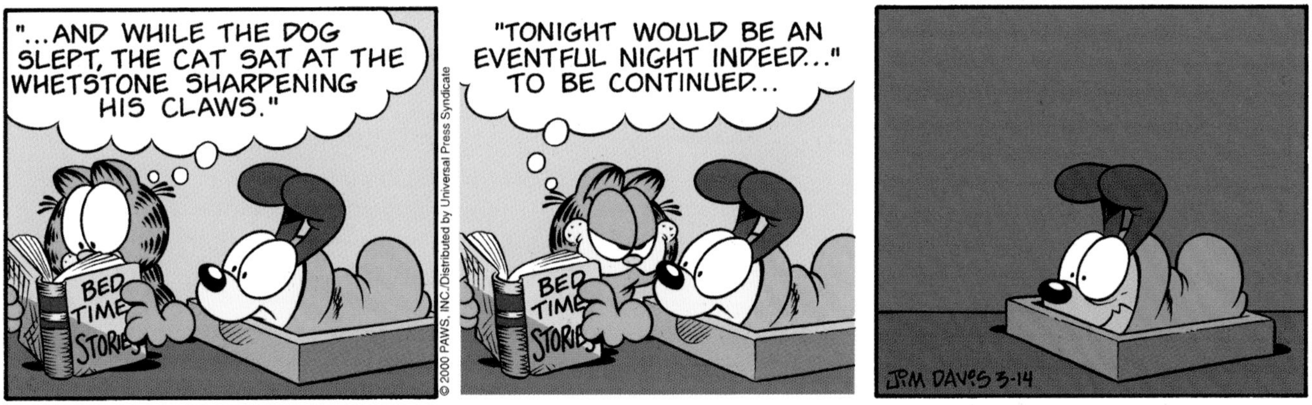
"...AND WHILE THE DOG SLEPT, THE CAT SAT AT THE WHETSTONE SHARPENING HIS CLAWS."
© 2000 PAWS, INC./Distributed by Universal Press Syndicate
BED TIME STORIES
"TONIGHT WOULD BE AN EVENTFUL NIGHT INDEED..." TO BE CONTINUED...
JIM DAVIS 3-14

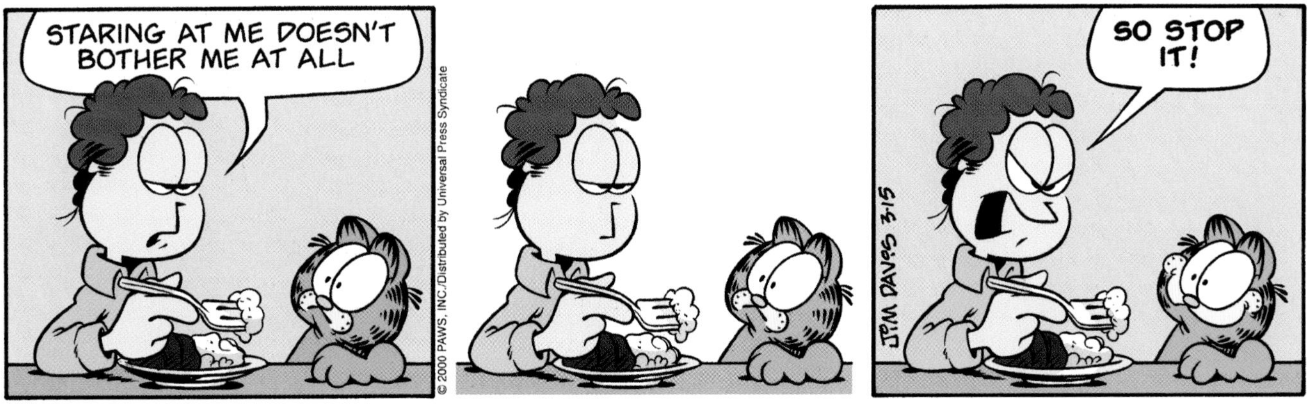
STARING AT ME DOESN'T BOTHER ME AT ALL
© 2000 PAWS, INC./Distributed by Universal Press Syndicate
SO STOP IT!
JIM DAVIS 3-15

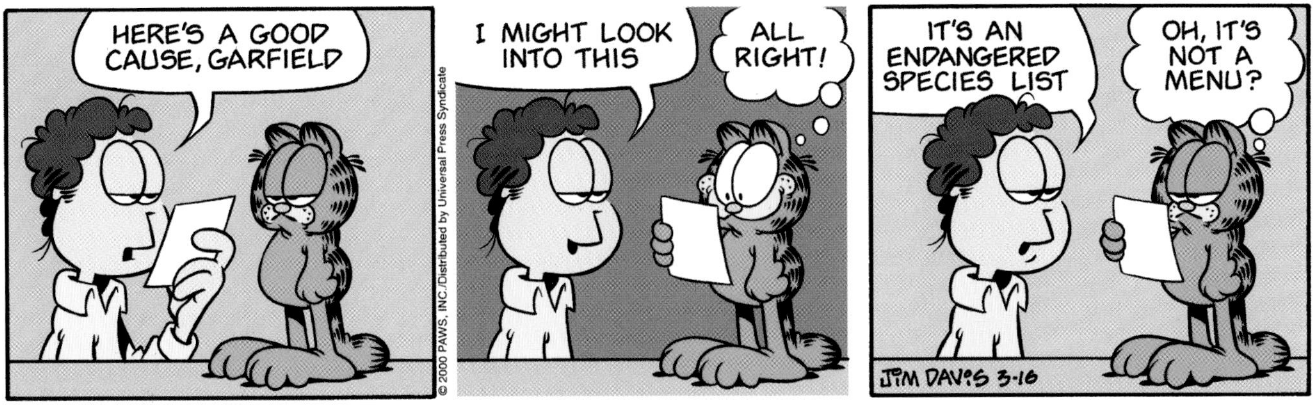
HERE'S A GOOD CAUSE, GARFIELD
© 2000 PAWS, INC./Distributed by Universal Press Syndicate
I MIGHT LOOK INTO THIS
ALL RIGHT!
IT'S AN ENDANGERED SPECIES LIST
OH, IT'S NOT A MENU?
JIM DAVIS 3-16

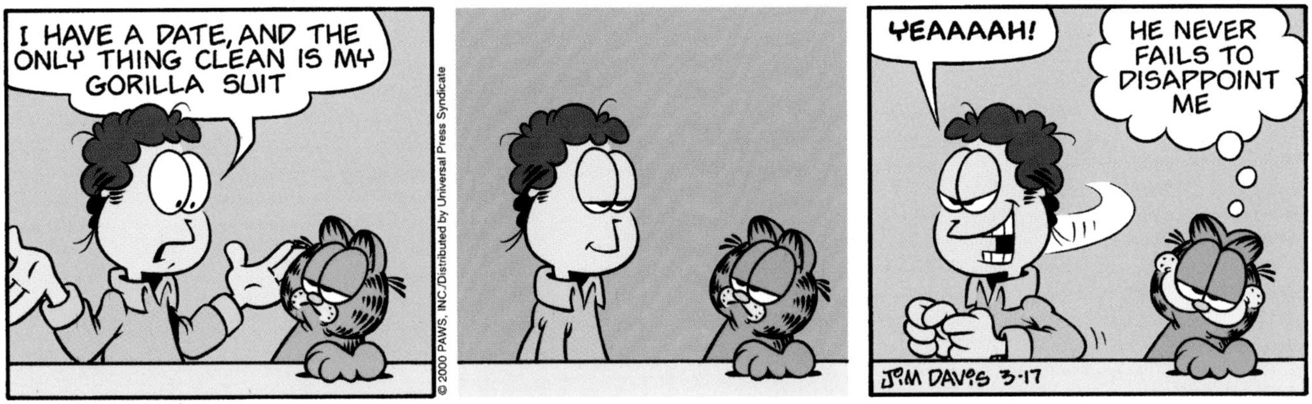
I HAVE A DATE, AND THE ONLY THING CLEAN IS MY GORILLA SUIT
© 2000 PAWS, INC./Distributed by Universal Press Syndicate
YEAAAAH!
HE NEVER FAILS TO DISAPPOINT ME
JIM DAVIS 3-17

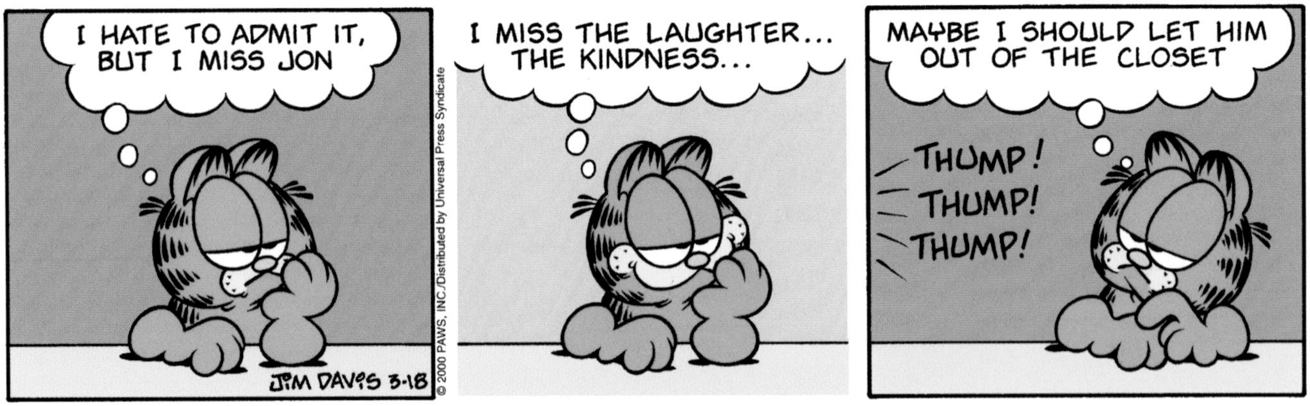
I HATE TO ADMIT IT, BUT I MISS JON
JIM DAVIS 3-18
© 2000 PAWS, INC./Distributed by Universal Press Syndicate
I MISS THE LAUGHTER... THE KINDNESS...
MAYBE I SHOULD LET HIM OUT OF THE CLOSET
THUMP!
THUMP!
THUMP!

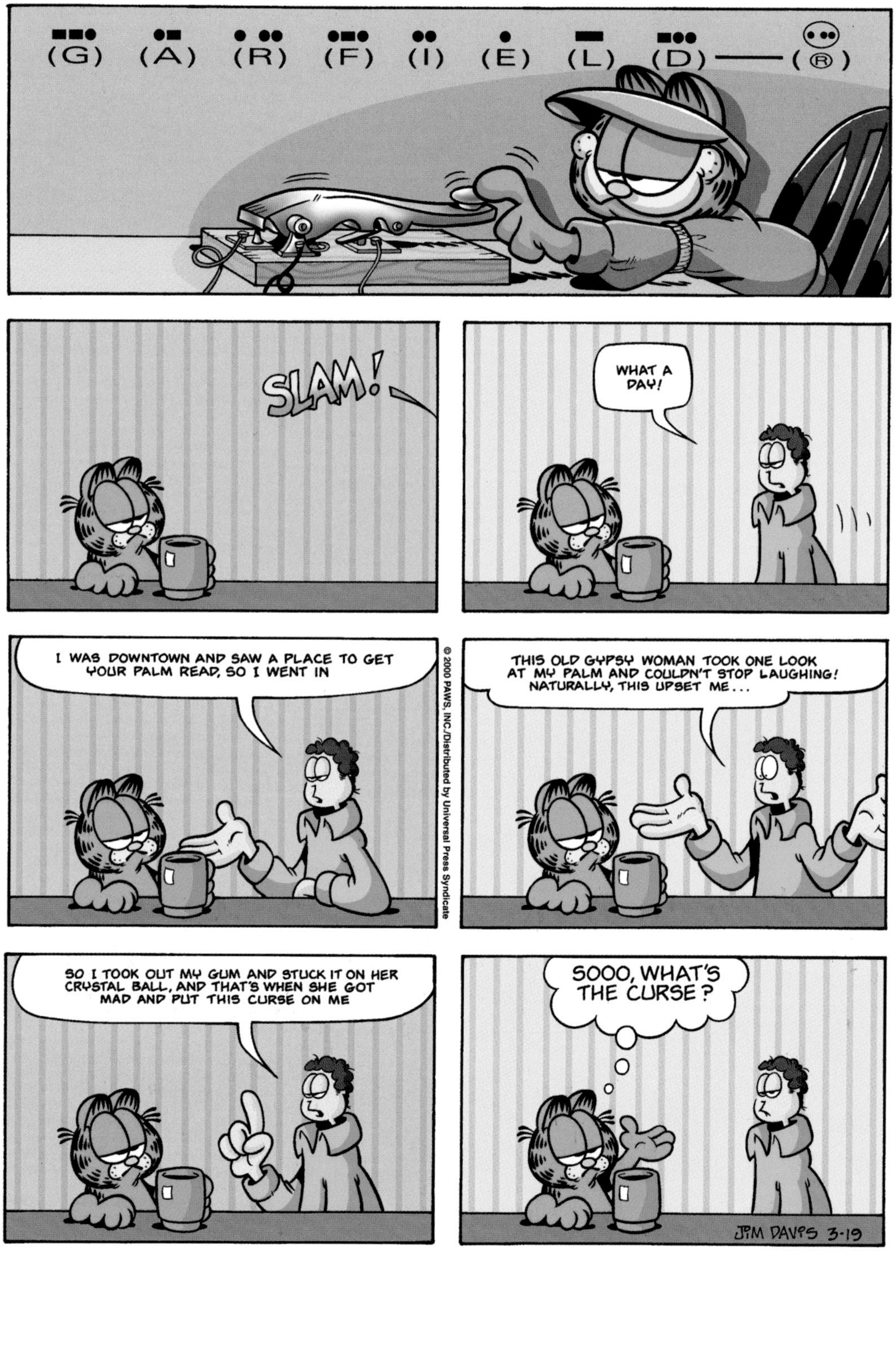
(G) (A) (R) (F) (I) (E) (L) (D) —— (®)
SLAM!
WHAT A DAY!
I WAS DOWNTOWN AND SAW A PLACE TO GET YOUR PALM READ, SO I WENT IN
THIS OLD GYPSY WOMAN TOOK ONE LOOK AT MY PALM AND COULDN'T STOP LAUGHING! NATURALLY, THIS UPSET ME...
SO I TOOK OUT MY GUM AND STUCK IT ON HER CRYSTAL BALL, AND THAT'S WHEN SHE GOT MAD AND PUT THIS CURSE ON ME
SOOO, WHAT'S THE CURSE?
JIM DAVIS 3-19

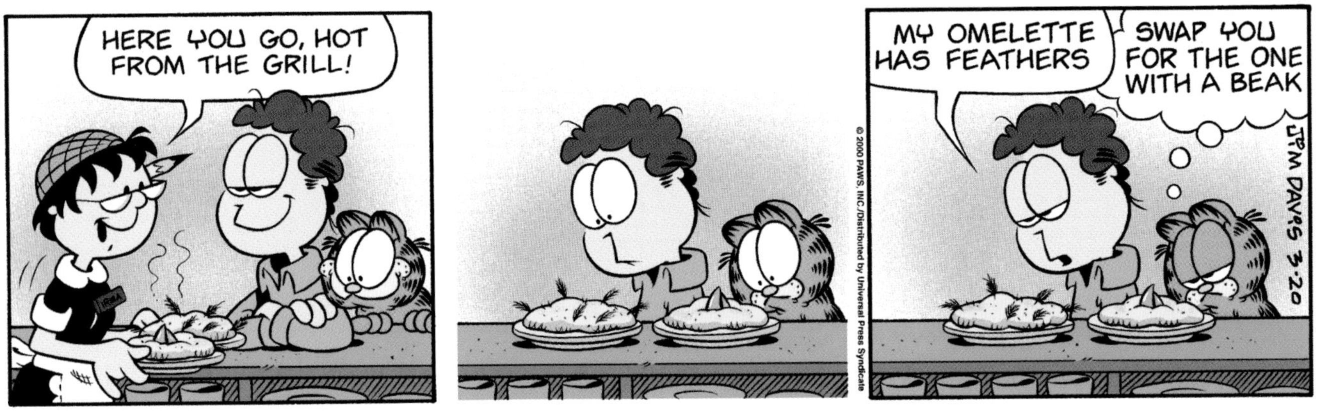
HERE YOU GO, HOT FROM THE GRILL!
MY OMELETTE HAS FEATHERS
SWAP YOU FOR THE ONE WITH A BEAK
JPM DAVIS 3·20
© 2000 PAWS, INC./Distributed by Universal Press Syndicate

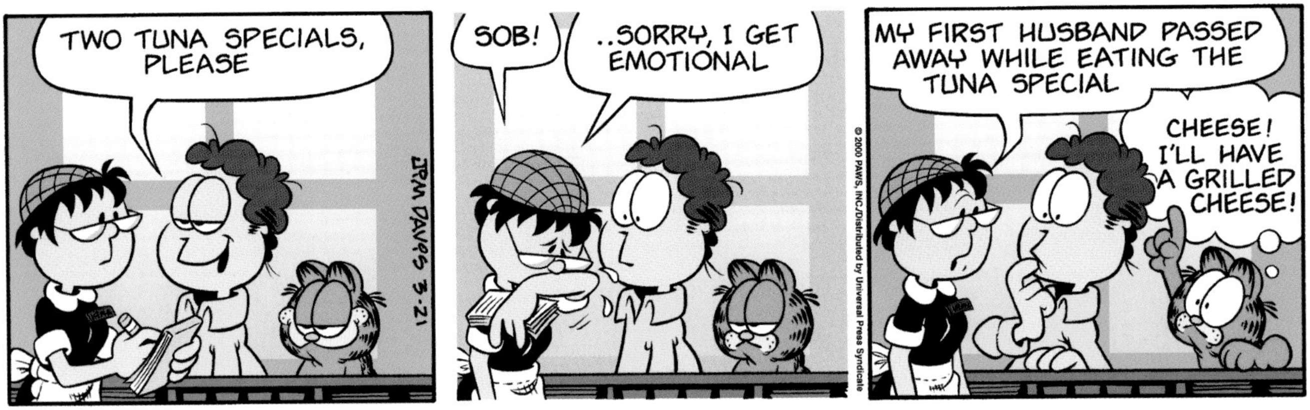
TWO TUNA SPECIALS, PLEASE
JPM DAVIS 3·21
SOB!
..SORRY, I GET EMOTIONAL
MY FIRST HUSBAND PASSED AWAY WHILE EATING THE TUNA SPECIAL
CHEESE! I'LL HAVE A GRILLED CHEESE!
© 2000 PAWS, INC./Distributed by Universal Press Syndicate

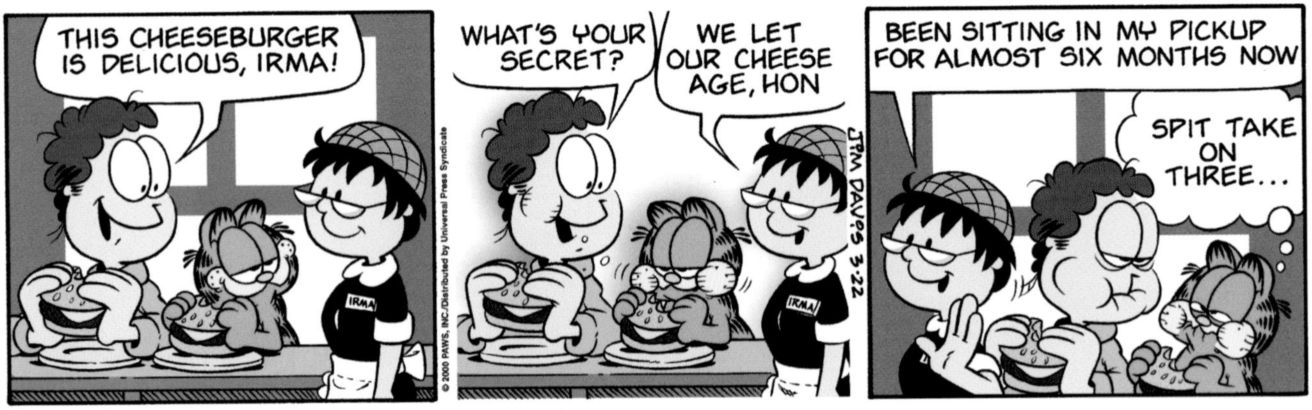
THIS CHEESEBURGER IS DELICIOUS, IRMA!
IRMA
WHAT'S YOUR SECRET?
WE LET OUR CHEESE AGE, HON
JPM DAVIS 3·22
BEEN SITTING IN MY PICKUP FOR ALMOST SIX MONTHS NOW
SPIT TAKE ON THREE...
© 2000 PAWS, INC./Distributed by Universal Press Syndicate

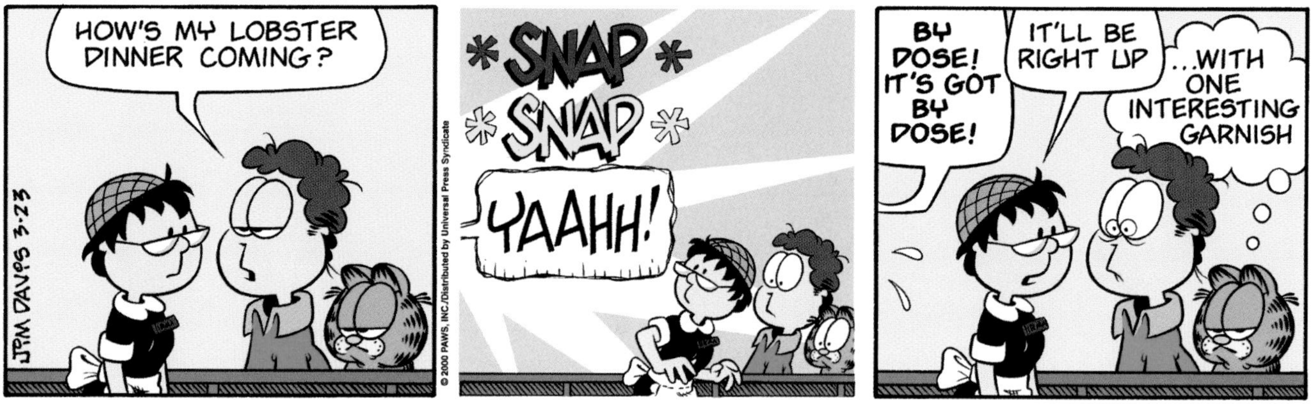
JIM DAVIS 3-23
HOW'S MY LOBSTER DINNER COMING?
© 2000 PAWS, INC./Distributed by Universal Press Syndicate
SNAP *SNAP*
YAAHH!
BY DOSE! IT'S GOT BY DOSE!
IT'LL BE RIGHT UP
...WITH ONE INTERESTING GARNISH

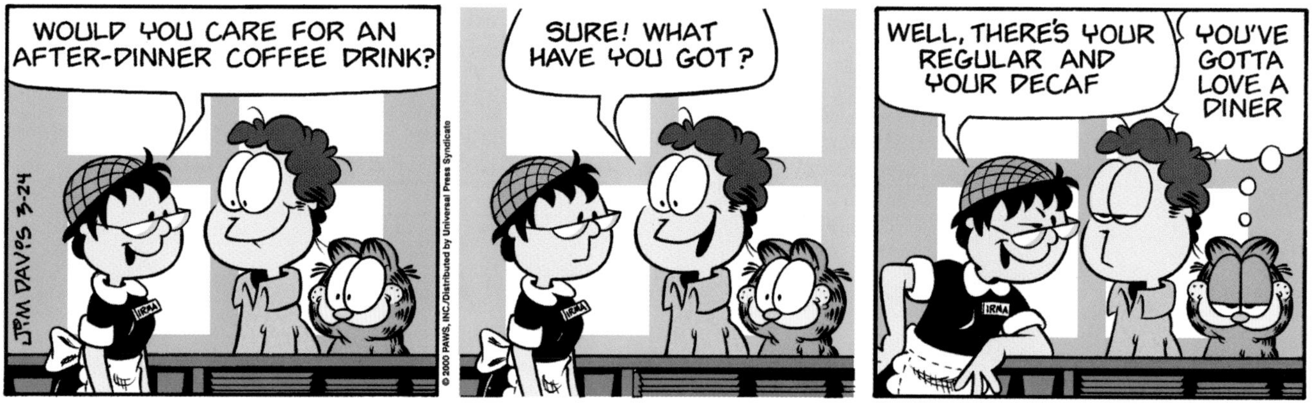
JIM DAVIS 3-24
WOULD YOU CARE FOR AN AFTER-DINNER COFFEE DRINK?
© 2000 PAWS, INC./Distributed by Universal Press Syndicate
SURE! WHAT HAVE YOU GOT?
WELL, THERE'S YOUR REGULAR AND YOUR DECAF
YOU'VE GOTTA LOVE A DINER

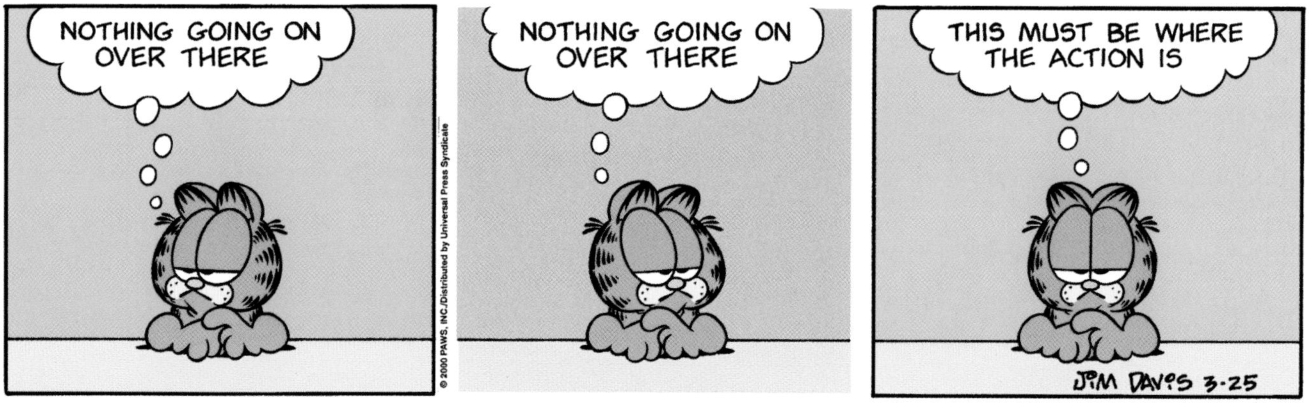
NOTHING GOING ON OVER THERE
© 2000 PAWS, INC./Distributed by Universal Press Syndicate
NOTHING GOING ON OVER THERE
THIS MUST BE WHERE THE ACTION IS
JIM DAVIS 3-25

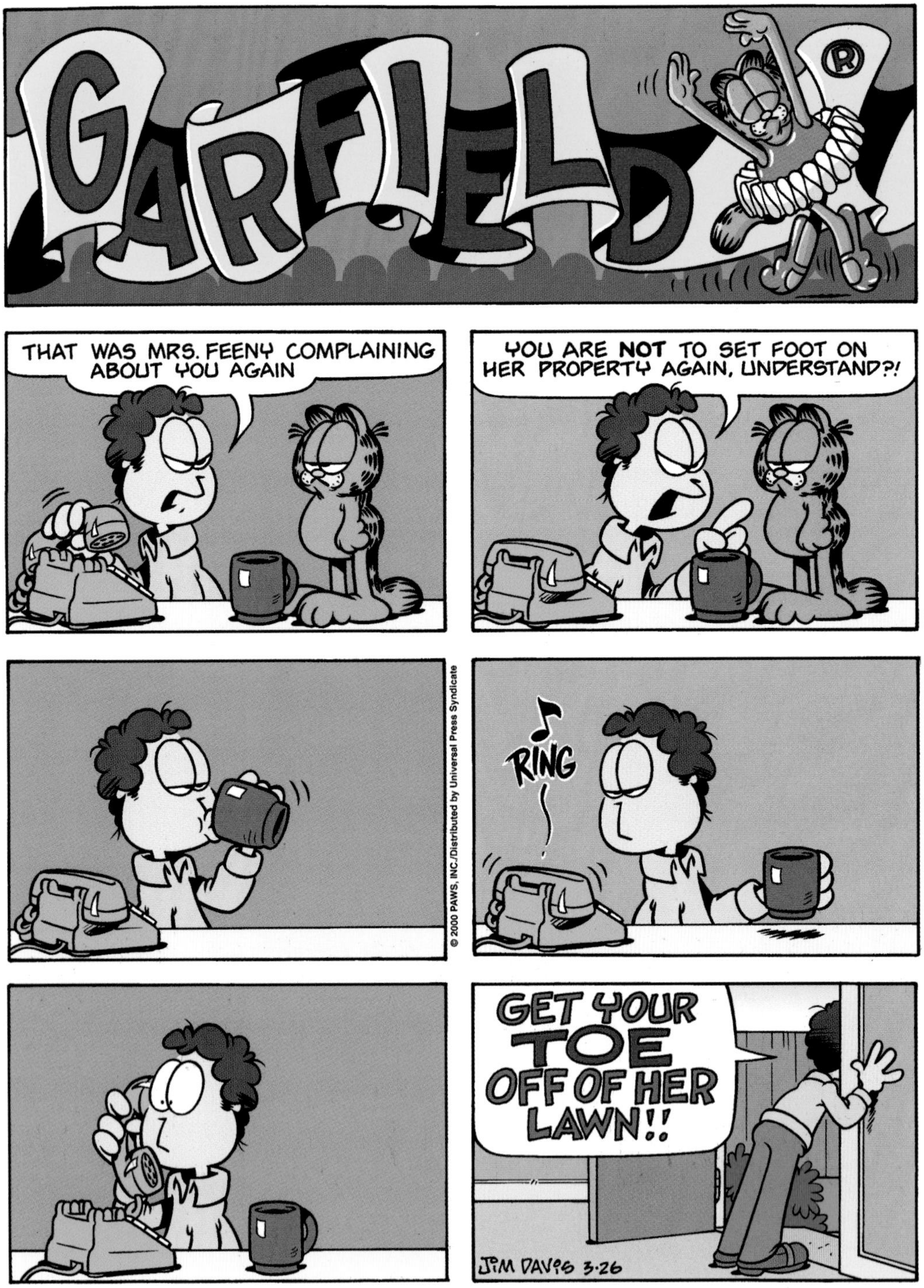
GARFIELD®
THAT WAS MRS. FEENY COMPLAINING ABOUT YOU AGAIN
YOU ARE NOT TO SET FOOT ON HER PROPERTY AGAIN, UNDERSTAND?!
© 2000 PAWS, INC./Distributed by Universal Press Syndicate
RING
GET YOUR TOE OFF OF HER LAWN!!
JIM DAVIS 3·26

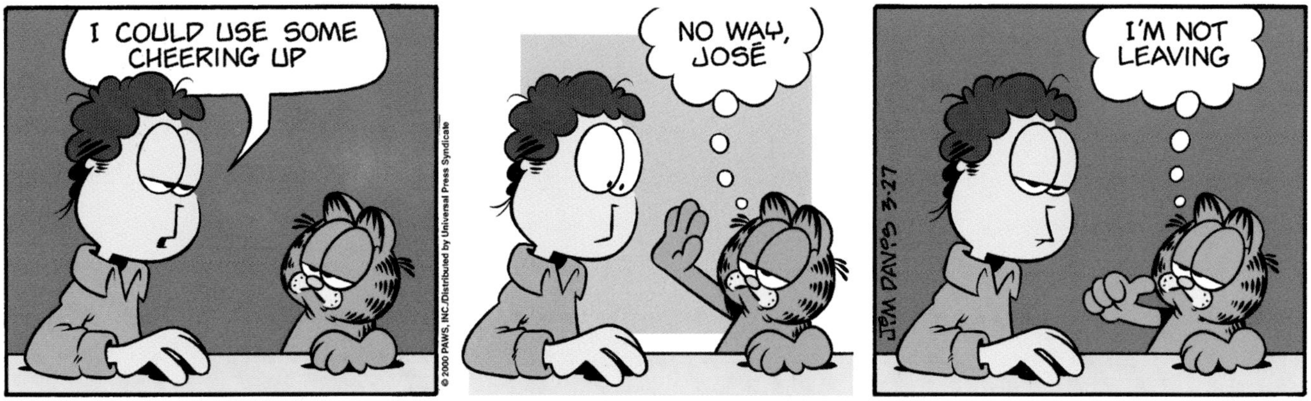
I COULD USE SOME CHEERING UP
NO WAY, JOSÉ
I'M NOT LEAVING
JIM DAVIS 3-27
© 2000 PAWS, INC./Distributed by Universal Press Syndicate

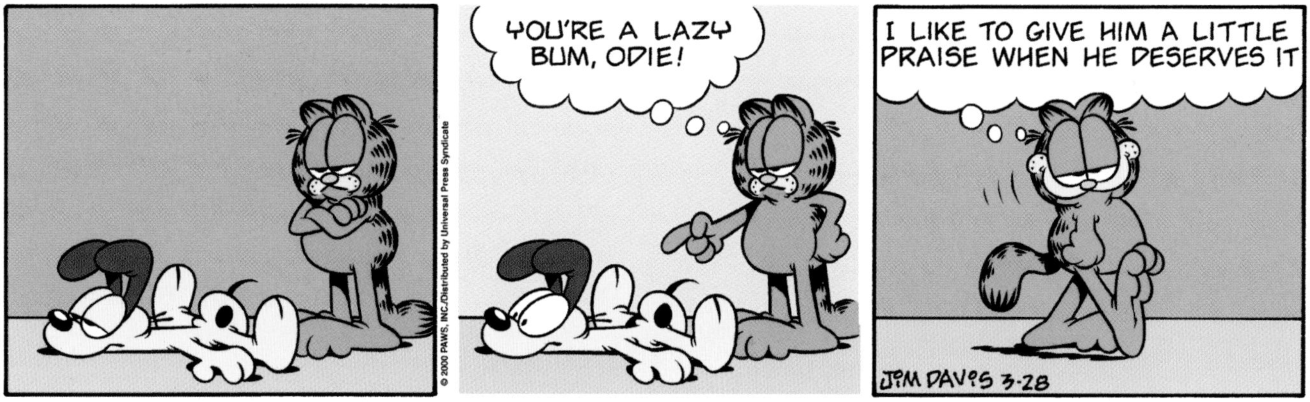
YOU'RE A LAZY BUM, ODIE!
I LIKE TO GIVE HIM A LITTLE PRAISE WHEN HE DESERVES IT
JIM DAVIS 3-28
© 2000 PAWS, INC./Distributed by Universal Press Syndicate

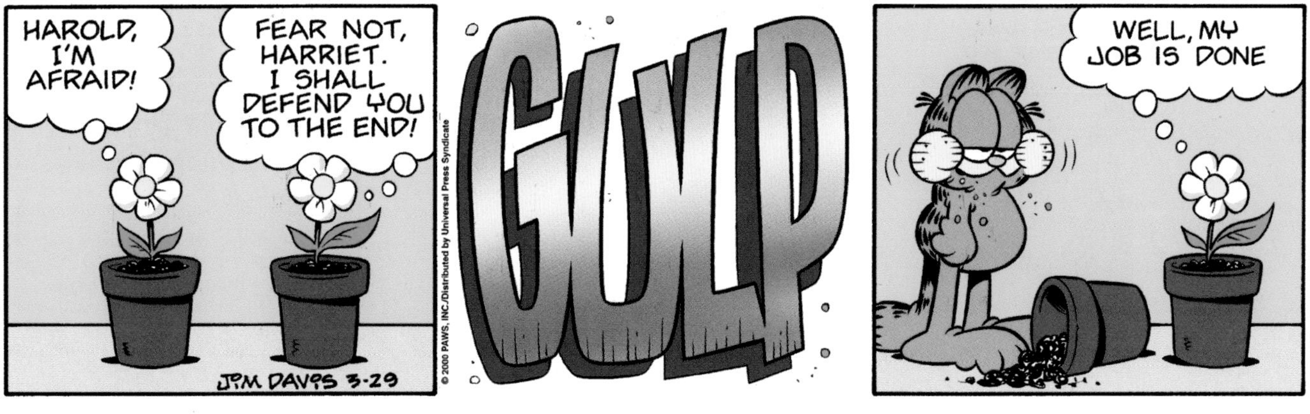
HAROLD, I'M AFRAID!
FEAR NOT, HARRIET. I SHALL DEFEND YOU TO THE END!
JIM DAVIS 3-29
© 2000 PAWS, INC./Distributed by Universal Press Syndicate
GULP
WELL, MY JOB IS DONE

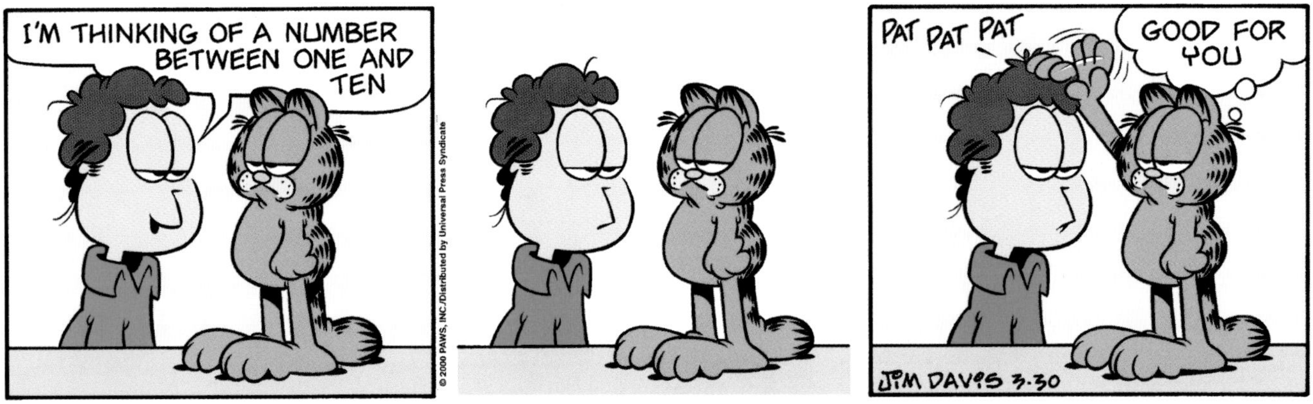
I'M THINKING OF A NUMBER BETWEEN ONE AND TEN
© 2000 PAWS, INC./Distributed by Universal Press Syndicate
PAT PAT PAT
GOOD FOR YOU
JIM DAVIS 3-30

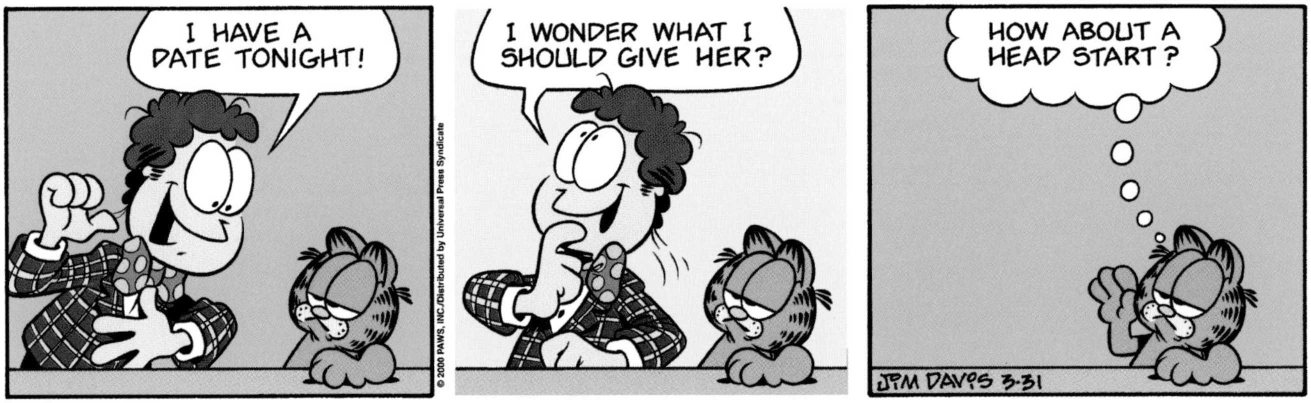
I HAVE A DATE TONIGHT!
© 2000 PAWS, INC./Distributed by Universal Press Syndicate
I WONDER WHAT I SHOULD GIVE HER?
HOW ABOUT A HEAD START?
JIM DAVIS 3-31

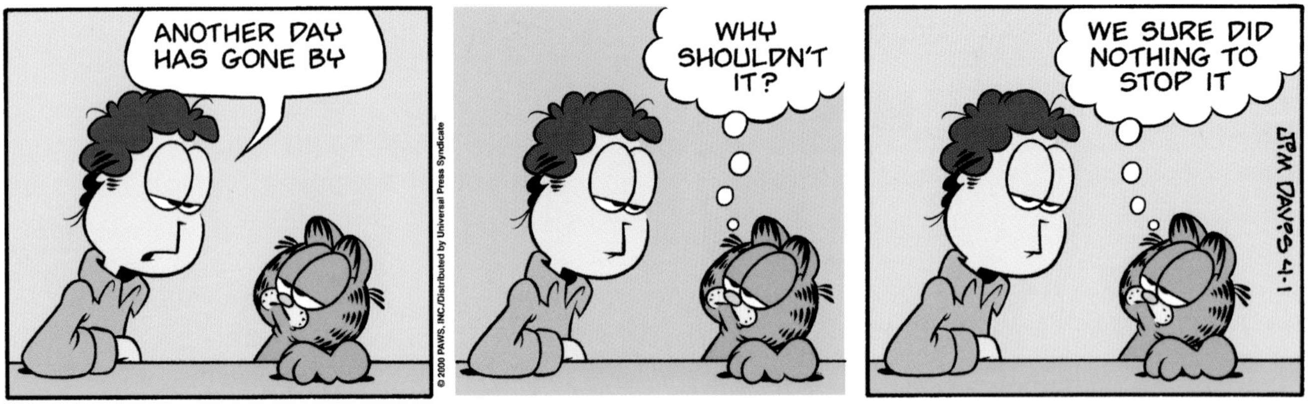
ANOTHER DAY HAS GONE BY
© 2000 PAWS, INC./Distributed by Universal Press Syndicate
WHY SHOULDN'T IT?
WE SURE DID NOTHING TO STOP IT
JIM DAVIS 4-1

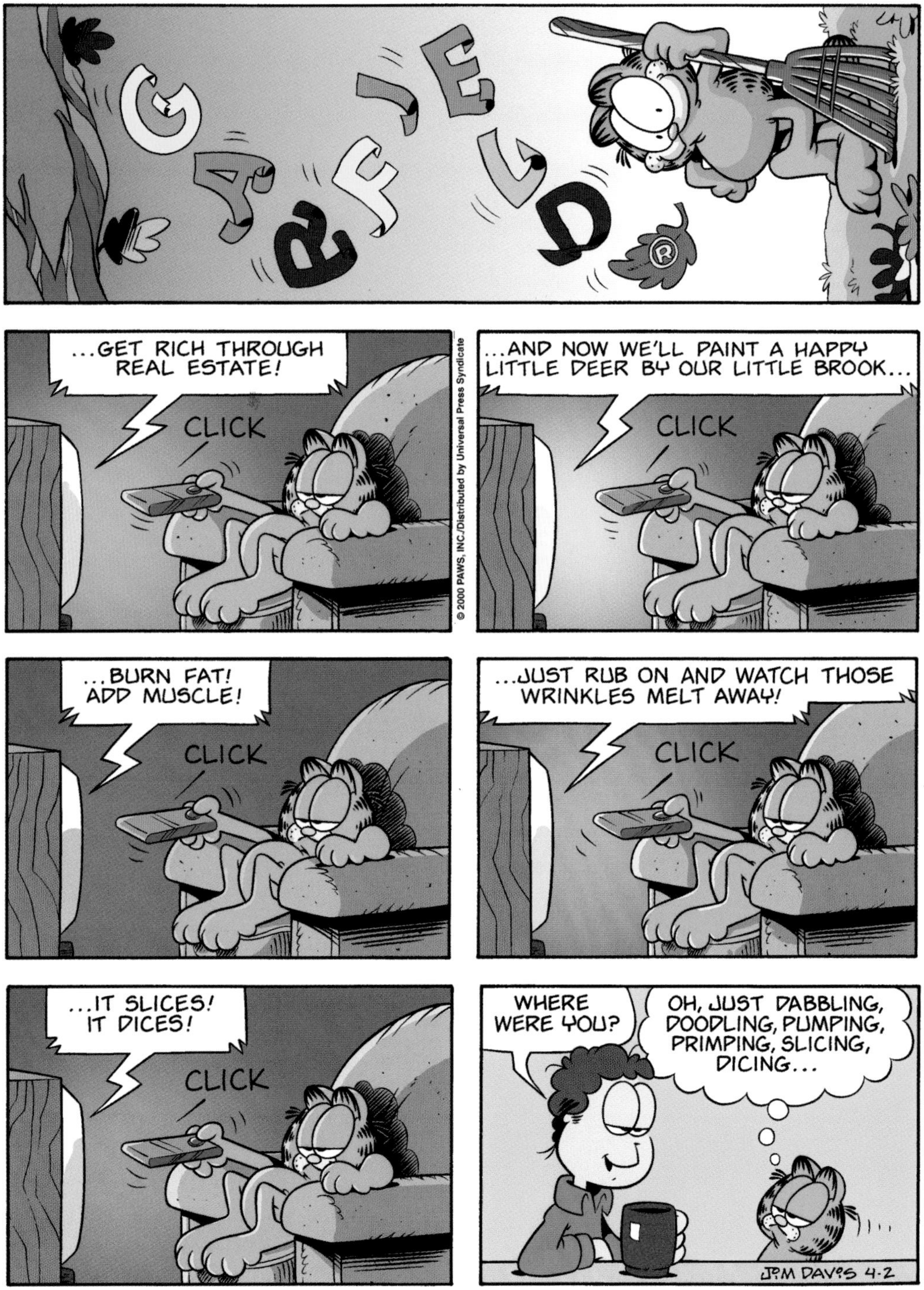
GARFIELD
...GET RICH THROUGH REAL ESTATE!
CLICK
© 2000 PAWS, INC./Distributed by Universal Press Syndicate
...AND NOW WE'LL PAINT A HAPPY LITTLE DEER BY OUR LITTLE BROOK...
CLICK
...BURN FAT! ADD MUSCLE!
CLICK
...JUST RUB ON AND WATCH THOSE WRINKLES MELT AWAY!
CLICK
...IT SLICES! IT DICES!
CLICK
WHERE WERE YOU?
OH, JUST DABBLING, DOODLING, PUMPING, PRIMPING, SLICING, DICING...
JIM DAVIS 4-2

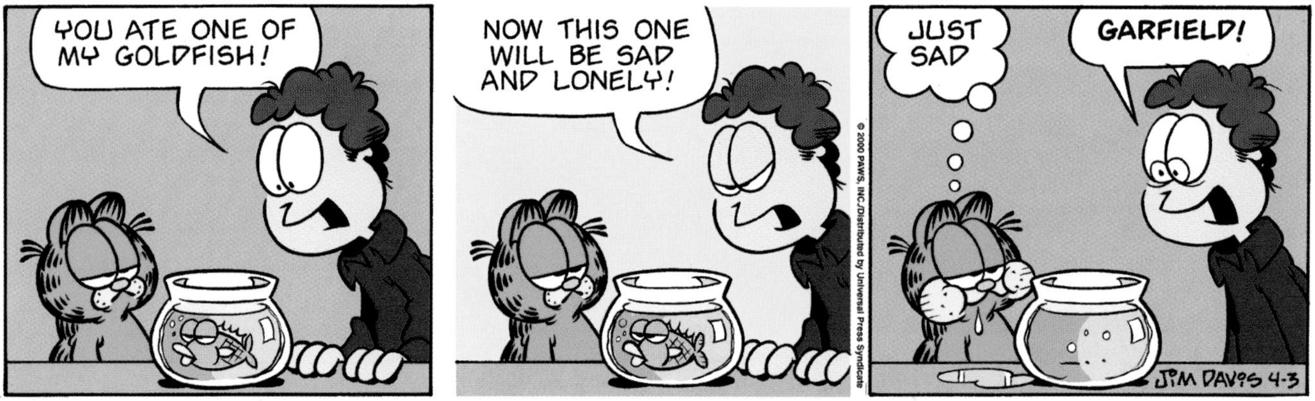
YOU ATE ONE OF MY GOLDFISH!
NOW THIS ONE WILL BE SAD AND LONELY!
© 2000 PAWS, INC./Distributed by Universal Press Syndicate
JUST SAD
GARFIELD!
JIM DAVIS 4-3

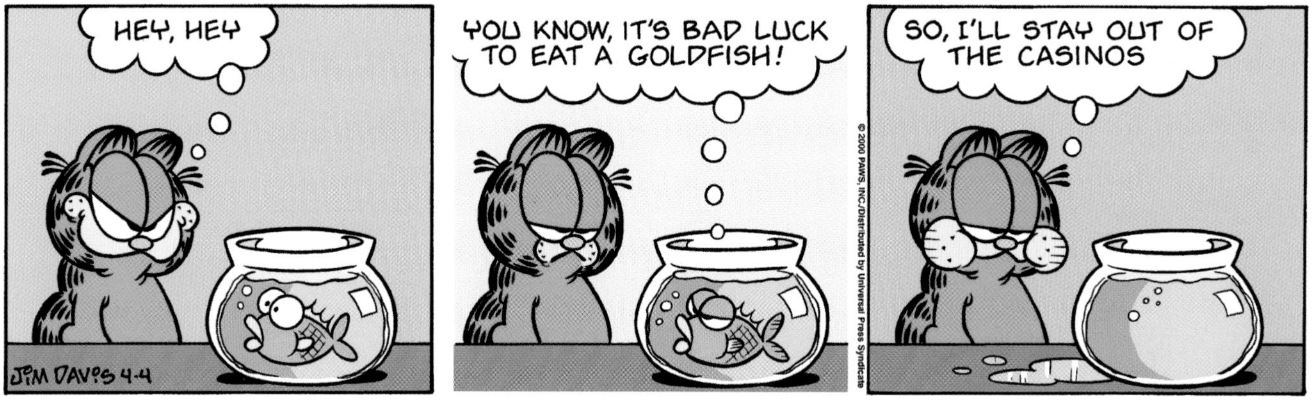
HEY, HEY
JIM DAVIS 4-4
YOU KNOW, IT'S BAD LUCK TO EAT A GOLDFISH!
© 2000 PAWS, INC./Distributed by Universal Press Syndicate
SO, I'LL STAY OUT OF THE CASINOS

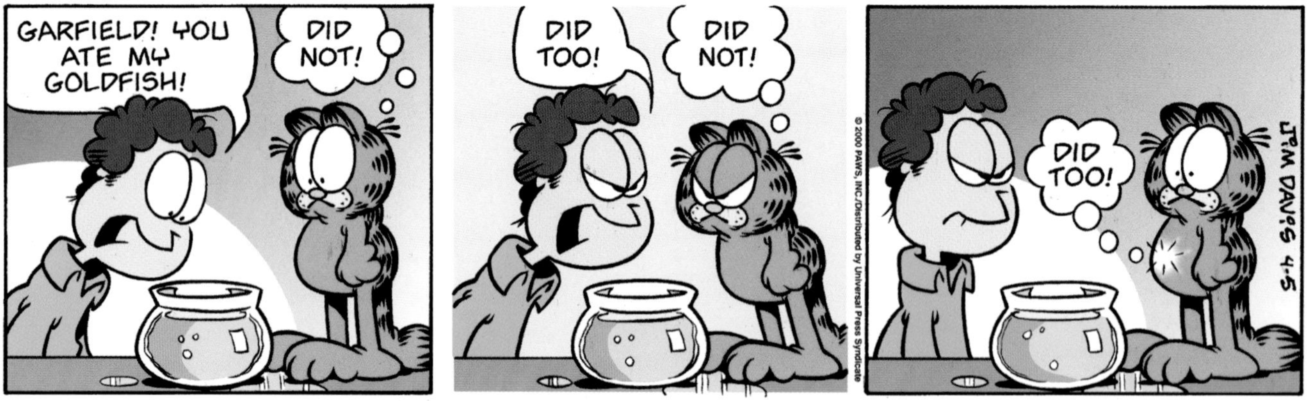
GARFIELD! YOU ATE MY GOLDFISH!
DID NOT!
DID TOO!
DID NOT!
© 2000 PAWS, INC./Distributed by Universal Press Syndicate
DID TOO!
JIM DAVIS 4-5

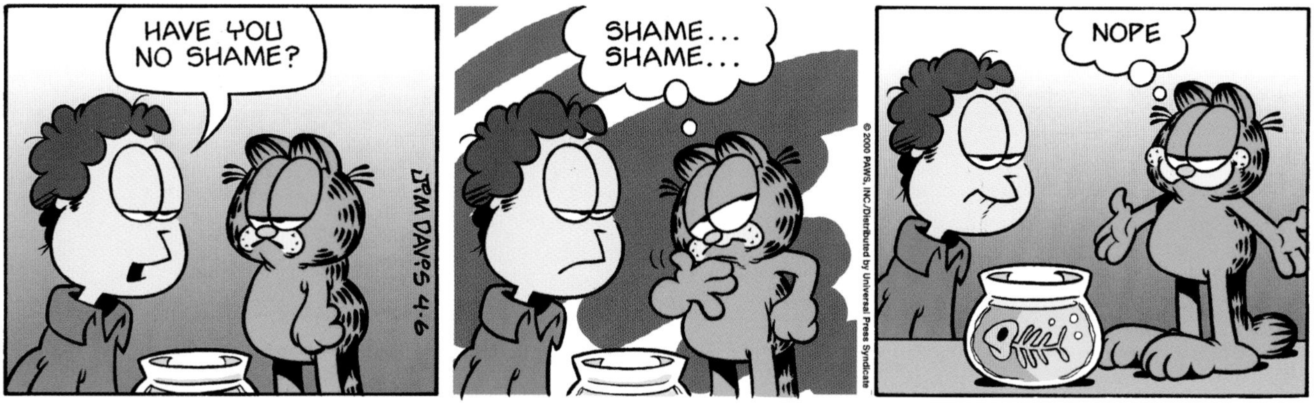
HAVE YOU NO SHAME?
JIM DAVIS 4-6
SHAME... SHAME...
© 2000 PAWS, INC./Distributed by Universal Press Syndicate
NOPE

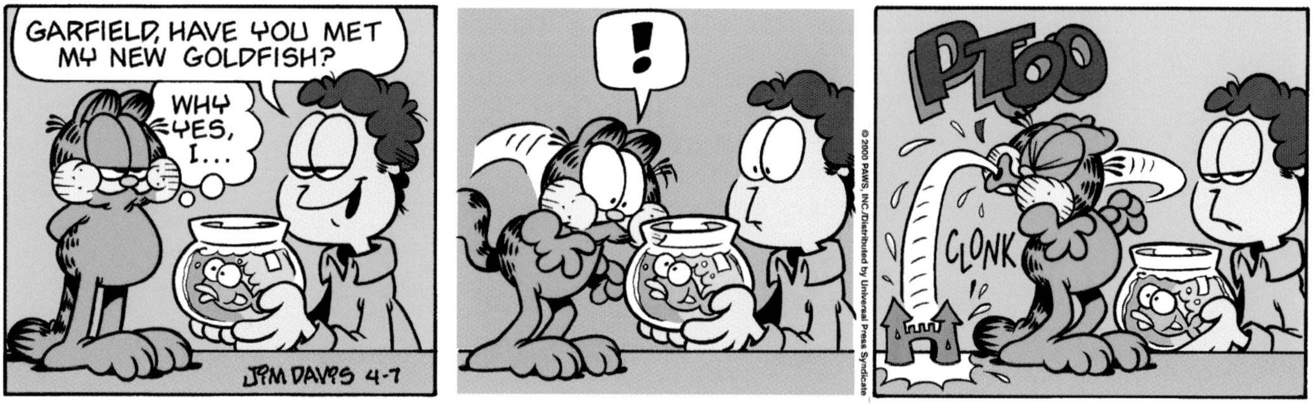
GARFIELD, HAVE YOU MET MY NEW GOLDFISH?
WHY YES, I...
JIM DAVIS 4-7
!
© 2000 PAWS, INC./Distributed by Universal Press Syndicate
PTOO
CLONK

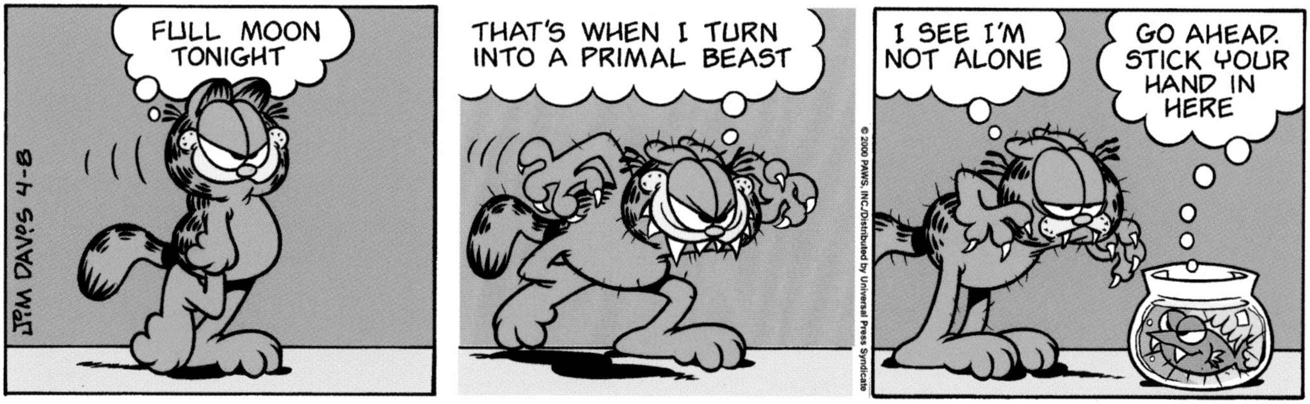
FULL MOON TONIGHT
JIM DAVIS 4-8
THAT'S WHEN I TURN INTO A PRIMAL BEAST
© 2000 PAWS, INC./Distributed by Universal Press Syndicate
I SEE I'M NOT ALONE
GO AHEAD. STICK YOUR HAND IN HERE

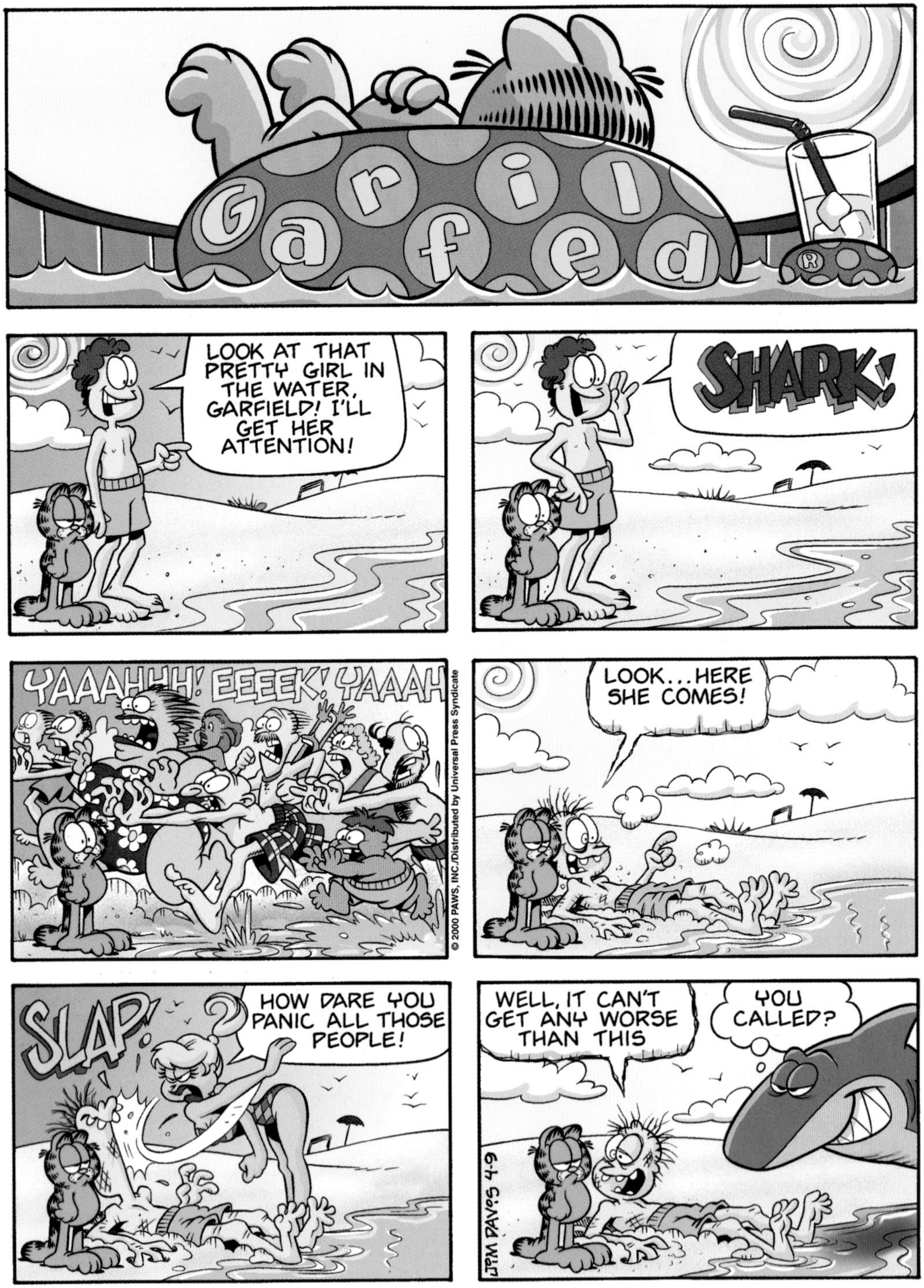
Garfield®
LOOK AT THAT PRETTY GIRL IN THE WATER, GARFIELD! I'LL GET HER ATTENTION!
SHARK!
YAAAHHH! EEEEK! YAAAH
LOOK...HERE SHE COMES!
SLAP!
HOW DARE YOU PANIC ALL THOSE PEOPLE!
WELL, IT CAN'T GET ANY WORSE THAN THIS
YOU CALLED?
JPM DAVIS 4-9
© 2000 PAWS, INC./Distributed by Universal Press Syndicate

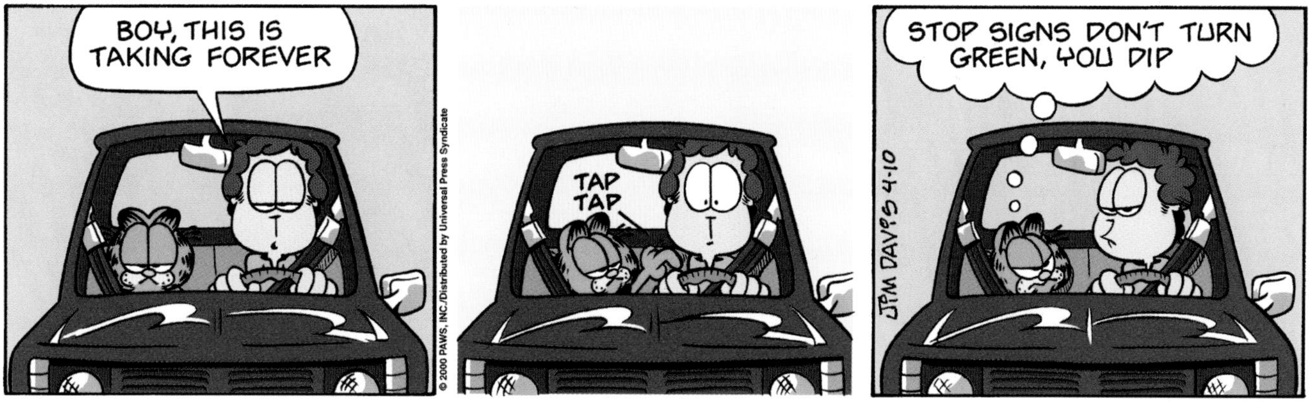
BOY, THIS IS TAKING FOREVER
TAP TAP
© 2000 PAWS, INC./Distributed by Universal Press Syndicate
JIM DAVIS 4-10
STOP SIGNS DON'T TURN GREEN, YOU DIP

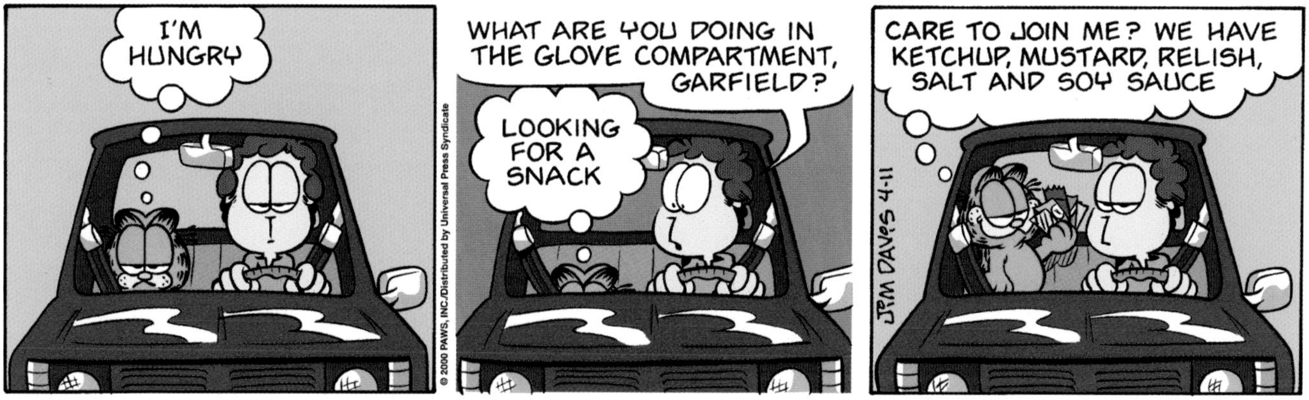
I'M HUNGRY
© 2000 PAWS, INC./Distributed by Universal Press Syndicate
WHAT ARE YOU DOING IN THE GLOVE COMPARTMENT, GARFIELD?
LOOKING FOR A SNACK
JIM DAVIS 4-11
CARE TO JOIN ME? WE HAVE KETCHUP, MUSTARD, RELISH, SALT AND SOY SAUCE

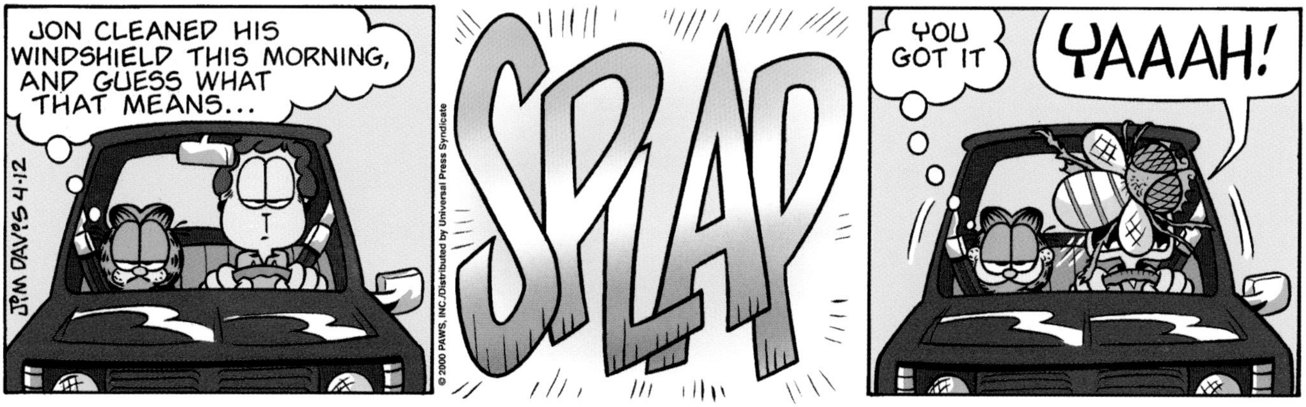
JON CLEANED HIS WINDSHIELD THIS MORNING, AND GUESS WHAT THAT MEANS...
JIM DAVIS 4-12
© 2000 PAWS, INC./Distributed by Universal Press Syndicate
SPLAP
YOU GOT IT
YAAAH!

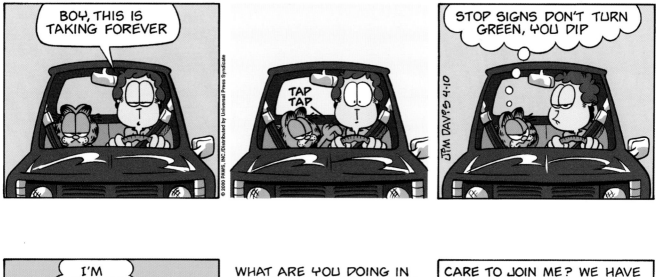

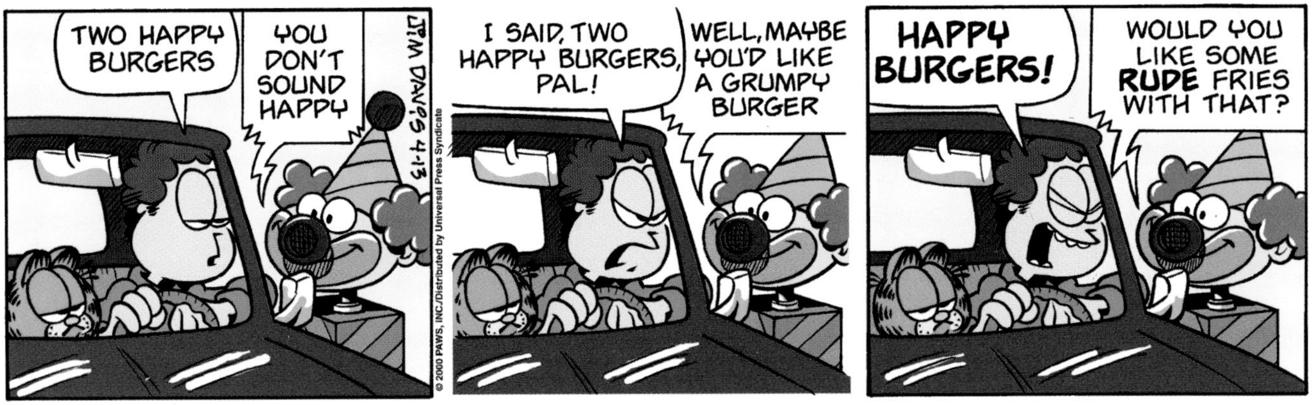
TWO HAPPY BURGERS
YOU DON'T SOUND HAPPY
JIM DAVIS 4-13
© 2000 PAWS, INC./Distributed by Universal Press Syndicate
I SAID, TWO HAPPY BURGERS, PAL!
WELL, MAYBE YOU'D LIKE A GRUMPY BURGER
HAPPY BURGERS!
WOULD YOU LIKE SOME RUDE FRIES WITH THAT?

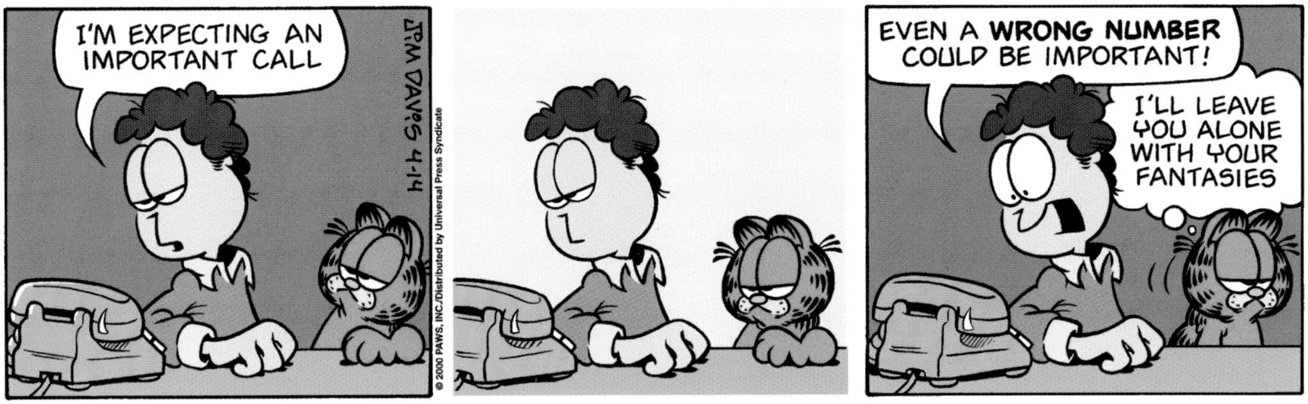
I'M EXPECTING AN IMPORTANT CALL
JIM DAVIS 4-14
© 2000 PAWS, INC./Distributed by Universal Press Syndicate
EVEN A WRONG NUMBER COULD BE IMPORTANT!
I'LL LEAVE YOU ALONE WITH YOUR FANTASIES

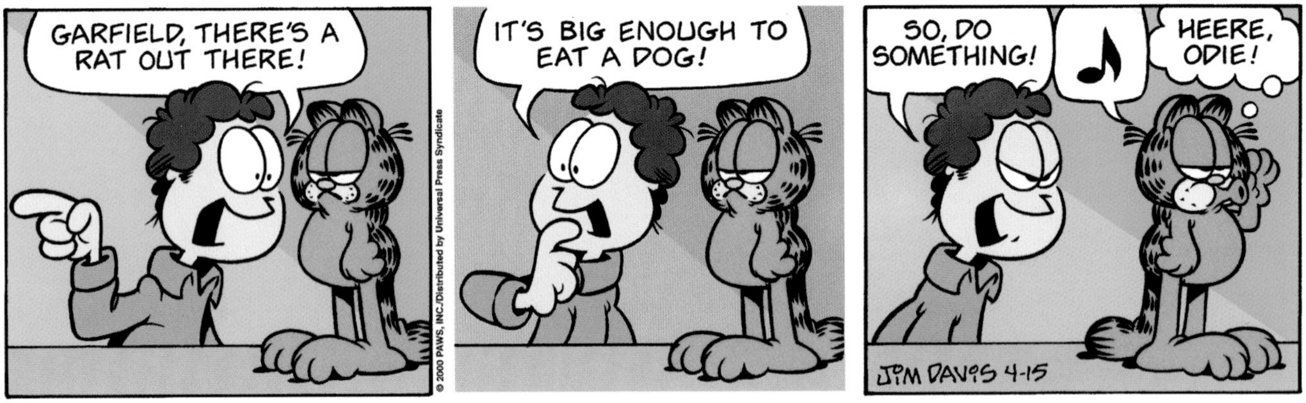
GARFIELD, THERE'S A RAT OUT THERE!
© 2000 PAWS, INC./Distributed by Universal Press Syndicate
IT'S BIG ENOUGH TO EAT A DOG!
SO, DO SOMETHING!
♪
HEERE, ODIE!
JIM DAVIS 4-15

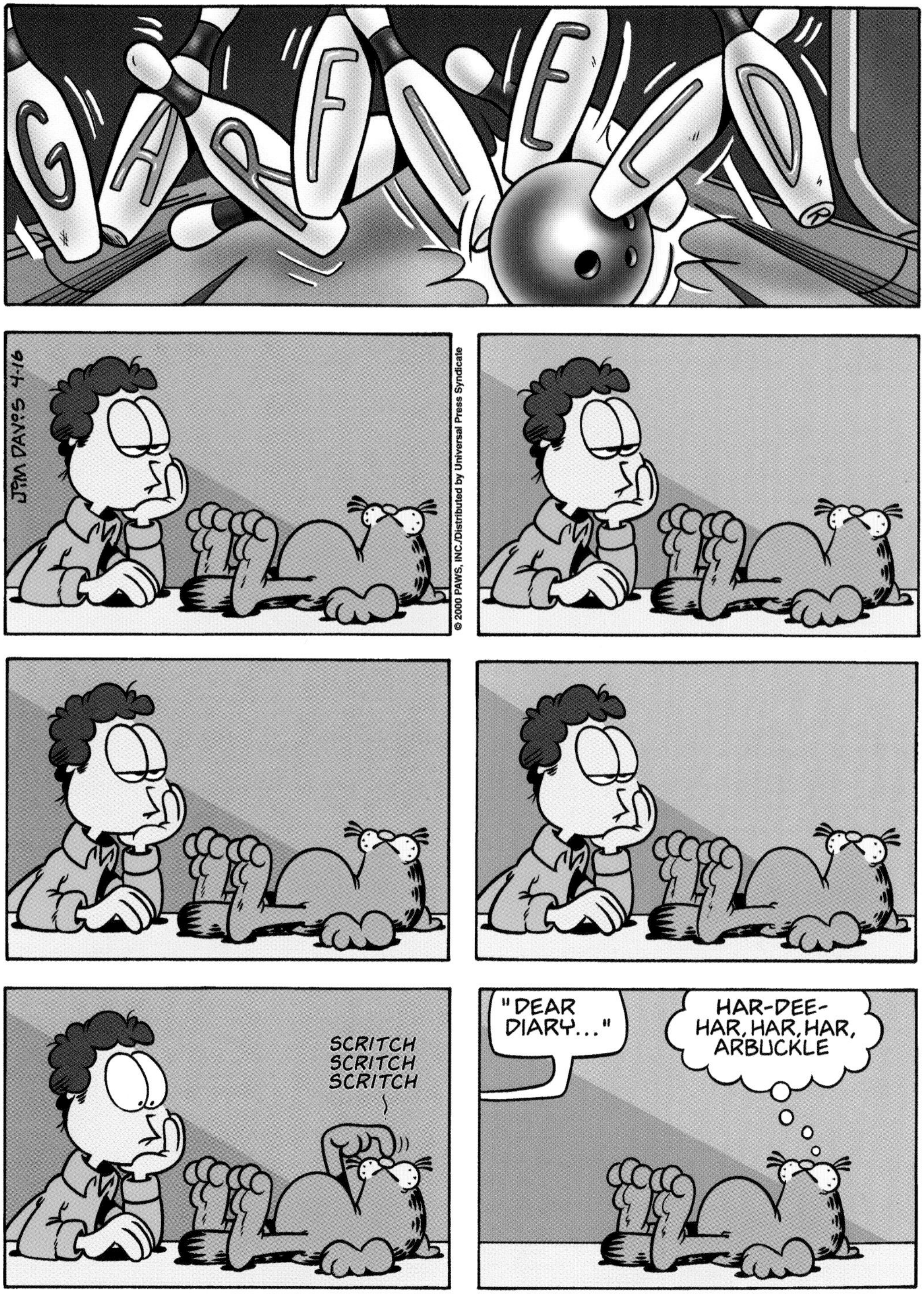
GARFIELD
JPM DAVPS 4-16
© 2000 PAWS, INC./Distributed by Universal Press Syndicate
SCRITCH
SCRITCH
SCRITCH
"DEAR DIARY..."
HAR-DEE-HAR, HAR, HAR, ARBUCKLE

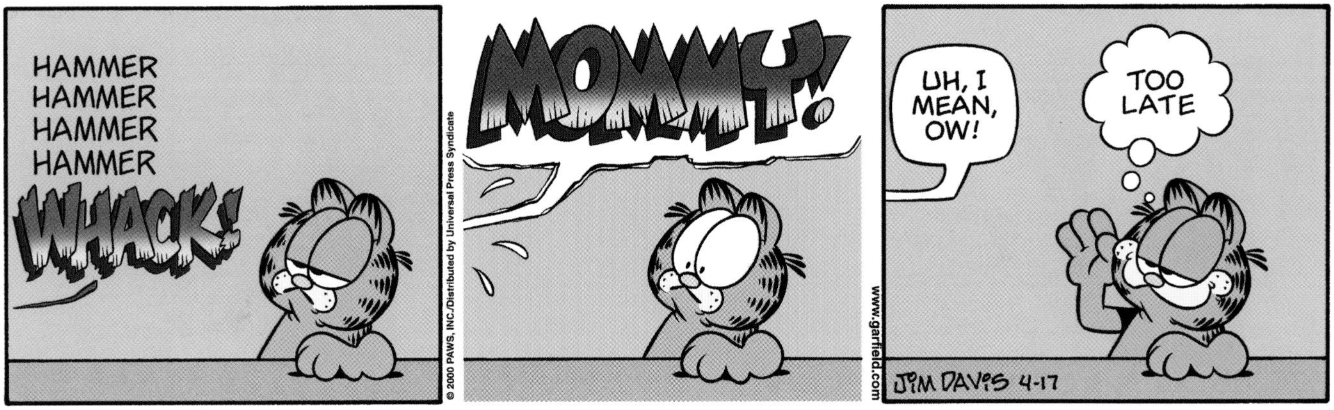
HAMMER
HAMMER
HAMMER
HAMMER
WHACK!
MOMMY!
UH, I MEAN, OW!
TOO LATE
© 2000 PAWS, INC./Distributed by Universal Press Syndicate
www.garfield.com
JIM DAVIS 4-17

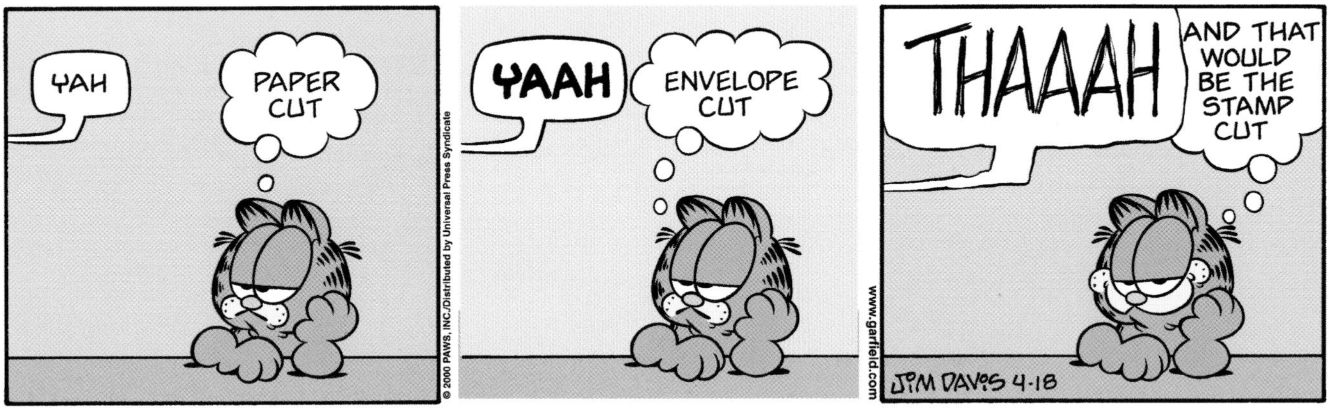
YAH
PAPER CUT
YAAH
ENVELOPE CUT
THAAAH
AND THAT WOULD BE THE STAMP CUT
© 2000 PAWS, INC./Distributed by Universal Press Syndicate
www.garfield.com
JIM DAVIS 4-18

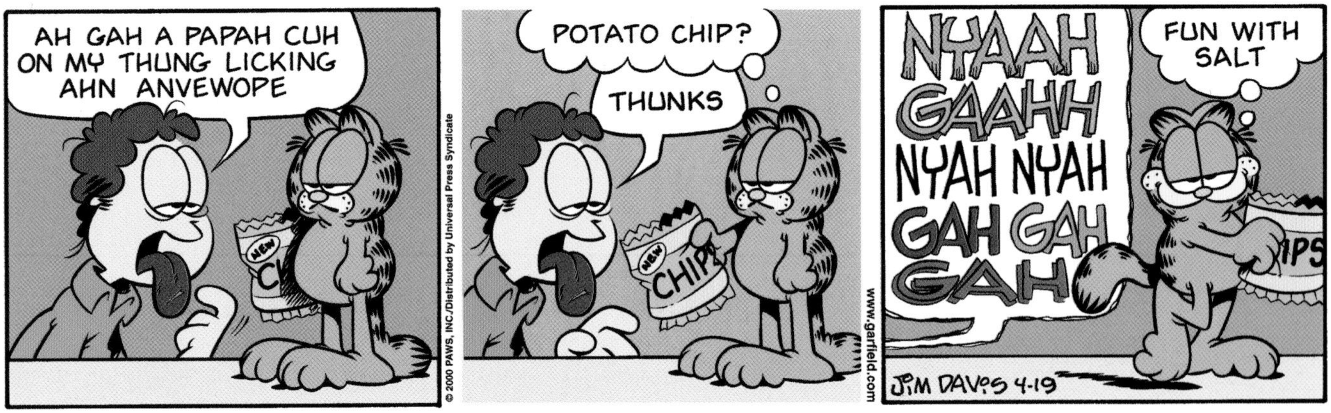
AH GAH A PAPAH CUH ON MY THUNG LICKING AHN ANVEWOPE
NEW
POTATO CHIP?
THUNKS
CHIPS
NYAAH GAAHH NYAH NYAH GAH GAH GAH
FUN WITH SALT
© 2000 PAWS, INC./Distributed by Universal Press Syndicate
www.garfield.com
JIM DAVIS 4-19

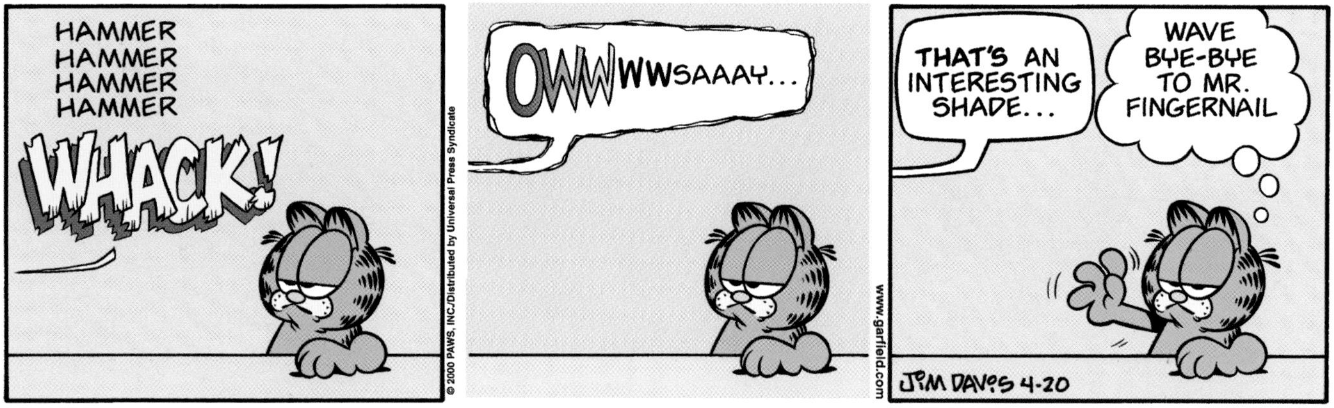
HAMMER
HAMMER
HAMMER
HAMMER
WHACK!
OWWWWWSAAAY...
THAT'S AN INTERESTING SHADE...
WAVE BYE-BYE TO MR. FINGERNAIL
© 2000 PAWS, INC./Distributed by Universal Press Syndicate
www.garfield.com
JIM DAVIS 4-20

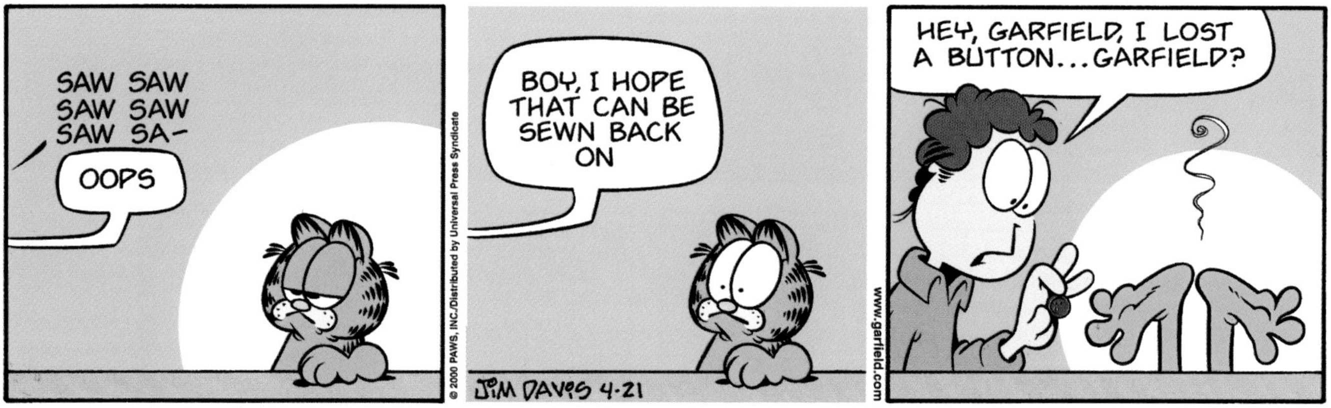
SAW SAW
SAW SAW
SAW SA-
OOPS
BOY, I HOPE THAT CAN BE SEWN BACK ON
HEY, GARFIELD, I LOST A BUTTON...GARFIELD?
© 2000 PAWS, INC./Distributed by Universal Press Syndicate
www.garfield.com
JIM DAVIS 4-21

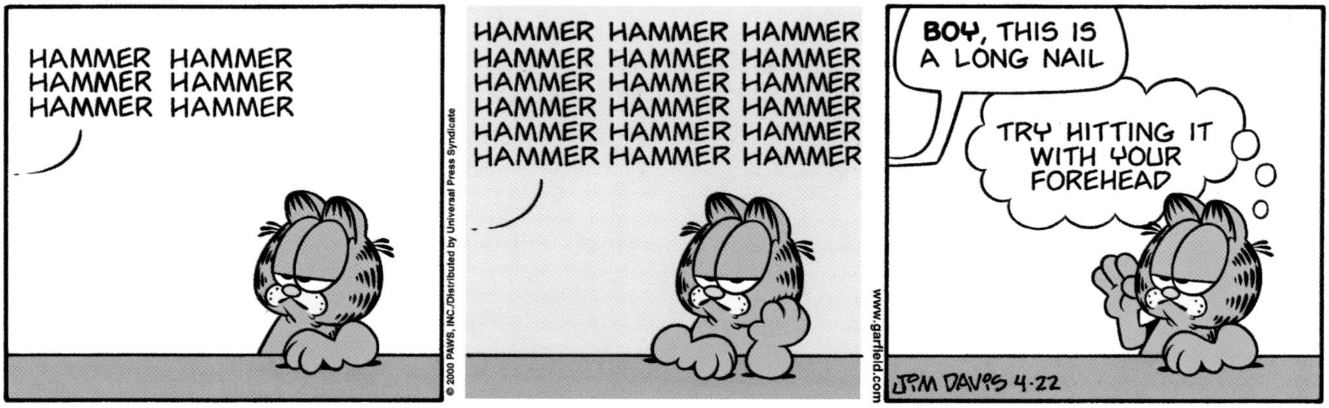
HAMMER HAMMER
HAMMER HAMMER
HAMMER HAMMER
HAMMER HAMMER HAMMER
HAMMER HAMMER HAMMER
HAMMER HAMMER HAMMER
HAMMER HAMMER HAMMER
HAMMER HAMMER HAMMER
HAMMER HAMMER HAMMER
BOY, THIS IS A LONG NAIL
TRY HITTING IT WITH YOUR FOREHEAD
© 2000 PAWS, INC./Distributed by Universal Press Syndicate
www.garfield.com
JIM DAVIS 4-22

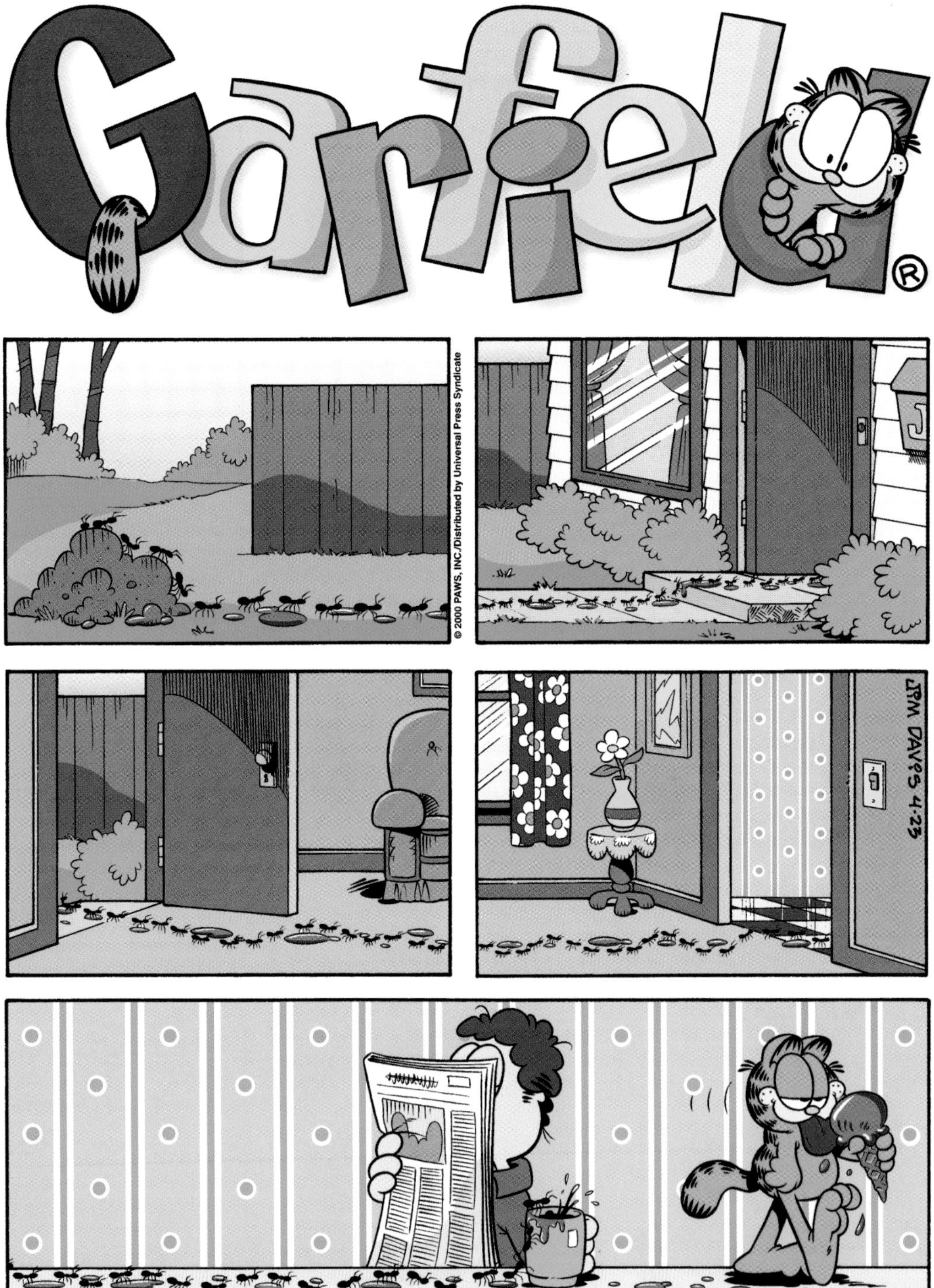
Garfield®
© 2000 PAWS, INC./Distributed by Universal Press Syndicate
JIM DAVIS 4-23

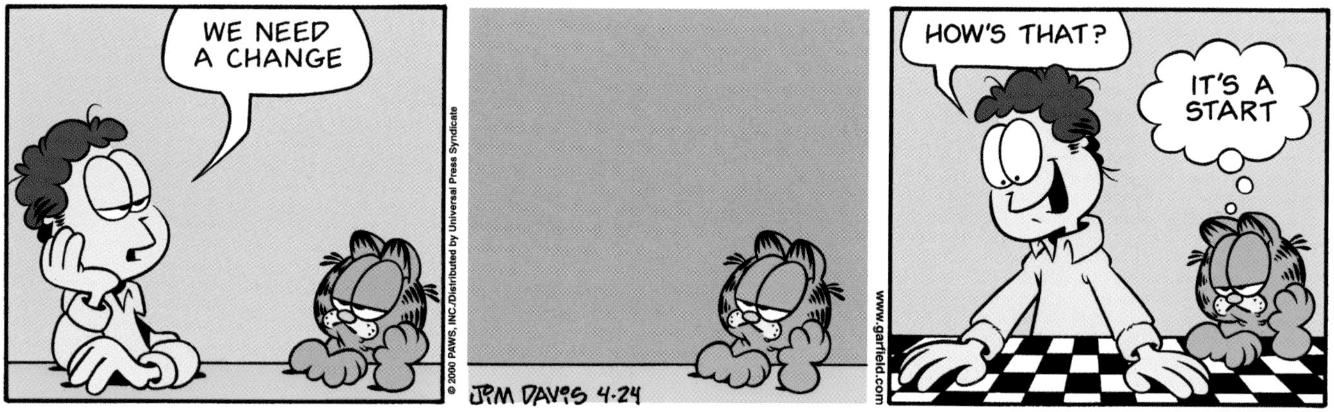
WE NEED A CHANGE
© 2000 PAWS, INC./Distributed by Universal Press Syndicate
JIM DAVIS 4-24
www.garfield.com
HOW'S THAT?
IT'S A START

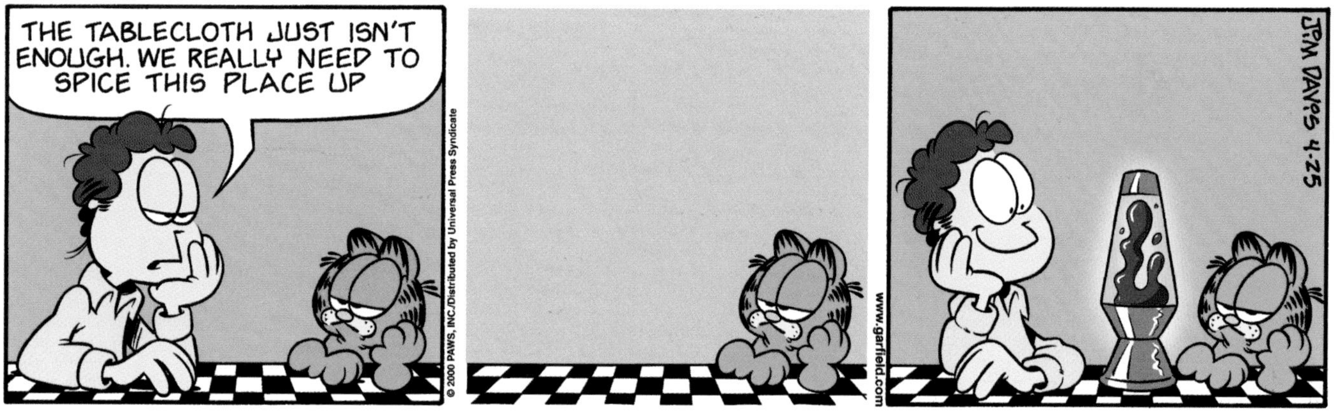
THE TABLECLOTH JUST ISN'T ENOUGH. WE REALLY NEED TO SPICE THIS PLACE UP
© 2000 PAWS, INC./Distributed by Universal Press Syndicate
www.garfield.com
JIM DAVIS 4-25

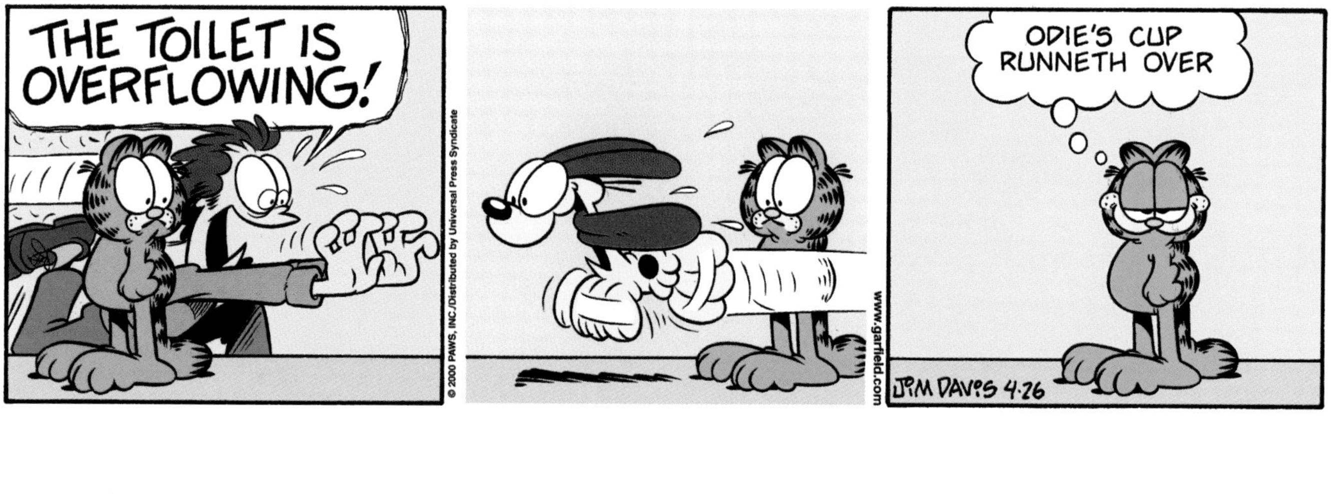
THE TOILET IS OVERFLOWING!
© 2000 PAWS, INC./Distributed by Universal Press Syndicate
www.garfield.com
JIM DAVIS 4-26
ODIE'S CUP RUNNETH OVER

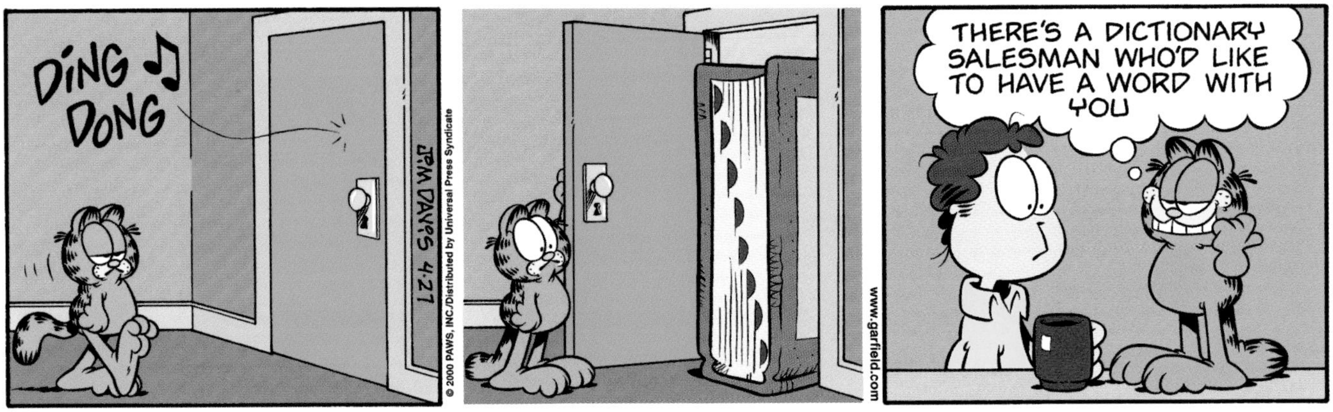
DING ♫ DONG
JIM DAVIS 4·27
© 2000 PAWS, INC./Distributed by Universal Press Syndicate
THERE'S A DICTIONARY SALESMAN WHO'D LIKE TO HAVE A WORD WITH YOU
www.garfield.com

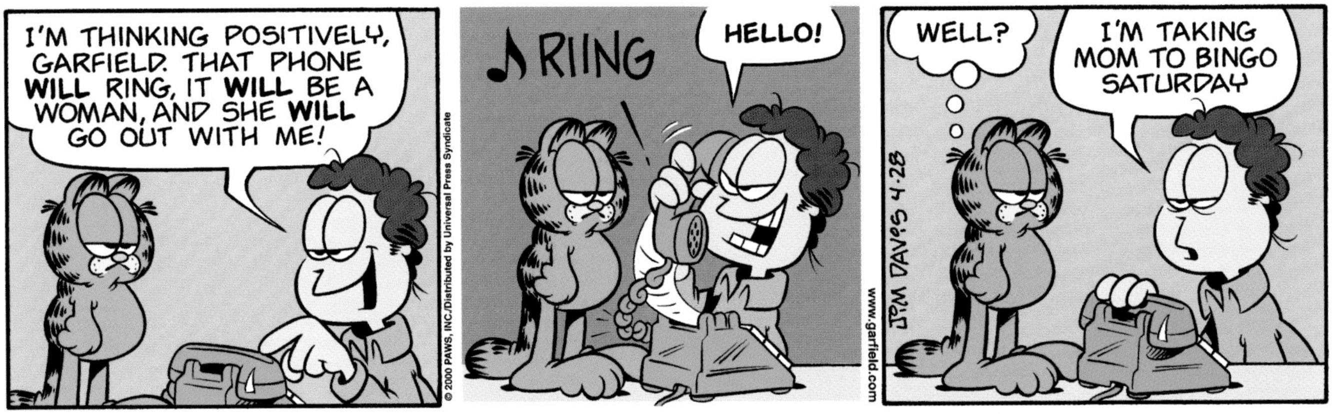
I'M THINKING POSITIVELY, GARFIELD. THAT PHONE **WILL** RING, IT **WILL** BE A WOMAN, AND SHE **WILL** GO OUT WITH ME!
© 2000 PAWS, INC./Distributed by Universal Press Syndicate
♪ RIING
HELLO!
WELL?
I'M TAKING MOM TO BINGO SATURDAY
JIM DAVIS 4·28
www.garfield.com

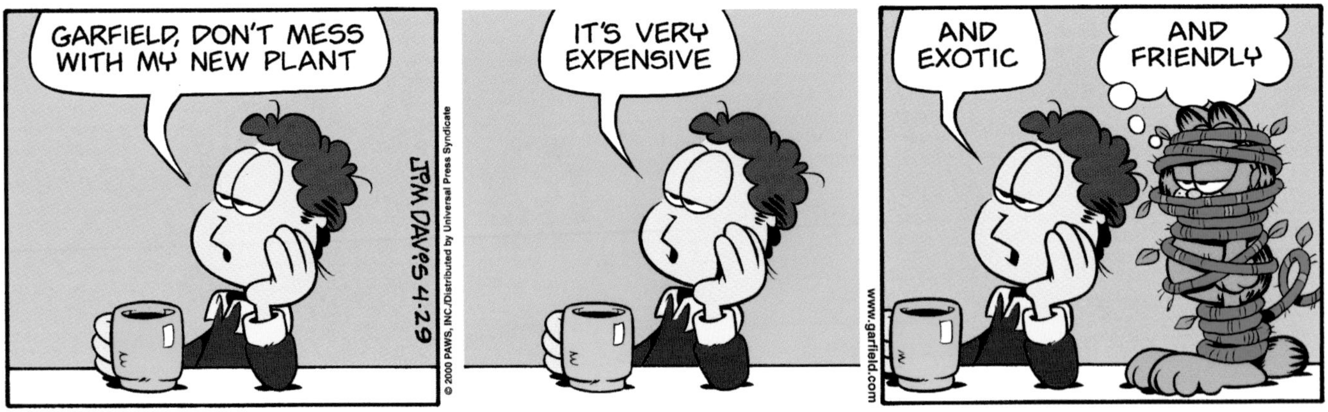
GARFIELD, DON'T MESS WITH MY NEW PLANT
JIM DAVIS 4·29
© 2000 PAWS, INC./Distributed by Universal Press Syndicate
IT'S VERY EXPENSIVE
AND EXOTIC
AND FRIENDLY
www.garfield.com

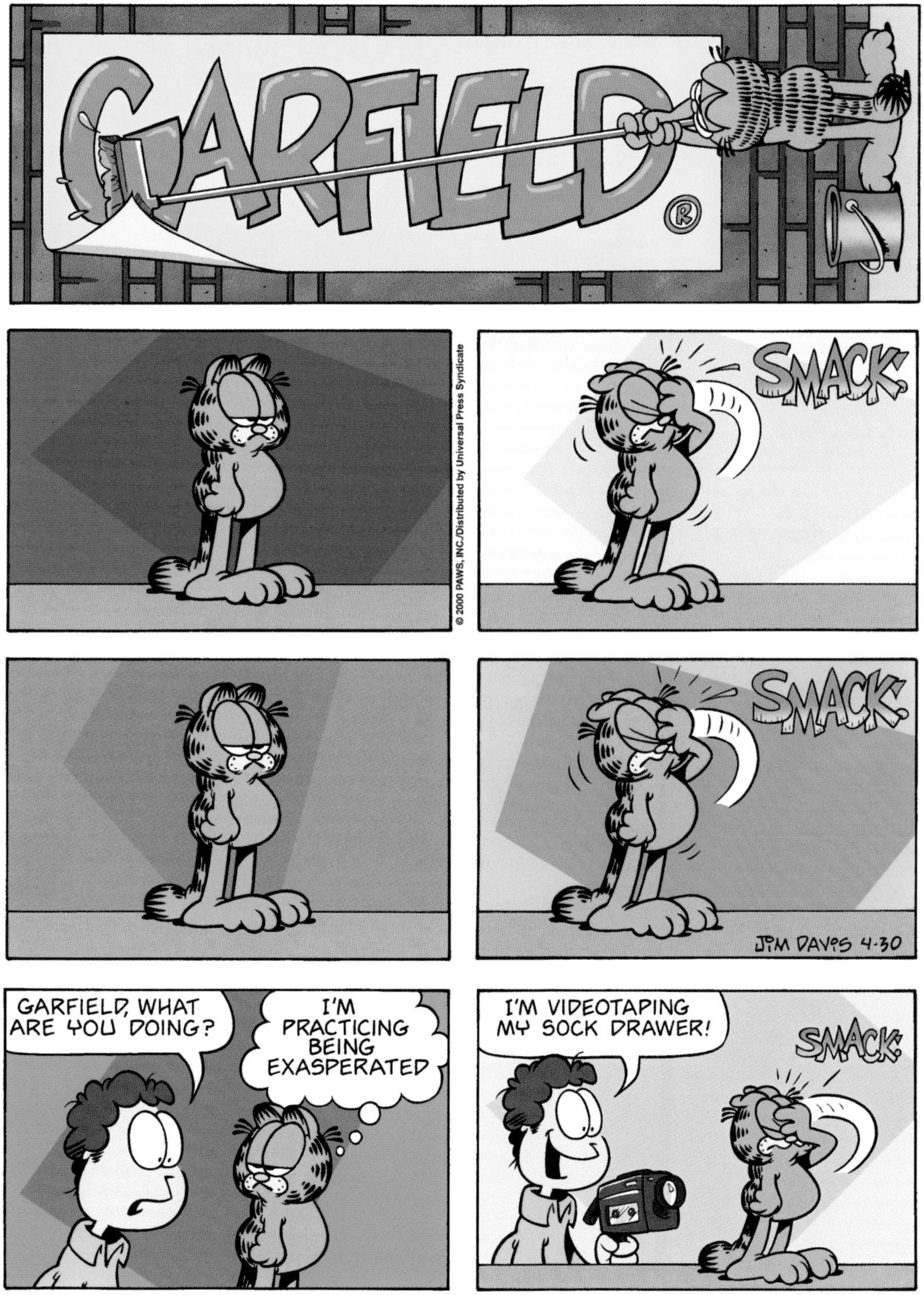
GARFIELD
© 2000 PAWS, INC./Distributed by Universal Press Syndicate
SMACK!
SMACK!
JIM DAVIS 4-30
GARFIELD, WHAT ARE YOU DOING?
I'M PRACTICING BEING EXASPERATED
I'M VIDEOTAPING MY SOCK DRAWER!
SMACK!

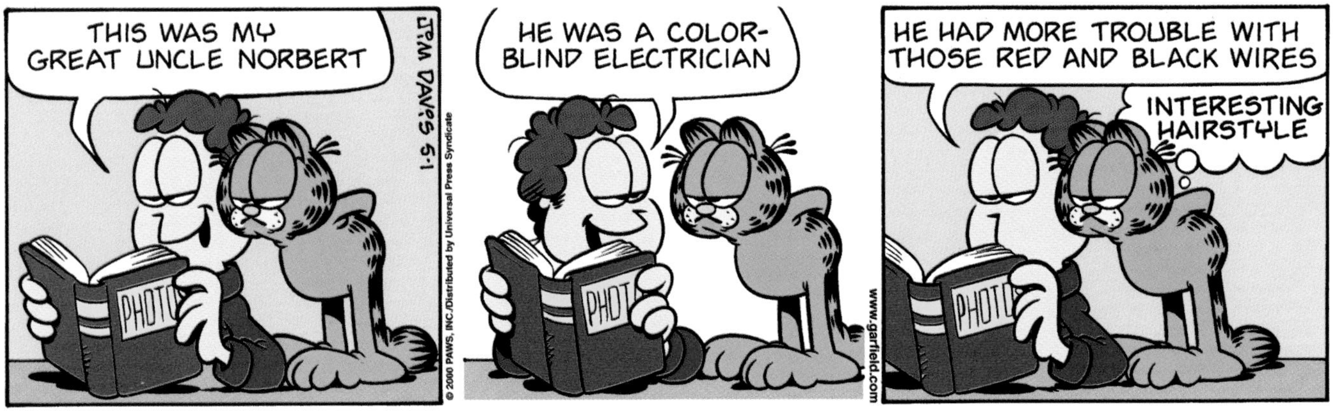
THIS WAS MY GREAT UNCLE NORBERT
JIM DAVIS 5-1
© 2000 PAWS, INC./Distributed by Universal Press Syndicate
HE WAS A COLOR-BLIND ELECTRICIAN
www.garfield.com
HE HAD MORE TROUBLE WITH THOSE RED AND BLACK WIRES
INTERESTING HAIRSTYLE

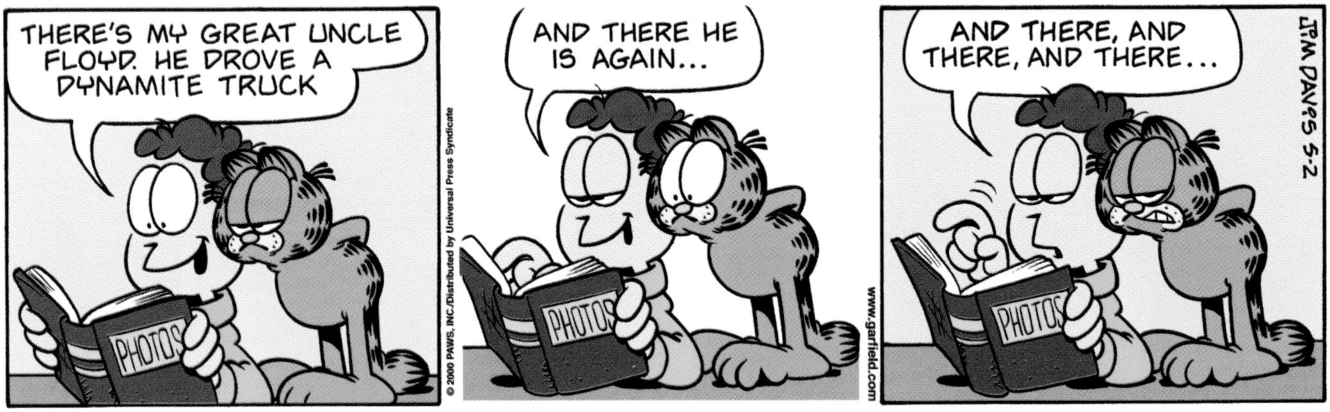
THERE'S MY GREAT UNCLE FLOYD. HE DROVE A DYNAMITE TRUCK
© 2000 PAWS, INC./Distributed by Universal Press Syndicate
AND THERE HE IS AGAIN...
www.garfield.com
AND THERE, AND THERE, AND THERE...
JIM DAVIS 5-2

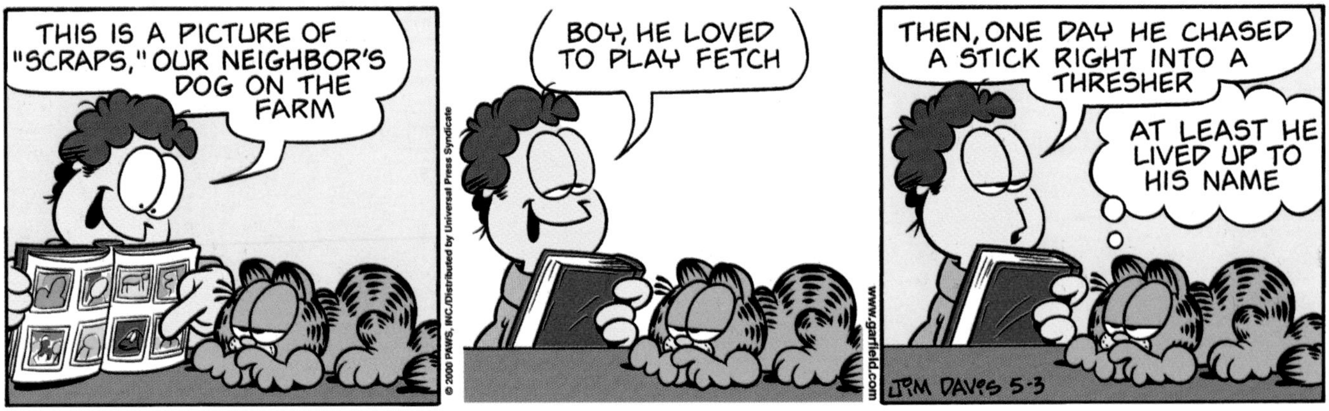
THIS IS A PICTURE OF "SCRAPS," OUR NEIGHBOR'S DOG ON THE FARM
© 2000 PAWS, INC./Distributed by Universal Press Syndicate
BOY, HE LOVED TO PLAY FETCH
www.garfield.com
THEN, ONE DAY HE CHASED A STICK RIGHT INTO A THRESHER
AT LEAST HE LIVED UP TO HIS NAME
JIM DAVIS 5-3

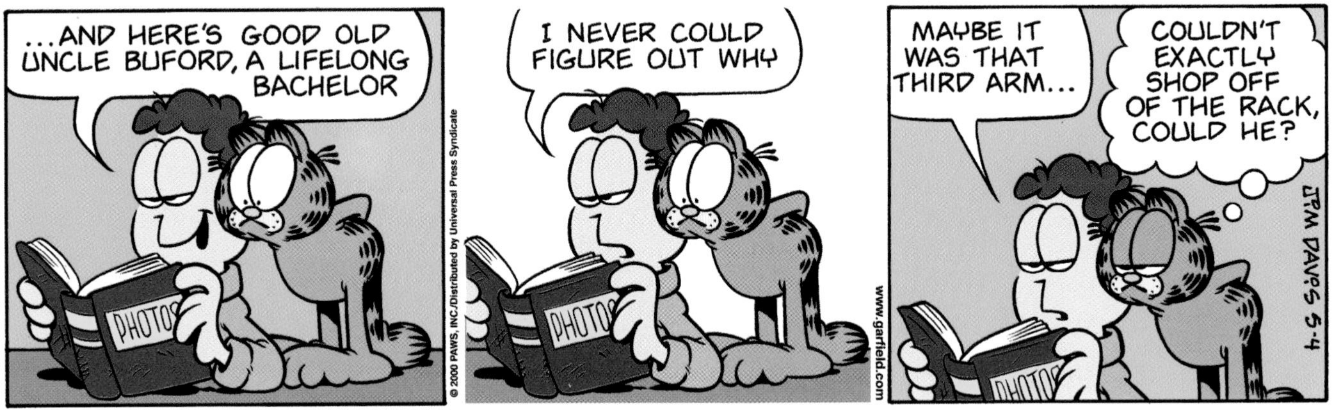
...AND HERE'S GOOD OLD UNCLE BUFORD, A LIFELONG BACHELOR
PHOTOS
I NEVER COULD FIGURE OUT WHY
PHOTOS
© 2000 PAWS, INC./Distributed by Universal Press Syndicate
www.garfield.com
MAYBE IT WAS THAT THIRD ARM...
COULDN'T EXACTLY SHOP OFF OF THE RACK, COULD HE?
JPM DAVIS 5-4

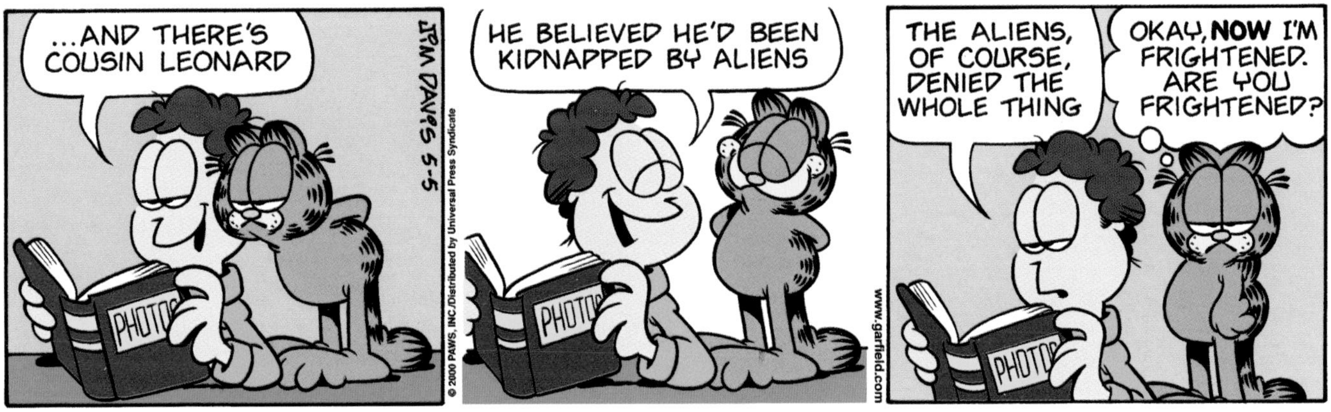
...AND THERE'S COUSIN LEONARD
JPM DAVIS 5-5
PHOTOS
HE BELIEVED HE'D BEEN KIDNAPPED BY ALIENS
© 2000 PAWS, INC./Distributed by Universal Press Syndicate
www.garfield.com
THE ALIENS, OF COURSE, DENIED THE WHOLE THING
OKAY, **NOW** I'M FRIGHTENED. ARE YOU FRIGHTENED?

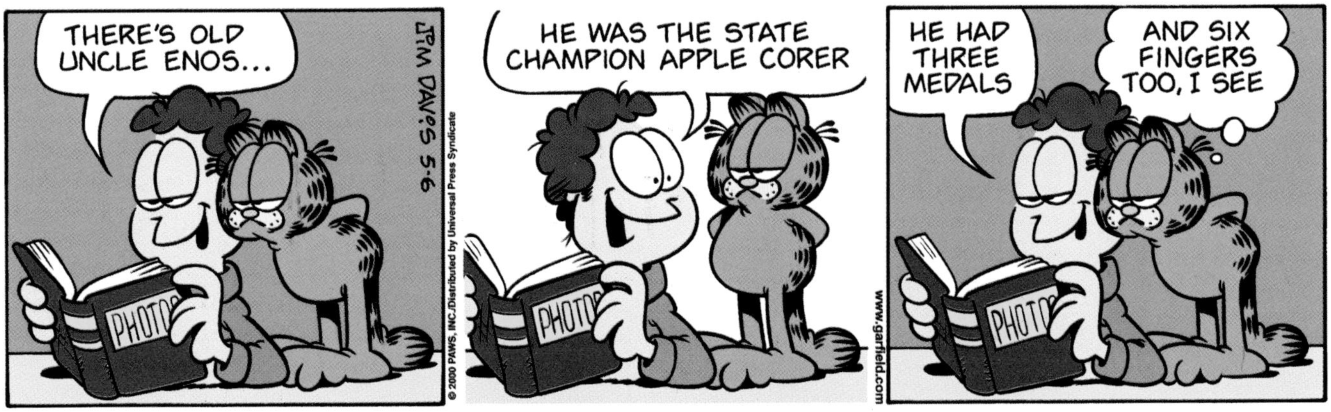
THERE'S OLD UNCLE ENOS...
JPM DAVIS 5-6
HE WAS THE STATE CHAMPION APPLE CORER
© 2000 PAWS, INC./Distributed by Universal Press Syndicate
www.garfield.com
HE HAD THREE MEDALS
AND SIX FINGERS TOO, I SEE

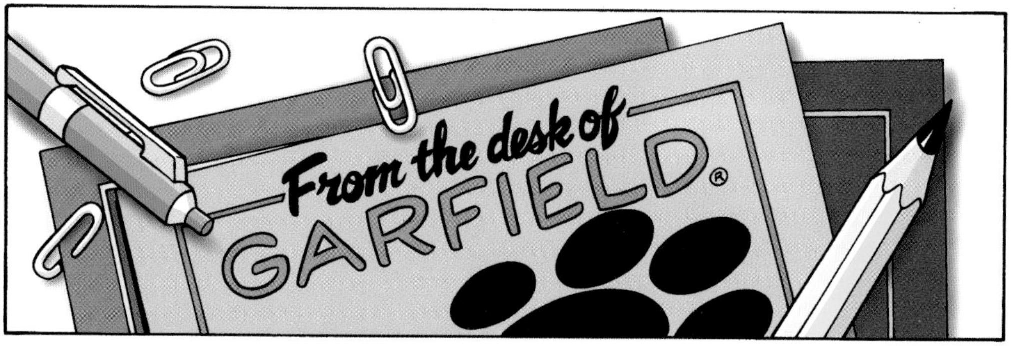
From the desk of
GARFIELD®

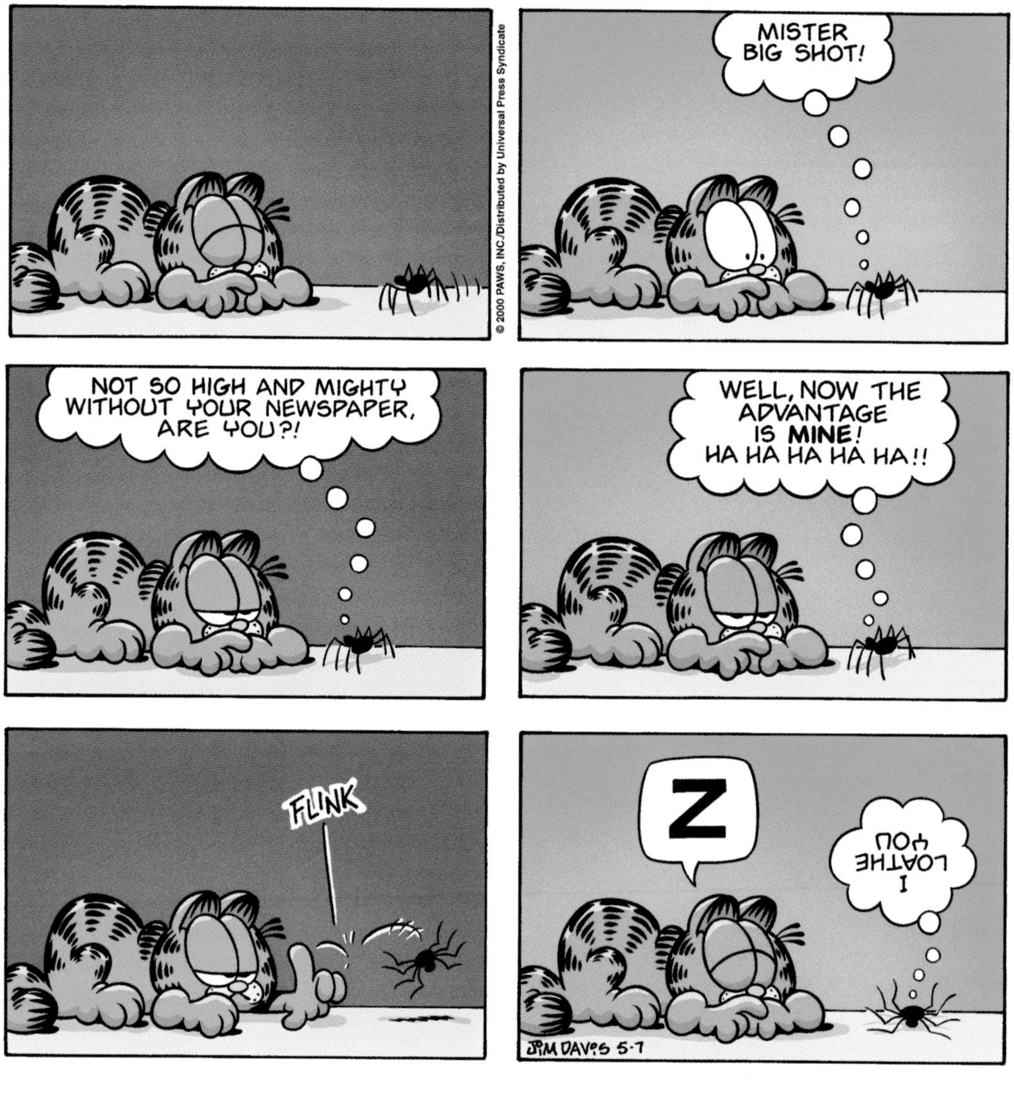
MISTER BIG SHOT!
NOT SO HIGH AND MIGHTY WITHOUT YOUR NEWSPAPER, ARE YOU?!
WELL, NOW THE ADVANTAGE IS **MINE**! HA HA HA HA HA!!
FLINK
Z
I LOATHE YOU
JIM DAVIS 5-7

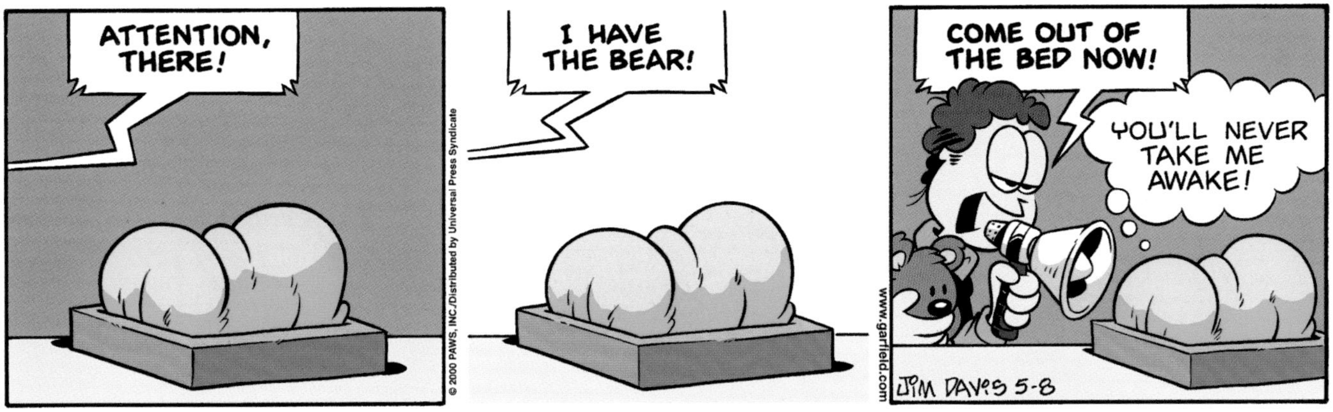
ATTENTION, THERE!
I HAVE THE BEAR!
COME OUT OF THE BED NOW!
YOU'LL NEVER TAKE ME AWAKE!
© 2000 PAWS, INC./Distributed by Universal Press Syndicate
www.garfield.com
JIM DAVIS 5-8

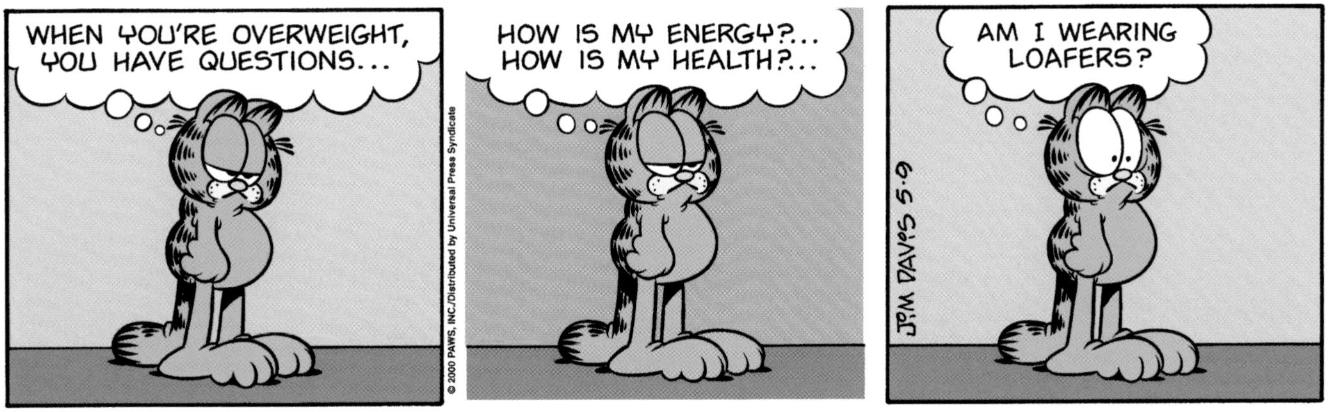
WHEN YOU'RE OVERWEIGHT, YOU HAVE QUESTIONS...
HOW IS MY ENERGY?... HOW IS MY HEALTH?...
AM I WEARING LOAFERS?
© 2000 PAWS, INC./Distributed by Universal Press Syndicate
JIM DAVIS 5-9

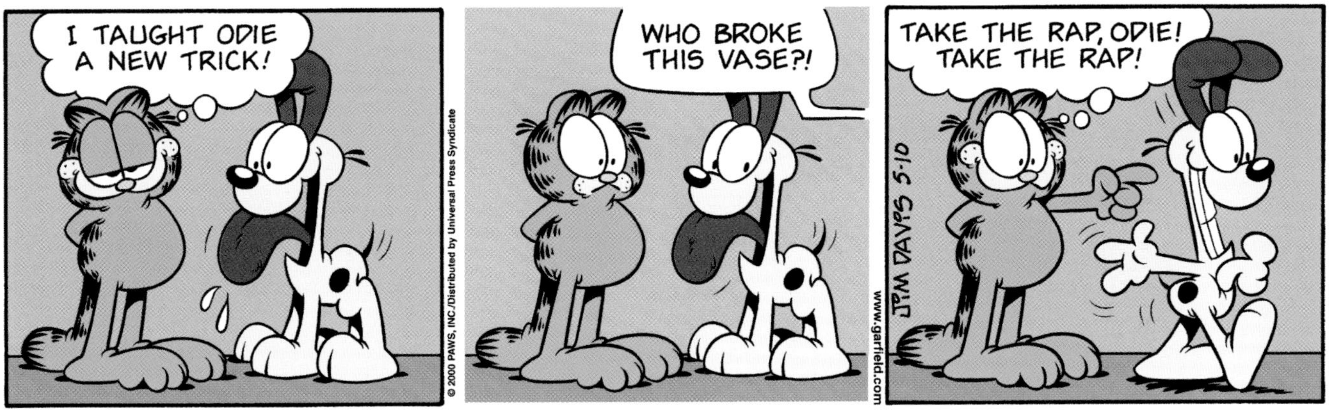
I TAUGHT ODIE A NEW TRICK!
WHO BROKE THIS VASE?!
TAKE THE RAP, ODIE! TAKE THE RAP!
© 2000 PAWS, INC./Distributed by Universal Press Syndicate
www.garfield.com
JIM DAVIS 5-10

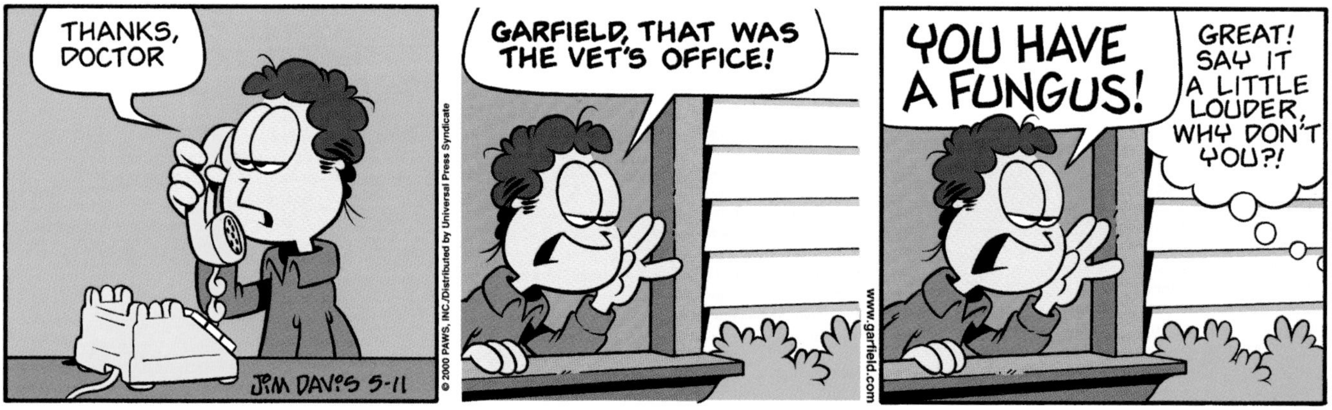
THANKS, DOCTOR
JIM DAVIS 5-11
© 2000 PAWS, INC./Distributed by Universal Press Syndicate
GARFIELD, THAT WAS THE VET'S OFFICE!
www.garfield.com
YOU HAVE A FUNGUS!
GREAT! SAY IT A LITTLE LOUDER, WHY DON'T YOU?!

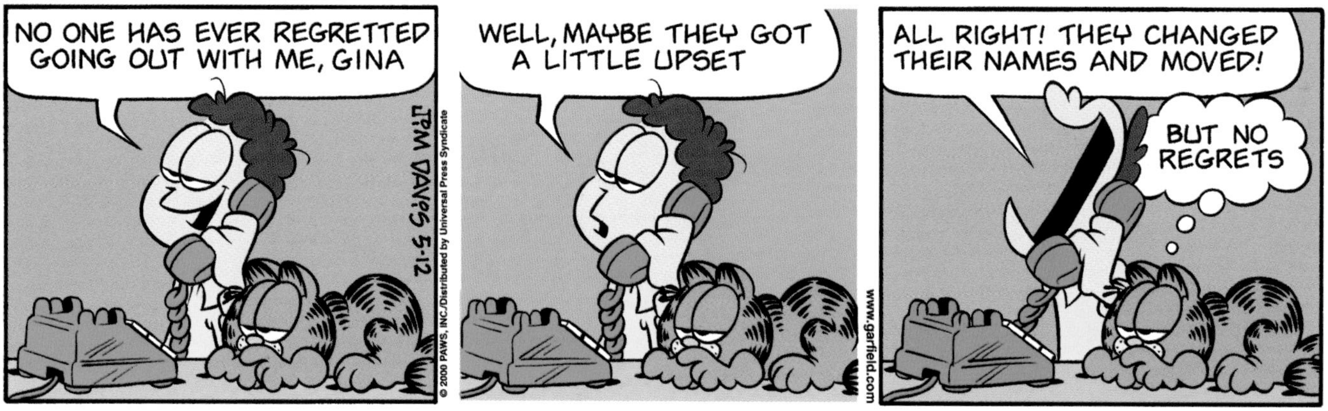
NO ONE HAS EVER REGRETTED GOING OUT WITH ME, GINA
JIM DAVIS 5-12
© 2000 PAWS, INC./Distributed by Universal Press Syndicate
WELL, MAYBE THEY GOT A LITTLE UPSET
www.garfield.com
ALL RIGHT! THEY CHANGED THEIR NAMES AND MOVED!
BUT NO REGRETS

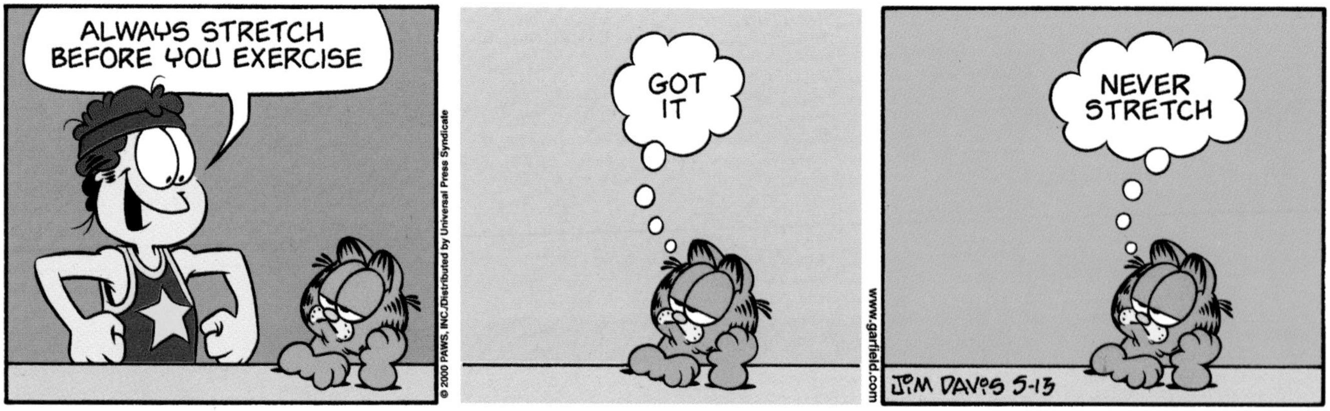
ALWAYS STRETCH BEFORE YOU EXERCISE
© 2000 PAWS, INC./Distributed by Universal Press Syndicate
GOT IT
www.garfield.com
NEVER STRETCH
JIM DAVIS 5-13

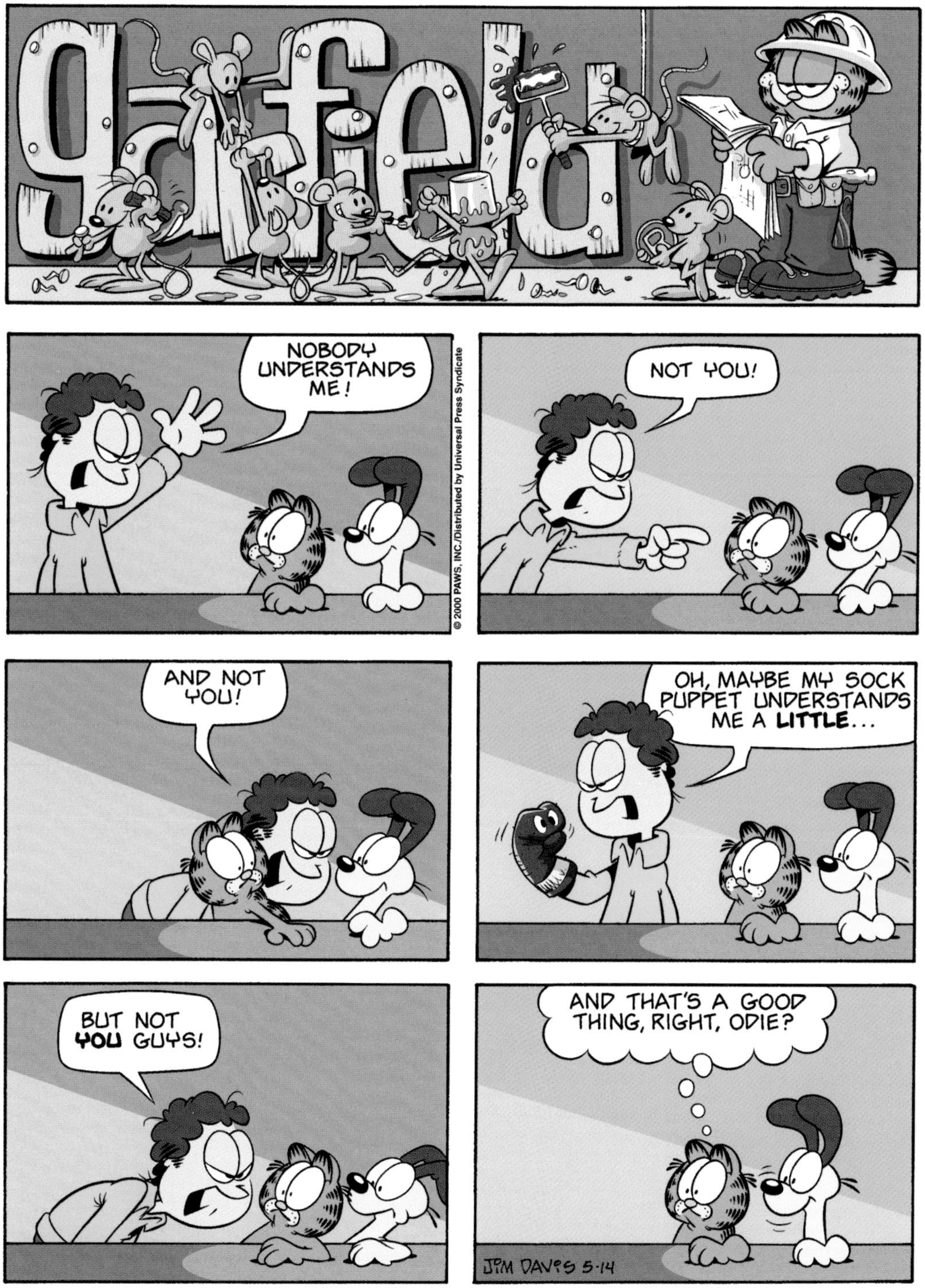
garfield
NOBODY UNDERSTANDS ME!
NOT YOU!
AND NOT YOU!
OH, MAYBE MY SOCK PUPPET UNDERSTANDS ME A **LITTLE**...
BUT NOT **YOU** GUYS!
AND THAT'S A GOOD THING, RIGHT, ODIE?
JIM DAVIS 5-14

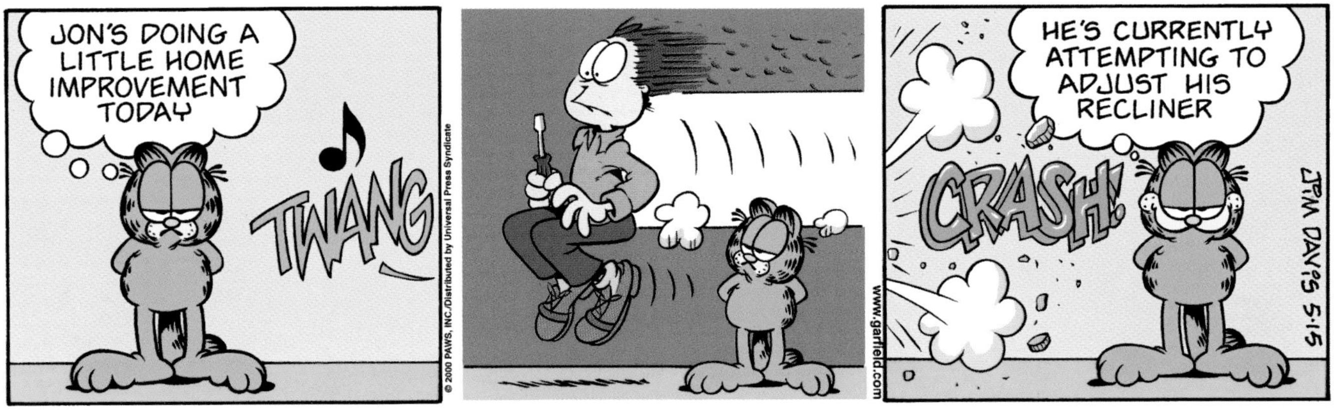
JON'S DOING A LITTLE HOME IMPROVEMENT TODAY
TWANG
© 2000 PAWS, INC./Distributed by Universal Press Syndicate
www.garfield.com
HE'S CURRENTLY ATTEMPTING TO ADJUST HIS RECLINER
CRASH!
JIM DAVIS 5-15

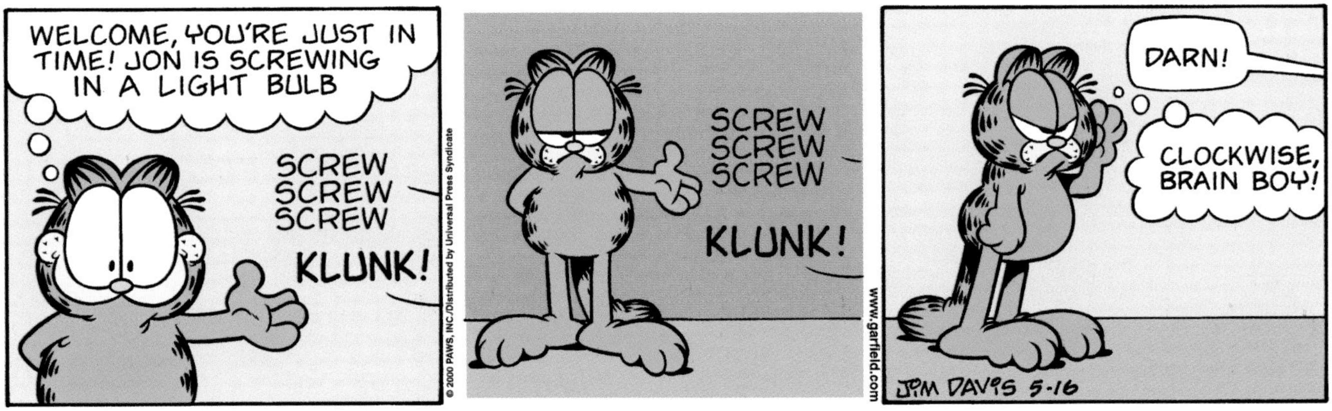
WELCOME, YOU'RE JUST IN TIME! JON IS SCREWING IN A LIGHT BULB
SCREW
SCREW
SCREW
KLUNK!
© 2000 PAWS, INC./Distributed by Universal Press Syndicate
SCREW
SCREW
SCREW
KLUNK!
www.garfield.com
DARN!
CLOCKWISE, BRAIN BOY!
JIM DAVIS 5-16

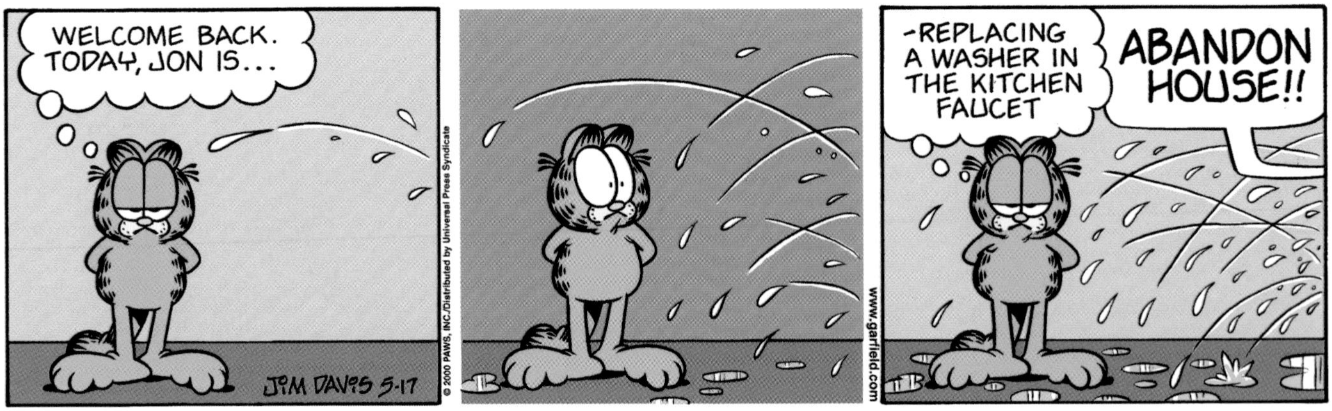
WELCOME BACK. TODAY, JON IS...
JIM DAVIS 5-17
© 2000 PAWS, INC./Distributed by Universal Press Syndicate
www.garfield.com
-REPLACING A WASHER IN THE KITCHEN FAUCET
ABANDON HOUSE!!

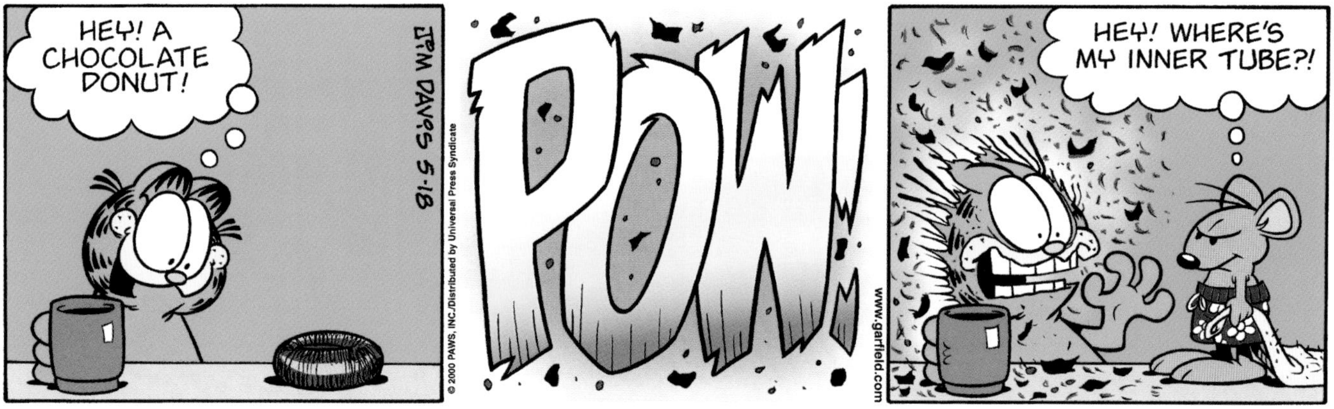
HEY! A CHOCOLATE DONUT!
JIM DAVIS 5-18
© 2000 PAWS, INC./Distributed by Universal Press Syndicate
POW!
www.garfield.com
HEY! WHERE'S MY INNER TUBE?!

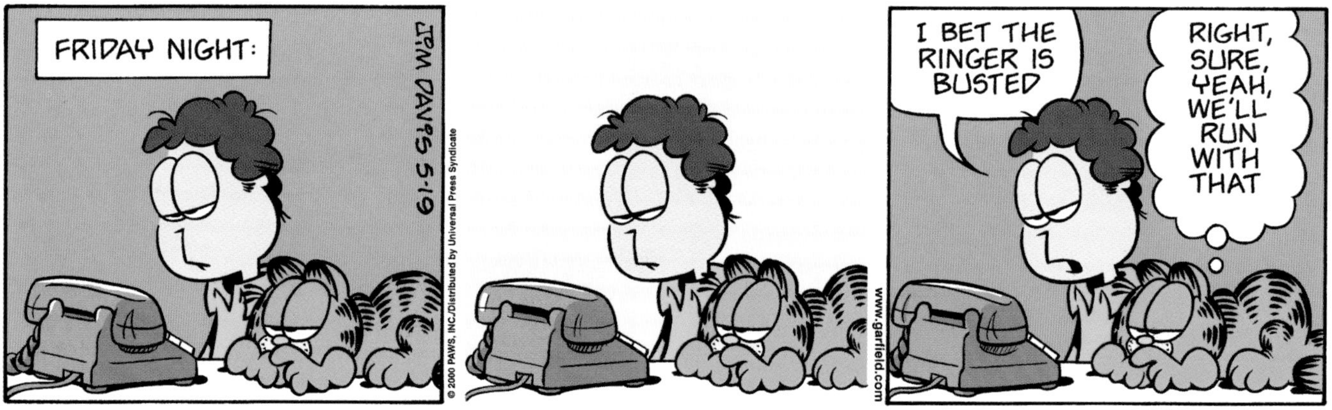
FRIDAY NIGHT:
JIM DAVIS 5-19
© 2000 PAWS, INC./Distributed by Universal Press Syndicate
www.garfield.com
I BET THE RINGER IS BUSTED
RIGHT, SURE, YEAH, WE'LL RUN WITH THAT

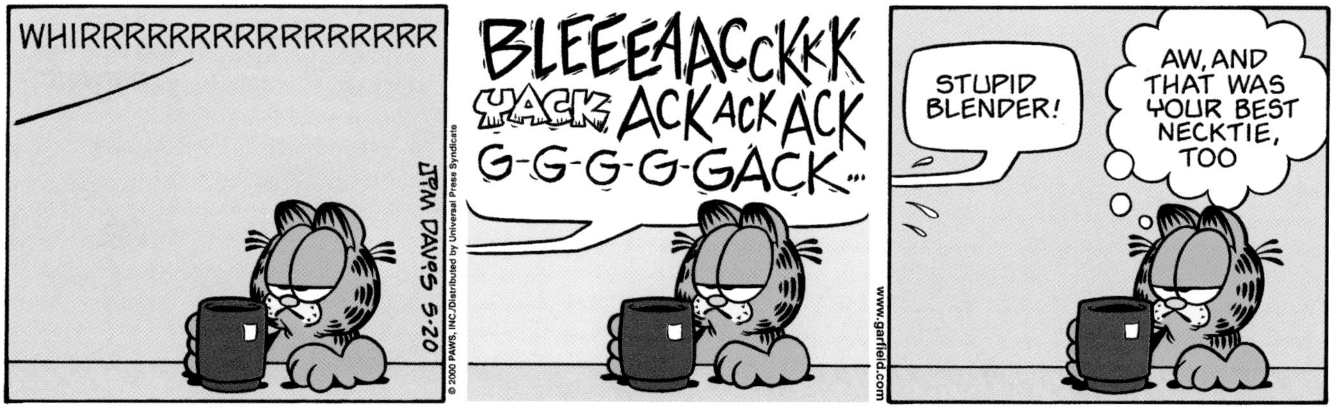
WHIRRRRRRRRRRRRRRRR
JIM DAVIS 5-20
© 2000 PAWS, INC./Distributed by Universal Press Syndicate
BLEEEAACCKKK YACK ACK ACK ACK G-G-G-G-GACK...
www.garfield.com
STUPID BLENDER!
AW, AND THAT WAS YOUR BEST NECKTIE, TOO

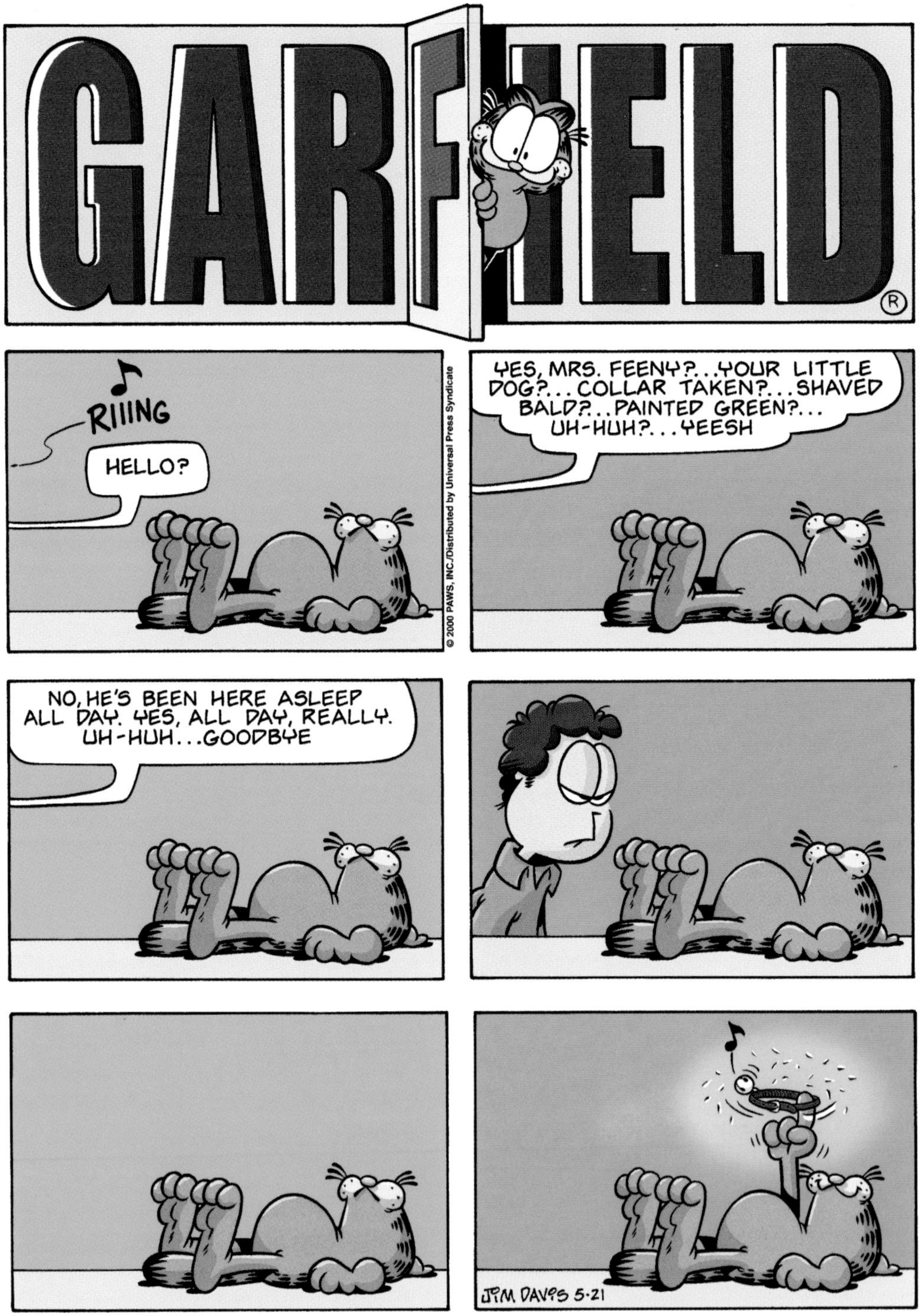
GARFIELD
RIIING
HELLO?
YES, MRS. FEENY?...YOUR LITTLE DOG?... COLLAR TAKEN?...SHAVED BALD?...PAINTED GREEN?... UH-HUH?...YEESH
NO, HE'S BEEN HERE ASLEEP ALL DAY. YES, ALL DAY, REALLY. UH-HUH...GOODBYE
JIM DAVIS 5-21
© 2000 PAWS, INC./Distributed by Universal Press Syndicate

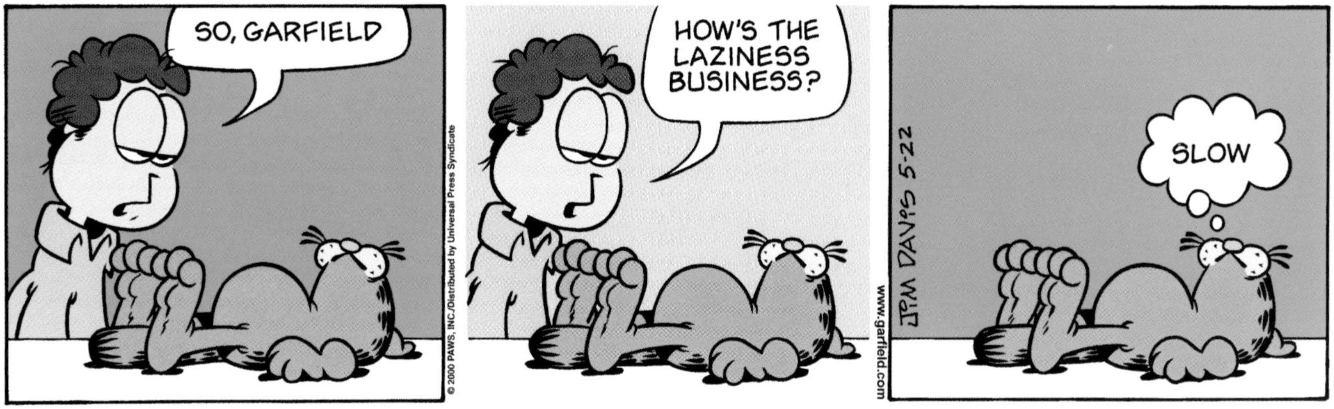
SO, GARFIELD
HOW'S THE LAZINESS BUSINESS?
SLOW
JIM DAVIS 5-22

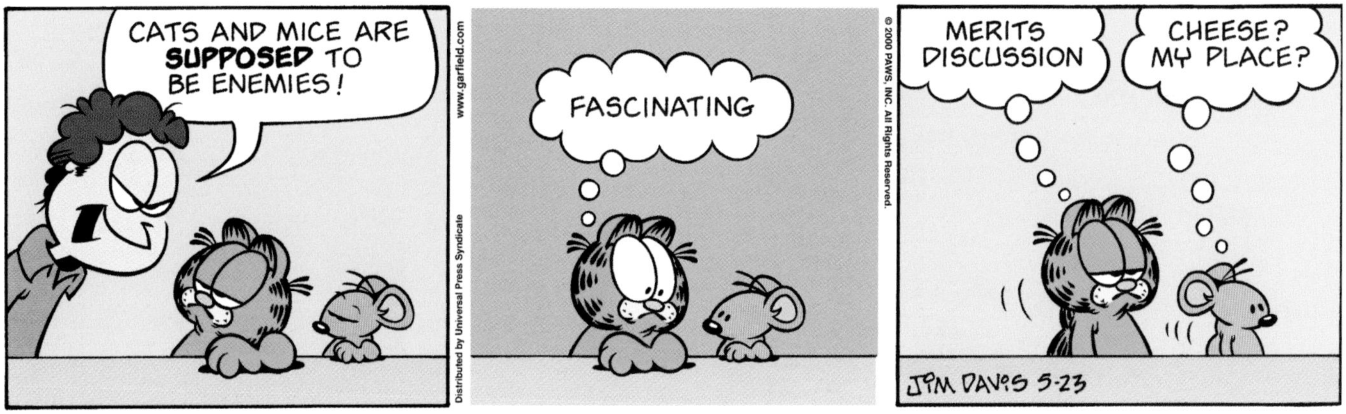
CATS AND MICE ARE **SUPPOSED** TO BE ENEMIES!
FASCINATING
MERITS DISCUSSION
CHEESE? MY PLACE?
JIM DAVIS 5-23

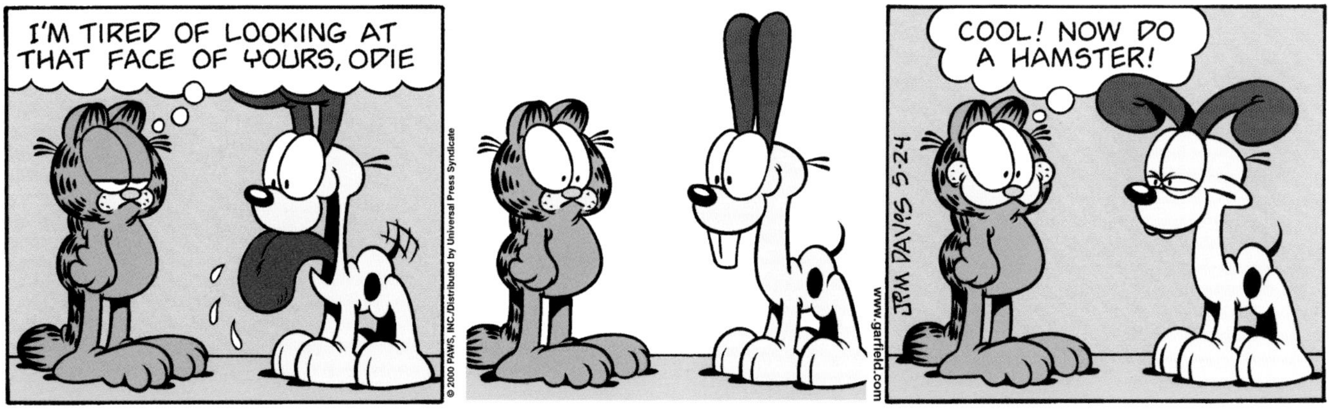
I'M TIRED OF LOOKING AT THAT FACE OF YOURS, ODIE
COOL! NOW DO A HAMSTER!
JIM DAVIS 5-24

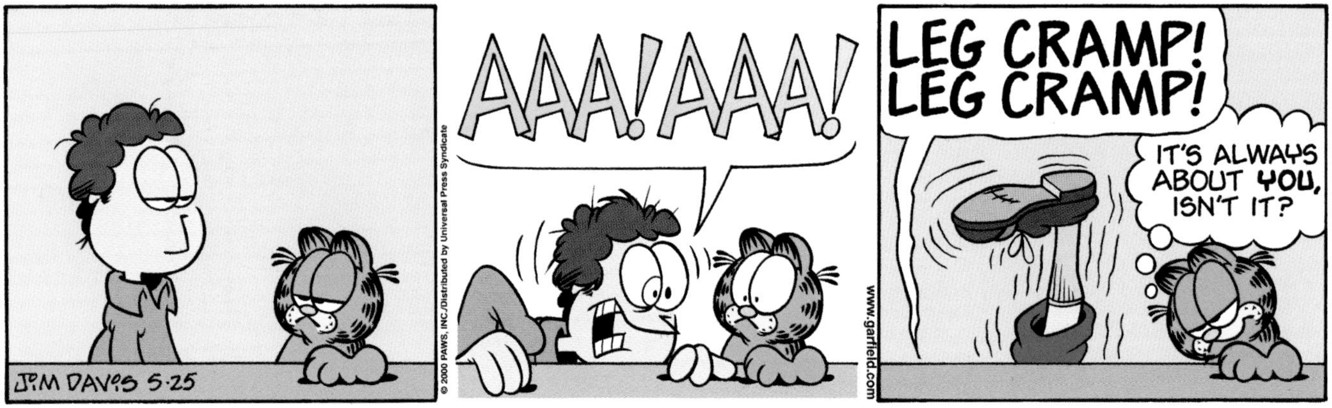
JIM DAVIS 5-25
AAA! AAA!
© 2000 PAWS, INC./Distributed by Universal Press Syndicate
LEG CRAMP! LEG CRAMP!
IT'S ALWAYS ABOUT YOU, ISN'T IT?
www.garfield.com

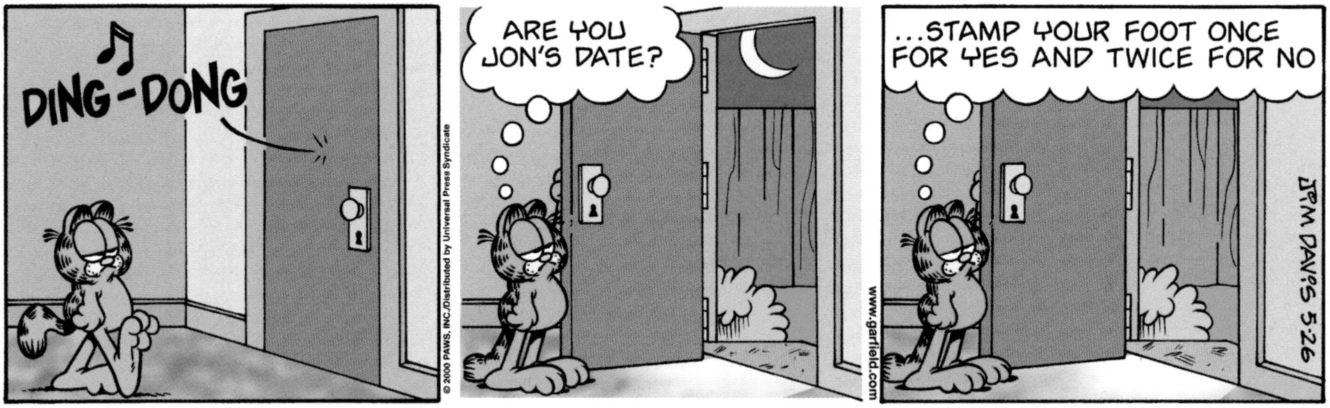
DING-DONG
© 2000 PAWS, INC./Distributed by Universal Press Syndicate
ARE YOU JON'S DATE?
www.garfield.com
...STAMP YOUR FOOT ONCE FOR YES AND TWICE FOR NO
JIM DAVIS 5-26

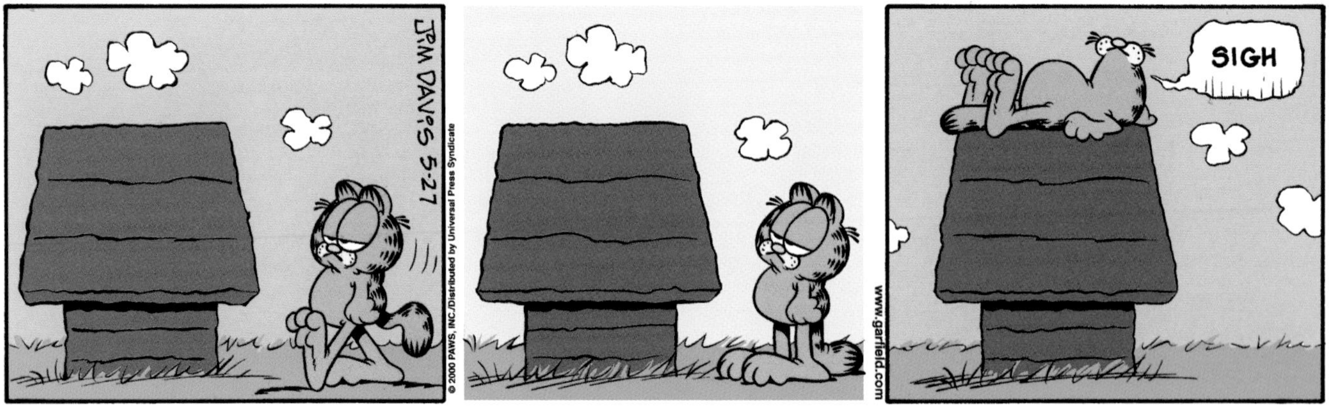
JIM DAVIS 5-27
© 2000 PAWS, INC./Distributed by Universal Press Syndicate
www.garfield.com
SIGH

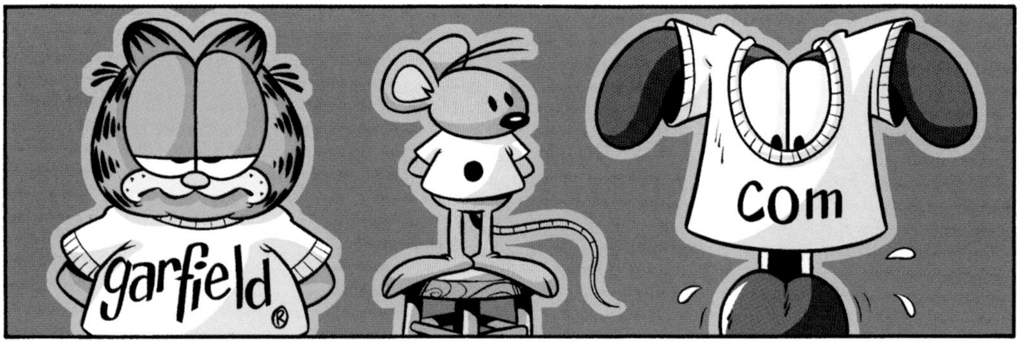
garfield®
com

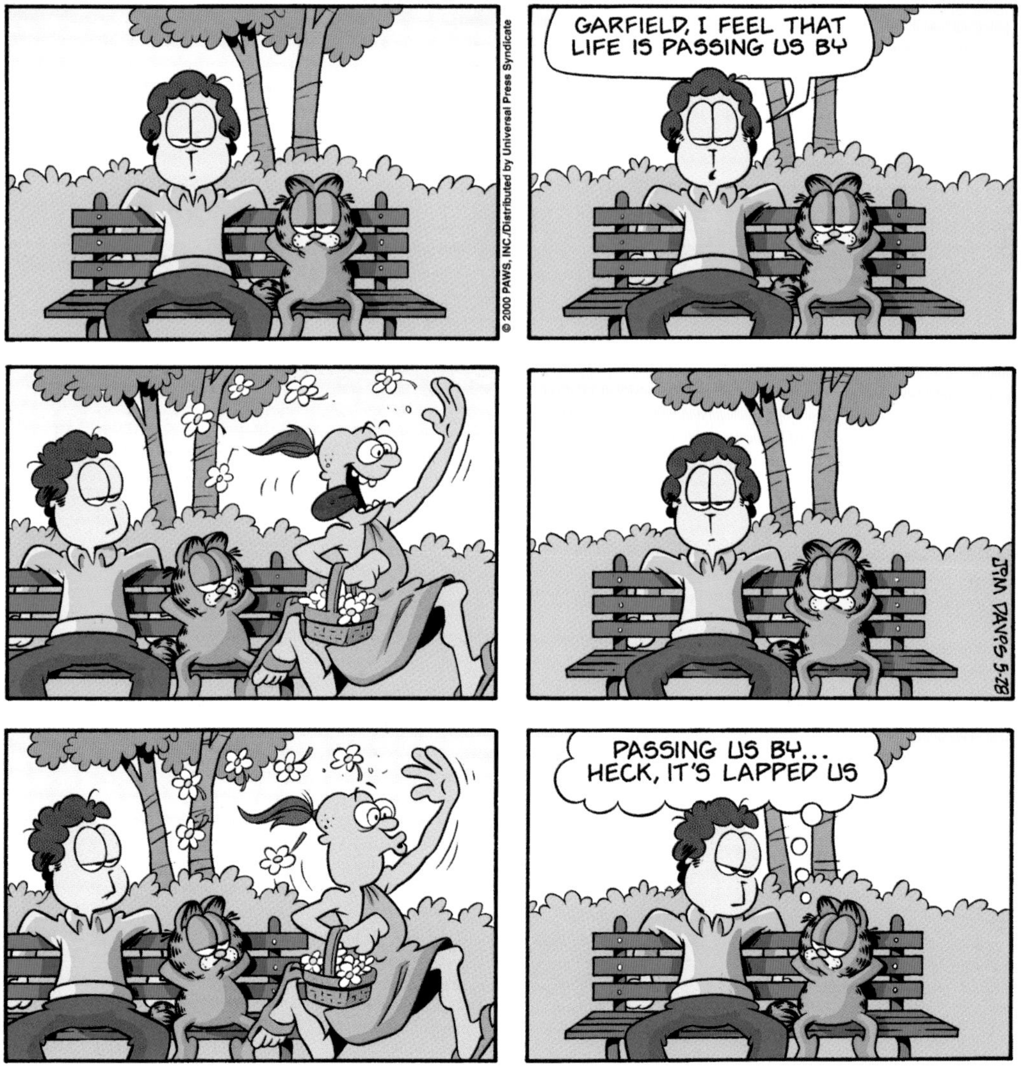
© 2000 PAWS, INC./Distributed by Universal Press Syndicate
GARFIELD, I FEEL THAT LIFE IS PASSING US BY
JIM DAVIS 5-28
PASSING US BY... HECK, IT'S LAPPED US

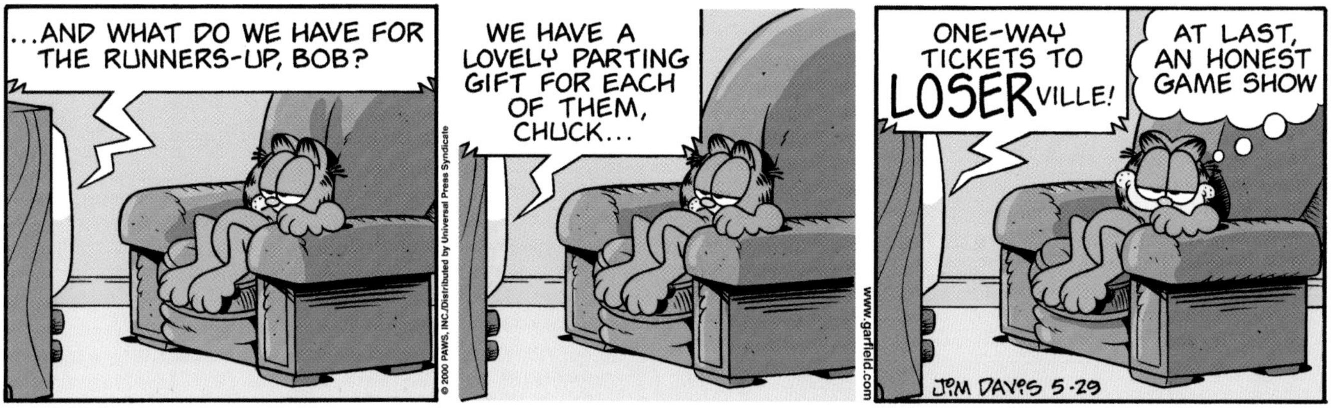
...AND WHAT DO WE HAVE FOR THE RUNNERS-UP, BOB?
WE HAVE A LOVELY PARTING GIFT FOR EACH OF THEM, CHUCK...
ONE-WAY TICKETS TO LOSERVILLE!
AT LAST, AN HONEST GAME SHOW
© 2000 PAWS, INC./Distributed by Universal Press Syndicate
www.garfield.com
JIM DAVIS 5-29

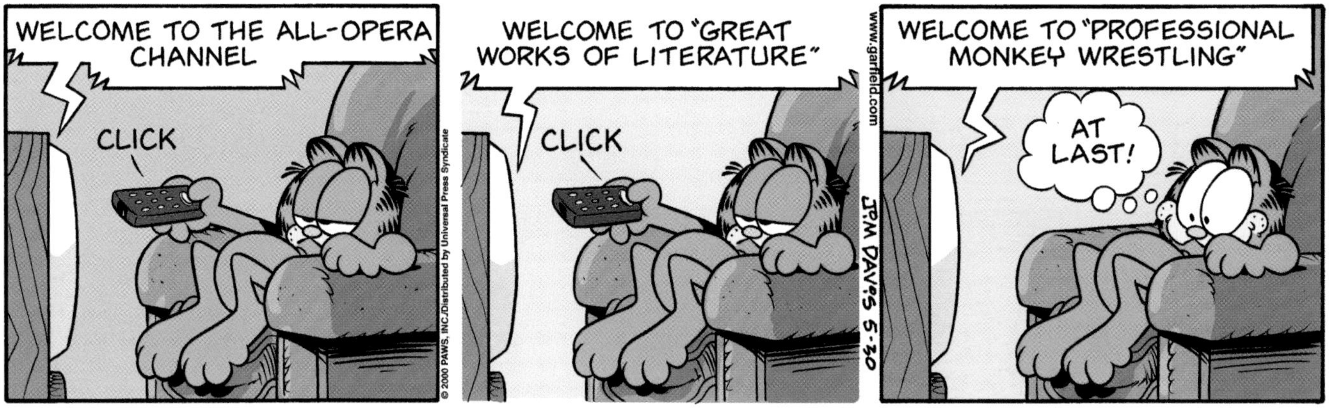
WELCOME TO THE ALL-OPERA CHANNEL
CLICK
WELCOME TO "GREAT WORKS OF LITERATURE"
CLICK
WELCOME TO "PROFESSIONAL MONKEY WRESTLING"
AT LAST!
© 2000 PAWS, INC./Distributed by Universal Press Syndicate
www.garfield.com
JIM DAVIS 5-30

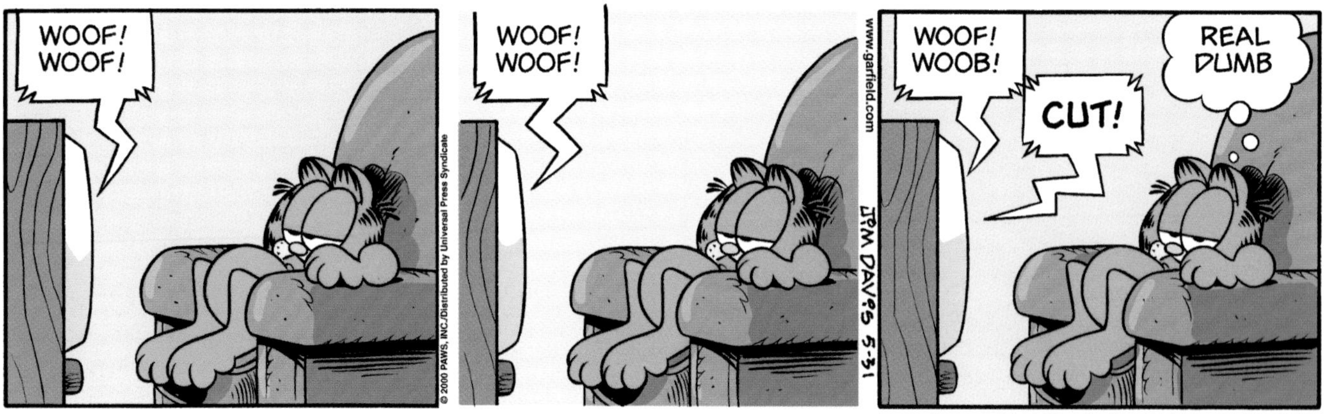
WOOF! WOOF!
WOOF! WOOF!
WOOF! WOOB!
CUT!
REAL DUMB
© 2000 PAWS, INC./Distributed by Universal Press Syndicate
www.garfield.com
JIM DAVIS 5-31

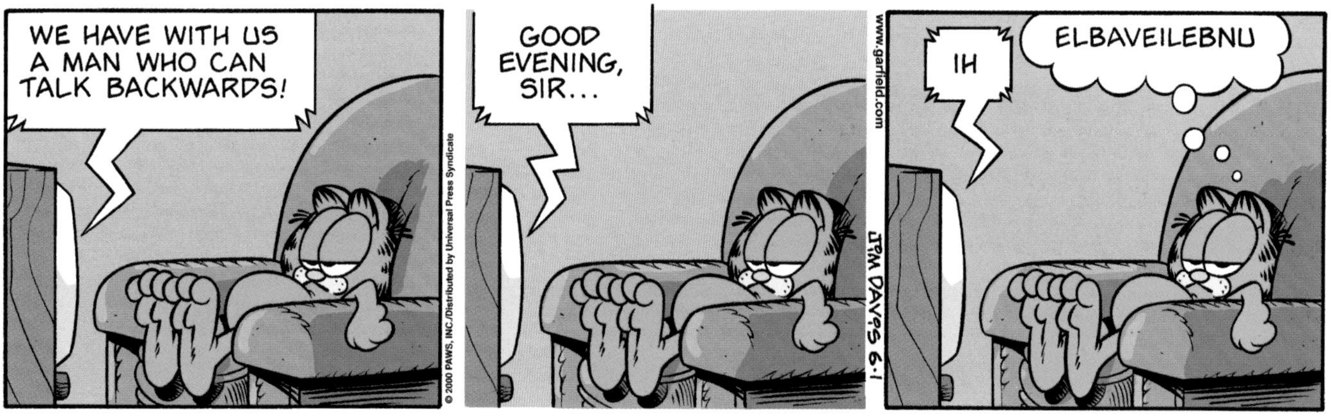
WE HAVE WITH US A MAN WHO CAN TALK BACKWARDS!
© 2000 PAWS, INC./Distributed by Universal Press Syndicate
GOOD EVENING, SIR...
www.garfield.com
JIM DAVIS 6-1
IH
ELBAVEILEBNU

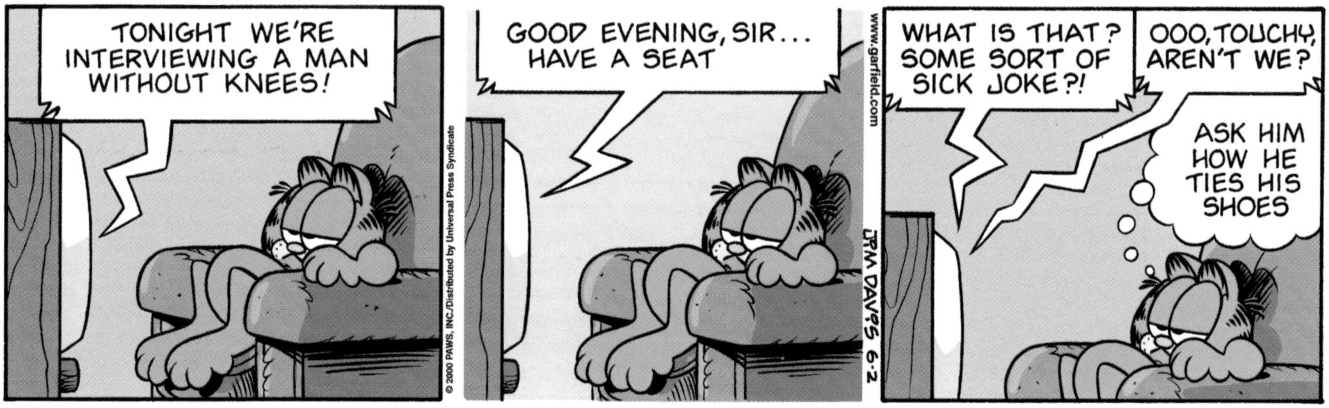
TONIGHT WE'RE INTERVIEWING A MAN WITHOUT KNEES!
© 2000 PAWS, INC./Distributed by Universal Press Syndicate
GOOD EVENING, SIR... HAVE A SEAT
www.garfield.com
JIM DAVIS 6-2
WHAT IS THAT? SOME SORT OF SICK JOKE?!
OOO, TOUCHY, AREN'T WE?
ASK HIM HOW HE TIES HIS SHOES

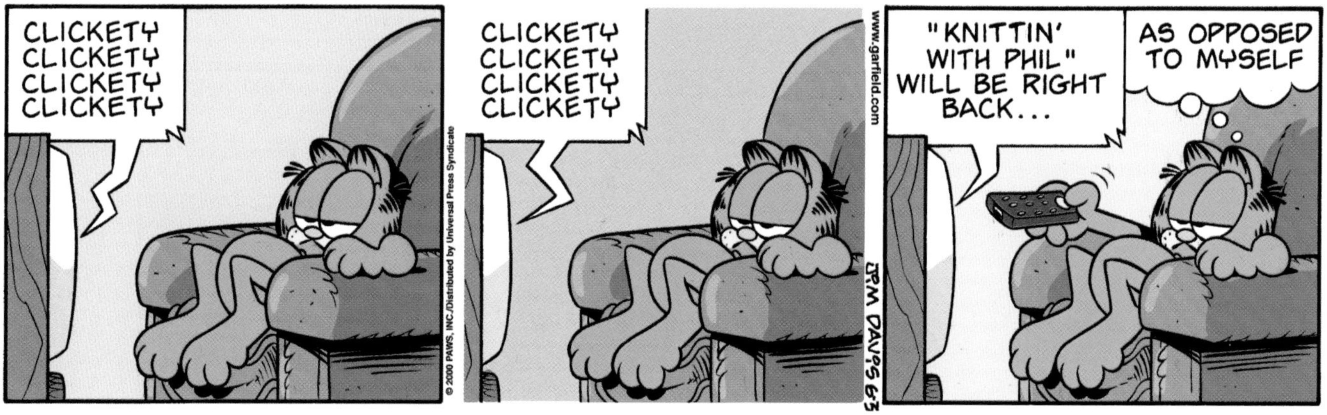
CLICKETY CLICKETY CLICKETY CLICKETY
© 2000 PAWS, INC./Distributed by Universal Press Syndicate
CLICKETY CLICKETY CLICKETY CLICKETY
www.garfield.com
JIM DAVIS 6-3
"KNITTIN' WITH PHIL" WILL BE RIGHT BACK...
AS OPPOSED TO MYSELF

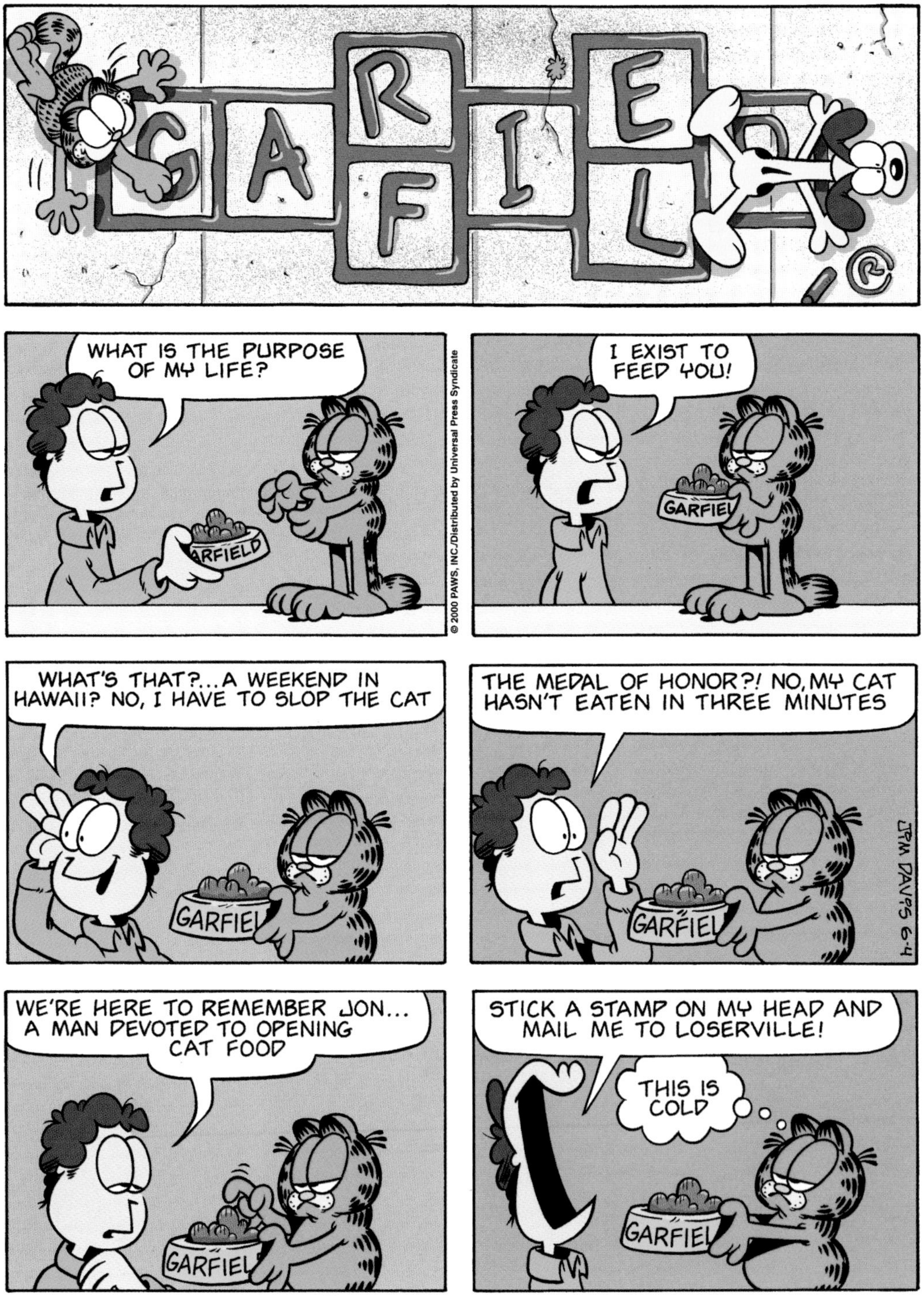
GARFIELD ®
WHAT IS THE PURPOSE OF MY LIFE?
GARFIELD
© 2000 PAWS, INC./Distributed by Universal Press Syndicate
I EXIST TO FEED YOU!
GARFIEL
WHAT'S THAT?...A WEEKEND IN HAWAII? NO, I HAVE TO SLOP THE CAT
GARFIEL
THE MEDAL OF HONOR?! NO, MY CAT HASN'T EATEN IN THREE MINUTES
GARFIEL
JPM DAVPS 6-4
WE'RE HERE TO REMEMBER JON... A MAN DEVOTED TO OPENING CAT FOOD
GARFIEL
STICK A STAMP ON MY HEAD AND MAIL ME TO LOSERVILLE!
THIS IS COLD
GARFIEL

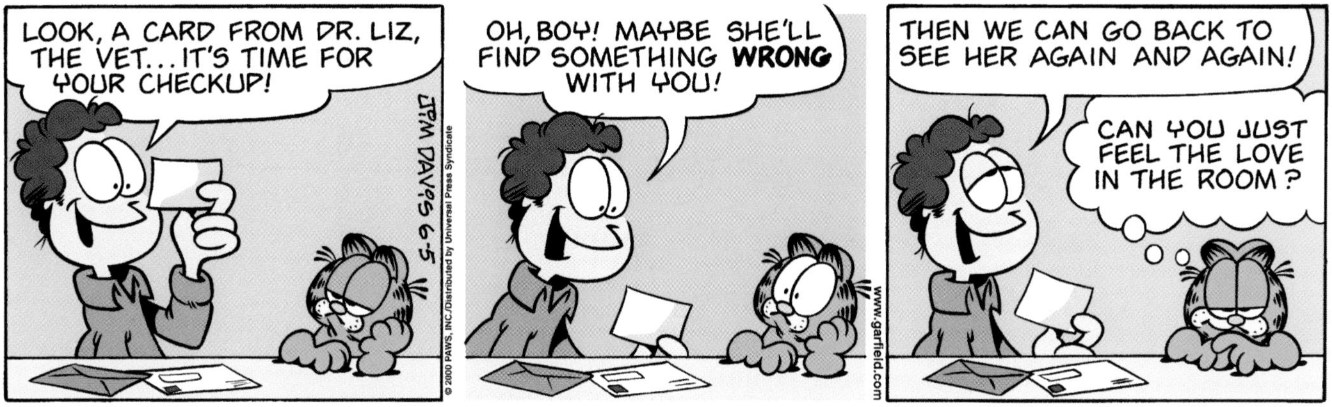
LOOK, A CARD FROM DR. LIZ, THE VET... IT'S TIME FOR YOUR CHECKUP!
JPM DAVIS 6-5
© 2000 PAWS, INC./Distributed by Universal Press Syndicate
OH, BOY! MAYBE SHE'LL FIND SOMETHING **WRONG** WITH YOU!
www.garfield.com
THEN WE CAN GO BACK TO SEE HER AGAIN AND AGAIN!
CAN YOU JUST FEEL THE LOVE IN THE ROOM?

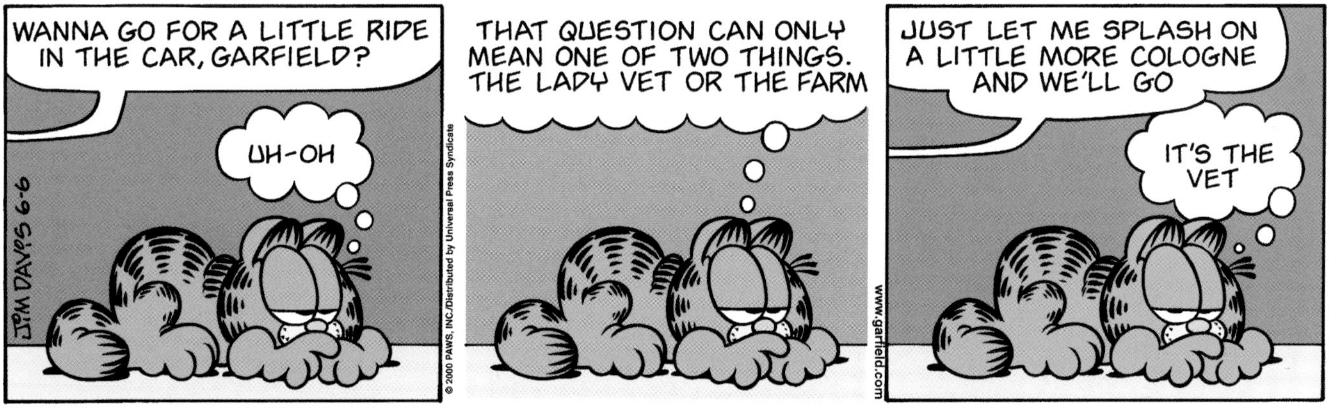
WANNA GO FOR A LITTLE RIDE IN THE CAR, GARFIELD?
UH-OH
JPM DAVIS 6-6
© 2000 PAWS, INC./Distributed by Universal Press Syndicate
THAT QUESTION CAN ONLY MEAN ONE OF TWO THINGS. THE LADY VET OR THE FARM
www.garfield.com
JUST LET ME SPLASH ON A LITTLE MORE COLOGNE AND WE'LL GO
IT'S THE VET

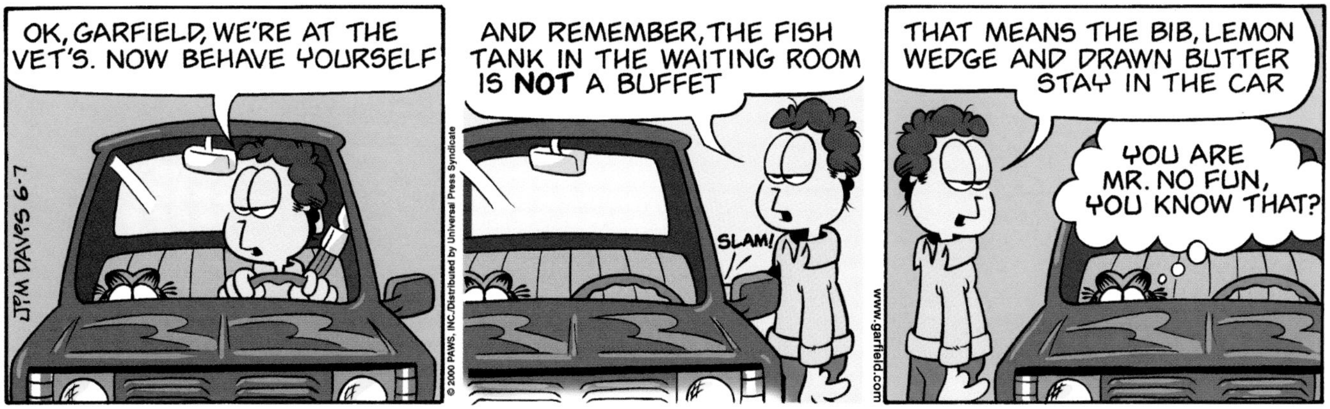
OK, GARFIELD, WE'RE AT THE VET'S. NOW BEHAVE YOURSELF
JPM DAVIS 6-7
© 2000 PAWS, INC./Distributed by Universal Press Syndicate
AND REMEMBER, THE FISH TANK IN THE WAITING ROOM IS **NOT** A BUFFET
SLAM!
www.garfield.com
THAT MEANS THE BIB, LEMON WEDGE AND DRAWN BUTTER STAY IN THE CAR
YOU ARE MR. NO FUN, YOU KNOW THAT?

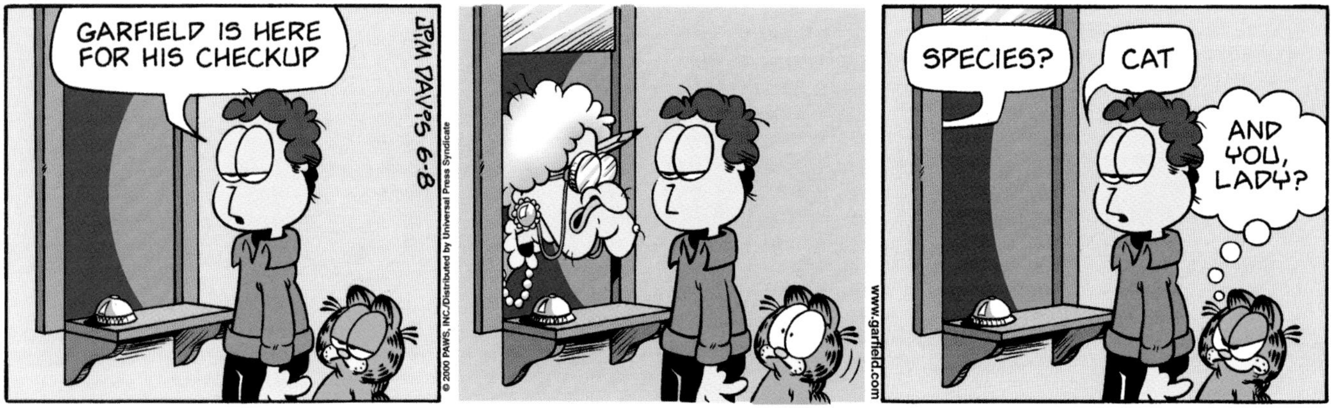
GARFIELD IS HERE FOR HIS CHECKUP
JIM DAVIS 6-8
© 2000 PAWS, INC./Distributed by Universal Press Syndicate
www.garfield.com
SPECIES?
CAT
AND YOU, LADY?

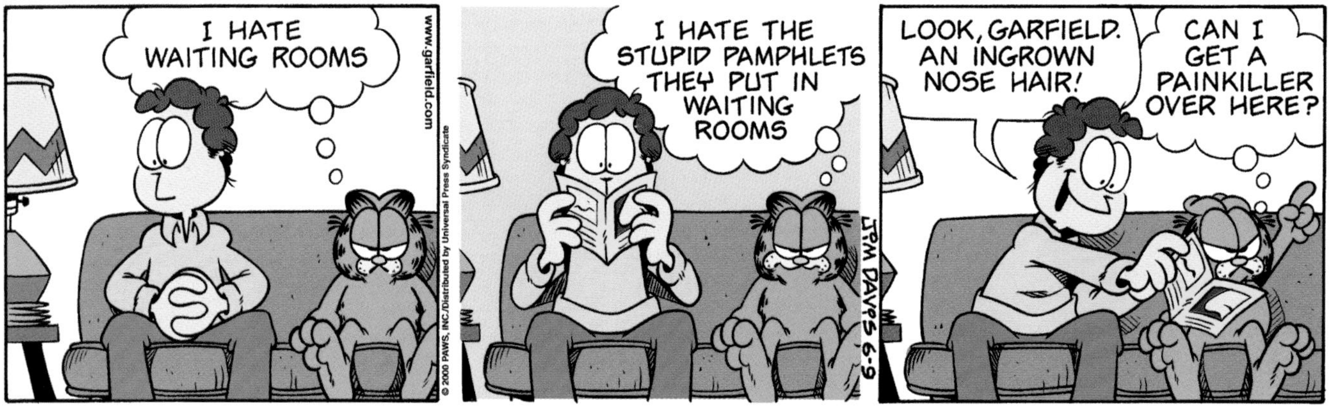
I HATE WAITING ROOMS
www.garfield.com
© 2000 PAWS, INC./Distributed by Universal Press Syndicate
I HATE THE STUPID PAMPHLETS THEY PUT IN WAITING ROOMS
JIM DAVIS 6-9
LOOK, GARFIELD. AN INGROWN NOSE HAIR!
CAN I GET A PAINKILLER OVER HERE?

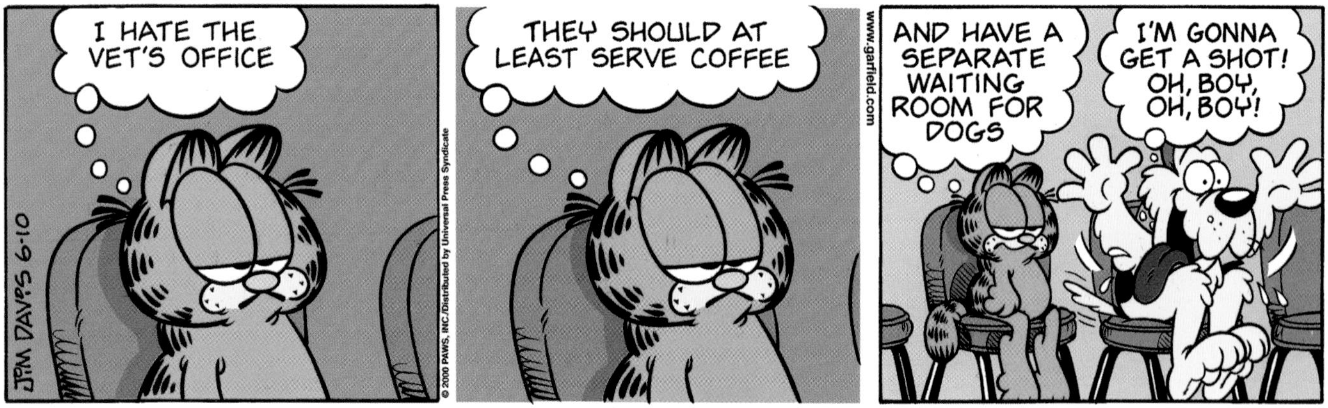
I HATE THE VET'S OFFICE
JIM DAVIS 6-10
© 2000 PAWS, INC./Distributed by Universal Press Syndicate
THEY SHOULD AT LEAST SERVE COFFEE
www.garfield.com
AND HAVE A SEPARATE WAITING ROOM FOR DOGS
I'M GONNA GET A SHOT! OH, BOY, OH, BOY!

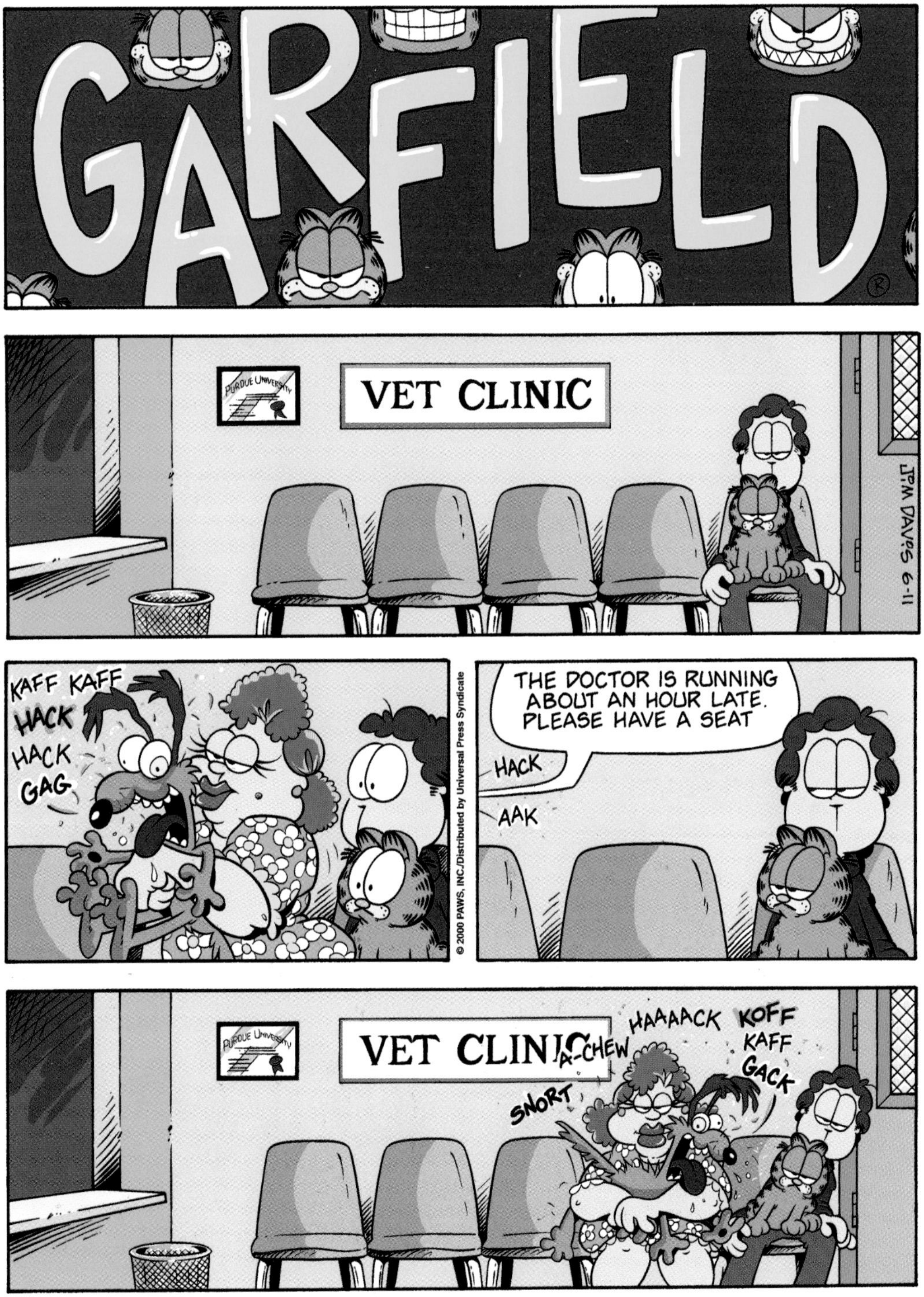
GARFIELD®
VET CLINIC
PURDUE UNIVERSITY
JPM DAVPS 6-11
KAFF KAFF
HACK
HACK
GAG
© 2000 PAWS, INC./Distributed by Universal Press Syndicate
THE DOCTOR IS RUNNING ABOUT AN HOUR LATE. PLEASE HAVE A SEAT
HACK
AAK
VET CLINIC
A-CHEW
HAAAACK
KOFF
KAFF
GACK
SNORT

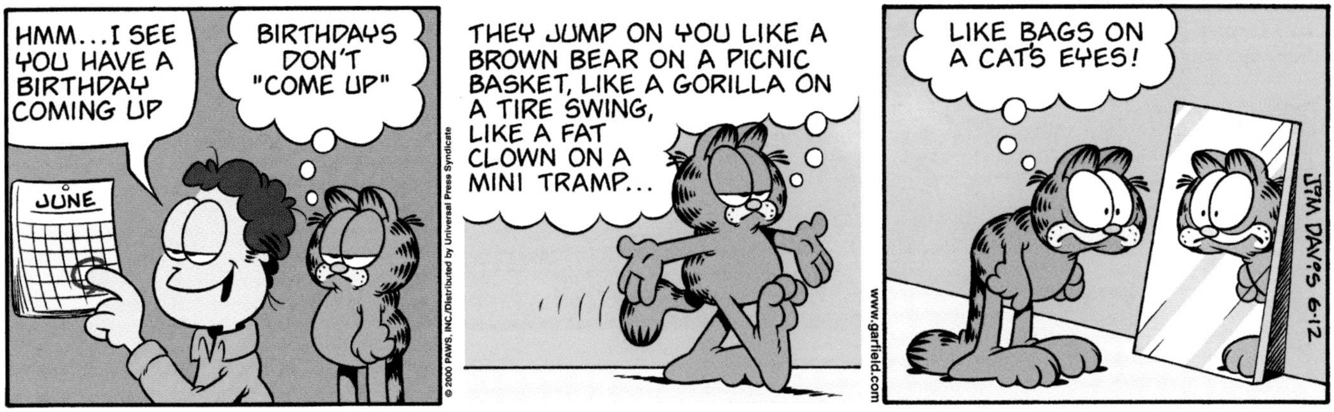
HMM...I SEE YOU HAVE A BIRTHDAY COMING UP
JUNE
BIRTHDAYS DON'T "COME UP"
© 2000 PAWS, INC./Distributed by Universal Press Syndicate
THEY JUMP ON YOU LIKE A BROWN BEAR ON A PICNIC BASKET, LIKE A GORILLA ON A TIRE SWING, LIKE A FAT CLOWN ON A MINI TRAMP...
www.garfield.com
LIKE BAGS ON A CAT'S EYES!
JIM DAVIS 6-12

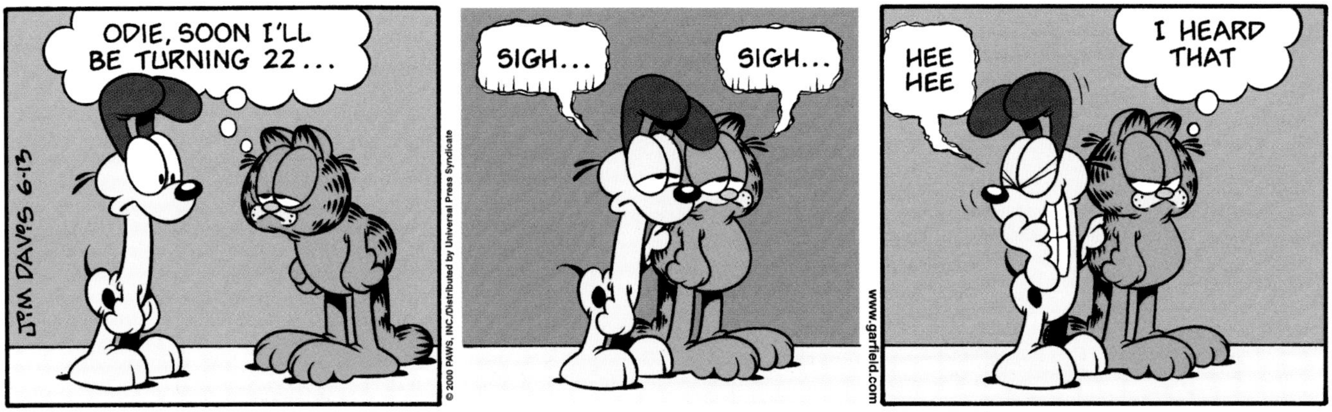
ODIE, SOON I'LL BE TURNING 22...
JIM DAVIS 6-13
© 2000 PAWS, INC./Distributed by Universal Press Syndicate
SIGH...
SIGH...
www.garfield.com
HEE HEE
I HEARD THAT

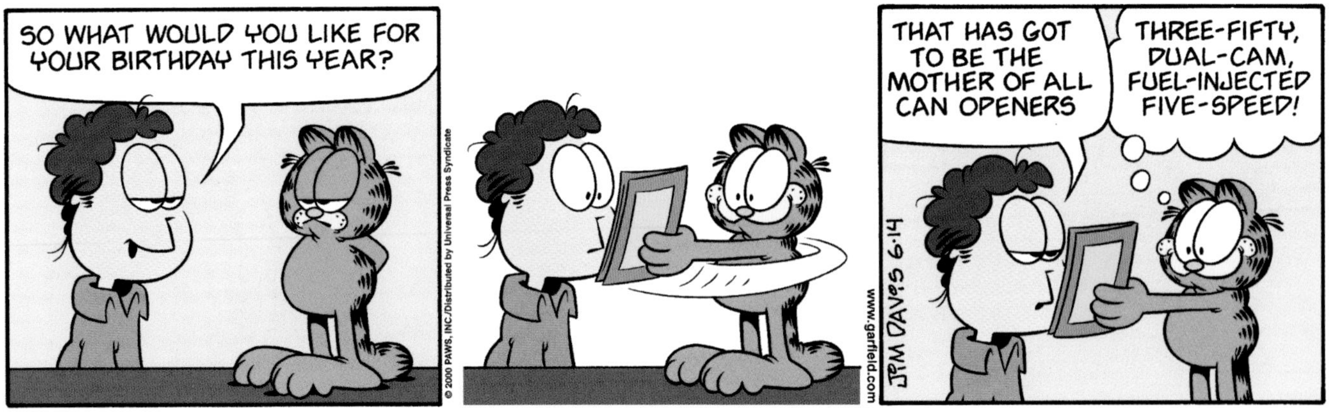
SO WHAT WOULD YOU LIKE FOR YOUR BIRTHDAY THIS YEAR?
© 2000 PAWS, INC./Distributed by Universal Press Syndicate
www.garfield.com
JIM DAVIS 6-14
THAT HAS GOT TO BE THE MOTHER OF ALL CAN OPENERS
THREE-FIFTY, DUAL-CAM, FUEL-INJECTED FIVE-SPEED!

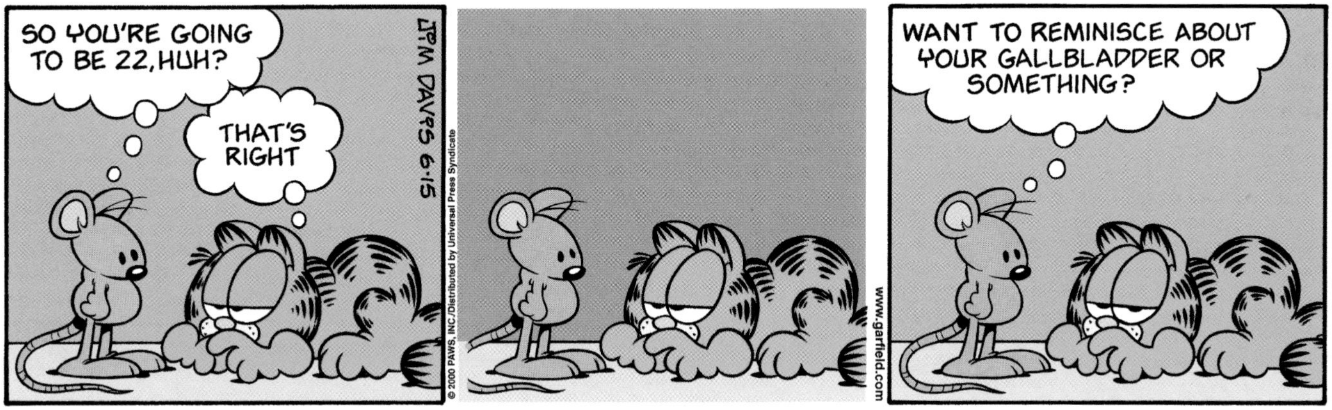
SO YOU'RE GOING TO BE 22, HUH?
THAT'S RIGHT
WANT TO REMINISCE ABOUT YOUR GALLBLADDER OR SOMETHING?
JIM DAVIS 6-15
© 2000 PAWS, INC./Distributed by Universal Press Syndicate
www.garfield.com

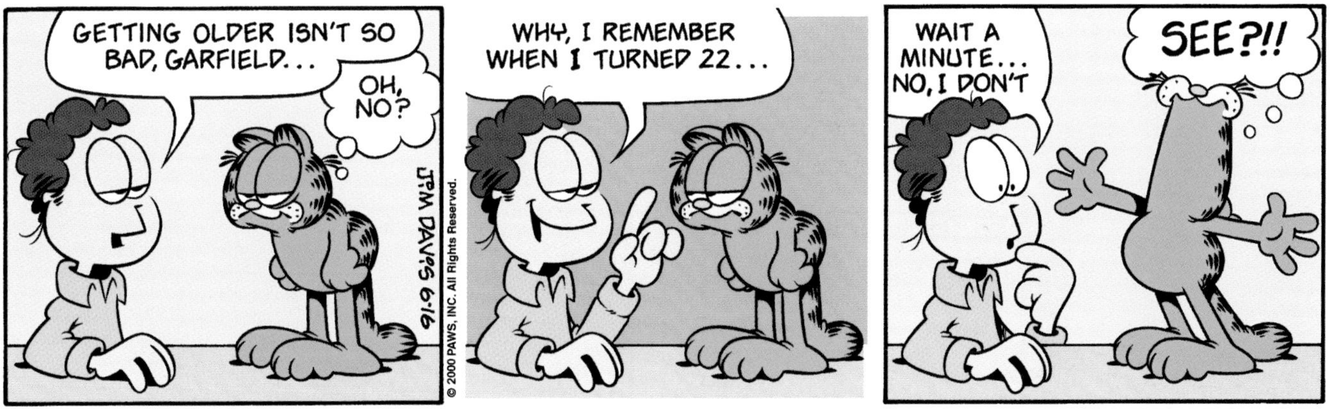
GETTING OLDER ISN'T SO BAD, GARFIELD...
OH, NO?
WHY, I REMEMBER WHEN I TURNED 22...
WAIT A MINUTE... NO, I DON'T
SEE?!!
JIM DAVIS 6-16
© 2000 PAWS, INC. All Rights Reserved.

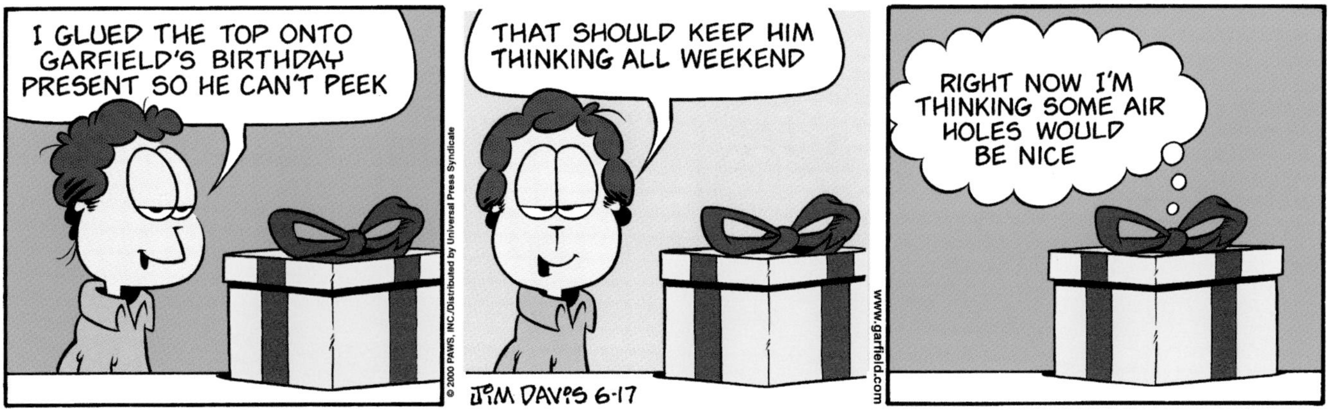
I GLUED THE TOP ONTO GARFIELD'S BIRTHDAY PRESENT SO HE CAN'T PEEK
THAT SHOULD KEEP HIM THINKING ALL WEEKEND
RIGHT NOW I'M THINKING SOME AIR HOLES WOULD BE NICE
JIM DAVIS 6-17
© 2000 PAWS, INC./Distributed by Universal Press Syndicate
www.garfield.com

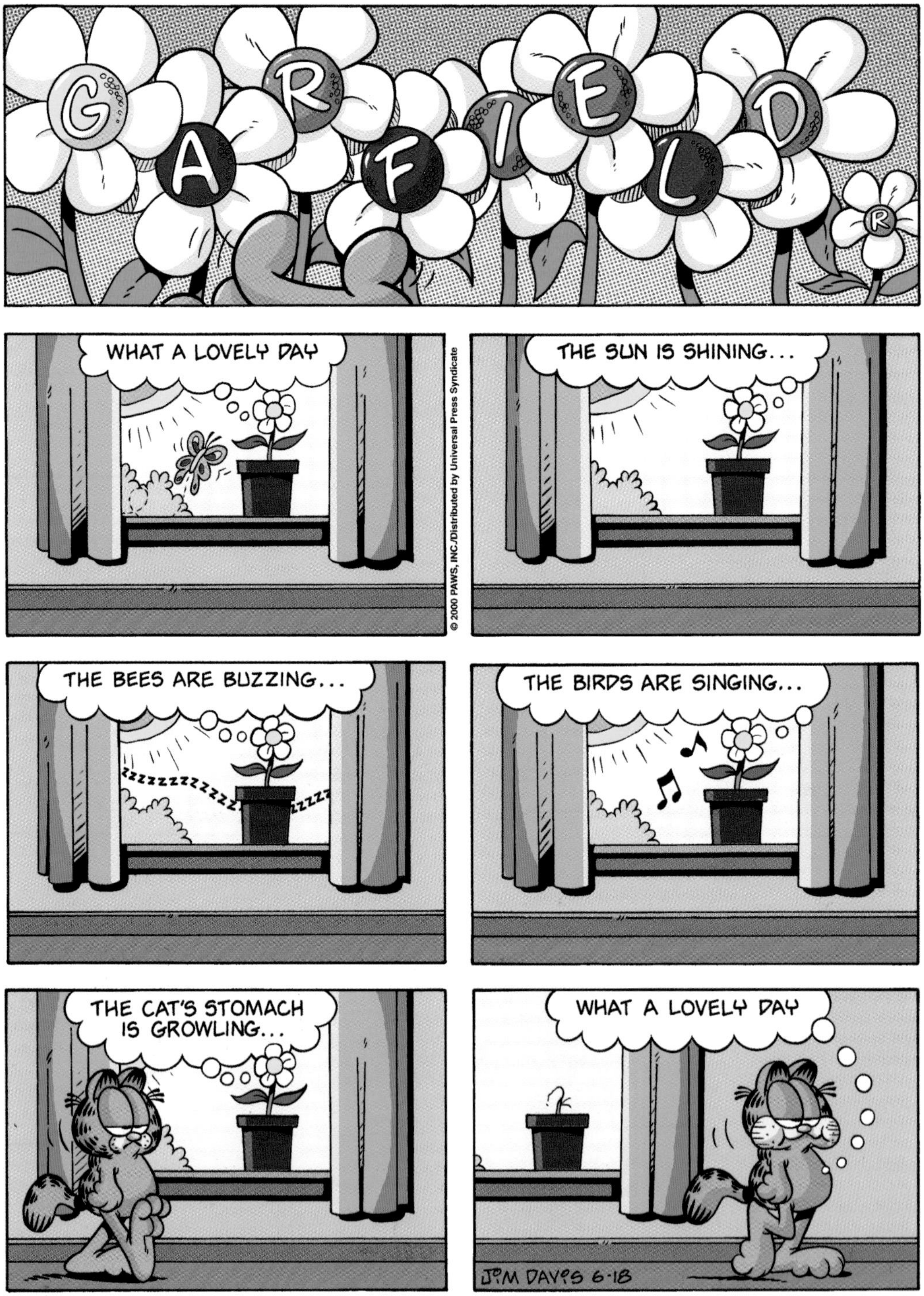
GARFIELD®
WHAT A LOVELY DAY
THE SUN IS SHINING...
THE BEES ARE BUZZING...
THE BIRDS ARE SINGING...
THE CAT'S STOMACH IS GROWLING...
WHAT A LOVELY DAY
JIM DAVIS 6-18
© 2000 PAWS, INC./Distributed by Universal Press Syndicate

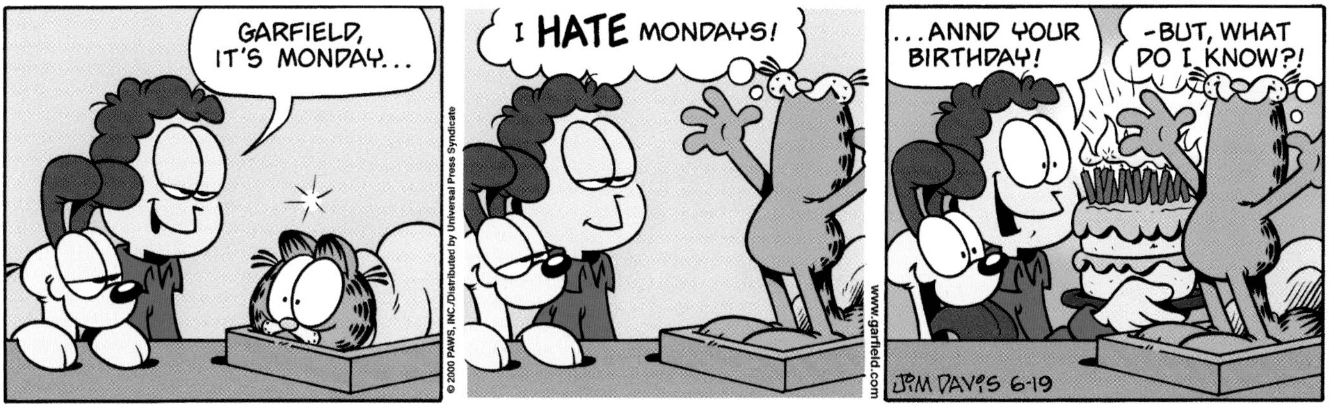
GARFIELD, IT'S MONDAY...
I HATE MONDAYS!
...ANND YOUR BIRTHDAY!
-BUT, WHAT DO I KNOW?!
JIM DAVIS 6-19
© 2000 PAWS, INC./Distributed by Universal Press Syndicate
www.garfield.com

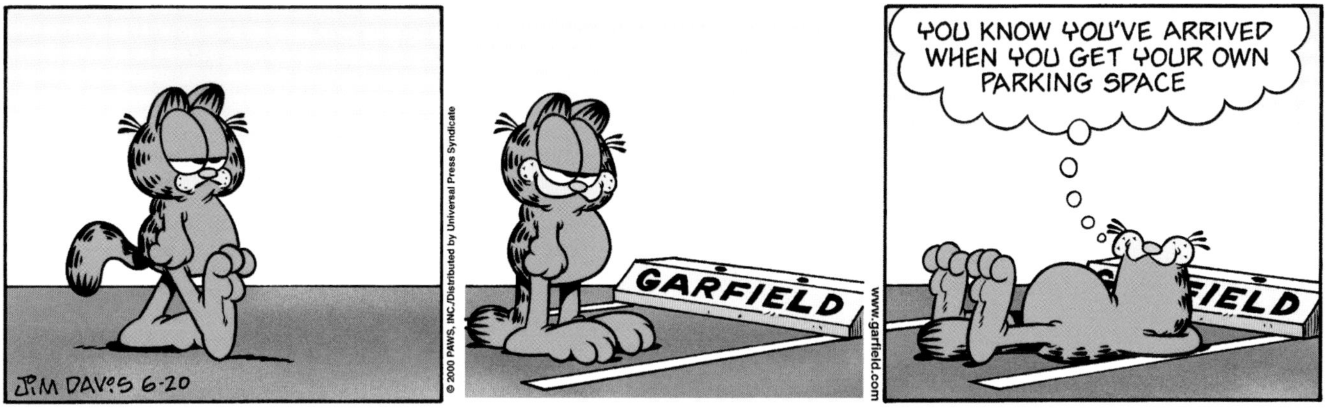
JIM DAVIS 6-20
GARFIELD
YOU KNOW YOU'VE ARRIVED WHEN YOU GET YOUR OWN PARKING SPACE
© 2000 PAWS, INC./Distributed by Universal Press Syndicate
www.garfield.com

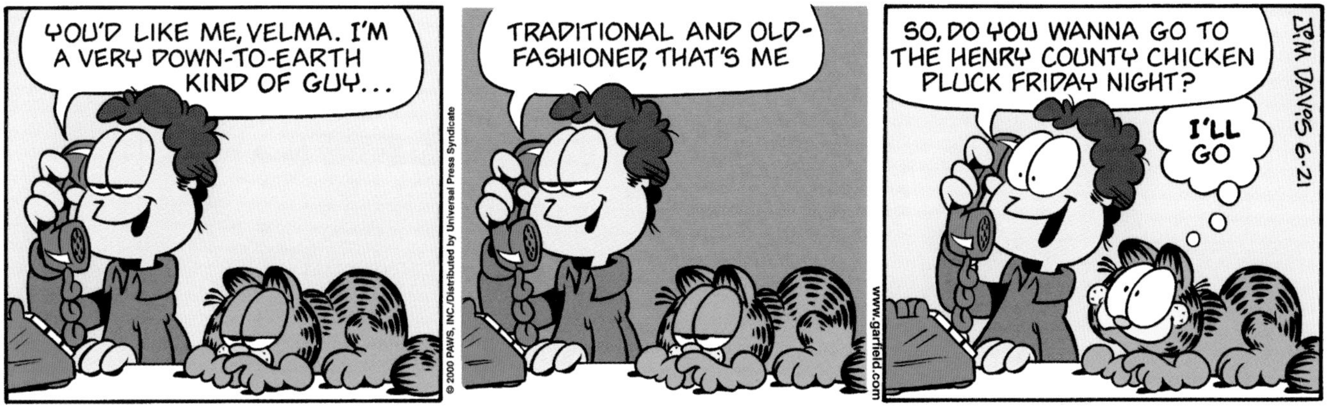
YOU'D LIKE ME, VELMA. I'M A VERY DOWN-TO-EARTH KIND OF GUY...
TRADITIONAL AND OLD-FASHIONED, THAT'S ME
SO, DO YOU WANNA GO TO THE HENRY COUNTY CHICKEN PLUCK FRIDAY NIGHT?
I'LL GO
JIM DAVIS 6-21
© 2000 PAWS, INC./Distributed by Universal Press Syndicate
www.garfield.com

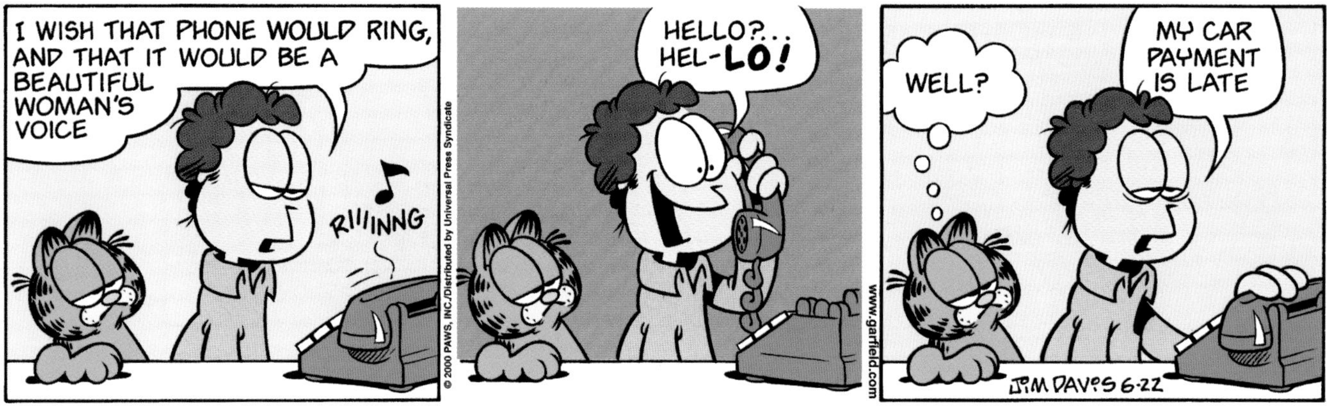
I WISH THAT PHONE WOULD RING, AND THAT IT WOULD BE A BEAUTIFUL WOMAN'S VOICE
RIIIINNG
© 2000 PAWS, INC./Distributed by Universal Press Syndicate
HELLO?... HEL-LO!
www.garfield.com
WELL?
MY CAR PAYMENT IS LATE
JIM DAVIS 6-22

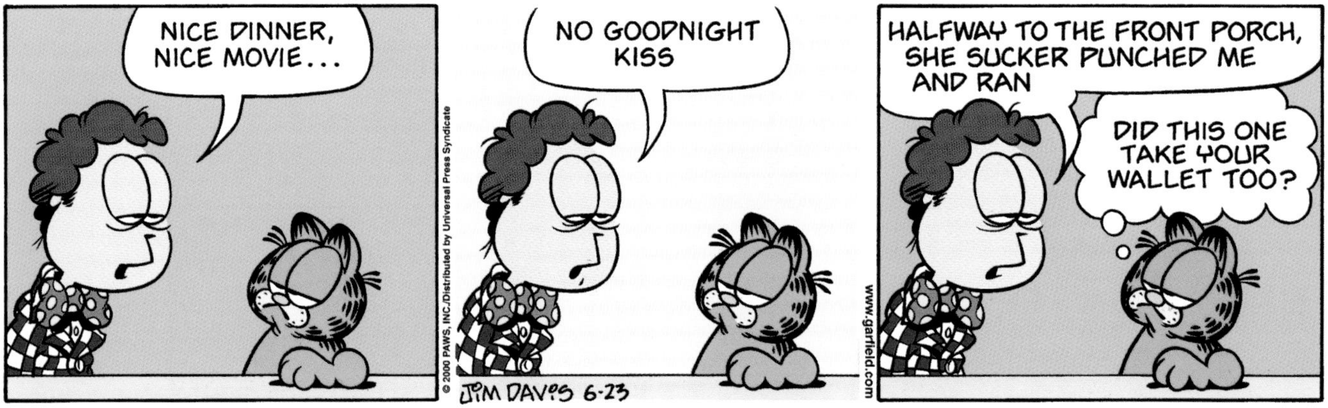
NICE DINNER, NICE MOVIE...
© 2000 PAWS, INC./Distributed by Universal Press Syndicate
JIM DAVIS 6-23
NO GOODNIGHT KISS
www.garfield.com
HALFWAY TO THE FRONT PORCH, SHE SUCKER PUNCHED ME AND RAN
DID THIS ONE TAKE YOUR WALLET TOO?

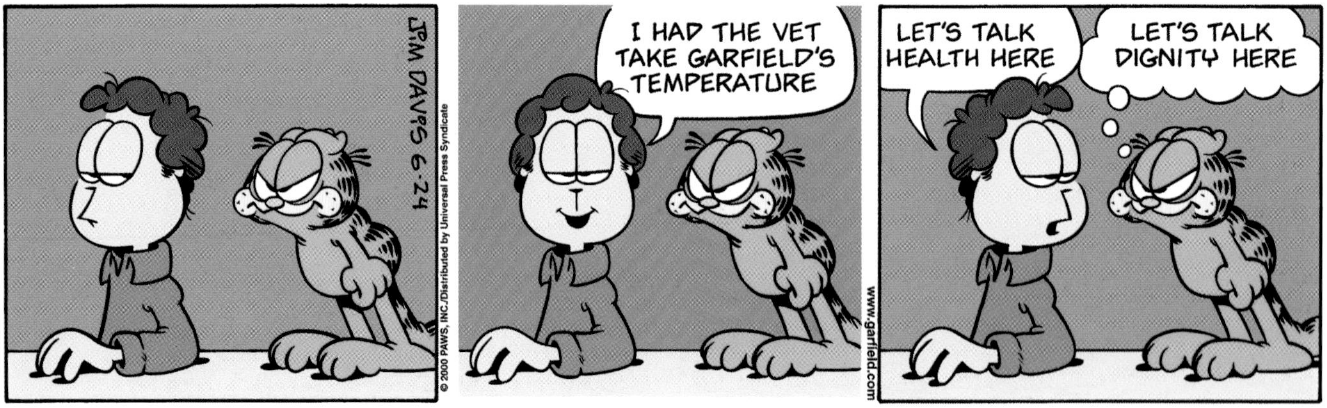
JIM DAVIS 6-24
© 2000 PAWS, INC./Distributed by Universal Press Syndicate
I HAD THE VET TAKE GARFIELD'S TEMPERATURE
www.garfield.com
LET'S TALK HEALTH HERE
LET'S TALK DIGNITY HERE

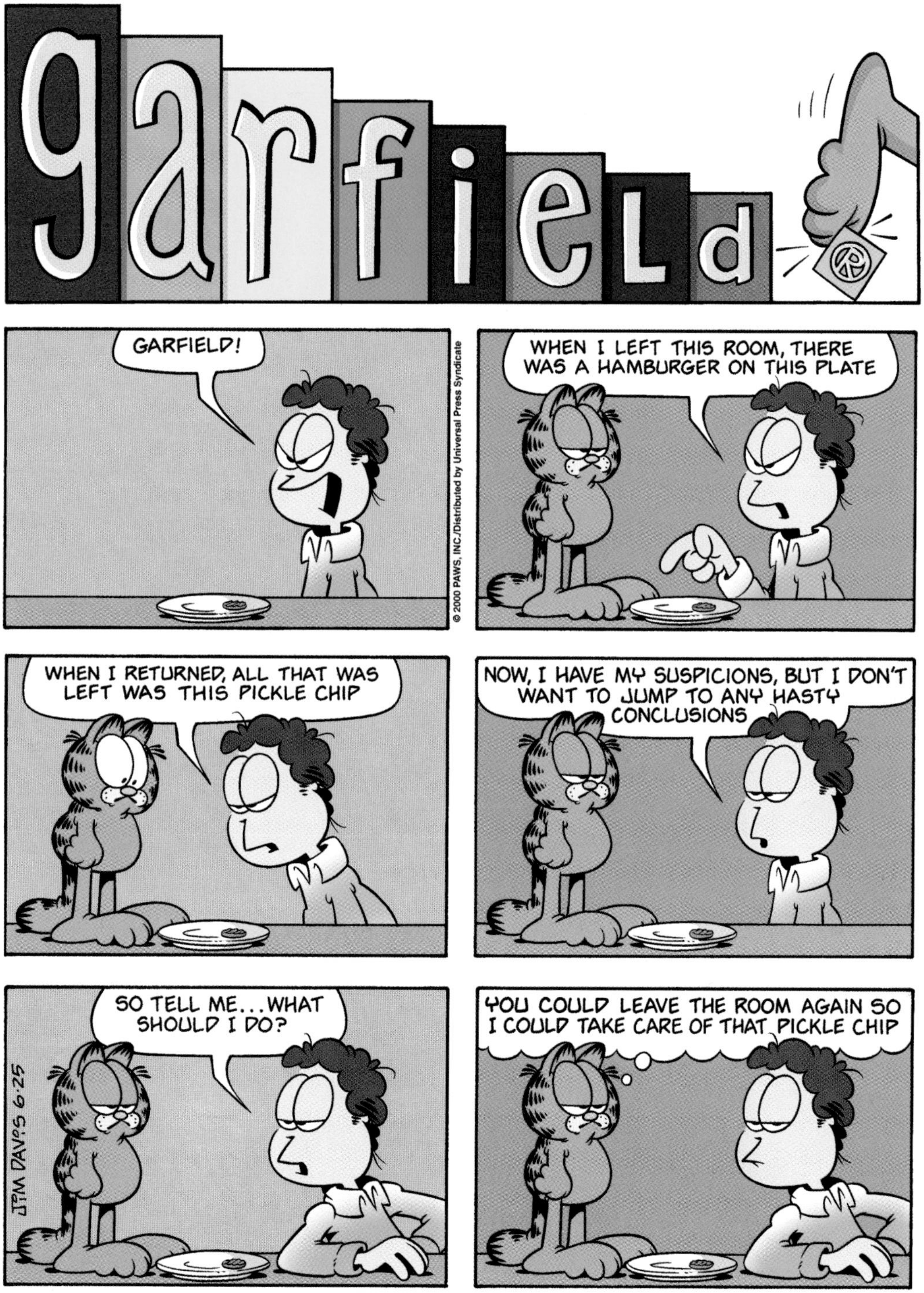
garfield
GARFIELD!
WHEN I LEFT THIS ROOM, THERE WAS A HAMBURGER ON THIS PLATE
WHEN I RETURNED, ALL THAT WAS LEFT WAS THIS PICKLE CHIP
NOW, I HAVE MY SUSPICIONS, BUT I DON'T WANT TO JUMP TO ANY HASTY CONCLUSIONS
SO TELL ME...WHAT SHOULD I DO?
JIM DAVIS 6-25
YOU COULD LEAVE THE ROOM AGAIN SO I COULD TAKE CARE OF THAT PICKLE CHIP

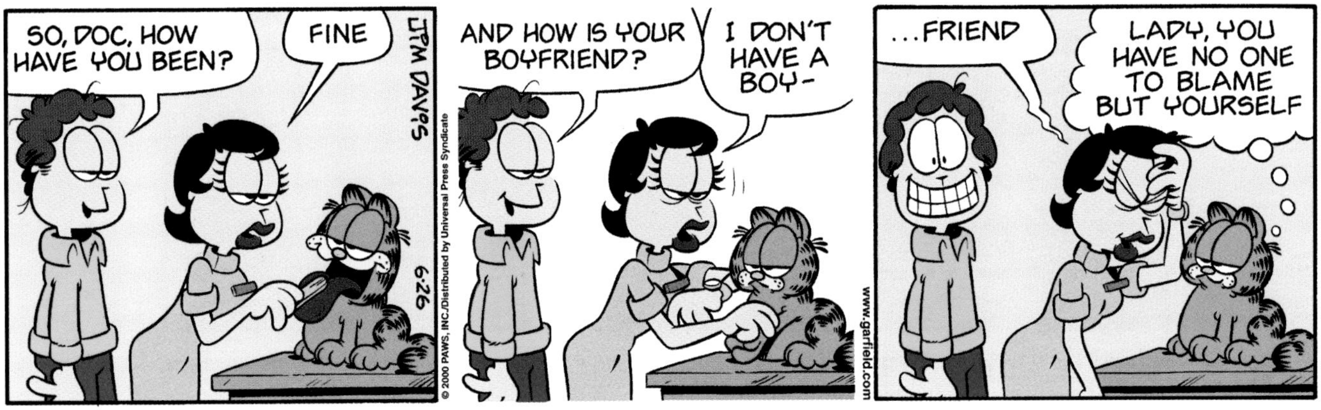
SO, DOC, HOW HAVE YOU BEEN?
FINE
JIM DAVIS 6·26
AND HOW IS YOUR BOYFRIEND?
I DON'T HAVE A BOY-
© 2000 PAWS, INC./Distributed by Universal Press Syndicate
...FRIEND
LADY, YOU HAVE NO ONE TO BLAME BUT YOURSELF
www.garfield.com

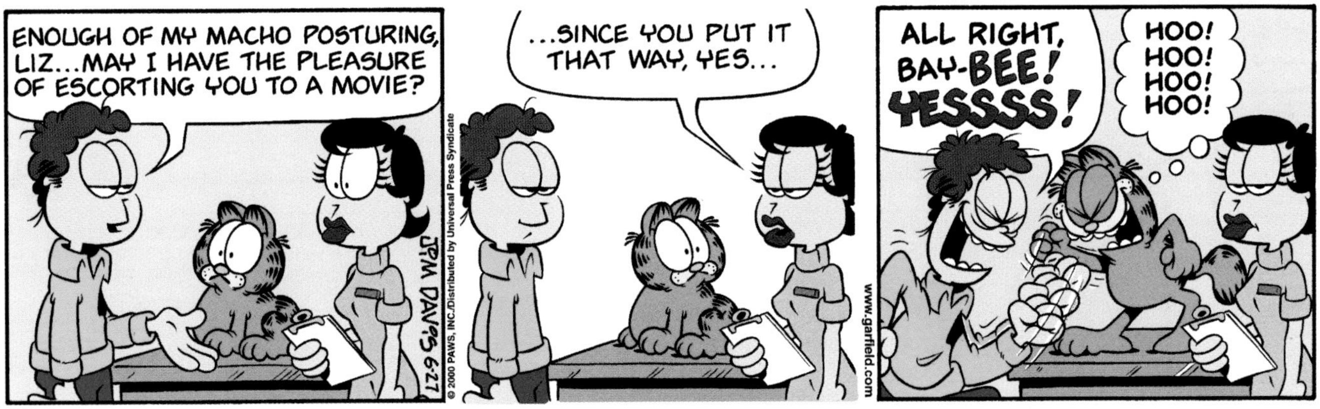
ENOUGH OF MY MACHO POSTURING, LIZ...MAY I HAVE THE PLEASURE OF ESCORTING YOU TO A MOVIE?
JIM DAVIS 6·27
...SINCE YOU PUT IT THAT WAY, YES...
© 2000 PAWS, INC./Distributed by Universal Press Syndicate
ALL RIGHT, BAY-BEE! YESSSS!
HOO! HOO! HOO! HOO!
www.garfield.com

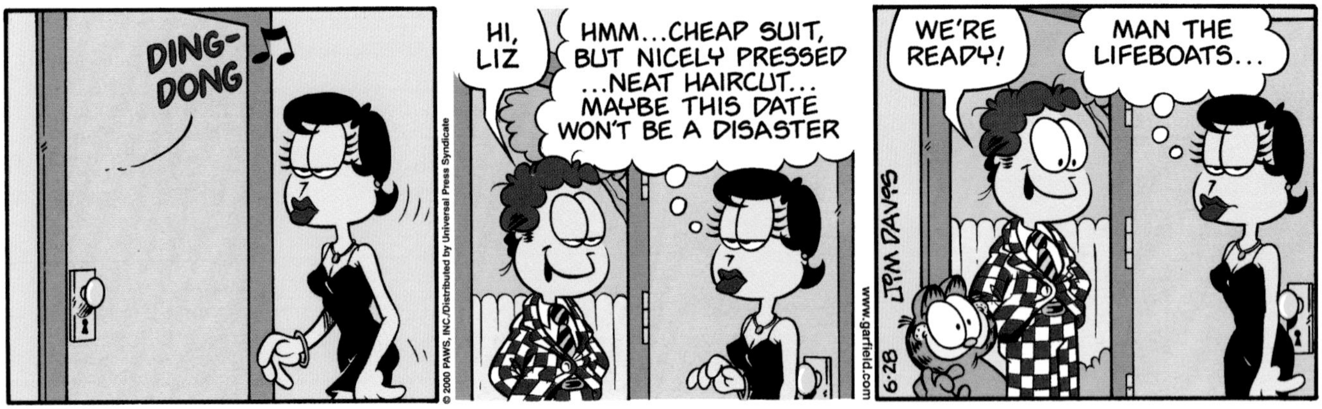
DING-DONG
HI, LIZ
HMM...CHEAP SUIT, BUT NICELY PRESSED ...NEAT HAIRCUT... MAYBE THIS DATE WON'T BE A DISASTER
© 2000 PAWS, INC./Distributed by Universal Press Syndicate
WE'RE READY!
MAN THE LIFEBOATS...
JIM DAVIS 6·28
www.garfield.com

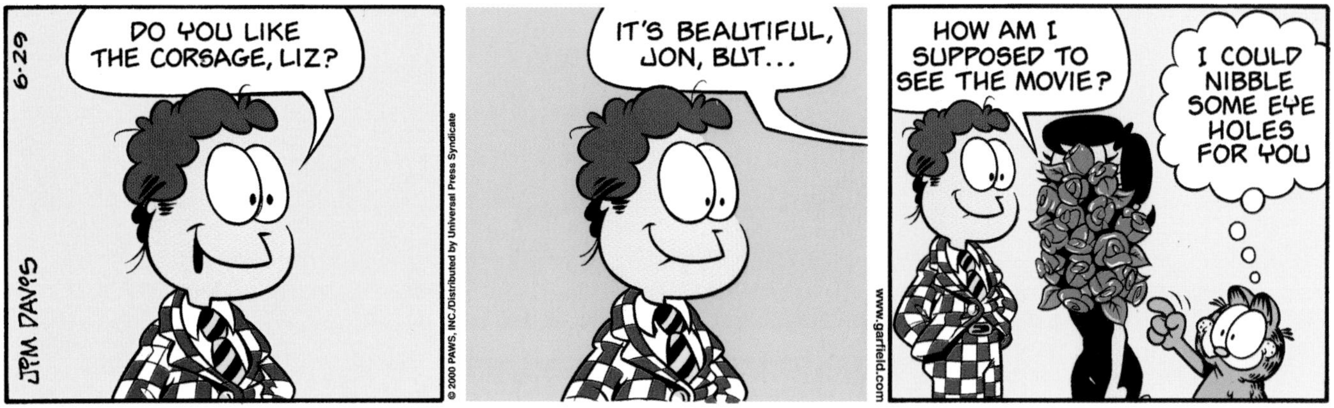
6-29
DO YOU LIKE THE CORSAGE, LIZ?
IT'S BEAUTIFUL, JON, BUT...
HOW AM I SUPPOSED TO SEE THE MOVIE?
I COULD NIBBLE SOME EYE HOLES FOR YOU

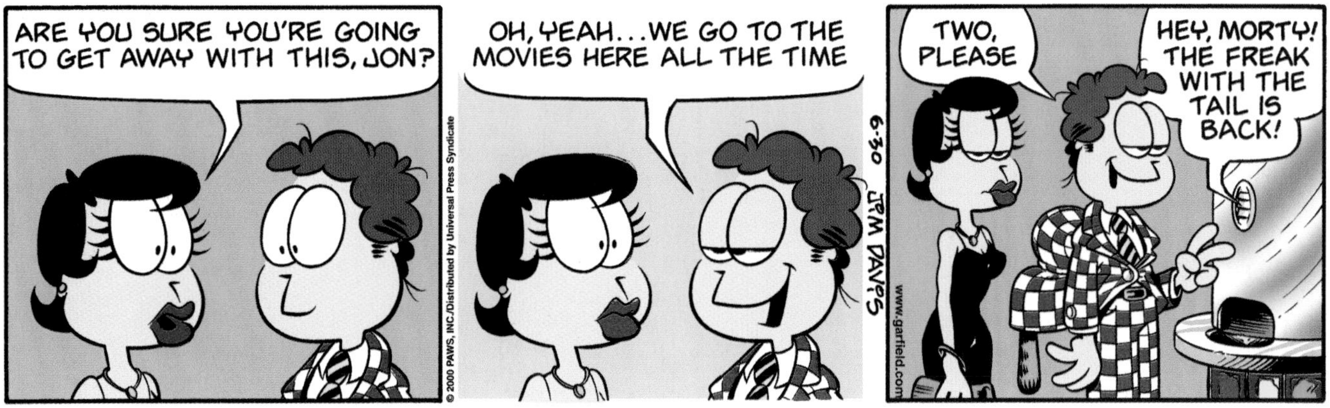
ARE YOU SURE YOU'RE GOING TO GET AWAY WITH THIS, JON?
OH, YEAH...WE GO TO THE MOVIES HERE ALL THE TIME
6-30
TWO, PLEASE
HEY, MORTY! THE FREAK WITH THE TAIL IS BACK!

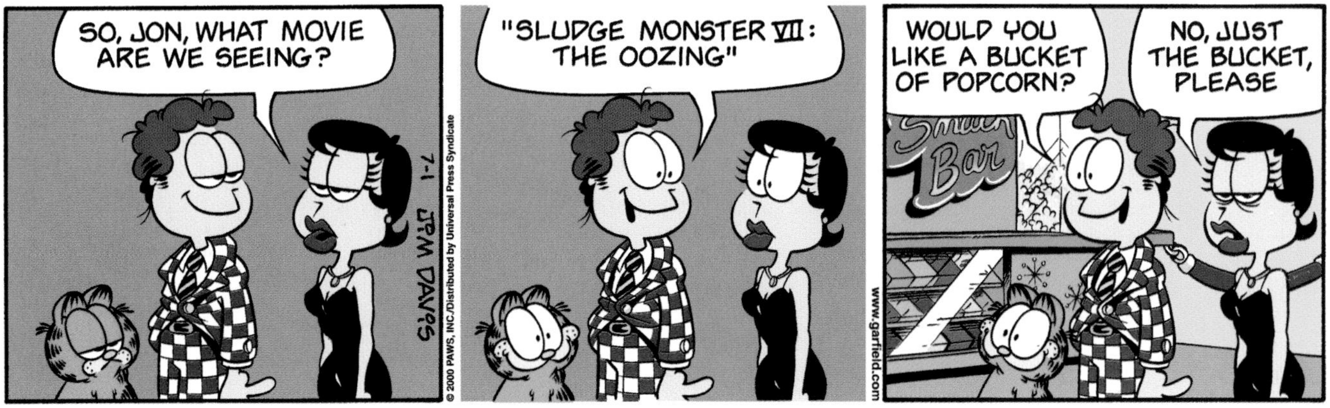
SO, JON, WHAT MOVIE ARE WE SEEING?
7-1
"SLUDGE MONSTER VII: THE OOZING"
WOULD YOU LIKE A BUCKET OF POPCORN?
NO, JUST THE BUCKET, PLEASE

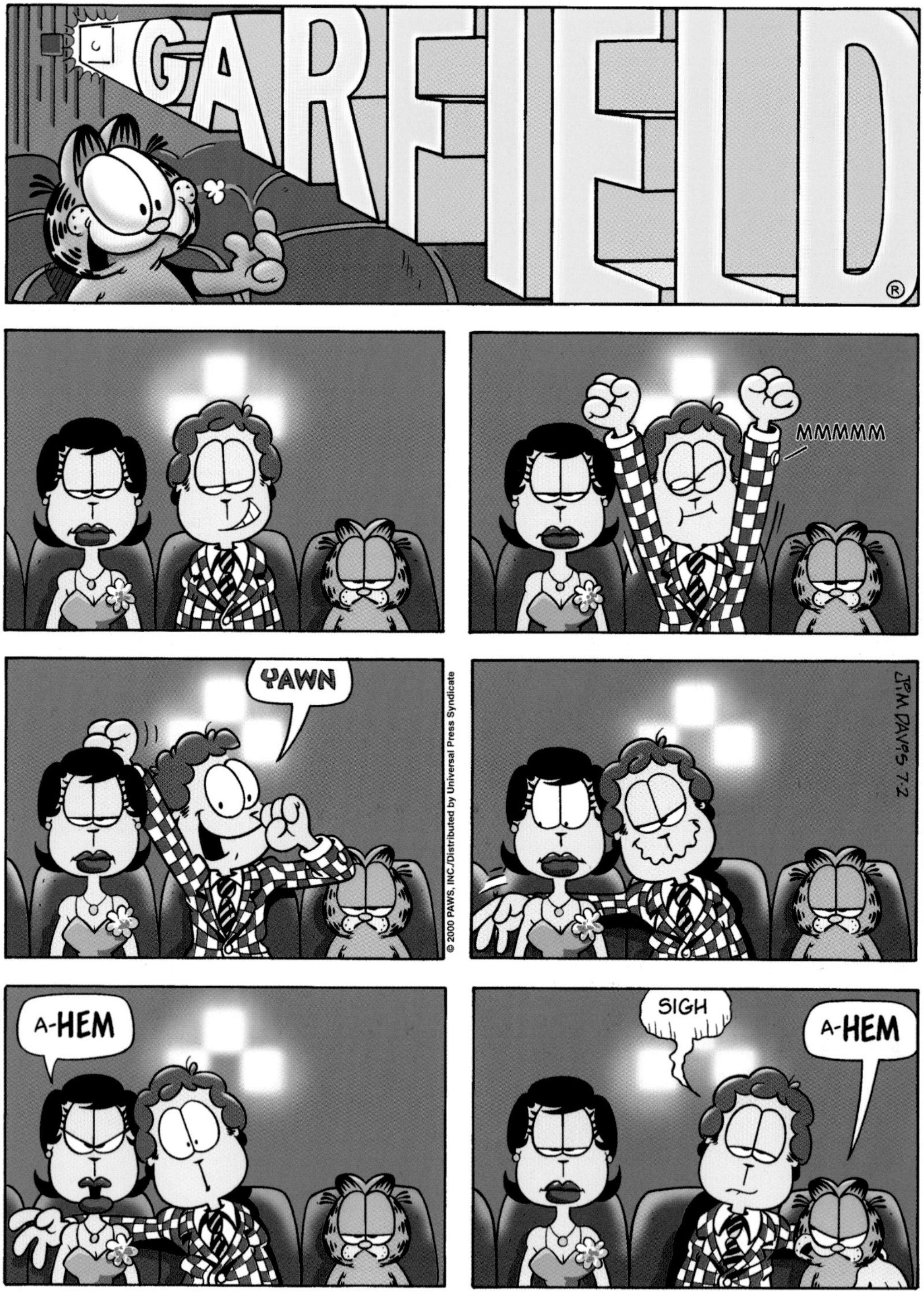
GARFIELD
MMMMM
YAWN
© 2000 PAWS, INC./Distributed by Universal Press Syndicate
JIM DAVIS 7-2
A-HEM
SIGH
A-HEM

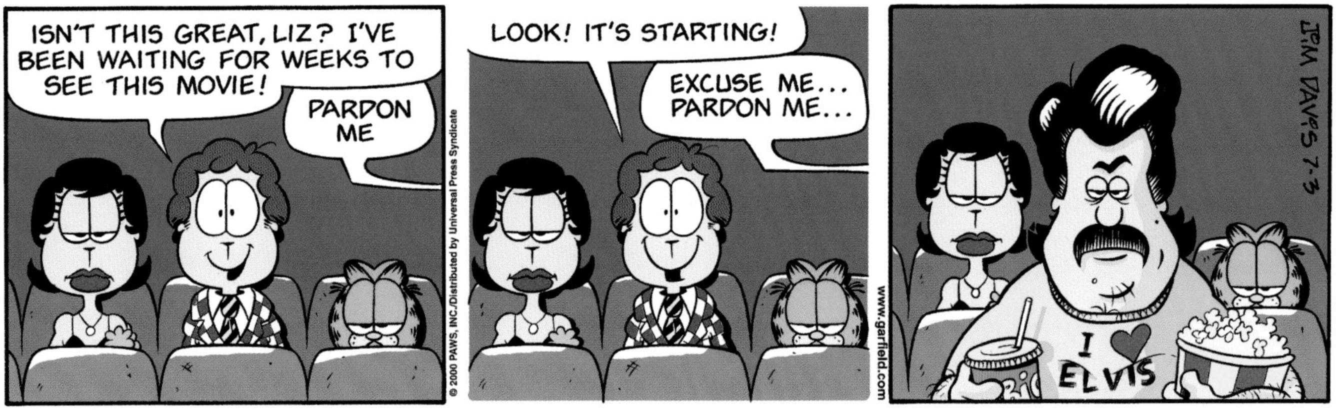
ISN'T THIS GREAT, LIZ? I'VE BEEN WAITING FOR WEEKS TO SEE THIS MOVIE!
PARDON ME
© 2000 PAWS, INC./Distributed by Universal Press Syndicate
LOOK! IT'S STARTING!
EXCUSE ME... PARDON ME...
www.garfield.com
JIM DAVIS 7-3
I ♥ ELVIS

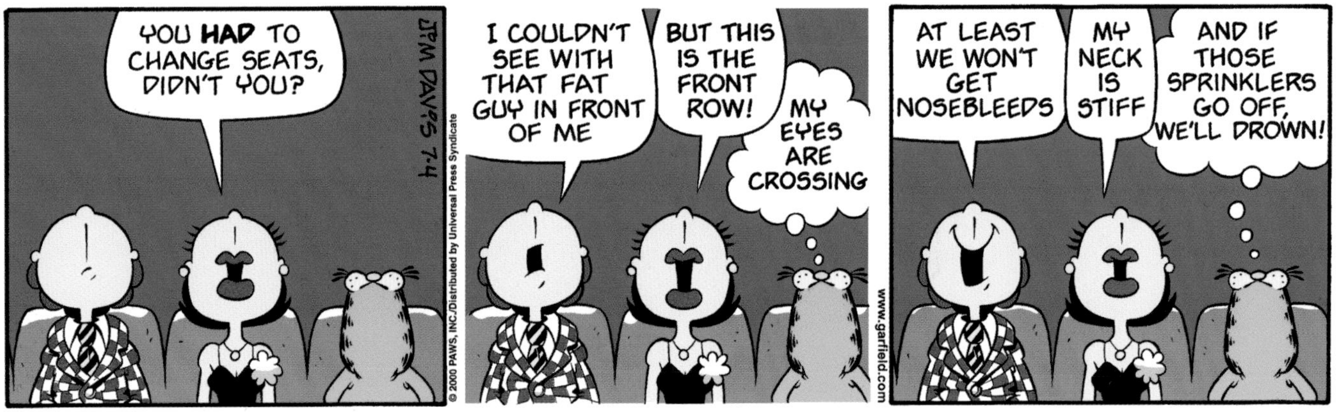
YOU **HAD** TO CHANGE SEATS, DIDN'T YOU?
JIM DAVIS 7-4
© 2000 PAWS, INC./Distributed by Universal Press Syndicate
I COULDN'T SEE WITH THAT FAT GUY IN FRONT OF ME
BUT THIS IS THE FRONT ROW!
MY EYES ARE CROSSING
www.garfield.com
AT LEAST WE WON'T GET NOSEBLEEDS
MY NECK IS STIFF
AND IF THOSE SPRINKLERS GO OFF, WE'LL DROWN!

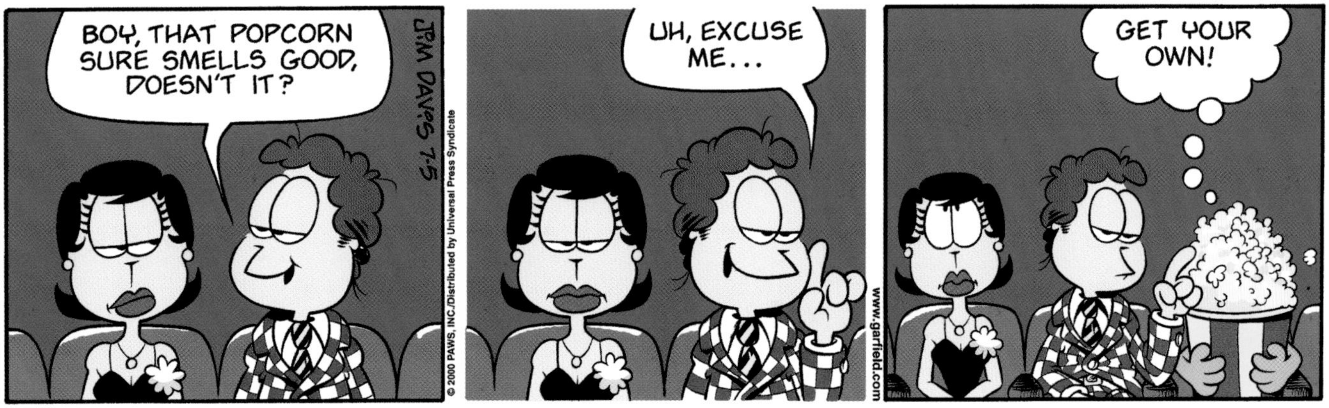
BOY, THAT POPCORN SURE SMELLS GOOD, DOESN'T IT?
JIM DAVIS 7-5
© 2000 PAWS, INC./Distributed by Universal Press Syndicate
UH, EXCUSE ME...
www.garfield.com
GET YOUR OWN!

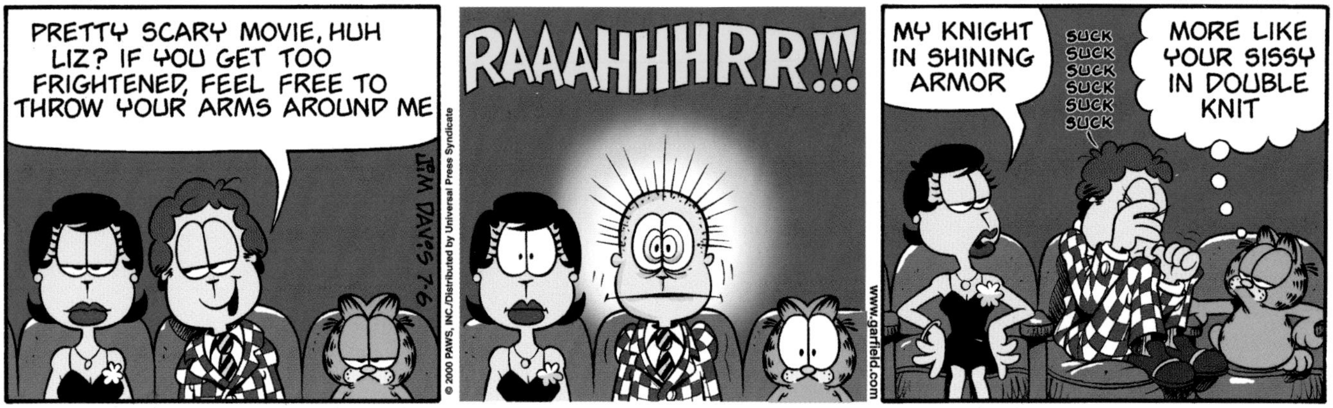
PRETTY SCARY MOVIE, HUH LIZ? IF YOU GET TOO FRIGHTENED, FEEL FREE TO THROW YOUR ARMS AROUND ME
JIM DAVIS 7-6
© 2000 PAWS, INC./Distributed by Universal Press Syndicate
RAAAHHHRR!!!
www.garfield.com
MY KNIGHT IN SHINING ARMOR
SUCK SUCK SUCK SUCK SUCK SUCK
MORE LIKE YOUR SISSY IN DOUBLE KNIT

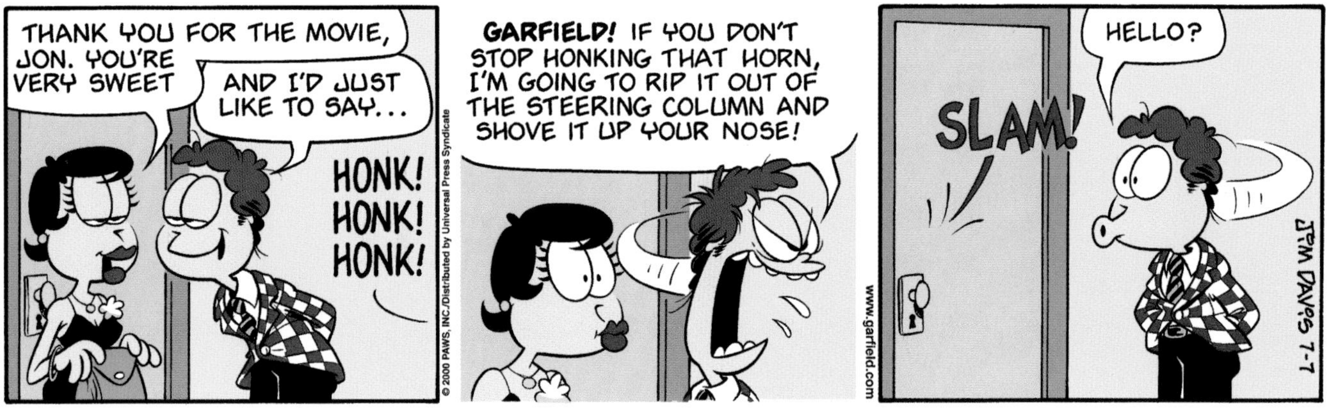
THANK YOU FOR THE MOVIE, JON. YOU'RE VERY SWEET
AND I'D JUST LIKE TO SAY...
HONK! HONK! HONK!
© 2000 PAWS, INC./Distributed by Universal Press Syndicate
GARFIELD! IF YOU DON'T STOP HONKING THAT HORN, I'M GOING TO RIP IT OUT OF THE STEERING COLUMN AND SHOVE IT UP YOUR NOSE!
www.garfield.com
SLAM!
HELLO?
JIM DAVIS 7-7

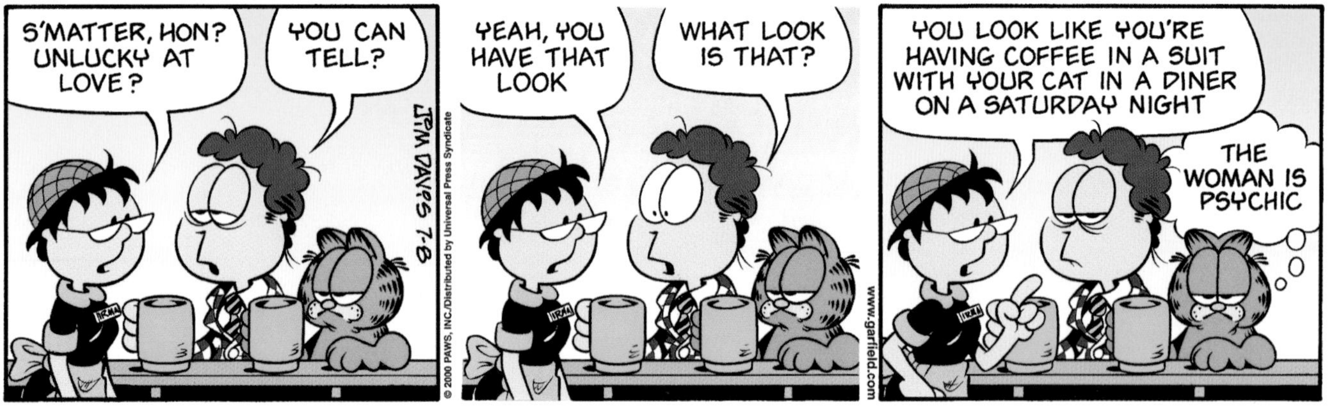
S'MATTER, HON? UNLUCKY AT LOVE?
YOU CAN TELL?
JIM DAVIS 7-8
© 2000 PAWS, INC./Distributed by Universal Press Syndicate
YEAH, YOU HAVE THAT LOOK
WHAT LOOK IS THAT?
www.garfield.com
YOU LOOK LIKE YOU'RE HAVING COFFEE IN A SUIT WITH YOUR CAT IN A DINER ON A SATURDAY NIGHT
THE WOMAN IS PSYCHIC

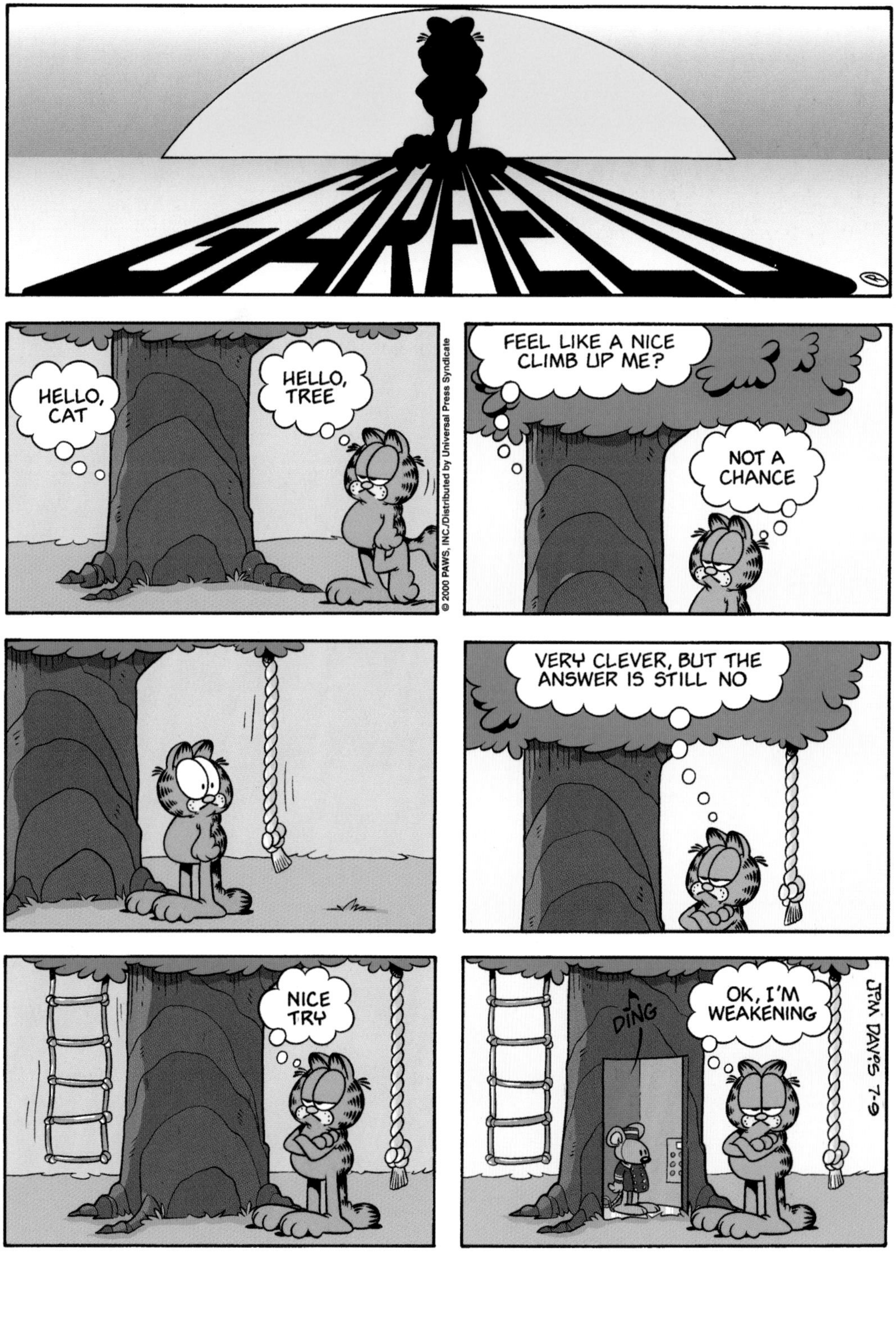

GARFIELD
HELLO, CAT
HELLO, TREE
© 2000 PAWS, INC./Distributed by Universal Press Syndicate
FEEL LIKE A NICE CLIMB UP ME?
NOT A CHANCE
VERY CLEVER, BUT THE ANSWER IS STILL NO
NICE TRY
DING
OK, I'M WEAKENING
JIM DAVIS 7-9

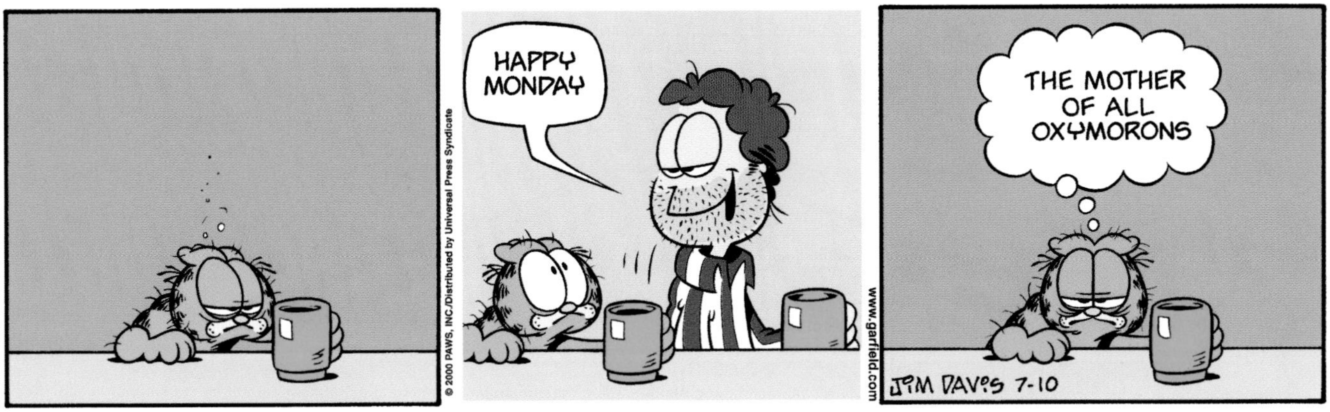
HAPPY MONDAY
THE MOTHER OF ALL OXYMORONS
© 2000 PAWS, INC./Distributed by Universal Press Syndicate
www.garfield.com
JIM DAVIS 7-10

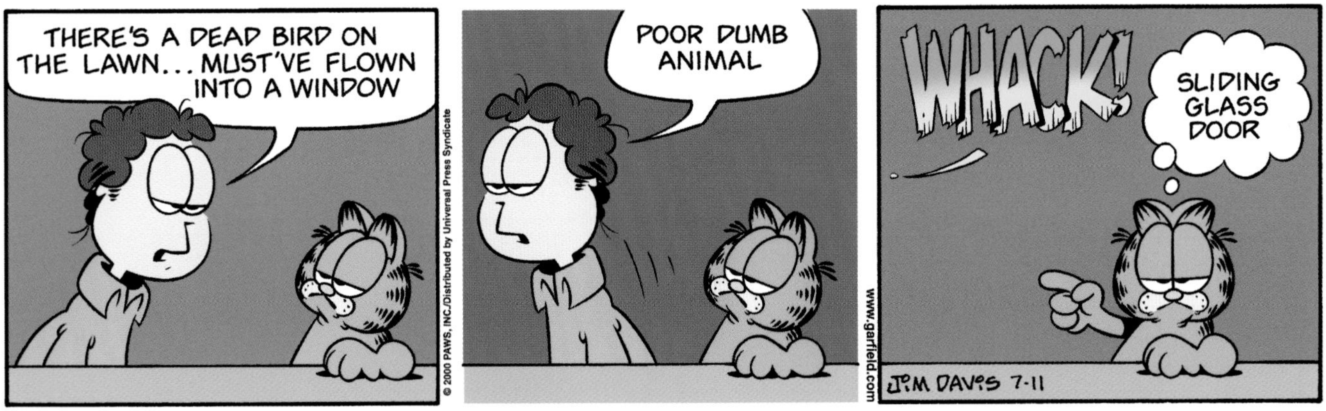
THERE'S A DEAD BIRD ON THE LAWN... MUST'VE FLOWN INTO A WINDOW
POOR DUMB ANIMAL
WHACK!
SLIDING GLASS DOOR
© 2000 PAWS, INC./Distributed by Universal Press Syndicate
www.garfield.com
JIM DAVIS 7-11

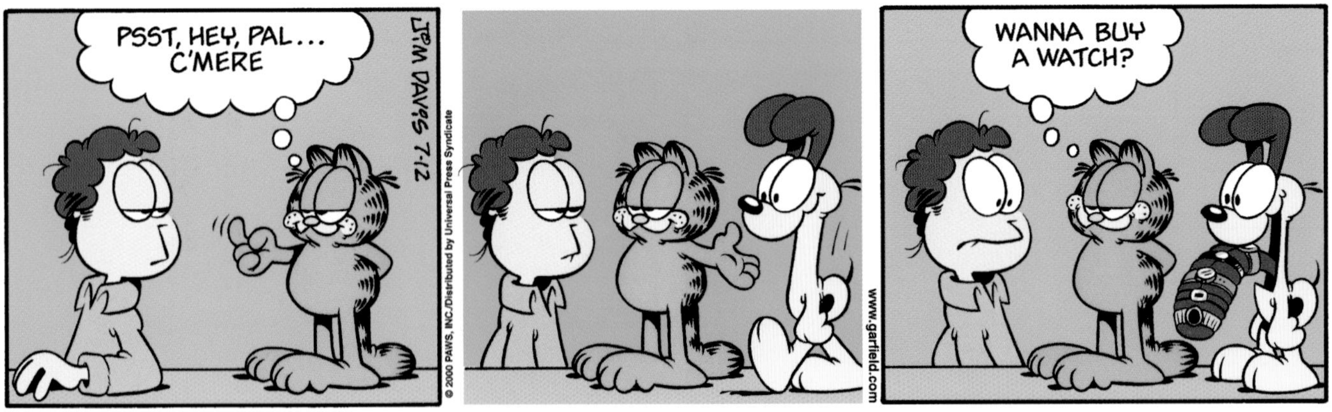
PSST, HEY, PAL... C'MERE
JIM DAVIS 7-12
WANNA BUY A WATCH?
© 2000 PAWS, INC./Distributed by Universal Press Syndicate
www.garfield.com

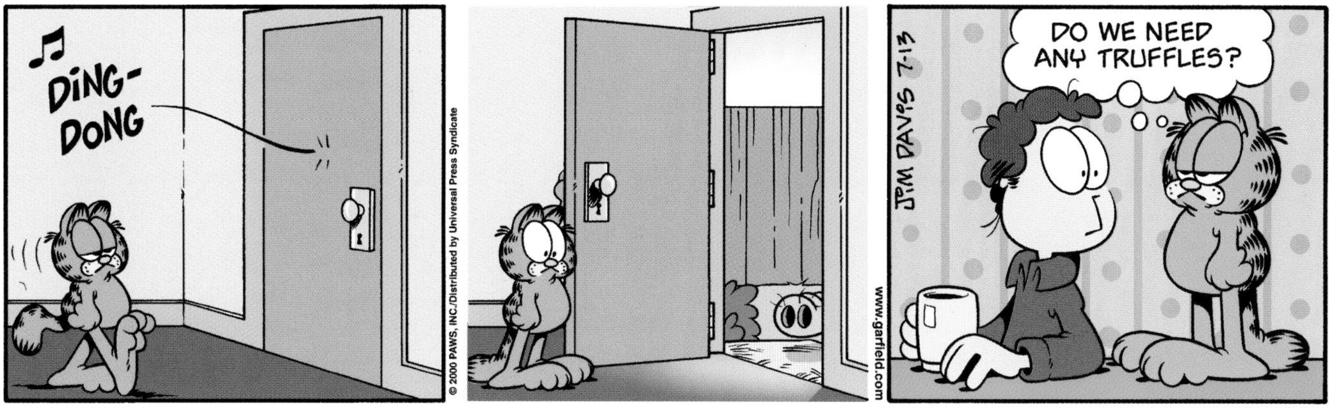
DING-DONG
© 2000 PAWS, INC./Distributed by Universal Press Syndicate
JIM DAVIS 7-13
www.garfield.com
DO WE NEED ANY TRUFFLES?

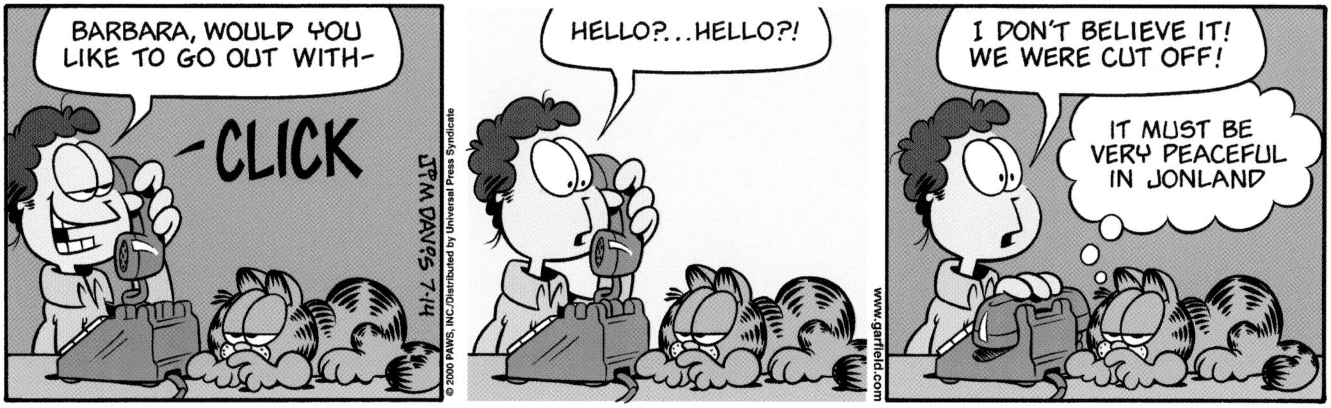
BARBARA, WOULD YOU LIKE TO GO OUT WITH-
-CLICK
JIM DAVIS 7-14
© 2000 PAWS, INC./Distributed by Universal Press Syndicate
HELLO?...HELLO?!
www.garfield.com
I DON'T BELIEVE IT! WE WERE CUT OFF!
IT MUST BE VERY PEACEFUL IN JONLAND

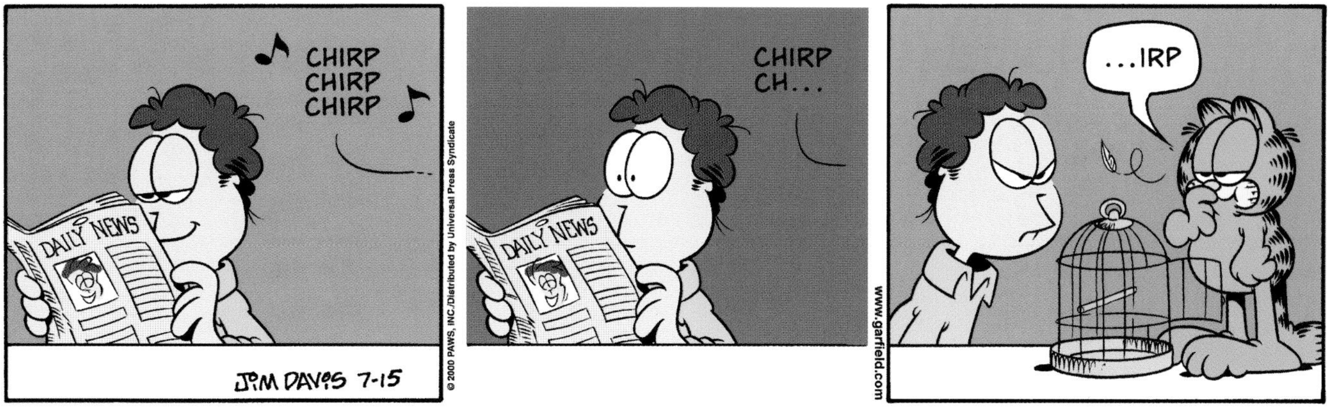
CHIRP CHIRP CHIRP
DAILY NEWS
JIM DAVIS 7-15
© 2000 PAWS, INC./Distributed by Universal Press Syndicate
CHIRP CH...
DAILY NEWS
www.garfield.com
...IRP

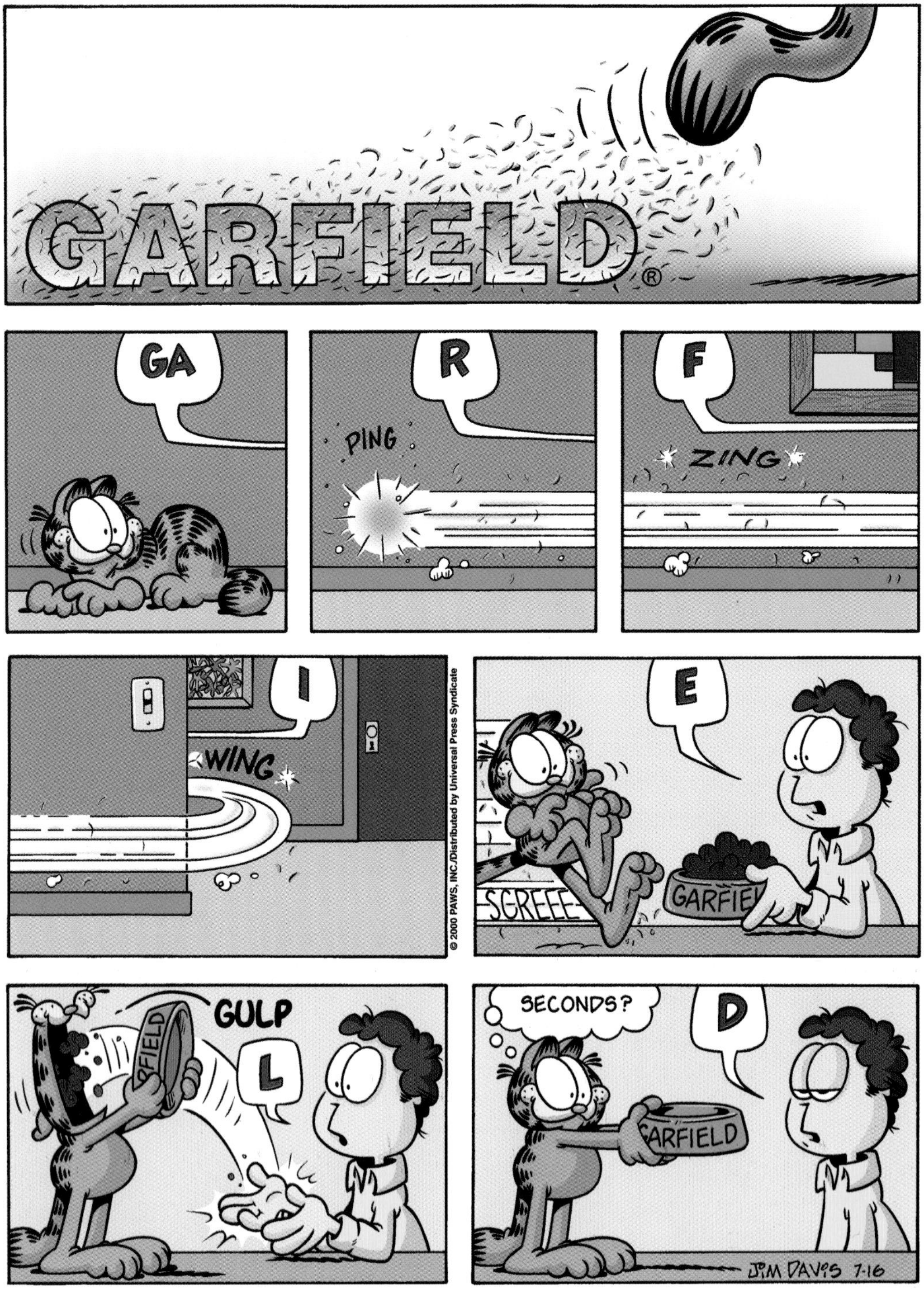
GARFIELD®
GA
R
PING
F
ZING
I
WING
© 2000 PAWS, INC./Distributed by Universal Press Syndicate
E
SCREEEE
GARFIELD
GULP
GARFIELD
L
SECONDS?
D
GARFIELD
JIM DAVIS 7-16

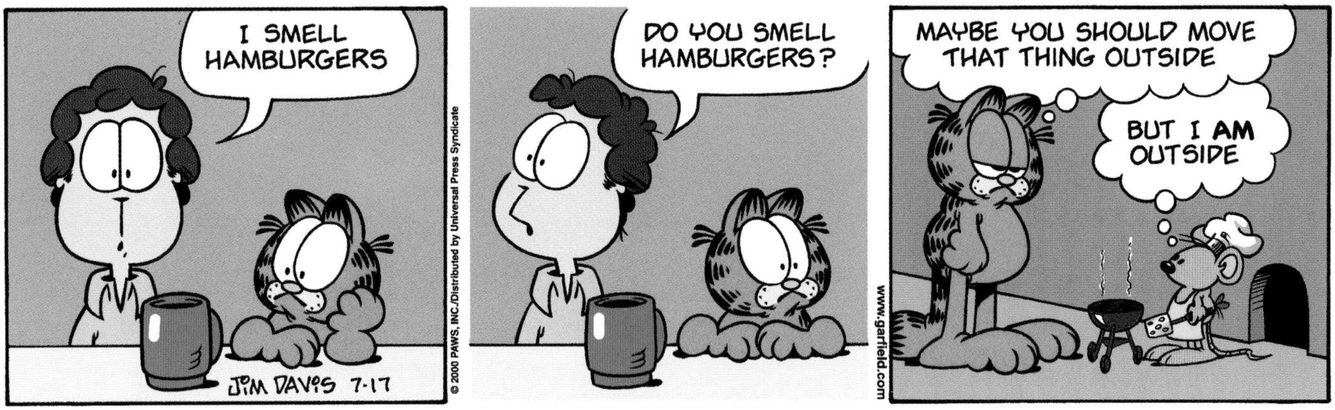
I SMELL HAMBURGERS
JIM DAVIS 7-17
© 2000 PAWS, INC./Distributed by Universal Press Syndicate
DO YOU SMELL HAMBURGERS?
www.garfield.com
MAYBE YOU SHOULD MOVE THAT THING OUTSIDE
BUT I AM OUTSIDE

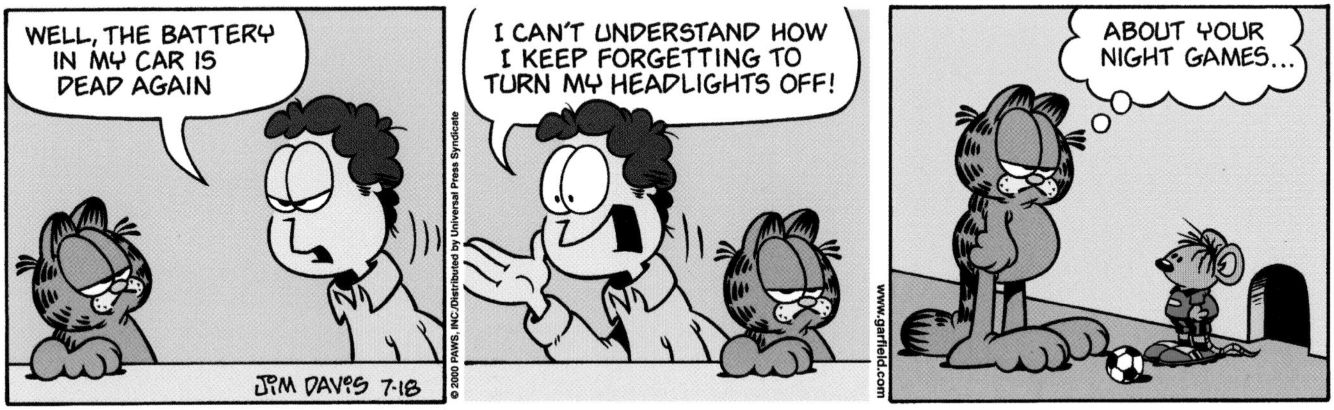
WELL, THE BATTERY IN MY CAR IS DEAD AGAIN
JIM DAVIS 7-18
© 2000 PAWS, INC./Distributed by Universal Press Syndicate
I CAN'T UNDERSTAND HOW I KEEP FORGETTING TO TURN MY HEADLIGHTS OFF!
www.garfield.com
ABOUT YOUR NIGHT GAMES...

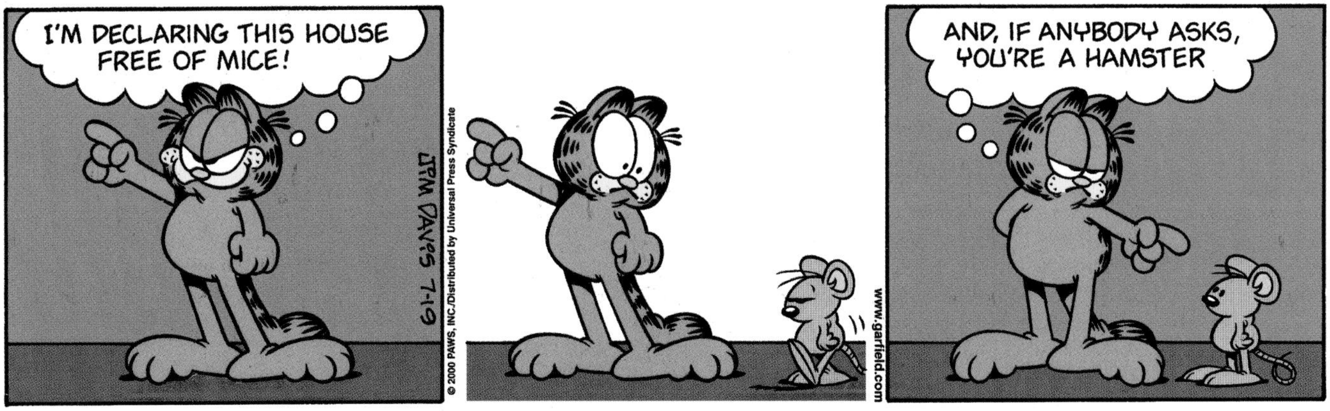
I'M DECLARING THIS HOUSE FREE OF MICE!
JIM DAVIS 7-19
© 2000 PAWS, INC./Distributed by Universal Press Syndicate
www.garfield.com
AND, IF ANYBODY ASKS, YOU'RE A HAMSTER

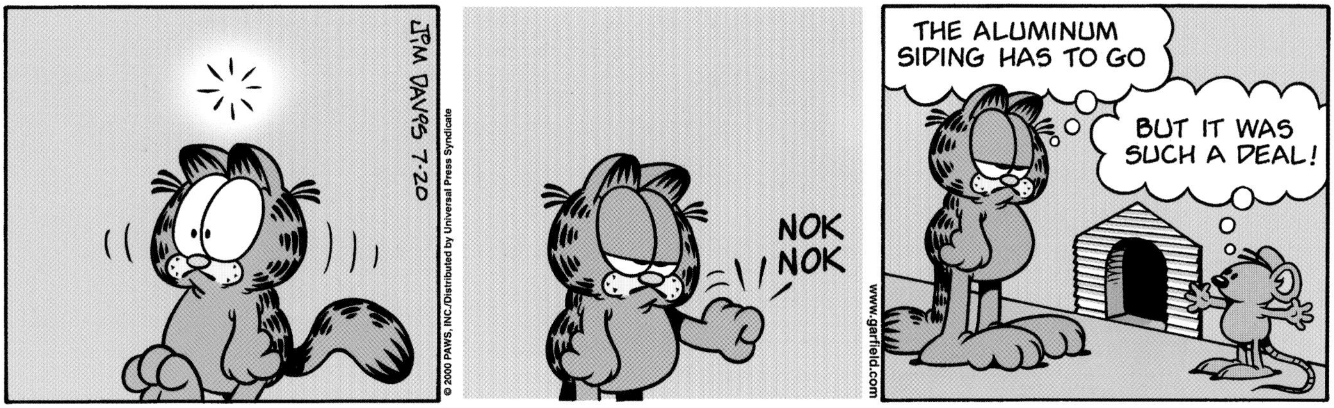
JPM DAVPS 7-20
© 2000 PAWS, INC./Distributed by Universal Press Syndicate
NOK
NOK
www.garfield.com
THE ALUMINUM SIDING HAS TO GO
BUT IT WAS SUCH A DEAL!

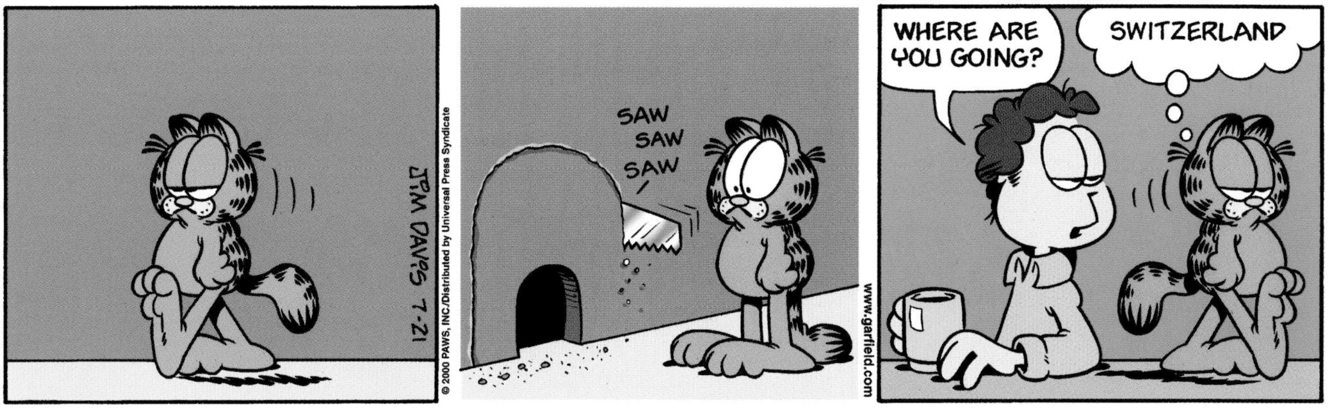
JPM DAVPS 7-21
© 2000 PAWS, INC./Distributed by Universal Press Syndicate
SAW
SAW
SAW
www.garfield.com
WHERE ARE YOU GOING?
SWITZERLAND

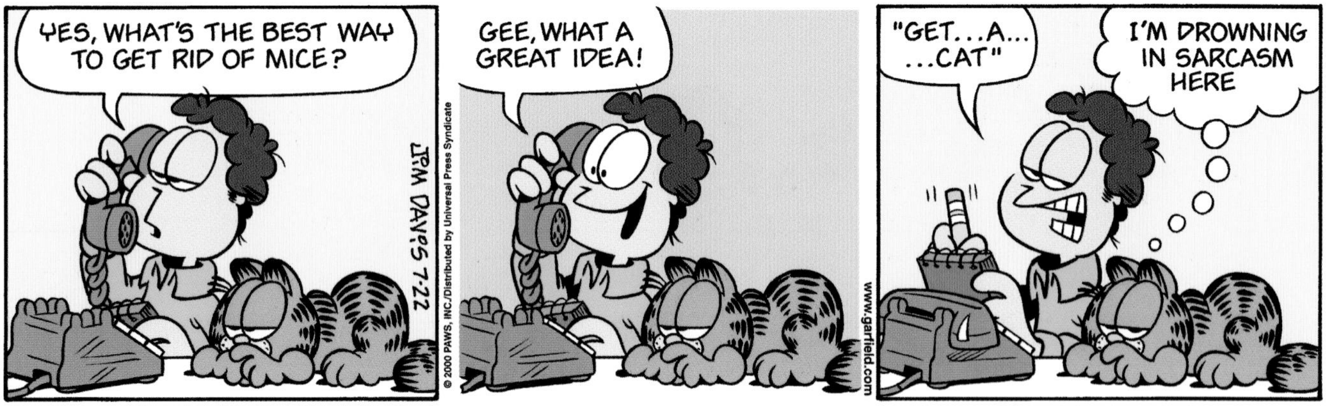
YES, WHAT'S THE BEST WAY TO GET RID OF MICE?
JPM DAVPS 7-22
© 2000 PAWS, INC./Distributed by Universal Press Syndicate
GEE, WHAT A GREAT IDEA!
www.garfield.com
"GET...A... ...CAT"
I'M DROWNING IN SARCASM HERE

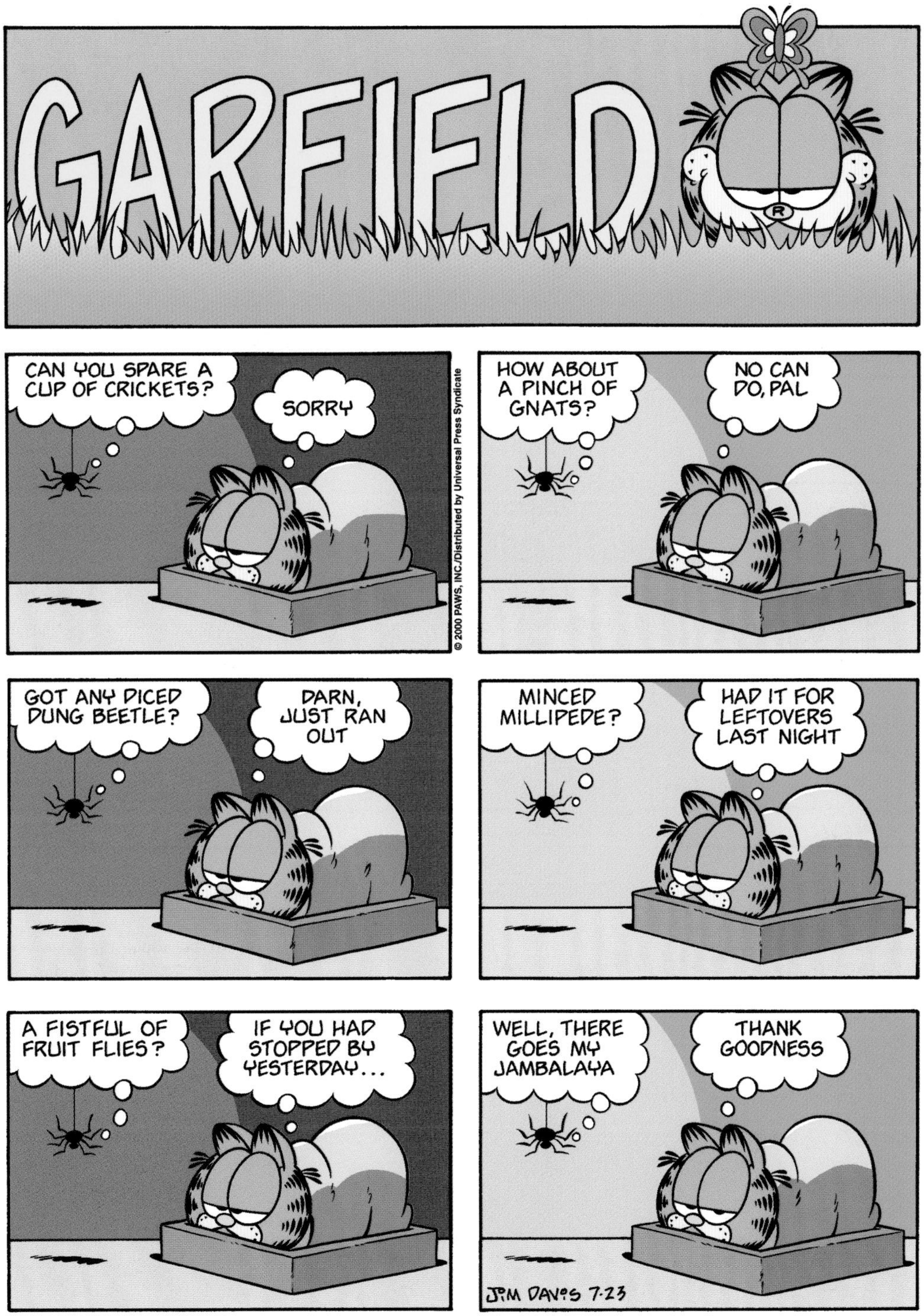
GARFIELD
CAN YOU SPARE A CUP OF CRICKETS?
SORRY
© 2000 PAWS, INC./Distributed by Universal Press Syndicate
HOW ABOUT A PINCH OF GNATS?
NO CAN DO, PAL
GOT ANY DICED DUNG BEETLE?
DARN, JUST RAN OUT
MINCED MILLIPEDE?
HAD IT FOR LEFTOVERS LAST NIGHT
A FISTFUL OF FRUIT FLIES?
IF YOU HAD STOPPED BY YESTERDAY...
WELL, THERE GOES MY JAMBALAYA
THANK GOODNESS
JIM DAVIS 7-23

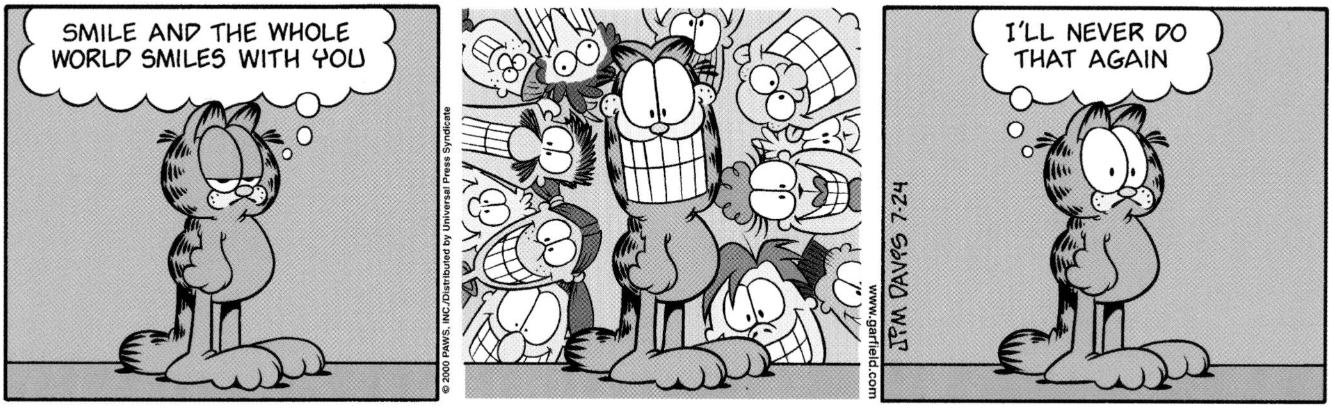
SMILE AND THE WHOLE WORLD SMILES WITH YOU
© 2000 PAWS, INC./Distributed by Universal Press Syndicate
JIM DAVIS 7-24
www.garfield.com
I'LL NEVER DO THAT AGAIN

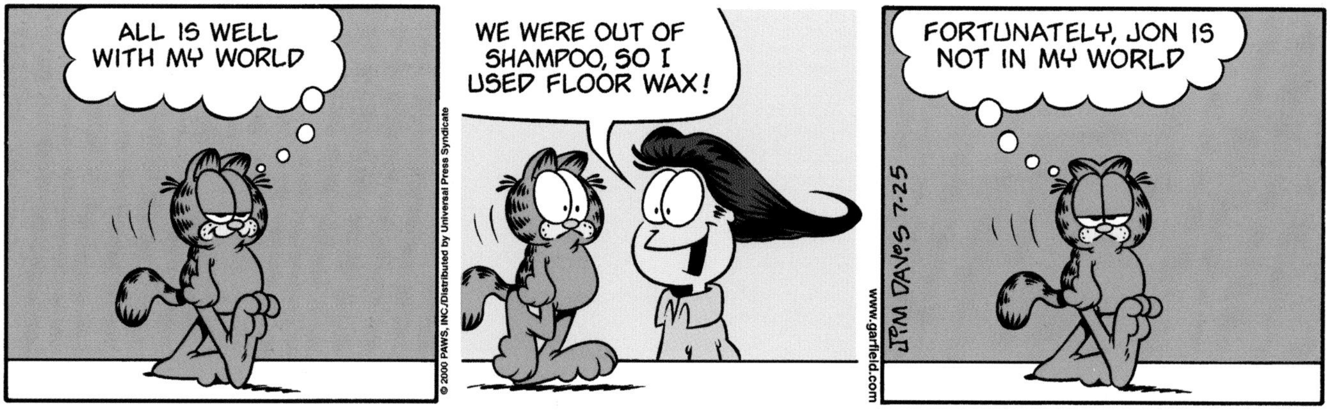
ALL IS WELL WITH MY WORLD
© 2000 PAWS, INC./Distributed by Universal Press Syndicate
WE WERE OUT OF SHAMPOO, SO I USED FLOOR WAX!
JIM DAVIS 7-25
www.garfield.com
FORTUNATELY, JON IS NOT IN MY WORLD

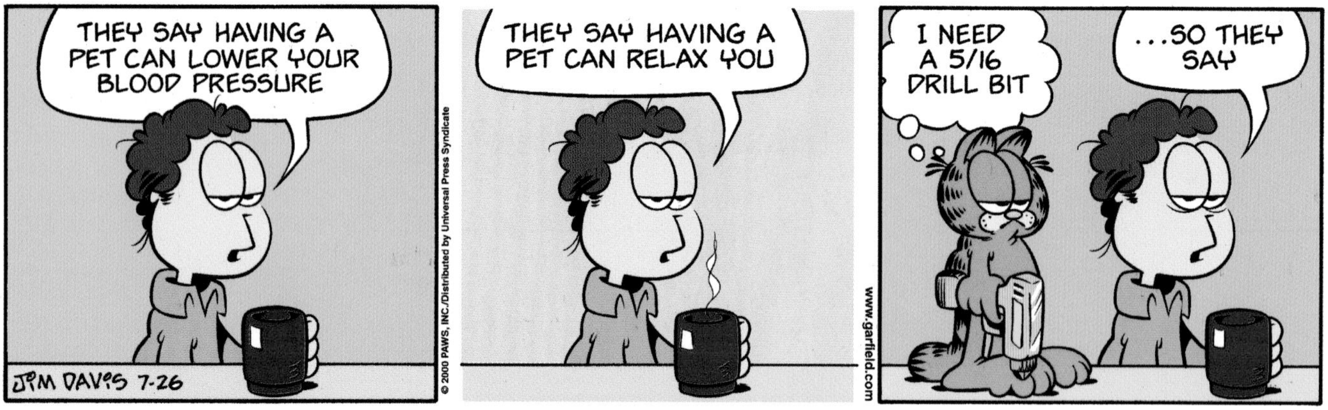
THEY SAY HAVING A PET CAN LOWER YOUR BLOOD PRESSURE
JIM DAVIS 7-26
© 2000 PAWS, INC./Distributed by Universal Press Syndicate
THEY SAY HAVING A PET CAN RELAX YOU
www.garfield.com
I NEED A 5/16 DRILL BIT
...SO THEY SAY

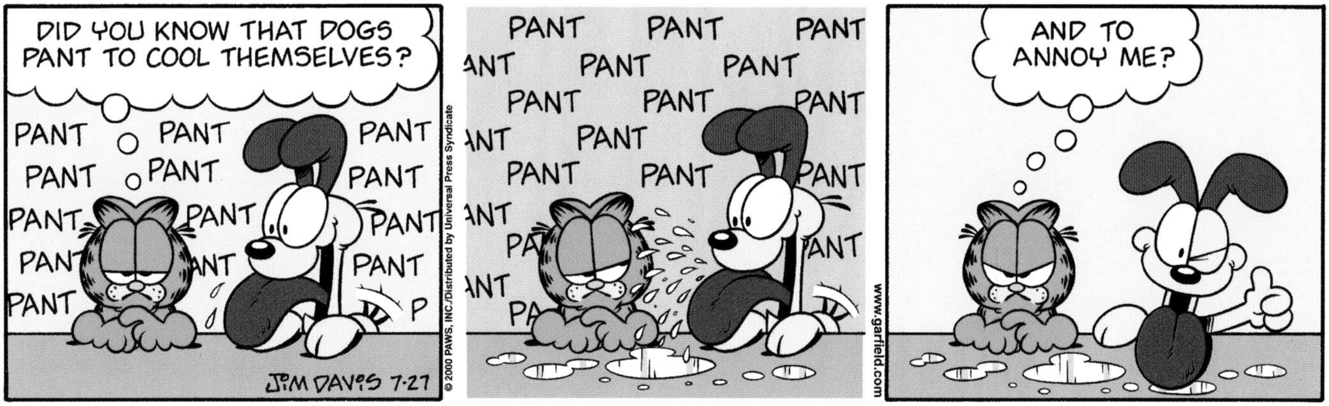
DID YOU KNOW THAT DOGS PANT TO COOL THEMSELVES?
PANT PANT PANT PANT PANT PANT PANT PANT
JIM DAVIS 7-27
© 2000 PAWS, INC./Distributed by Universal Press Syndicate
PANT PANT PANT PANT PANT PANT PANT PANT PANT
AND TO ANNOY ME?
www.garfield.com

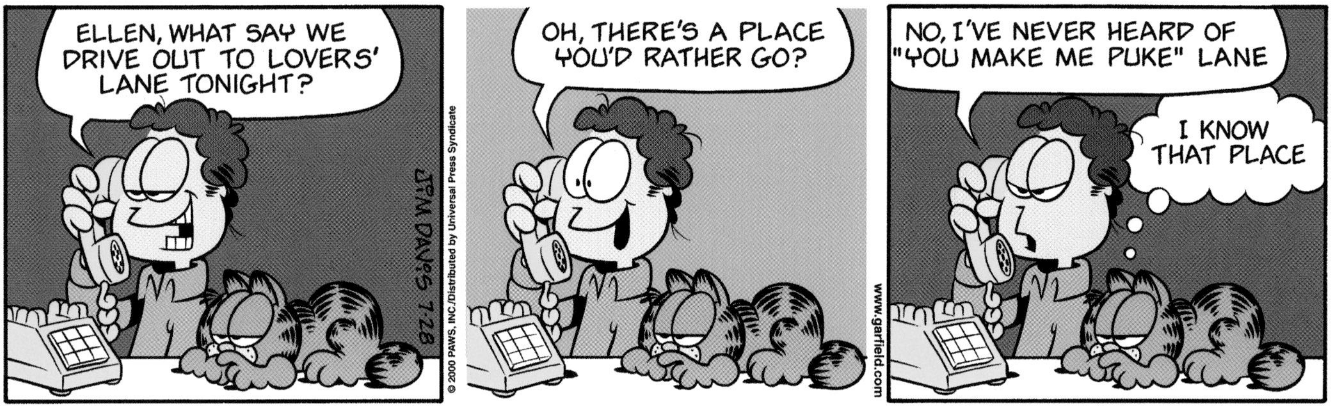
ELLEN, WHAT SAY WE DRIVE OUT TO LOVERS' LANE TONIGHT?
JIM DAVIS 7-28
© 2000 PAWS, INC./Distributed by Universal Press Syndicate
OH, THERE'S A PLACE YOU'D RATHER GO?
NO, I'VE NEVER HEARD OF "YOU MAKE ME PUKE" LANE
I KNOW THAT PLACE
www.garfield.com

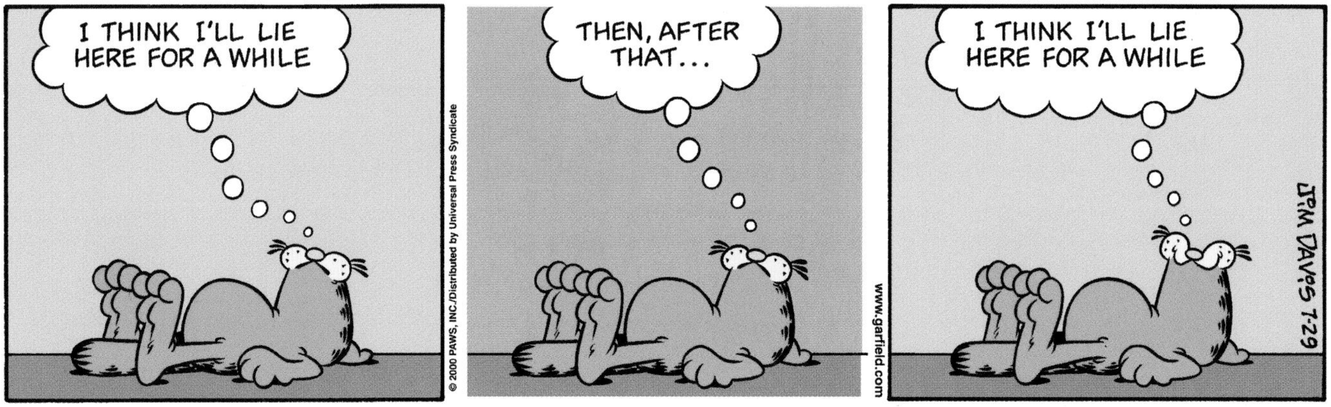
I THINK I'LL LIE HERE FOR A WHILE
© 2000 PAWS, INC./Distributed by Universal Press Syndicate
THEN, AFTER THAT...
I THINK I'LL LIE HERE FOR A WHILE
JIM DAVIS 7-29
www.garfield.com

Other GARFIELD titles published by Ravette ...

Pocket Books

		ISBN	Price
Am I Bothered?	(new)	978-1-84161-286-7	£3.99
Below Par		978-1-84161-152-5	£3.50
Compute This!		978-1-84161-194-5	£3.50
Don't Ask		978-1-84161-247-8	£3.99
Feed Me		978-1-84161-242-3	£3.99
Get Serious		978-1-84161-265-2	£3.99
Gotcha!		978-1-84161-226-3	£3.50
I Am What I Am		978-1-84161-243-0	£3.99
I Don't Do Perky		978-1-84161-195-2	£3.50
Kowabunga		978-1-84161-246-1	£3.99
Light Of My Life		978-1-85304-353-6	£3.50
Pop Star		978-1-84161-151-8	£3.50
S.W.A.L.K.		978-1-84161-225-6	£3.50
Wan2tlk?		978-1-84161-264-5	£3.99
What's Not to Like?	(new)	978-1-84161-285-0	£3.99

New titles available Feb 2008

	ISBN	Price
No. 59 - Time to Delegate	978-1-84161-296-6	£3.99
No. 60 - Numero Uno	978-1-84161-297-3	£3.99

Theme Books

	ISBN	Price
Behaving Badly	978-1-85304-892-0	£4.50
Cat Napping	978-1-84161-087-0	£4.50
Creatures Great & Small	978-1-85304-998-9	£3.99
Entertains You	978-1-84161-221-8	£4.50
Healthy Living	978-1-85304-972-9	£3.99
Pigging Out	978-1-85304-893-7	£4.50
Slam Dunk!	978-1-84161-222-5	£4.50
Successful Living	978-1-85304-973-6	£3.99
The Seasons	978-1-85304-999-6	£3.99

Gift Books (new)

	ISBN	Price
Keep your attitude I have my own	978-1-84161-278-2	£4.99
Don't Know, Don't Care	978-1-84161-279-9	£4.99
I Don't Do Ordinary	978-1-84161-281-2	£4.99
Get a Grip	978-1-84161-282-9	£4.99

2-in-1 Theme Books

	ISBN	Price
All In Good Taste	978-1-84161-209-6	£6.99
Easy Does It	978-1-84161-191-4	£6.99
Lazy Daze	978-1-84161-208-9	£6.99
Licensed to Thrill	978-1-84161-192-1	£6.99
Out For The Couch	978-1-84161-144-0	£6.99
The Gruesome Twosome	978-1-84161-143-3	£6.99

Classic Collections

	ISBN	Price
Volume One	978-1-85304-970-5	£6.99
Volume Two	978-1-85304-971-2	£5.99
Volume Three	978-1-85304-996-5	£5.99
Volume Four	978-1-85304-997-2	£6.99
Volume Five	978-1-84161-022-1	£6.99
Volume Six	978-1-84161-023-8	£6.99
Volume Seven	978-1-84161-088-7	£5.99
Volume Eight	978-1-84161-089-4	£5.99
Volume Nine	978-1-84161-149-5	£6.99
Volume Ten	978-1-84161-150-1	£6.99
Volume Eleven	978-1-84161-175-4	£6.99
Volume Twelve	978-1-84161-176-1	£6.99
Volume Thirteen	978-1-84161-206-5	£6.99
Volume Fourteen	978-1-84161-207-2	£6.99
Volume Fifteen	978-1-84161-232-4	£5.99
Volume Sixteen	978-1-84161-233-1	£5.99
Volume Seventeen	978-1-84161-250-8	£6.99
Volume Eighteen	978-1-84161-251-5	£6.99

Little Books

	ISBN	Price
C-c-c-caffeine	978-1-84161-183-9	£2.50
Food 'n' Fitness	978-1-84161-145-7	£2.50
Laughs	978-1-84161-146-4	£2.50
Love 'n' Stuff	978-1-84161-147-1	£2.50
Surf 'n' Sun	978-1-84161-186-0	£2.50
The Office	978-1-84161-184-6	£2.50
Zzzzzzz	978-1-84161-185-3	£2.50

Treasuries

	ISBN	Price
Treasury 7	978-1-84161-248-5	£10.99
Treasury 6	978-1-84161-229-4	£10.99
Treasury 5	978-1-84161-198-3	£10.99
Treasury 4	978-1-84161-180-8	£10.99
Treasury 3	978-1-84161-142-6	£9.99

All Garfield books are available at your local bookshop or from the publisher at the address below.

Just tick the titles required and send the form with your payment and name and address details to:-
RAVETTE PUBLISHING, Unit 3, Tristar Centre, Star Road, Partridge Green, West Sussex RH13 8RA

Prices and availability are subject to change without prior notice.

Please enclose a cheque or postal order made payable to Ravette Publishing
to the value of the cover price of the book and allow the following for UK p&p:-
70p for the first book + 40p for each additional book, except Garfield Treasuries, when please add £3.00 per copy.